PRAISE FOR THE TOGETHER LEADER

"We've all seen the most earnest, well-intentioned leaders miss the mark because they lack an airtight plan to get their most mission-critical work done. *The Together Leader* provides a clear, groundbreaking roadmap for maximizing systems, structures, people, and most all of, leaders themselves, in order to yield excellent results. This book is as useful for a not 'together' novice, as it is for a high-functioning leader with undiscovered blind spots to fine tune. I'm not exaggerating when I say that regardless of where you are in your leadership journey, Maia's book will change your life."—Paula White, executive director, Regional Achievement Centers, New Jersey Department of Education

"Maia Heyck-Merlin has proven her ability, on so many stages, to help teachers reach their goals on student development, time management, and personal balance. And now, with *The Together Leader*, she is inviting leaders to join the movement. This book pairs practical advice with compelling anecdotes to help mission-driven leaders revolutionize the way they do business, and the way their organizations reach their ambitious goals."—Emily McCann, president, Citizen Schools

"No one on the planet is better qualified to write about 'togetherness' than Maia Heyck-Merlin. Her book is a gift to mission-driven leaders who want to be more effective, more reliable, more productive—in other words, who want to have a bigger impact on the world. It is filled with easy-to-use, concrete, practical tools and advice, and on top of that it is a joy to read. I love this book!"—Jerry Hauser, chief executive officer, The Management Center

"As someone who has clung to her copy of *The Together Teacher*, *The Together Leader* is a welcome addition to my professional library. In *The Together Leader*, Maia reminds us that mission-driven work is done in service of the greater good, and that the mission-driven leader needs a strong foundation of organizational support to effectively reach that goal. *The Together Leader* enables leaders to create that foundation of organizational support within their team. I'm grateful to Maia for helping my team establish 'togetherness,' as it has aided our ability to work in service of students with disabilities, their families, and the schools that serve them."—Christina Foti, chief executive director, Special Education Office–Division of Specialized Instruction and Student, New York City Department of Education

"There's not a mission-focused leader out there who wouldn't benefit from reading this book. Whether you are trying to change the world on a shoestring or leading from within a major institution, *The Together Leader* delivers the comprehensive customizable set of tools you need to manage your time and that of others for maximum impact and minimum burnout."—Alex Johnston, founder and president, Impact for Education

"*The Together Leader* is the real deal for leaders and leadership teams who want concrete tools to help manage their time and for execute their priorities in our age of information overload. The tools and techniques outlined in this book will bring clarity and organization to anyone who uses them. It will be a tune-up for some and a lifesaver for many."—Jay Altman, chief executive officer, FirstLine Schools

"Maia is uniquely qualified to support educators in this critical arena. Her framework has benefited our staff tremendously in separating the urgent from the merely important, focusing our time and energy on what matters most."—Paymon Rouhanifard, superintendent, Camden City School District

"With clarity and compassion, Maia delivers strong advice on being a 'together' leader in the mission-driven workplace. Filled with smart storytelling, clear examples, and actionable steps, *The Together Leader,* is a must-read for anyone in the nonprofit sector."—Elisa Villanueva Beard, chief executive officer, Teach for America

"Maia tells it like it is—leading a school or team requires a level of 'togetherness' and 'with-it-ness' that is just never taught. Leaders are too often overwhelmed or even blindsided by the daily demands of their jobs. Maia provides the mindset and tools necessary for leaders to prioritize, plan, and protect their time. Her approach has helped hundreds of our team members—they will help you as well."—Dave Levin, cofounder, KIPP: Knowledge is Power Program

"*The Together Leader* has helped me maximize my time as a leader. Not only do I have more time dedicated to supporting my team, I have developed the systems necessary to think both short and long term, review critical plans with care, and make better decisions on behalf of the children I serve. Maia's tips on organization have helped me become a better leader."—Jennifer Cheatham, superintendent of schools, Madison Metropolitan School District

"You can have all the vision, dedication, and talented team members in the world, but if you can't organize yourself as a leader, you can't possibly reach maximum impact. Using the techniques Maia describes in this must-read book, hundreds of Leading Educators' teacher leaders have improved their team management abilities. The payoff of their 'togetherness': increased student learning and opportunity in life."—Jonas Chartock, chief executive officer, Leading Educators

"As nonprofit leaders we must do the work that matters most. Trouble is, precious time can get swallowed up by out-of-control inboxes, endless meetings, and urgent requests. To keep important work on track, *The Together Leader* gives leaders the practices and tools to connect the big picture with their daily work. Our Education Pioneers team regularly uses Maia's teachings and trainings because we believe strongly in their effectiveness to drive mission-critical work forward."—Scott Morgan, founder & chief executive officer, Education Pioneers

"What Maia did for teachers in *The Together Teacher*, she has now done for leaders. As our best teachers transition into leadership roles, their lives change in ways that require new levels of 'togetherness'—they have to be responsive, mobile, and reliable without the comfort of their own classroom or a predetermined schedule. Her practical, bite-sized, applicable tools and techniques are the difference between surviving and thriving as a school leader. This book goes well beyond time management. It helps leaders successfully ensure that 'the right things are done by the right people at the right times' so they can spend their time doing what matters most – helping teachers and students be successful."—Gail McGee, career pathways senior manager, Houston Independent School District

"*The Together Leader* is an invaluable resource for our organization in helping individuals and teams align and maximize their time in service of schools. Whether it's the weekly worksheet or the long-term comprehensive calendar, our teammates rave about Maia's resources—they're practical, timely, and can be put to use right away. Personally, I've learned an immense amount from Maia on how to maximize my own time to best benefit my organization. I know leaders everywhere will put the practices in this book to use for themselves and for their organizations."—John Maycock, cofounder and president, The Achievement Network

"*The Together Leader* provides incredibly useful strategies that empower leaders to manage their priorities more effectively. We use Maia's strategies and guidance in leadership teams across our network to ensure that our leaders are executing our vision in the most skillful and strategic ways."—Katie Severn, president & chief academic officer, DC Prep

"The ideas and systems Maia provides are practical yet life-changing. She understands the unique demands of mission-driven leadership. This book provides the tools necessary to tackle challenges head on. By reflecting on and implementing these thoughtful strategies, leaders are guaranteed to save time and energy, enacting a strategy this is sustainable and that allows them to retain their passion for leading in the long-term!"—Amanda Delabar, principal, Tubman Elementary, DC Public Schools

"Empowering … Tool agnostic … Balanced … Maia is more than just a great presenter and a treasure trove of tools. She empowers leaders to meet their professional goals by balancing their personal priorities in ways that are smart and sustainable. Readers will be empowered by Maia's practical insight on how to create effective systems that any leader can replicate and apply to their daily practice. *The Together Leader* is essential for central office leaders, principals, assistant principals, aspiring leaders, and principal supervisors, instructing them on how best to protect their time both personally and professionally."—Michele Mason, executive director, Leadership Development, Charlotte-Mecklenburg Schools

THE
TOGETHER
LEADER

THE
TOGETHER
LEADER

Get Organized for Your
Success—and Sanity!

Maia Heyck-Merlin

The
Together
Group™

JB JOSSEY-BASS™
A Wiley Brand

Published by Jossey-Bass
A Wiley Brand
One Montgomery Street, Suite 1000, San Francisco, CA 94104-4594—www.josseybass.com

Jossey-Bass books and products are available through most bookstores. To contact Jossey-Bass directly call our Customer Care Department within the U.S. at 800-956-7739, outside the U.S. at 317-572-3986, or fax 317-572-4002.

Wiley publishes in a variety of print and electronic formats and by print-on-demand. Some material included with standard print versions of this book may not be included in e-books or in print-on-demand. This material may be found on the author's website, **www.thetogethergroup.com**. For more information about Wiley products, visit **www.wiley.com**.

Library of Congress Cataloging-in-Publication Data

978-1-118-98752-0 Paperback
978-1-118-98753-7 ePub
978-1-118-98754-4 ePDF

Cover Design: Wiley

Printed in the United States of America

FIRST EDITION

PB Printing 10 9 8 7 6 5 4 3 2

To Doug McCurry and Dacia Toll, who modeled the entire leadership package and enabled this book to happen

CONTENTS

SECTION ONE: SET THE STAGE · 1

Chapter 1: Leading in a Mission-Driven Context · 3

What Do You Mean by *Mission-Driven Work*? • What Do You Mean by *Togetherness*, Anyway? • Why Togetherness Matters Even More in Your Context • My Own Togetherness Journey • Why This Book Is Different • How This Book Is Organized • How Each Chapter Is Organized • How to Use This Book • Notes on Terminology and Methodology • Togetherness Is a Means to an End

Togetherness Talks: Shawn Mangar

Chapter 2: Take Stock: Assess Your Togetherness Level · 15

Overview and Objectives • Togetherness Levels • The Tools You Need • Reader Quiz: Togetherness Tools • Routines Rule • Mind-Sets Matter (More Than Anything) • Build the Habit • Don't Go on an Organizational Binge • Let's Jump In

Togetherness Talks: Natalie Rubio

SECTION TWO: GET CLEAR ON YOUR PURPOSE · 27

Chapter 3: Set Goals: Define the Direction · 29

Seen and Heard • Overview and Objectives • How Do I Set Yearly Goals? • How Do I Set Quantitative Goals? • Create a Time Line for Goal Setting—and Put Someone in Charge • Reviewing Goal Progress • Start Strong

See It In Action: Goal Setting Start to Finish

ACKNOWLEDGMENTS

The Together Leader was a long time coming. And it would never have arrived without a ton of support. I certainly didn't invent the To-Do List, but I have been inspired and encouraged by many to share my own unique approach to Togetherness. Two Together and rapidly growing non-profits, Teach For America and Achievement First, collectively employed me for over a decade and let me observe, experiment and eventually train widely across both organizations while I was technically doing "other jobs." So many people have invited me deep into their organizations, their schools, and even their homes to allow me to paint a rich picture of Together Leaders. And because of all of those observations, I've been able to curate and narrate effective practices back to you.

To the thousands of Together Leader workshop and webinar participants: thank you for sharing your stories, results, and passion. Every time I deliver a workshop, I'm reminded why we need so many more mission-driven leaders fighting the good fight. I'm especially grateful to organizations that have welcomed me in to share so much about their people and practices: The Achievement Network, TNTP, KIPP, the Relay Graduate School of Education, YES Prep, Achievement First, The Ewing Marion Kauffman School, Teach For America, Citizen Schools, and more. There are countless other organizations mentioned within the book, but the ones listed here tolerated my e-mails, visits, questions, and more over countless years. And a huge thank-you to the leaders I've coached who agreed to open the doors and share their tools, mind-sets, and routines throughout this text. There are too many of you to list individually but just know I have a spreadsheet and I'm thanking you all profusely. You've dealt with my requests for interviews, requests for documents, and requests for more interviews with grace and enthusiasm.

There are many pioneering authors on the topics of priorities, habits, rituals, energy, and productivity. To Tony Schwartz, Brigid Schulte, Tom Rath, Steven Covey, David Allen, David Levitan, and Laura Vanderkam: thank you for setting the stage, going first, doing the hefty research, and helping me apply your concepts to my particular sector.

I'm so grateful to those who have been brave (or unfortunate) enough to lead *me*: Antoinette Bienemy and Jim Geiser, my two principals; Jerry Hauser, Nicole Baker Fulgham, and Jeff Wetzler, my managers at Teach For America; Dacia Toll and Doug McCurry, my co-bosses at Achievement First. Thanks for consistently modeling *why* a leader needs to be Together.

Norman Atkins, Dan Konecky, Aaron Suffrin, the whole Relay GSE team, Jay Altman, and Mike Goldstein have always championed my work and served as wise mentors. I'm grateful to a team of professional supports, including Rusty Shelton and the entire team at Shelton Interactive, Lee Kirby, Nicole Garner, and Lee Weiner. We have been together for a long time now, and I'm grateful for your various areas of content expertise. Kate Gagnon and her wonderful team at Jossey-Bass supported this project from the very start. They joined me at workshops, refined the table of contents, ensured every ounce of text flowed smoothly and every image printed clearly.

Many people donated their most precious resource (their time) to read entire copies of this book. Allie Rogovin, you are the epitome of a Together Leader. Thank you for being my first cold reader. Trusted advisors Scott McCue, Randall Lahann, Kim Marshall, and Giselle Wagner brought their collective decades of leadership experience to offer wise feedback in the book's earliest stages. Genna Weinstein and Kate McCabe: thank you for serving as such trusted thought partners and consistently replying to my spazzy text messages. I also want to thank Kate Berger, Shawn Mangar, Erica Williamson, Chris Hines, Ron Gubitz, Emily Stainer, Maggie Goldstein, Sean Precious, and Amanda Cahn for being ever-available on the bat-phone; fellow author Elena Aguilar for being a source of practical advice and constant cheerleading in the home stretch; and many thanks to the countless others, too many to name, who gave input on the initial table of contents.

A big thanks to Shelby Lee Keefer and Evan Jenkins, who functioned as my work best friends while in graduate school and looking for acting work on Broadway, respectively, for handling social media, travel booking, and myriad other thankless tasks that kept us moving. A deep shout-out of gratitude goes out to Kendra Rowe Salas and her rotating cast of actors (including, occasionally, her husband!), who seamlessly handle every back-office part of my work, from project management to inventory to website to newsletters to accounting. Kendra, this book would not be possible without you doing so much to free up my brain to think and write. To Meghan Pierce, book production coordinator, researcher, fact checker, art logger, recipe sharer extraordinaire: thank you for handling my creativity with such flexibility and encouragement. You can make a spreadsheet, spot an inconsistency, and find a million solutions like *no* other. And to Marin Smith, my dear friend and colleague of almost a decade: thank you for your editorial support. You bring more of my voice to my stuff than even I do sometimes! And last, to Josh Lowitz, my pretend boss: here's to another five years.

I'm eternally grateful to have a strong group of people who support my home life, especially my dear girlfriends who don't mind late-night phone calls when I return from airports, provide vacation memos with meal plans, and potluck planning documents. And WoMos: thanks for all the gold stars over the past few years. You keep me going. Daysi Espinoza takes wonderful care of my children, especially when I'm on the road for multiple days at a time. My husband, Jack Levner, tolerates my musings, reflections, and practice sessions—and maintains a strong commitment to our family Google Calendar. Last but never least, thank you to my kids, Ada and Reed, who know how to put their shoes away in cubbies and can read calendars already. I see a Together Student on the horizon …

CONTENTS | WEBSITE RESOURCES

For downloadable tools, templates, samples, and other useful items please visit my.thetogethergroup.com. You'll find simple instructions on how to create an account in the back of the book, "How to Access Website Resources."

All Chapters

- Reader Reflection Guide (Reflection Questions + Reader Quizzes)
- Additional Resources and Helpful Links

Chapter 3: Set Goals: Define the Direction

- Ewing Marion Kauffman School Goals
- YES Prep Houston's Goals Powerpoint
- ANet's Goal-Setting Dashboard
- ANet's State of the Organization Agenda
- Rocketship's Annual Planning Process & Time line
- Rocketship's Annual Planning Kickoff Agenda
- ANet's Quarterly Stepback Agenda
- YES Prep Houston's State of the School
- TPSD Ops Goal Review Spreadsheet
- Talent Development Team Responsibilities
- Diana A's School Leadership Roles Chart
- YES Prep Houston's Role & Responsibilities
- Team Ops Big Rocks Calendar
- CANO Scorecard
- YES Prep Houston's School Director HIRs

SECTION 1

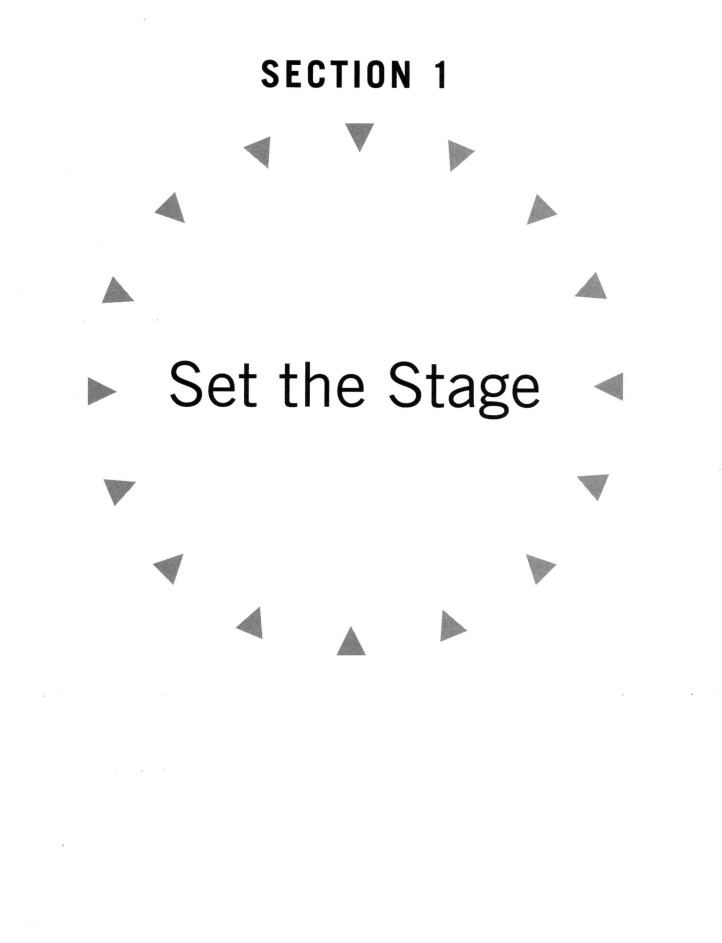

Set the Stage

CHAPTER 1

Leading in a Mission-Driven Context

It was June 17, 2003, 12:30 PM. I had no choice. I pulled my car over on a residential Houston street, threw down the driver's seat, and curled up for a catnap. In approximately sixty minutes, I'd be training fifty veteran educators on how to support rookie teachers over the summer. But right then, I needed to sleep. My backseat was packed to the brim with training materials and supplies hastily thrown into boxes. The address and directions for the training were scrawled on the back of an envelope. Oh, and did I mention I had another session scheduled for the very next day that I had not yet planned?

Now how did I get in this precarious predicament, you may ask? A dreadful combination of a new job, unclear roles and responsibilities, not enough sleep, poor delegation, and lack of preparation. I was an *un*-Together Leader, and I had hit a breaking point. And the stakes were high. We were preparing teachers to go in front of students. So on this day almost fifteen years ago, I made a vow to never, ever get myself into that kind of situation again.

Perhaps you empathize? You, too, may be trying to juggle the high volume of work and responsibility thrown at you every day. Maybe you have all your to-dos reasonably under control but wish you could be more planned ahead. Or maybe you're just exhausted and looking for a better way?

This book can work for you if you are a new manager. It can work for you if you've shifted careers from the corporate world into the nonprofit sector and you're thoroughly confused about the culture. Or maybe you've made the move from teaching to school or district leadership, or you've quickly realized your MBA was practical but didn't teach you how to prioritize in a world of limited resources. Or maybe you have been in your role for a few years and you realize that lack of Togetherness is holding you back from achieving your goals or securing a promotion. Perhaps you are trying to get your own mission-driven work off the ground. You may have unlimited vision and passion but require finer execution skills to make your dream a reality. Regardless of who you are, let this book be your guide in managing your time, energy, people's work, meetings, projects, and stuff. If we leaders are not Together, we will not get the ambitious results we want for our organizations. But if we are Together (along with a few other things), big and meaningful change *can* happen.

Some of you may have read my first book, *The Together Teacher*, a guide for teachers and other folks who work on a fixed schedule in on-your-feet environments without much discretionary time. But now you're a leader, and you have a different challenge: choice. You get to *choose* how you use your time. It's wonderful and daunting all at once.

WHAT DO YOU MEAN BY *MISSION-DRIVEN WORK*?

There are many, many books, blogs, apps, hacks, and more designed to boost your productivity and hone your time-management skills. This book is unique because it's designed for leaders in *mission-driven* settings who do their own work *and* manage the work of others. By mission driven, I simply mean anyone whose work ultimately serves the greater good. It doesn't have to be limited to nonprofit work, either. A mission-driven leader could be the person who oversees a community theater group, a Sunday school director, a chief financial officer of a housing organization, or a school principal.

So why is mission-driven work so different? In my work coaching leaders, I've seen mission-driven leaders face these specific challenges:

- The problems we are trying to eliminate (homelessness, poverty, and environmental concerns, just to name a few) or create solutions and innovations for are enormous, urgent, and critical.

- Our work is never ending. Resources are limited. We are often both managers *and* makers.

- Our goals can and should be ambitious. The volume of our work is intense.

- The emotional toll of our work cannot be understated. In any given week, leaders face tough conversations about apartment evictions, breaking up fights between students, or big layoffs.

It is no wonder that many mission-driven leaders are overwhelmed and ineffective and eventually burn out.

WHAT DO YOU MEAN BY *TOGETHERNESS,* ANYWAY?

What does a Together Leader look like anyway? What is my definition of Togetherness? I'm *deliberately* not using the term *organized* because, well, just being organized is simply not enough for a busy leader with an important mission at stake. I see Togetherness as a combination of prioritized, planned, efficient, organized, flexible, predictable, intentional, and reliable.

In the painful personal example that opened this book, a more Together Leader may have thought, "Maia knew the training for the veteran teachers was incredibly high stakes. Because she regularly reviewed her calendar three months in advance, she knew it was coming down the pike. Because it was a new training, she proactively scheduled a series of meetings with her deputy director to outline the objectives, create the activities, and design the practice in the month leading up to the training. Because Maia realized that the materials aspect of the workshop would be a huge crunch, she carefully delegated production to a summer intern and set several meetings to check on progress. The day before the training, she ran one more dress rehearsal; invited her deputy director to ask her the tough questions she anticipated would come up in the trainings; packed the materials in her car; printed out directions, a premade pacing guide, and a sheet to take questions and contact info; laid out her outfit; and got a good night's sleep." *That* leader would have been much more Together—and clearly would get to a better outcome, via planning, prioritizing, delegating, anticipating challenges, and operating efficiently.

> Togetherness means being
>
> - Prioritized
> - Planned
> - Efficient
> - Organized
> - Flexible
> - Predictable
> - Intentional
> - Reliable

Of course, Togetherness is just *one* aspect of effective leadership. There are so many more facets of people management, such as setting vision, investing in others, leading with heart, designing strategy, marketing and selling ideas, and so on. There are tons of books, executive courses, and grad school syllabi that cover this stuff. This book, however, focuses on just one aspect of leadership, one I believe is often neglected or discounted. There are very few classes in high school, college, or graduate school that really teach you how to design and execute personal, team, and organization-wide systems to reach your goals. As you head deeper into the following chapter, you will find several self-assessments about your tools, routines, and mind-sets to help you determine your Togetherness strengths as well as where you may have some gaps.

WHY TOGETHERNESS MATTERS EVEN MORE IN YOUR CONTEXT

I entered my first job as a nonprofit leader at Teach For America immediately after working as a classroom teacher—where I basically had *no* time. Teaching was an efficiency and prioritization game. But in my new role, everything was suddenly about choices: how to use my time, how to spend our limited money, and which staff to hire and when. With each new decision I was reminded of whose future was at stake. Yikes!

Togetherness is a means to an end. You can lead a strong organization without being completely Together. Many top-notch organizations do not subscribe to a culture of Togetherness and instead place strong value on turning on a dime, dropping everything to pursue an opportunity, and swooping in to flawlessly solve a crisis. I respect this. And a small percentage of people want this excitement on a daily basis for the rest of their lives.

The former chief talent officer in me would argue that this approach, though invigorating, will not build the teams and organizations we want over time. People get burnt out by late-night, never-ending meetings, and eventually even the most mission-dedicated individuals decide they want more time with their families. **The Together Leader is about finding the right balance between systems and spontaneity so that you can meet all of your organization's goals—and have a life!**

FAQ

Can this book work for me if I am not a mission-driven leader? I've grappled with this question myself, but the answer is yes. I actually believe everything in this book can be applied to any busy leader. Go for it!

On the flip side, it's also possible to be incredibly Together yet highly ineffective. I'm sure you have all met the color-coded colleague with her notebook always at the ready along with a specific set of pens and a very neat desk. But at the end of the year, she actually didn't accomplish any of her goals. This person often has a very mechanically clean calendar but doesn't always prioritize. She might get the next steps from meetings accomplished without issue but can't stop to reflect on if she is actually doing things that will ensure she reaches her goals.

Can you be effective without being Together? Yes, but only for a short period of time. Eventually your disorganization will catch up with you in *some* way, whether it's your team getting tired of operating in crisis mode, losing enough sleep that you get sick all the time, or your family forgetting what you look like.

The goal is to be Together *enough* to achieve your goals, do your job to the best of your ability, and enjoy your life. This can happen when you and your organization routinize all predictable work, make processes more efficient, and ruthlessly plan ahead. I want you to have more headspace to think innovatively and creatively, react smoothly to true emergencies, and minimize as much job-related stress and overwhelmedness as possible.

MY OWN TOGETHERNESS JOURNEY

It all started with my button collection when I was two years old … just kidding! In reality, I've been fortunate to work in leadership roles for several high-performing nonprofits and school districts. And I've served as a Together coach and trainer for organizations, traditional school districts, stand-alone charter schools, and more. I've directly coached leaders in start-up mode, those in rapid-growth mode, and veteran leaders trying to sustain systems. And my own Togetherness journey directly mirrors the way I decided to set up this book. Just as I had to learn to create and define systems for myself, systems for my teams, and then systems for my organizations, you will likely follow a similar path over the course of your career.

As I settled into my first nonprofit leadership role as an executive director at Teach For America, I needed to set a clear direction for my team. This helped me appreciate measurable goals, detailed plans to accomplish an ambitious set of objectives, and transparent roles and responsibilities.

After that, I oversaw a large summer teacher-preparation program that required me to manage an even larger team, this time spread out across the country. Together we learned about the value of managing our energy and ourselves to pull off a successful summer.

Following that, I took on an executive-level role in a growing charter school organization. Oh, and I got married and had two kids of my own. And so I really came to value organization-wide practices to support Togetherness—my organization and my family were rapidly scaling! Similar to you, I was interested in creating good in the world—*and* having a life.

WHY THIS BOOK IS DIFFERENT

Lots of good resources already exist on time management and leadership. Check out my website, www.thetogethergroup.com, for my ongoing list of favorite books, articles, and blogs. So why write (or read) another one? What's out there seems to split into two camps: the technical and the philosophical. On the technical side are outstanding titles such as *Getting Things Done* by David Allen and *Total Workday Control Using Microsoft Outlook* by Michael Linenberger. For those who want to focus on prioritization and the philosophy of leadership,

The 7 Habits of Highly Effective People and *First Things First*, both written by the dearly beloved Steven Covey, and *168 Hours* by Laura Vanderkam, are amazing. And I'm a big fan of *Your Best Just Got Better* by Jason Womack and *The Power of Habit* by Charles Duhigg for routines, habits, and efficiencies.

Yet none of these speaks directly to the unique challenges faced by leaders in mission-driven settings. Effective writing and training on Togetherness has to be practical—focused on tools and rituals—and neutral—applicable to anyone who leads people—whether in a school building, nonprofit, central office, or volunteer organization. I can't tell you what your goals or priorities should be, but I sure can help you achieve them by helping you ask the right questions, build the right tools, and develop the right rituals for yourself.

My work is rooted in this mind-set: *What is good is what works.* I draw best practices from many of the cited titles, but the bulk of my research and examples come directly from the thousands of workshop participants and many coaching clients I have been privileged to learn from in the past decade. I've been welcomed into high-performing nonprofits, strong school districts, advocacy organizations, and rural schools. And I've been fortunate enough to coach leaders of all levels directly in their own environments, which enables me to bear witness to every single emergency, interruption, and crisis that can throw off a well-planned day. You will see many of my past clients featured in this book. Quite deliberately, I have chosen people and organizations who get strong results but are not wild perfectionists.

One of my biggest observations is that the Togetherness journey is personal, specific to one's own habits, preferences, and organizational culture. I am not going to sell you a particular gadget, lock you into one specific app, or require you to purchase a certain planner. I'm remarkably indifferent about specific tools, but I'm a staunch believer in strong routines, planning, boundaries, and communication. And I'm going to really push you to ensure your goals are clear and your actions are aligned to meet them.

HOW THIS BOOK IS ORGANIZED

The Together Leader is organized into five sections. It is designed to be read sequentially, though I invite you to pick and choose chapters based on your specific needs. In between sections, you will also find real-life examples of how organizations have put systems into action. And peppered throughout, you will find vignettes of real-life leaders facing common challenges. Last, scattered between chapters, you will get to read Togetherness Talks from real-life mission-driven leaders, most of whom still continue in their current capacities—though a few have moved on to new ventures. In the case of a job move, I chose to keep the position listed at the time of the sample for consistency. But everyone's samples are active and the real deal. In several cases, we created cleaner versions if there was an issue with readability or pared down a document so you could dive more deeply but know this content is not invented! Almost all the tools and templates you'll see throughout the book can be found on my website, www.thetogethergroup.com, using the passcode provided with the book. There you will also find additional samples, videos, and modifiable templates.

Section 1: Set the Stage

These initial chapters set the stage for why productivity and time management in your unique, mission-driven context is so important. This section also helps you evaluate your current strengths and gaps as they relate to tools, routines, and mind-sets.

Chapter 1: Leading in a Mission-Driven Context: You are here! This chapter is designed to preview the what, why, and how of the book.

Chapter 2: Take Stock: Assess Your Togetherness Level: This chapter is full of quizzes and assessments to help you determine your current level of Togetherness and set your purpose for reading.

Section 2: Get Clear on Your Purpose

This section places our focus on preparing for your course, taking a long view, and making sure your priorities are in order:

Chapter 3: Set Goals: Define the Direction: This chapter ensures your goals are in order, you have time to systematically review progress, and your organization has a predictable calendar.

See It in Action: Goal Setting Start to Finish: How an organization sets and reviews its goals.

Chapter 4: Break Down the Goals: Create a Priority Plan: This chapter helps you boil down your Yearly Goals into a three-month path of clear actions that in turn should drive your calendar and meetings!

See It in Action: Wrist, Elbow, and Shoulder: How a leader articulates what she cares most about in her team's work.

Chapter 5: Align Your Meetings: Make a Meeting Matrix: Because leaders spend a ton of time in meetings, this chapter is designed to test your meeting schedule against your priorities—and communicate to others accordingly.

Section 3: Get Yourself Together

This section is designed to ensure your personal organization systems are securely Together! Even if you are already moderately Together, I recommend you spin through this section to confirm that your methods are airtight. You may also get some new ideas to tune up existing systems!

Chapter 6: Get Macro: Design a Comprehensive Calendar: In this chapter, I will take you through the development of a macro view of your calendar to ensure it reflects the priorities developed in the previous section.

Chapter 7: Strategic Procrastination: Design a Later List: The calendar cannot survive on its own! In this chapter, I help you capture all of the To-Dos related to your priorities—and consolidate all those other pesky To-Dos just running around!

Chapter 8: Reconcile Your Time and To-Dos: Create Your Weekly Plan: This chapter is where I get *really* specific, or micro, about your plan for the week.

Chapter 9: Keep It Together: Routines and Checklists: No tools work by themselves. They need care, love, and feeding. This chapter pushes you to set daily, weekly, and monthly rituals to keep Togetherness moving forward.

Chapter 10: Hold That Thought: Save It for Later! This chapter helps you separate your thoughts from your To-Dos so you can refer back to those good ideas in the future.

See It in Action: What Should I Carry? How a leader stays Together during a typical week—and what to carry!

Section 4: Get Your Team and Organization Together

This section describes the tools, systems, and routines necessary to function as a Together Team.

Chapter 11: Keep E-mail in Its Place: Drowning in e-mail? Is your team constantly pinging each other all day long? Get clear on communications in this chapter.

Chapter 12: Project Design, Planning, and Communication: More Than Just Spreadsheets! Some projects call for more detailed plans that you can easily share with others, or you may manage someone who leads very detailed projects. If so, you'll find help here.

Chapter 13: Become a Dynamic Duo: Maximize Your Assistant: If you are fortunate to have some administrative or operational support, you will benefit from this chapter, which helps you make the most of this important partnership.

See It in Action: The Management Memo: Check out a Management Memo from a leader who clearly articulates expectations to his teams.

Section 5: Put It All Together

In the final section of the book, I discuss how to synthesize all of your new tools and systems.

Chapter 14: Keep Track of Stuff, Space, and Knowledge: The physical clutter cannot be overlooked, nor can all of those documents lie around. This chapter helps you control that chaos.

Chapter 15: Create a Culture of Togetherness: I will share ideas about how to infuse Togetherness into your entire organization—from hiring to evaluation.

Chapter 16: Conclusion: Keep It All Together: Now that we've tackled systems for self, team, and organization, let's keep ourselves honest as the rubber hits the road!

And peppered throughout the book are Common Challenges that I see leaders face on a daily basis, whether they're drowning in e-mail, shifting priorities, or moving to different organizations.

HOW EACH CHAPTER IS ORGANIZED

Most chapters follow a predictable rhythm:

Seen and Heard. These quotes are directly from my workshop and webinar participants.

Overview and Objectives. The purpose of the tool and overview of objectives are given.

The Model. The models show the structure of each tool and share the thought process behind it.

The Examples. Each chapter includes two to three examples of actual tools from real-life leaders who use a variety of different products.

Build Your Own. These are step-by-step instructions on how to build your own tool, select the right product, and address common pitfalls.

The Routine. This section describes how to use your tool during the busy workday—and how to stay committed!

Start Strong. These are bullet points of how to quickly get started and a summary of the time commitment required.

HOW TO USE THIS BOOK

First get your own systems up to snuff, as described in section 1 and section 2. After you feel super sharp, move to team systems, going slowly to accommodate your colleagues' habits, preferences, and appetites. To make the most of the resources in this book, you could also try the methods listed in the following sections.

Independently with the Reader Reflection

I recommend downloading or printing out the Reader's Reflection Guide from my website, www.thetogethergroup.com. Here you will find diagnostics, discussion and thinking questions, and bulleted summaries to wrap up each section. Tuck a printed copy inside the cover of the book or keep a soft copy open on your desktop. If you complete the Reader Reflection as you review each chapter, I guarantee you will feel well equipped to tackle each aspect of Togetherness!

Accountability Partners

You could also read this book with a partner on your team, in your organization, or even in another organization. Select a chapter per week, share answers from the Reader Reflection, and examine the corresponding samples on my website. Working together, you can take the self-assessments and quizzes, share artifacts, and brainstorm roll-out processes with your teams. You might even send each other drafts of your tools.

Improve Team Performance

You could read this book as an entire team to see what concepts and rituals stick the most as a group. However, I do *not* recommend that you make portions of this book mandatory; that will quickly backfire on you in the form of quiet rebellion. In my experience, people get motivated to get it Together when they have a clear reason for digging in, such as increasing sustainability or better meeting their own goals.

Regardless of the approach you take to reading, I do recommend going into this book with some sort of clear plan of how you will digest, practice, and apply the tips and tools. Keep a list of ideas on a sticky note, a running document on your laptop, or in your Reader Reflection Guide. If you don't have a plan, you will walk away feeling overwhelmed—which is exactly what I *don't* want to happen!

NOTES ON TERMINOLOGY AND METHODOLOGY

Finally, a word about terminology: I could have easily titled this book *The Together Manager* or *The Together Supervisor*. I just like the word *leader* best. It feels more all-encompassing of all that we do and everything we try to accomplish. Throughout the book, however, I will use the terms interchangeably. There are lots of articles about the fair and valid differences among the different job titles, but I'm not here to debate them. I'm here to help you manage the time you have to support a cause you believe in. Call yourself what you want, because *you* are in charge.

Similarly, I know there are many names for support staff, but I'm going to use *assistant* and let you translate that to your own context. And instead of using the technical term *direct reports*, I'm most often going to say *team members*. Last, although some of you work for nonprofits, schools, charter school management companies, religious institutions, school districts, and more, I'm going to use the blanket term *organization* instead of *company* or *district*.

This enables me to be as neutral as possible to meet your various needs. Everyone is working with a mission in mind.

In almost all cases, I'm using real people and real organizations who have agreed to open their calendars and habits to you. I'm sure there are many Together leaders and organizations not represented. I always love to gather new examples, so please do feel free to send them my way via my website. Not one of my featured people or organizations is perfect in every way. We all have areas to work on in our own Togetherness journeys. But every single person, team, and organization profiled here is putting forth a concerted effort to keeping Together to help meet professional and personal goals—whatever they may be.

TOGETHERNESS IS A MEANS TO AN END

In case you cannot already tell, I'm a huge fan of clear expectations, organizational routines, and planning for the unexpected. This is *not* a book about being organized just to have a clean desk. This book is to help you feel and *be* more successful driving toward your mission—and maybe, just maybe, having a life along the way! This book is focused on helping you think about your own time—and your people's time—as a manager. This book is about developing tools, habits, and systems to effectively and efficiently lead a team. This book is about creating plans for expected work so we can deal with the unanticipated stuff when it inevitably arises. This book is the nuts and bolts of effective time management in a leadership role at a mission-driven organization: how to weigh the urgent call that comes through against the need to revamp staff orientation, how to plan purposefully for a meeting, and then follow up. This book is not about color-coding, alphabetizing, or creating perfect paper files. In fact, there will be multiple times I encourage messiness and improvisation.

Togetherness matters *more* in mission-driven work—and no one has taught it—until now!

Togetherness Talks: Shawn Mangar

Name: Shawn Mangar

Title: Founding principal of Baychester Middle School (NYC Department of Education)

Why Togetherness matters: My workload is endless but my time isn't. Togetherness allows me to make the most of every minute.

Tell me about the mission and scope of your work. What are you most proud of?

My goal was to develop an organization that places the needs of students above all else while simultaneously providing staff with the best resources and opportunities to excel at one of the hardest jobs in the world. I'm proud of the fact that we've taken our student community service commitment from an ideal to a reality by ensuring every student has the opportunity to actively support the Bronx community with their advisory class each year.

At 10 AM on any given workday, what might I find you doing?

A typical day involves reigniting the best friend status of two middle students, providing instructional feedback to teachers, and planning or leading teacher training.

What is your favorite Together Tool and why?

I'm a huge fan of the software program Flow. It allows me to focus on my priorities, break down larger projects into bite-sized pieces, and monitor the deliverables of our team.

Tell me how you start and end each day to remain Together.

I begin every morning with a ten-minute meeting with my secretary, Elsa. We preview the day and discuss any tasks that need to get done. I end each workday with a fifteen-minute meeting with my codirector, Liz. We support each other by staying focused on the big rocks and holding ourselves accountable to our To-Do Lists for the next day or week.

What is a challenge you still face with Togetherness?

I'm addicted to e-mail and ESPN .com. I'm working on allocating specific time frames each day for checking e-mail and focusing on one task at a time without self-interruptions.

How do you remain focused when the work is swirling around you?

I often take a five-minute break and go interact with our students at recess or gym. This instantly puts me in a better mood. Our students have the ability to motivate me without even knowing it. After time with them, I head back to my desk to write everything down and reprioritize as needed.

What happens when you get interrupted or ambushed?

In the moment, I tend to deal with the problem at hand. Afterwards, I like to take a step back and identify the organizational breakdown that led to the interruption and strategize about how I can prevent it from occurring in the future.

It's 10 AM on a Saturday morning. What keeps you rejuvenated and renewed?

Saturdays involve taking a spin class with my wife or playing Battleship with my nieces and nephew.

What have you learned to let go?

I've let go of organizing e-mails into specific file folders and ironing my school embroidered polo.

CHAPTER 2

Take Stock
Assess Your Togetherness Level

Togetherness is a means to an end—strong results and retention of great people, I would argue. But you may have picked up this book for a number of other very valid reasons. At the beginning of workshops, I usually have all leaders write on a card what they hope their Togetherness outcome will be and the benefit they think it will have. I get all kinds of thought-provoking responses, but some of my favorites include these:

- Balanced so I can do my job for a long time
- Consistent so my team knows what to expect
- Proactive so I feel like I'm moving the most important work forward
- Focused so I can make progress toward goals
- Intentional so I make thoughtful decisions

Reader Reflection
What is *your* Togetherness goal? What impact will it bring to you? Your intention can change over time, so this is a question worth asking yourself a few times per year.

OVERVIEW AND OBJECTIVES

This chapter will describe different levels of Togetherness, ask you to take an honest self-assessment, and set your purpose for how and where to focus your reading.

In this chapter, you will do the following:

- Define your current level of Togetherness and envision your next steps.
- Articulate the mind-sets necessary to execute Togetherness.
- Identify the key tools required to pull off Togetherness.
- Determine how you will build the habits and keep them alive.

TOGETHERNESS LEVELS

In my experience, people fall along a few different levels on the Togetherness spectrum (figure 2.1). This book will work for you no matter where you are—but it helps to know, so you can target your growth and next steps!

Level 1: I need to hunt and gather! This is the earliest stage of Togetherness. If this describes you, it's likely that your desk, bag, and in-box are a complete mess. You may leave a trail of paper or digital breadcrumbs in your wake. You keep a lot of stuff "in your head." You may be stressed, overwhelmed, and prone to missing deadlines. If you are a hunter-gatherer, your Together Task is to write everything down and locate all important items.

Level 2: I need to consolidate! You know where your To-Dos are (written on whiteboards, sticky notes, and other locations), but you have *too* many systems going on. You have the right instincts but the wrong habits. You may be considered a "promiscuous organizer," one who hops from system to system without a faithful commitment. If you are a consolidator, it's time to reel in all of those To-Dos, dates, deadlines, and projects and get them in one single location.

Level 3: I need to plan! You know where everything is and it's all in one place. You rarely miss deadlines and you have a strong sense of your work—in the day-to-day. But you are not as planned ahead as you would like to be. You may fall prey to the lure of the lusty checkmark, becoming easily distracted by the immediate work right in front of you but forgetting to look ahead. If you are a planner, you will focus on planning beyond a single day or week.

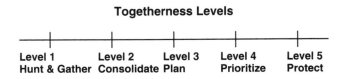

Figure 2.1 Togetherness Spectrum

Level 4: I need to prioritize! You know where everything is in your world, and your To-Dos and deadlines are reasonably planned out. You get a lot of stuff done, but is it the right stuff? Have you proactively determined what is *most* important in your work and figured out how to let everything else fall in place around it? If you are a prioritizer, your job is to engage in the painful process of identifying your most important work and building structures to support it.

Level 5: I need to protect! Ah, the final stage of Togetherness ... the protector. You've gathered, consolidated, planned, and prioritized. Now you need to fiercely protect your time to focus on the most important work. You set clear boundaries with colleagues, bosses, and team members; your focus and discipline are razor sharp. You are rarely distracted by emergencies, and people feel a slight level of trepidation when randomly interrupting you. If you are a protector, you will focus on articulating expectations with your team and others.

Reader Reflection

What is your current level of Togetherness? Where do you need to focus?

THE TOOLS YOU NEED

Mind-sets and routines matter most (and more on those in a minute), but you will also need a set of practical tools to support yourself on your journey. Not all leaders will need all tools; I encourage you to use the self-assessment later in this chapter to help you pick and choose the ones best for you. For example, if you scored low in the questions about prioritization, then you should double down on creating a Priority Plan. Let's take a peek at our guiding graphic—something I affectionately call Maia's Togetherness Tools (figure 2.2).

Figure 2.2 The Togetherness Tools

Let's review the definitions of each tool I will share in this book.

Yearly Goals. The outcomes you are responsible for achieving over the course of a year; you may also have longer-term goals, a vision statement, or a strategic narrative to describe where you want to be in three to five years.

Roles and Responsibilities: These clearly describe who does what across your organization.

Annual Activities: Different than your Yearly Goals, your Annual Activities outline recurring work that must be done at certain times per year.

Priority Plans. Three-month extractions from your Yearly Goals that name what matters most for you and your team; they also define the high-level actions needed to arrive at the desired outcomes.

Project Plans. Step-by-step work plans to achieve desired outcomes on cross-functional projects.

Meeting Matrix. An articulation of who you meet with, when, and why; this helps shape each meeting's required preparation and standing agenda items.

Comprehensive Calendar. A long-term, macro view of your calendar that reflects your priorities.

Later List. A long-term and total list of To-Dos, organized and grouped in some logical fashion.

Meeting Notes. Systematic methods for planning, facilitating, and following through on your various meetings to ensure time is well spent and aligned with your priorities.

Thought Catchers. A unified place to record your thoughts for people, teams, or topics to reference at a more appropriate time.

Weekly or Daily Worksheet. An hour-by-hour view of your time and To-Dos for the week ahead, created *before* the week starts.

Management Memo. An outline of meeting, planning, and communications expectations for your team.

Working Agreements. An organization-wide understanding of communication and Togetherness agreements.

Don't worry if all of these definitions feel daunting at the moment. These are not all fourteen-page documents that you will spend hours creating. Some of them may be as simple as a handwritten list.

READER QUIZ: TOGETHERNESS TOOLS

Now that you have seen where you fall on the spectrum of Togetherness, let's drill down into some specific tools and habits. *Warning:* I am going to get graphic here. This self-assessment is designed to rigorously examine your current habits. Don't feel bad about your work—I *know* you are getting it done. This is all about getting a little better and a little stronger! If you would like to take the quiz digitally, be sure to download the Reader Reflection Guide from www.thetogethergroup.com.

Quiz
Togetherness Assessment
After reading each statement, consider your current practice and rank yourself on a scale of one to three in table 2.1, table 2.2, and table 2.3. Three means you don't think your system could get better, two means you get mixed results from your current system, and one means you don't have a system. And yes, if you must, you can have good-day and bad-day answers!

Table 2.1 Togetherness Assessment: Section 1

Section 1: Get Yourself Together	Rating
1. My calendar reflects my goals and priorities. There is time blocked for proactive work.	
2. I have everything in one place. For example, all deadlines are in one calendar.	
3. I have a place to note immediate To-Dos that pop up during the day.	
4. I have a place to record longer-term action items and I regularly refer back to them.	
5. I can easily select the most important thing to do at any given moment.	
6. I have a method for tracking delegated work, deadlines, and feedback.	
7. I reliably follow up from meetings.	
8. I can easily access reference information, data, and other needed tools with little wasted time.	
9. I am able to focus for a sustained period of time during work blocks.	
10. I complete tasks efficiently with little procrastination.	
11. I can accurately predict how long my To-Dos will take to complete.	
12. It is always appropriate to use my system. For example, if I am digital, I can always access my tools.	
13. My system is highly portable; it is easy for me to carry it everywhere all the time.	
14. My system is synchronized across all devices and gadgets.	
15. If applicable, I use administrative supports to their fullest.	

The tools that will help you most master the outcomes in this assessment are at the foundation of the Togetherness Tools: Comprehensive Calendar, Later List, Weekly/Daily Worksheet, Thought Catchers, and Meeting Notes.

Table 2.2 Togetherness Assessment: Section 2

Section 2: Get Your Team Together	Rating
1. I have a strong sense of my team's goals and priorities, and we discuss progress regularly.	
2. My team knows which results I care about most and why; they keep me in the loop on the right stuff.	
3. I have regular standing meetings focused on the right topics, at the right times, with strong follow-through.	
4. My team has articulated expectations for management routines and rhythms, such as meeting preparation.	
5. Roles and responsibilities are clearly articulated and regularly reviewed.	
6. There are clear expectations for planning tools required, such as Project Plans and Priority Plans.	
7. Our communication agreements are clear and concise. We know when to use e-mail versus other vehicles for communication.	
8. I have systematic and regular methods for communicating information to my team in a manageable format.	
9. My team is clear on which decisions are made by whom and why. Decisions are anticipated in advance.	

The tools that will help you most master the outcomes in this assessment work their way up the Togetherness Tools with a focus on Priority Plans, Roles and Responsibilities, Meeting Matrix, Project Plans, and Communication Agreements.

Table 2.3 Togetherness Assessment: Section 3

Section 3: Get Your Organization Together	Rating
1. We have thoughtful, recurring, and predictable goal-setting cycles.	
2. We carefully allocate team time and resources to meet those goals.	
3. Our organization chart is current, clear, and communicated.	
4. We have systems to capture knowledge, learnings, documents, and data.	
5. We onboard, train, and support practices of Togetherness for our new employees.	
6. We use shared technology, such as consistent calendar tools, to their fullest potential.	
7. When an emergency or opportunity arises, we have conversations about how and if we will adjust resources.	

The tools that wlil help you most here sit at the top of the Together Tools: Onboarding Overviews, Yearly Goals, Annual Activities, Organizational Charts, and Scorecards.

Reader Reflection

Examine your responses.

- What strengths emerged that you didn't know you had?
- Did any gaps get exposed? Which ones? Why?
- Which overall section had the highest scores? Lowest?

If you had any one section rated below the others, I would suggest starting there.

ROUTINES RULE

No Together Tool exists in a vacuum. Any tool needs a routine to create it and keep it alive. Over time, I've observed the routines present in the most Together (and successful) leaders.

Quiz

Routines Rule Assessment

Please review each of the routines in table 2.4 and rate yourself on a scale of one to three. Three means you consistently act in accordance with the routine. Two means you sometimes act in line with the statement. One means you do not adhere to this routine at all.

Table 2.4 Routines Rule Assessment

Routines Rule	Score
1. I pause and reprioritize each day when needed.	
2. I pause and plan ahead on a weekly basis.	
3. I pause and plan ahead each month or quarter.	
4. I have checklists or templates for regularly occurring events.	
5. I plan my workload with my energy levels in mind.	
6. I have methods for batch processing similar types of work.	
7. When an emergency arises, I have a method for analyzing and deciding on its importance.	

If you had low marks for any of these statements, I suggest focusing on routines in chapter 9.

Reader Reflection

Examine your responses.

- Where are your routines strong? Why?

- Did any gaps get exposed? Which ones? Why?

MIND-SETS MATTER (MORE THAN ANYTHING)

Now that you have examined your tools and routines, there is one more missing element—mind-sets! This is perhaps most important.

Quiz

Mind-Sets Matter Assessment

Please review each mind-set in table 2.5 and rate yourself on a scale of one to three. Three means you consistently act in accordance with the mind-set. Two means you sometimes act in line with the statement. One means you do not adhere to this mind-set at all.

Table 2.5 Mind-Sets Matter Assessment

Routines Rule	Score
1. **The more planned you are, the more flexible you can be.** Although some people utterly abhor scheduling every moment, I promise that detailed planning will feel good. When a crisis or opportunity arises, you'll actually know and be able articulate the trade-offs on your time. Most of us automatically swing toward the urgent. Although that may often be the right move, I want you to understand what you are sacrificing to do so.	
2. **Whether we like it or not, our credibility is on the line.** We've all been there. You know how quickly you identify those people who will deliver for you and those who will not? Well, people are doing the same about you, too! If we bottleneck decisions, wait two months to answer e-mails, or show up to meetings unprepared, people will judge us quickly. If we run a bumpy hiring process or turn in a grant report late, the consequences are dire—for our personal reputations and the success of our organizations.	
3. **If you base your success on completing a daily To-Do List, you will never feel successful.** The work you do is too big and important to complete each day. And even when you do check things off your list, I'm sure you or someone else dreams up other items to accomplish. Instead of crossing off To-Dos from a list, I want to you to think constantly, "Am I doing the right thing at the right time?" Togetherness is not about ticking things off a list but rather ensuring the right things are done by the right people at the right times.	

(continued)

Table 2.5 Continued

Routines Rule	Score

4. **Predictable routines and systems enable us to focus on bigger, bolder, more creative work!** You *could* read a book like this and actually *over*-implement its ideas. You *could* have your takeaway be that every second of the day has to be mapped out and is *never* moveable. But that is not what we're going for here. What I'm pushing you to do is to routinize as much predictable work as possible in order to free up your brain and time for the bigger and more creative work.

5. **There are no perfect tools, only consistent routines.** Try as you might to find one, no perfect productivity tool exists—though some are clearly better than others. It's your *use* of the tool that will have the greatest impact. Whether you run from a pack of index cards in your back pocket or an app'd-out (is that a word?) iPad, each tool will only be as good as its user.

6. **Clear and up-front expectations are way better than back-end cleanup.** At your first read, some of the suggested structures in this book could be perceived as micromanaging. But if they're designed and implemented with the right spirit and good doses of input, I promise they can be incredibly empowering to your teams. Most people learn what their managers want via observation and osmosis. Let's stop wasting time by making people guess and just be clear instead!

7. **As we go, so go our teams.** You know when you've stayed up late and sent that e-mail with the 11:30 PM time stamp? Well, you are being watched and emulated, whether you like it or not. Whatever you model will be what follows in your organization. I want you to live your own expectations for Togetherness so your habits don't become the default. Unless, of course, they're the right ones!

8. **We have greater agency over our time than we believe we do.** You may think you don't have control over your time, but I promise you do. Everyone has some level of agency, from the office manager who is frequently interrupted by parents to the district HR professional who is constantly pulled into grievance battles. Claiming your power usually starts with communicating a point of view on where you think your time should go and then asking others to help you protect it.

9. **Just because you set boundaries doesn't mean you don't care about the mission.** This one kills me. Given the importance of our organization's goals to better society, many mission-driven leaders feel guilty for having personal lives. I'm fine with you being all-in—and I'm right there with you. That said, we all need to eat well, sleep enough, and be healthy—or else our organizations don't get what they deserve.

10. **There is no magical priority fairy.** "I am not sure what my priorities even *are*." That's something I hear over and over. Well, make a guess, put them on paper, and share them with someone who can help you confirm and revise. No one else is going to magically spout off your priorities! This one's on you.

Reader Reflection
Which of these mind-sets surprise you? Resonate with you? Why?

BUILD THE HABIT

Sometimes, the mind-sets are there and you've picked up some good tools and routines. But staying consistently Together on an ongoing basis (e.g., "being in a committed relationship" with your system) is a real challenge. There are many ways to build habits; I recommend Charles Duhigg's *The Power of Habit* if you want to learn more. But in the meantime, here are a few things I've learned along the way on my own journey:

1. **Remember your guiding light.** Be clear on *why* you are reading this book and embarking on your own Togetherness journey. I like to plan ahead so I can deliver great workshops, write well, and spend time with my family. I also like to sleep enough because without that, well, nothing goes well! What's your big purpose?

2. **Make it easy on yourself.** I was in my late thirties while writing this book and decided I needed an exercise habit once and for all. I did a few small things like move my workout clothes into a drawer in my bedroom (from the office closet where they were previously living), bought doubles of toiletries so I could shower at the gym, and got a bike to vary my workouts. I knew sheer willpower alone would not make me exercise; I also had to take some small steps to make it easier on myself. How can you make keeping Together easy on yourself?

3. **Enlist others.** I hedged on writing this book a year longer than I should have, even though I knew I had it in me! But once I let Jossey-Bass know I was interested and started telling workshop participants I was going to do it, I was too chicken not to deliver. Publicly state your intention and let others help keep you honest!

Reader Reflection
What supports will you leverage as you build your Togetherness habit?

DON'T GO ON AN ORGANIZATIONAL BINGE

One common mistake I see people make is to go all out all at once. Such as the minute you read this whole book, you run to Staples and spend a million dollars, or you totally app out your smartphone and tablet (even though you hate technology), or you tell your team you are no longer available for anything. Go slooooowwww, and spread this work out over time.

Table 2.6 Togetherness Timeline

Month	Tool
Month 1	Set Yearly Goals and Roles and Responsibilities
Month 2	Individual Scorecards, Priority Plans, and Meeting Matrix
Month 3	Comprehensive Calendar, Later List
Month 4	Weekly Worksheet, Thought Catchers
Month 5	Project Plans and Communication Agreements
Month 6	Make a Plan for Space and Stuff

Whether you are creating new tools, building new habits, or establishing new routines, take it one thing at a time. I recommend approaching the book in the order shown in table 2.6.

Although the book is designed to have each chapter build on the ones before it, there is no harm in skipping around to meet your immediate needs. Plus, the sooner you feel successful, the faster you will build the habits!

LET'S JUMP IN

The rationale has been set, you believe I'm a credible character, and you understand that this book is about *way* more than just organizing your e-mail and crossing To-Dos off a list. You are ready for action! In the next section, we'll make sure that your goals are tight, you have a plan to regularly review them, and it is clear who does what!

Togetherness Talks: Natalie Rubio

Name: Natalie Rubio

Title: Director, Effective Teacher Fellowship, Houston Independent School District

Why Togetherness matters: So I can have a full life!

Tell me about the mission and scope of your work. What are you most proud of?
I have the privilege of driving work to ensure that our kids in Houston ISD have effective, novice teachers. I'm proud of our work's impact and influence, and I'm more proud to be paying it forward as an HISD alumna.

At 10 AM on any given workday, what might I find you doing?
I have the privilege of driving work to ensure that our kids in Houston ISD have effective, novice teachers. I'm proud of our work's impact and influence, and I'm more proud to be paying it forward as an HISD alumna.

What is your favorite Together Tool and why?
The Thought Catcher is my favorite tool because it minimizes countless e-mails and texts and gives others the perception that I have an elephant's memory.

Tell me how you start and end each day to remain Together.
I start each day with a 5 AM Cross-Fit class, and I end each day cuddling my husband and my ARC notebook. I don't want to lose either one! And a text message or call from my college-student daughter – at the start or end of the day – helps me remain Together.

What is a challenge you still face with Togetherness?
Exercising flexibility and patience when others around me—internally or externally—lack Togetherness.

How do you remain focused when the work is swirling around you?
In the summer months in Houston, I drive to a local refresqueria for a raspa (snow cone). Any other time, I drive to a campus our team supports and then plant myself in a classroom. Being in the presence of kids always grounds me and reminds me why I grind the way I do. It's all for them.

What happens when you get interrupted or ambushed?
This doesn't happen a ton because of our team's Beast Mode flag system (see chapter 8 for more!). When it does, I ensure that I schedule a few fifteen- to thirty-minute buffers every day.

It's 10 AM on a Saturday morning. What keeps you rejuvenated and renewed?
I'm generally eating a *huge* breakfast after a Suicide Saturday CrossFit class.

What have you learned to let go?
I've learned that it's not a good use of time to try and coach mind-set and attitude. What I can control and influence are the ways I coach and manage performance, and at the end of the day, the results are what matter for our kiddos!

Get Clear on Your Purpose

CHAPTER 3

Set Goals
Define the Direction

SEEN AND HEARD

"Individually we're generally efficient and mostly organized, but as a team we're a mess—it's unclear what our goals are and what we are working toward."

"I think roles and responsibilities aren't transparent to the people on my team. They are constantly wanting to be told exactly what to do, which makes me feel like I always have to figure it out for them before they actually can do things."

OVERVIEW AND OBJECTIVES

There are many wonderful resources on goal setting out there. This book will not introduce any more. I actually almost *didn't* include this chapter at all because there is already so much literature on the topic. However, when pen (or keyboard!) came to paper, I realized this book couldn't exist without a nod to the need for incredibly clear and purposeful direction. Ultimately, this direction should help us decide what we do each day when we arrive at work.

Whether your goals are SMART (strategic, measurable, ambitious, realistic, and time bound), targets, benchmarks, or currently nonexistent, you need to have some sort of grand idea of where you and your team are headed. In this chapter, you will find resources on goal setting, anecdotes about how organizations set goals, ideas for keeping them alive, and, of course, instruction on how to align your time and your organization's time to reviewing

Figure 3.1 The Togetherness Tools

the goals. This last step is where the real magic happens. You will also find sections on articulating roles and responsibilities and holding people accountable to outcomes.

If the process of yearly goal setting is going to hold you back from implementing the rest of the tools and routines in this book, I recommend skipping this chapter and coming back around to it at the end of reading. But please promise to return, because everything must tie back to our goals!

In this chapter, you will do the following:

- Articulate your goals in a clear and simple fashion.
- Cascade your organization's goals from team to individual.
- Plan to review your goals at regular intervals.
- Align your goal-setting process to your organization's calendar.
- Ensure job roles and responsibilities and scorecards are clearly articulated in order to achieve goals.

Right now, we are at the very top of the Togetherness Tools. The goals we set here will ultimately define how we spend our days (see figure 3.1)!

HOW DO I SET YEARLY GOALS?

Now before you go running for the hills because goal setting is *the* thing everyone told you that you *must* do before you do *anything* else on this earth, please understand that I'm operating under the assumption that you already have decent goals in place *or* you are so deep in start-up mode that thinking one year ahead sounds absolutely ridiculous.

You may have to attend a mountaintop retreat to figure out what your organization stands for, or it may be as easy as just writing down the goals you all carry in your heads. But at some point, you will have to decide what you care about the most and put it on paper for the next year—and beyond.

You are welcome to select any method you wish, but if you want to go simple, I think SMART goals are the best place to get started. You do not need to hire a management consultant to lead your team through a complicated process. Just choose some items that matter the most and try to keep it simple. If you do not already have a clear picture of how you define your endgame, I'd recommend picking up a copy of *Managing to Change the World* by Allison Green and Jerry Hauser. Read their chapter on SMART goals before you get started here. And if you find yourself up late at night hyperlinking spreadsheets, back up and make it simpler. Let's peek into two different models. The first is from a small organization in Kansas City, the Ewing Marion Kauffman School. The CEO, Hannah Lofthus, shared her model with me (see figure 3.2).

Yearly Goals

1: Build on strong school academic and culture performance

Academic Metrics

- 1.25 years growth on all assessments
- 75% proficiency on Missouri Assessment Program (MAP)
- Curriculum and assessments aligned for grades 5–8 by June
- High school opens in August

Culture Metrics

- 95% lifework completion
- 95% average daily attendance
- 75% student retention rate in grades 5–8
- 75% stakeholder satisfaction
- College readiness continuum by June

2: Planning and documenting systems for growth

Metrics

- Training manual for all positions created by June
- All necessary operations functions and services are properly documented
- Each department has a continuum of development and benchmark goals for current year and beyond
- Beginning, middle, and end of year audits of all project plans

3: Create world class talent: Cement staff leadership development

Metrics

- 100% of staff have scheduled one-on-one meetings with direct manager
- >85% of teachers agree or strongly agree that they are receiving adequate professional development
- Internal candidates for Principal, Dean of Students, Director of Special Education, and Director of Operations
- Chief level leadership team expanded by June
- Succession plans in place for CEO, Principals, Dean of Students, and Director of Operations
- Partnership with external human capital organization expanded or created

Figure 3.2 Ewing Marion Kauffman School Goals

I like that her sample includes

- Inspirational big buckets, such as "Create world-class talent!" This keeps the mission alive and is way more motivational than just a list of numbers on a spreadsheet.
- A combination of quantitative outcomes, "More than 85% of teachers agree or strongly agree they are receiving adequate professional development," and measurable activities, "training manual for all positions created by June."
- It's short. The full version is just two pages, and it is easy to share, publish, and review.

Let's peek into a school sample. I like an example from Eric Newcomer, a school director at YES Prep Public Schools, in Houston, Texas. Figure 3.3 and Figure 3.4 show an excerpt from his goals PowerPoint presentation.

There are several reasons why I like Eric's view of his school goals:

- The goals are connected to broad categories, such as student achievement and staff retention.
- The presentation is very simple so it can be easily shared and published.
- They are highly measurable so progress can be tracked.

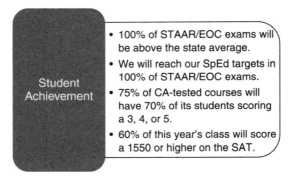

Figure 3.3 YES Prep Presentation Slide

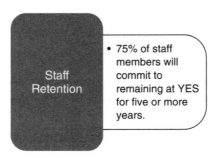

Figure 3.4 YES Prep Presentation Slide

HOW DO I SET QUANTITATIVE GOALS?

If you don't currently have measurable goals, and you would like to get started, I would go back to the SMART chapter in *Managing to Change the World*. In sum:

- Decide what you and your constituents care about most.

- Plan how you will measure progress.

- Review past data to determine how much effort you want to increase or if maintaining steady is okay for now.

- Compare your past data and goals to those from similar organizations.

FAQ: Should I set goals for *everything*?
You should set goals for the outcomes you care about most. What doesn't get measured doesn't get done.

You need goals so your Togetherness practices steer you toward the outcomes you want to achieve. We work in mission-driven contexts where the stakes for success are high. If we don't know what we are ultimately shooting for, it can be hard to know if we have done right for the world. Time is our most limited resource, so we need to direct it to the right stuff.

FAQ: What if I work in a start-up or an organization where the goals are not clear?
This does make the situation a lot more challenging. That said, you must figure out what you are shooting for so that you can figure out if you have accomplished what you'd hoped. There are a few approaches you can take. Review your job description, your office's mission, your boss's calendar, your board's stated desires, and your constituents' wishes, and put something on paper that resembles Hannah's and Eric's models. Then share it with your boss or board and ask if it looks directionally on track. You have to start somewhere!

Reader Reflection
How clear are my organization's or team's goals? If you don't currently have any goals, start by listing yours in the table in the Reader Reflection Guide for this chapter.

CREATE A TIME LINE FOR GOAL SETTING—AND PUT SOMEONE IN CHARGE

Most organizations set Yearly Goals in line with a natural cycle, whether that be the fiscal year, school year, or testing calendar. The best organizations all take time to reflect backwards and improve performance for the following year. Your goals should ultimately drive how you spend your time each day. Togetherness is about more than just checking things off a list; I want you to be constantly asking yourself, "Am I doing the right work at the right time?"

The Achievement Network's Goal-Setting Time Line

Once you have your big goals in place, you'll usually need to involve colleagues from the rest of your organization to either ratify them or set their own to support yours. The Achievement Network (ANet), a nonprofit organization based in Boston, sets the following goal-setting cycle to follow their fiscal year:

June: Yearly Goals are proposed to leadership team.

July: Team leaders introduce organization goals to team and set team level goals.

August: Individual performers set their own metrics for annual evaluations.

September: Goals are presented back to organization, board, and other constituents.

Looks good, right? ANet's goals cascade down from organization to individual. But Michelle Odemwingie, the chief of staff for ANet, said, "Our process has actually evolved over time. We've come to learn that not all goals need to be set at the same time of the year because we don't receive all data points back at the same point in the year. And theoretically we could have the senior leadership team sit in a dark room and name what they want to see happen, but that would lack the level of clarity and buy in that is essential to ensuring that our organizational [anizational] goals are a living, breathing part of the way that we all orient and operate as one team." ANet laid out a dashboard that helps them chart out goals, metrics, targets, and a clear process for owners and timing. Figure 3.5 shows their dashboard template.

I love the clarity of ANet's goals, process, and owners. This is the place where many organizations lose focus. But here's how ANet stays aligned:

- There is space to provide key dates when the target is proposed by the senior leadership team with an acknowledgment that not all targets can be set on the same time line.

- Each goal has a clear owner and identifies who is consulted and helps set the target.

- The dashboard has a clear place to update ongoing progress with the status review.

Goals are rarely set in isolation. Their creation usually involves some back and forth among multiple parties, and they may have to be adjusted in light of shifting data or landscapes. But goals for the organization, team, and self need to be set via a clear process. This way your

Current Year's Org-Wide Goals		Metric	Last Year's Target	Proposal for 2015–16	Recommendation Owner	Consult/ Helpers	Initial Target proposed	Final target confirmed by S team	Status
School and student learning	Students	% of schools making student gains or sustaining high performance							
	Teachers	TBD (currently Teaching Composite measuring teachers' usage of standards and data to shape instruction)							
	Leaders	% of schools that meet practice goals							
Partnership strength and growth	Value	School leader Net Promoter Score							
	New?	Teacher Net Promoter Score							
	Retention	% school renewal							
	Growth	# partner schools							
Org health and sustainability	Staff engagement	% organizational strength (Gallup 12)							
	Core values	% agreement ANet lives core values							
	Finances	Cost per school							

Figure 3.5 ANet Goal-Setting Dashboard

organization can put the right resources—time, money, and people—toward a shared vision. In the absence of this, your organization's mission may get unintentionally diffused.

After the goal-setting time line is in place, meeting agendas must match. ANet sets an annual "state of the organization agenda" to reflect on the past year and kick off the year ahead.

As you can see in figure 3.6, there is a significant amount of time dedicated to the following:

- Thinking beyond a year
- Reviewing Yearly Goals across various dimensions, such as student performance and school practice
- Looking ahead for their must wins (more on these Priority Plans in chapter 4)

Figure 3.7 is another example from Rocketship Education that illustrates their entire goal-setting process and time line from start to finish. This process is not only to set goals, but also to allocate resources. The finished template that each team fills out includes initiatives and people and monetary resourcing that they'll need to do their work toward those goals.

I specifically like a few things in Rocketship's example:

- The cascading process from the senior leadership teams (SLTs) to department heads
- The HR team setting aside time to check in with team leaders
- Key initiatives being finalized by March 17 before all goals are set (presumably to ensure teams have enough resources)

Not only did Rocketship put time and thought into their goal-setting and prioritization process but also they held a thoughtful kick-off meeting to invest and train their team leaders. Let's peek at their agenda in figure 3.8.

Because there is often collaboration across key initiatives or staffing across projects, it makes sense to do some organization- and team-level planning before teams set goals in isolation.

Reader Reflection
What is your organization's goal-setting time line? Do you need a kick-off meeting to introduce the process?

Put the Right Person in Charge
Once you have your goals and a clear time line in place to set them, someone must be appointed to be in charge of monitoring progress, aligning meetings to goal reviews, and

July Offsite
State of the Org Agenda
Wednesday, July 8
9am - 11am

Objectives:

- Welcome everyone and celebrate milestones
- Reflect on year's events that shaped us and our work
- Reflect on year at ANet
- Kick off the day that kicks off our year ahead

I.   People News

    A. Sharing and naming the New Faces in the organization

    B. Celebrating personal milestones across the organization (weddings, house purchases, babies, marathons, graduations other ...)

II. Year beyond ANet

    A. Headlines and current events that shaped our perspective

    B. Education landscape news that impacted our schools

III. Year at Anet

    A. Reflections from the moments we shared during Friday Team Check-Ins

    B. Takeaways from our 10 Year Anniversary Calls

    C. Progress on this year's Must Wins

    D. Anchoring in our refresh of our 2020 Strategy

IV. Review of our Annual Goals

    A. Student Performance

    B. School Practice Change

    C. Teaching Composite

    D. Partnership Strength

    E. Partnership Growth

    F. Org Health Survey & Core Values

V.   Looking Ahead

    A. Sharing of next year's Must Wins

    B. Preview of Org Goals where we are headed

VI. Core Values Champion

Figure 3.6 ANet's State of the Organization Agenda

Annual Planning Process and Timeline

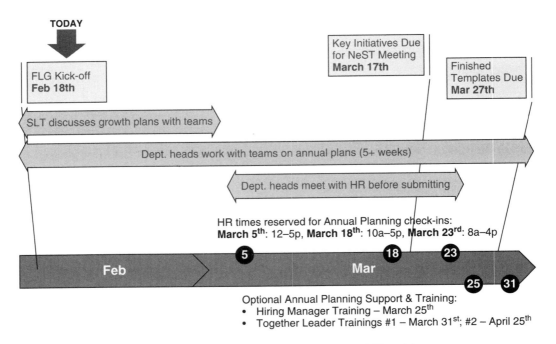

Figure 3.7 Rocketship Education Annual Planning Process and Time Line

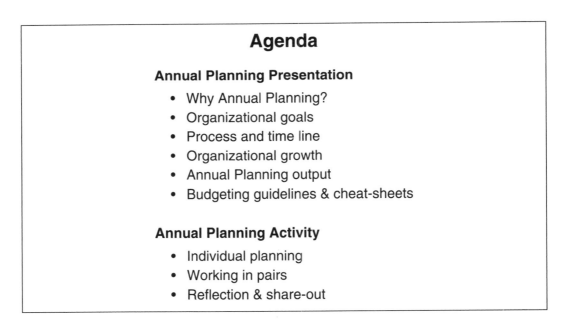

Figure 3.8 Rocketship Education Annual Planning Kick-Off Agenda

identifying if the organization is spending time and resources on work that is not connected to the goals. The leader of the goal-setting process does not have to be the most senior person at the table. This role often falls to the chief of staff or director of human capital, but a hard-charging assistant who understands how to communicate and navigate could also take the reins.

Michelle, the chief of staff for ANet you met previously, oversees their process from start to finish: "I have to project manage to ensure that they are set in a way that is both ambitious and feasible and then continue to ensure that the senior leadership team is actively engaging and managing toward these goals throughout the year in my support of the CEO." But Michelle's role doesn't stop there. She also helps influence how organizational time is used at meetings. She says, "I also own the design of the organization-wide step backs and state of the organization addresses to ensure that the whole organization feels confident and clear on what we are driving toward and how we are doing to empower managers and team leaders to adjust course as necessary."

What matters is that this person overseeing the goal process is outstanding at creating and communicating complex time lines, producing directions and summaries, and presenting information back to the leadership. Of course, it also helps if he or she is very organized, well respected, and can inspire and motivate others.

Reader Reflection

Who's the right person to take charge of your goal-setting process? Why? How can you set him or her up for success?

REVIEWING GOAL PROGRESS

Goals are all fine and good, but let's be real: a lot of organizations—maybe yours—put a lot of time and effort into setting them, only to leave them sitting dusty on a shelf for the rest of the year. In this section, you will see how to review progress toward your goals at an organization or team level. Let's return to examples from ANet and add in some other nonprofit and school-based models to help us think through this.

An Organization-Wide Goal-Review Process

ANet carefully calibrates review of progress at quarterly intervals by setting full-day meetings to look at progress toward goals.

In figure 3.9, you can see the time and effort ANet devotes to reflecting on the following:

- The overall state of the network
- Survey data
- Obsessions and must-wins (which are basically their Yearly Goals and priority plans)

Q4 Stepback: District of Columbia Network

June 17

Objectives:

- Collaboratively analyze EOY network data to develop hypotheses about the root causes of our successes and places to improve.
- Reflect on the progress we have made toward our overall Network Goals and Must-Wins this year.
- Generate concrete ways we can directly and indirectly communicate our Advance Equity Core Value through our work.
- Develop near-final Network Must-Wins and key metrics that will guide our work in the upcoming year.
- Celebrate the impact of our work as a team and the contributions of coaches, as this is our last step-back with them in their current role.

Norms:

What norms should we hold ourselves to?

- Everyone participates
- Assume best intent
- Active listening

Agenda Topic	Main Objectives/Outcomes
Opening/Warm-Up (9:15am-9:30am)	• Opener
State of the Network (9:30am-10am)	• Define where we currently stand as a network in relation to our annual goals.
EOY Survey	• Capturing EOY Practice Tracking Evaluations Nuances
Workbook/Practice Data (10am-12pm)	• EOY Survey: Overall goals, Leader/Coach perception, School level satisfaction

Figure 3.9 ANet's Quarterly Step-Back Agenda

Agenda Topic	Main Objectives/Outcomes
Lunch (12pm-1pm) Shout-outs	
Advance Equity (1:00pm-2:00pm)	What are some of the different ways we can directly and indirectly communicate our Advance Equity Core Value through our work with our partners?
Q4 Reflections on Obsessions and Must-Wins (2pm-3:45pm)	• Where did we see progress? • What feels most urgent to make progress? • Metric brainstorm • Q1 Obsession Planning (TBD)
Closing/Reflection (3:45-4pm)	• Warm/cool feedback on the day
	• Shout-outs

Figure 3.9 Continued

A School-Based Goal Review

Eric from YES Prep also reviews progress toward goals with his entire team several times per year. He calls this meeting the "state of the school" (figure 3.10).

During this meeting, Eric reviews the goals set for the school (described previously) and updates his team on progress toward them.

> As a school leader, it's my responsibility not only to establish a clear vision of success for my school but also to keep my staff informed about the progress we're making toward that vision. There's often a lot of excitement about goals when they're rolled out at the beginning of the year, but that excitement can dissipate if goals aren't revisited. That's why I think it's really important to take some time—roughly thirty minutes—in the fall, in the spring, and at the very end of the year to share and discuss data related to our vision of success. Staff members appreciate the transparency, and I think they get reenrolled in goals through the process.

Figure 3.11 is an example of a slide Eric has used to update his team on their student achievement progress.

And then Eric takes it just one step further and asks his team to reflect on progress as well (figure 3.12).

Figure 3.10 YES Prep's State of the School

Student Achievement

- CAs: our performance improved from T1: 62% to T2: 72%, and we're within reach of our goal for the year.
- STAAR/EOC benchmarks: 71% of our courses are above the state average.
- SpEd
  - December STAAR updates: all SpEd and ELL students who had an outstanding EOC from a previous grade level passed.
  - SpEd CA passing rates: T1: 38%, T2: 44%
- SAT: 38% of our seniors earned a 1550 or better.

Figure 3.11 YES Prep's Student Achievement

Personal Reflection

- On an index card, please identify something you just learned about the progress we've made toward our vision of success and share about something that you or the school has done that you are proud of.
- On another index card, please write to a colleague thanking him or her for something specific he or she has done to help us make progress toward our vision of success.

Figure 3.12 YES Prep's Staff Reflection

A Team-Level Goal-Review Process

Shannon Donnelly, an operations team leader at Teach For America, a nonprofit focused on education equity, uses a unique approach. She and her team maintain a live spreadsheet in Google Docs (see figure 3.13 for an excerpt, and the full sample is available on my website, www.thetogethergroup.com). Once per quarter, each project is subjected to the following measures, reported by the owner of the work. This is a great method to track goals and activities.

- Status: on track, pending. or off track

- Risk-level forecast: sunny, partly sunny, chance of rain, or cloudy

- Any additional updates from the project driver

Shannon describes the process that she and her team follow: "Once per quarter, I spend an hour reviewing to make sure I feel like my team is on track with its work to reach our goals. I have to prioritize this time because it is not much fun to sit and review a huge spreadsheet line by line. It's worth it though, because inevitably, I usually find something off track where I should have been paying more attention. It refocuses the team—and me—for the rest of the quarter."

By creating a deliberate time, place, and process to check on goals, ANet, YES Prep, and Teach For America are each able to keep their ultimate goals in sight while they do their day-to-day work. They can make smart, well-informed decisions about how their organizations should allocate time, money, and human resources to meet their goals and serve their missions!

Reader Reflection

When and how will you monitor progress toward your organization or team goals? Who reports on the status of progress toward goals? Do you need to arrange your meeting cycles around your goal cycle?

Get Clear on Who Does What—and Make Sure Everyone Else Is Clear, Too!

Now that you have the goals, the time line for creation, and the process to review progress, how will the work actually happen? Too often, we commit to goals without understanding *who* is expected accomplish them and in what manner. This section focuses on clearly defining the human resources required to achieve those goals you care so much about!

Many of you work in organizations that are rapidly scaling, expanding, or shifting missions. It can be hard to keep up! But we have to at least start with a point of view on who is doing what. We can't create systems to support goals unless this is clear first. You'll need just

TPSD Ops Portfolio of Work

			Q1: Initial Updates; November		
Workstream	Project	Driver	Status - Select from drop-down list	Risk Level - Select from drop-down list	Updates - Please explain your choices, and note any innovations
Conferences	African-American CMOC Summit Operations	Ahmed	On Track	Sunny	Last year's summit closed out

This year's contract signed |
| F&C - Audit Prep | Audit Prep | Allison, Marianne | Pending | Chance of Rain | Struggling to invest partners in new approach; potential disconnect with TPSD Ops expectation and G&C expectation |

Figure 3.13 TPSD Operations Goal-Review Spreadsheet

four foundational documents to get started. In this section, we will discuss how to establish and communicate clarity on the front end through the use of these tools:

- An **organizational chart** that is relatively legible and shows various teams and functions
- A simple **roles and responsibilities document** so everyone understands who owns what
- A **scorecard** per role so it is clear who owns which outcomes (made popular by the wonderful book *Who: The A Method for Hiring* by Geoff Smart and Randy Street)
- Create a list of **annual activities** that your team accomplishes on a yearly basis

Organizational Charts

One of the first questions I ask my clients is, "Can I see your organizational chart?" This is not because I want to get all hierarchical on them but rather because I need to understand where resources lie, who communicates with whom and when, and how complexly the organization is organized. Large Fortune 500 companies have wildly complicated organization charts produced by management consultants who know details of PowerPoint that you and I have never even heard of. Don't let that intimidate you. Just take the time to spell out how you see your organization or your team functioning using SmartArt in PowerPoint or a flowchart software such as Gliffy. You can even just sketch by hand if you are designing an organization from scratch. If you don't lay this out now, it will be hard to figure out who is responsible for which of those goals you thoughtfully set in the first section of this chapter.

When I built new teams at Teach For America and Achievement First, I wasn't even sure what kind of resources and people I would need. So, based on each unique context, I approached composing Organizational Charts in the following two ways.

Start with the People

When I founded a talent development team at Achievement First, my charge was fairly clear up-front: infuse talent practices into all levels of the organization. To do this, I needed to assign work to the capable people I had on my team in logical ways that motivated them. I kept a simple PowerPoint on hand, shown in figure 3.14, which helped me keep track of the roles and responsibilities I assigned to each person. I monitored what work needed to be done to achieve our goals, what each talented individual liked and had skill in doing, and what projects we were taking on from other teams.

Start with the Work

On the flip side, I had to figure out which work lived with which level of person. I had to figure out *new* work, meaning work that had never been done before—before even hiring anyone to help with it. After considering our goals, I created an organizational chart by starting with the work that needed to be done and dividing it up somewhat logically by

Talent Development: Responsibilities by Individual

Dir., School Leader and Teacher Recruitment	Dir., Talent Strategy & Operations	Director, Engagement and Evaluation	Director, Leadership Dev'p
-**Lead School Leader Recruitment, Selection, and Long-Term Cultivation** (build ongoing relationships with organizations, schools, universities)	-**Coordinate all recruitment and talent goal setting and planning processes** (co-create goals, strategies, benchmarks, and calendars)	-**Design and execute evaluation Process for AF Central and Schools** (PES, LES, 360 feedback, training, informal structures, tool design, analysis)	-**Lead all aspects of Leadership Fellows program** (attract, recruit, design, execute, coach in an ongoing and supportive basis)
-**Head Hunters** (build relationships in respective geographies and nationally with various schools, non-profits, universities)	-**Ensure we are being data-driven in all choices** (retention statistics and presentation, high yield sources, present recommendations to RDs)	-**Lead AF Central Management and Leadership Training** (execute high quality trainings for AF Central team leaders)	-**Develop instructional excellence** (design, identify, plan and manage our group of master teachers)
-**Rally the Troops—Internal and External** (strategically deploy the right people to events, matriculate, train principals, etc.)	-**Oversee and liaise for all marketing efforts** (work with Marketing to get teacher folders, website, opportunities)	-**Feedback mechanisms—Lead organizational health and network support surveying** (design, execution, analysis, recommendations)	-**Lead our competency development process and definition of excellence** (teachers, leaders, etc.)
-**Lead search for emerging markets** (where else should we be sourcing, what are untapped sources, what are other pockets of potential)	-**Study and articulate what makes our best people truly our best** (study our most effective people, refine selection model, create interview templates)	-**Lead our school evaluation efforts** (lead and coordinate annual school review process)	-**Maintain a list of needs and design additional training modules for schools as needed**
-**Communicate with Principals and School Leaders** (communicate regularly and maintain great relationships with schools)	-**Develop a systematic talent identification approach** (maintain list of new markets, deploy relationship-builders as needed)	-**Ensure we have a real-time understanding of the talent landscape** (create, develop, execute Talent Reviews, systematic succession planning)	-**Help Team Recruit by maintaining a list of great external PD sessions we can offer**
-**Manage 2–3 Teacher Recruiters** (lead recruitment teams in respective geographies)	-**Build back office infrastructure systems to support growth** (Virtual Rolodex, mass marketing time lines, irecruiter, clear and inspiring role descriptions)	-**Strategic Compensation** (development of compensation philosophy, communication, articulation, and design)	-**Develop and support additional teacher leader opportunities** (grade level leads, coaches, Saturday tutors)
-**Maintain relationships with top candidates** (sprinkle magic and love on all top candidates in a strategic way)	-**Coordinate AF Central hiring processes and selection tool support** (lead senior searches, train directors in hiring)	-**Champion Engagement of our Team** (design and execute a monthly communication mechanism, recognition of team, clear on-boarding processes, AF "volunteers")	-**Coordinate development and manage syllabus for Dean, Principal, and Principal in Residence trainings** (develop objectives, scope and sequence, combination of project management, etc.)
	-**Manage relationships with external talent sources** (Broad, Ed Pioneers, Net Impact, etc.)		-**Consider a culturally consistent teaching excellence award** (research, design, implement, reflect)

Figure 3.14 Talent Development by Individual

"bucket": recruitment, operations, evaluation, and development. After that, I started hiring and assigning who should take on what job. As more colleagues joined the team, I shifted job descriptions and roles and responsibilities to keep people motivated—but the structure remained logical (see figure 3.15).

Reader Reflection

Review your current organizational chart(s). Is it clear which team is responsible for which goals? Are reporting lines clear? If you don't currently have an organizational chart for your team or organization, pause to sketch one now!

Roles and Responsibilities

Now let's discuss actually assigning the work to your teams. It's very useful to have an all-in-one-place version of roles and responsibilities for internal uses and external needs. This way, when your boss or board asks, "Who's responsible for *x*?" your answer is ready to go. When you are asked to take on a new venture, you can thoughtfully plan for who will own what and include any needed adjustments to his or her current workload. This is also helpful if goals shift for your entire team or if you need to adjust goal responsibilities over the course of the year.

Internal Roles and Responsibilities. As organizations grow and responsibilities shift, it can be unclear who is in charge of what, especially if this changes each year. Diana Archuleta, a school director at Phillis Wheatley Community School in New Orleans, took the time to spell out all areas of activity and who the lead was on each (figure 3.16).

Diana got clear on each area of responsibility, work within that area, and who the leads were across the schools. This is important to ensure clarity of who is responsible for what—and who is ultimately responsible for achieving the organization's goals. For example, in the school culture and behavior section, the "counseling/support to high school and college" responsibilities sit squarely with AS, a member of Diana's team. This means AS is also responsible for the goals related to this area of responsibility. It is beneficial to assign owners to every single bucket of work or activity on your team, but it doesn't mean that person has to *do* all of that work. It just means they are fundamentally in charge of ensuring it happens! I also love that this example is in Excel so that it can be easily sorted by person. Another benefit is the immediate team can easily review this to see where they overlap with someone else.

External Roles and Responsibilities. When I first started working at Teach For America, everyone e-mailed a wonderful guy named Isaac to get help with IT issues. However, as we grew rapidly and so did the IT team, poor Isaac could no longer handle every

Talent Development: Responsibilities by Title

VP, Talent	Talent Associate	Talent Assistant	Dir., Talent Recruitment & Selection (2)	Dir., Talent Marketing	Director, Leadership Development	Director, Talent Services
-Lead overall Talent team -Serve as an organizational talent champion -Lead school evaluation process -Ensure overall talent practices and policies align with our core competencies -Coach/counseling to key managers	-Project owner of all trainings (Dean Trainings, Leadership Fellows, AF Network trainings) -Manage long-term pipeline building (Contact Management system inputting and next steps) -Ensure our reach is widespread (manage entire organization to follow up with candidates) -Lead network-wide communication efforts (design and execute monthly network newsletter) -Lead external monthly blasting to Alumni, Friends, Family of AF	-Scheduling (Travel, appointments, etc. for MHM) -Support (creating reading packets, binders, summarizing articles) -Office management (vendor contact, mail services, maintaining contact lists) -Resource for all staff trainings (assist Associate with aspects of trainings)	-Head Hunters (build relationships in respective geographies and nationally) -School Leader Recruitment and Long-Term Cultivation (build ongoing relationships with organizations, schools, universities) -Manage Recruitment Associates (lead recruitment teams in respective geographies) -Maintain top candidates (spend time with top candidates) -Define selection model (study our most effective teacher, refine selection model)	-Drive all message development (articulating the signature experience of AF Central and Schools) -Liaison to Julie for website (user-friendly, messages, attraction on website) -Liaison to outside design firm (printed materials, print ads, pamphlets, video) -Data Guru (retention statistics and presentation, high yield sources, analysis of talent review, present recommendations to Recruitment Directors) -Lead search for emerging markets	-Lead all aspects of Leadership Fellows program (attract, recruit, design, execute) -Leadership of all aspects of Dean and Principal training (develop objectives, scope and sequence, etc.) -Develop Master Teacher program to retain our best people (design, identify, plan and manage our group of master teachers) -Oversee Talent Review process (create, develop, execute, recommend) -Lead AF network development efforts (design trainings, learning plans)	-Lead network talent initiatives (attracting, job descriptions, recruiting, sourcing, networking events, interviewing for AF Central) -Lead all aspects of performance management (network PGPs, Admin Surveys, LESs, PESs) -Serve as lead consultant for all personnel issues -Determine appropriate and competitive compensation packages -Lead all staff policy development needs -Lead workforce planning efforts

Figure 3.15 Talent Development by Title

School Leadership Roles, Responsibilities, and Systems Overview

Area of Responsibility	Whole School Lead	Lower School Lead	Middle School Lead
School Culture and Behavior			
Student Parent Handbook			
Overview of Core Academic Program	LH		
Overview of RTI	CB		
Overview of SpEd	SE DCs		
Counseling/support to high school & college			
Parent/Family Info Sessions	AS		
High School Tours (schedule of visits)	AS		
Student Application Tracking	AS		
School Environment			
Lab Data Displays	RM		
Classroom Data Displays	LH	DS	AO
Public Spaces	RM		
Coordination with Facilities Management	CJ		
Teaching & Learning			
Annual Calendar			
Assessment Calendar	LH	DCs	DCs
Daily/Weekly Schedule			
Upkeep/Updates	LH	DS	AO
Coverage Expectations	LH	DS	AO
Math Curriculum			
Curriculum plan: course offerings, defining features, time	LH	GA	GA
Scope and sequence	LH	GA	GA
Unit Plans	LH	GA/AB	GA
Lesson Plans	LH	AB/AS	GA
Intervention/RTI	CB	CB	CB
Special Education	LH/GA	LC	IM
Curriculum Resources (ordering and management)	GA	AB/AS	GA

Figure 3.16 School Leadership Roles Chart

single question. To alleviate problems such as this, successful organizations get very clear on roles and responsibilities and even make cheat sheets like this one from Corey Crouch, a school director at YES Prep Public Schools. This way, your people can operate independently to get what they need without always bothering the team leader.

In figure 3.17, Corey laid out whom to go to for common issues and challenges. But she didn't just sit in a room and create this by herself. She discussed the idea with her leadership team, aligned her vision with theirs, and then published to her team. A good roles-and-responsibilities chart helps prevent the common time-suck for leaders I call the *hallway ambush*. This is when you are asked a question that is on someone's mind right at that moment about something you have nothing at all to do with, but you just happened to be the person standing right there. Of course, we don't want to be rude and just say, "Refer to the chart!" But we can nicely explain that we are running to a meeting, so please check

Person	Questions and Topics
School Director	• Campus vision and priorities • Campus Report Card • Employment concerns/updates • Personal time off (PTO) requests • General concerns, suggestions, questions • Colleague concerns
Director of Academics/Dean of Instruction	• Instructional best practices • Common Assessments • State testing • Teacher Continuum • Student Achievement Forecast (SAF) • Academic data analysis • Instructional PD opportunities • Grading
Dean of Students	• Student culture • Discipline • Parental/family relations • Students of concern (academics/behavior) • Trips/Force FUNctions • Service • Advisory • Credit earning (HS) • Student handbook
Operations Manager	• Facilities • Scheduling • Supplies • Student records • School calendar
Director of College Counseling	• Graduation requirements • SAT/PSAT/AP testing • Senior Signing Day/Graduation • Student opportunities
Grade Level Chair	• Grade level culture • Basic student discipline
Student Support Counselor	• Student emotional concerns • Parent concerns regarding their students • Student programming

Figure 3.17 YES Prep's Roles and Responsibilities

with so and so! This kind of articulation also keeps ownership of goals front and center. For example, the dean of students is fundamentally in charge of the student culture goals. He may certainly have support from others (similar to ANet's examples of goal supporters), but this articulation also makes it clear to his team that he owns student culture.

It is sometimes hard to control your constituents and stakeholders, whether they are families, principals, donors, or vendors, but it can't hurt to try! Is it clear to your end users whom they reach out to for what? Now, of course, anyone can always reach out to you, but over time, you may not want all of those e-mail requests in your in-box! So, let's communicate!

FAQ: What if you are not even sure where to start?

This is a challenge in especially large organizations. Amanda Cahn, a former leader in the New York City Department of Education, shared her strategy: "I would often try to develop my own contact in other departments or divisions. Sometimes we had a go-to person assigned for all informational questions and he/she helped fan out into the larger department."

Reader Reflection

How aligned are the roles and responsibilities to goals on your team? How clear are roles and responsibilities to internal and external constituents? How do you know?

Outline Your Annual Activities

During the process of goal setting, you may find yourself or your team stumbling into a set of activities or standard operating procedures and decide you want to document these annual happenings as well.

Ever since I saw a team version of annual activities from a school site operations team, I've been in love (see figure 3.18). The entire team got together and mapped out on one page their large events, key deadlines, and big projects by start month. If you look closely (the sample is also available on my website, www.thetogethergroup.com), you'll see how this team sliced its goals by month and job category, such as August HR.

There are a number of things I love about this example:

- It serves as a communication tool across the team. "Oh, I didn't realize *you* were working on this. Great, I can focus on something else."

- It serves as a communication tool with constituents. "Oh, you are curious when the handbook comes out? It's in August!"

- It anticipates the workload. "Oh, my goodness, July looks nuts with school readiness. Can we move the computer project to another month?"

This is intentionally *not* a strategic plan or outline of measurable Yearly Goals. It is literally just a list of tasks, organized by month and category, to help keep the team on the same page. However, annual activities support your goals by ensuring that all of the regular work keeps humming along.

Team Ops: Big Rocks Calendar

June	July	August	September
• NY Per Pupil Due	• NY Per Pupil Reconciliation	• NY Per Pupil Due	• DSO cohort joint meeting (9/16)
• DSO cohort meetings (6/14 & 6/21)	• Computer Project	• Deep dive: Facility	• School Readiness celebration
• End-of-year trips	• School Readiness	• FRL: VP of Ops communicated FRL expectations to DSOs	• School readiness DSO cohort debrief
• DSO led end of year close-out	• New Staff Training (7/23-7/27)	• FRL: VP of Ops coordinates w/IC product team to clear out LY data as appropriate so new info can be entered	• DSO school readiness self-reflection & calibration w/RDOs & principals
• <u>Data:</u> Spring report cards	• <u>HR:</u> New staff paperwork due (7/1)	• Readiness: VP of Ops visits all campuses	• <u>Finance:</u> (NY) Audits
• <u>Data:</u> (CT) ED166 due	• CT board meetings (7/26)	• <u>HR:</u> Revised employee handbook published	• Back to school nights (continue)
• <u>HR:</u> Continue collecting new staff & renewal paperwork	• NY board meetings (7/23)	• <u>HR:</u> Attendance bonus/sabbatical pay-outs	• BOY F&P (8/15-9/30)
• Ops BHAG setting	• Budvar meetings	• Back to School Nights begin	• IA1 (9/29-10/11)
• <u>EOY F&P</u> (5/1-6/15)	• KPI reporting		• CT board meetings (9/21-9/26)
• EOY DRP (6/6)	• Plan DSO cohort scope and sequence		• NY board meetings (9/26)
• IA 5 (6/4-6/21)	• Annual Refresh of Big Rocks & Little Rocks Ops Calendars		• CT: Enrollment snapshot (10/1)
• EOY Regents [NY HS only]* (6/13-6/22)	• Annual Refresh of Ops Manager Toolkit, PGP, IDP		• Budvar meetings
• Budvar meetings	• Annual Refresh of Ops Scorecard & Deep Dives		• KPI reporting
• KPI reporting			

Figure 3.18 "Big Rock" Calendar

Reader Reflection

How will your annual activities articulation help support your Yearly Goals? Complete the template in the Reflection Guide.

Scorecards to Accomplish Goals and Measure Annual Activities

A job description alone isn't really enough to measure progress, though it is certainly necessary to hire the right people. But what about after the right people are hired? Geoff Smart and Randy Street, authors of the wonderful book *Who: The A Method for Hiring,* describe the process of setting a role-specific scorecard with the following three buckets:

- Mission
- Outcomes
- Competencies

Outside of an actual job description, a scorecard for each role may be helpful in articulating progress toward goals—especially if some of the goals are more project- or activity-based in nature. Figure 3.19 is an example from Collegiate Academies in New Orleans that shows all three elements.

2014–2015 SCORECARD: Morgan C, President

Mission: Collegiate Academies will create and support schools that prepare all scholars for college success.			
President OUTCOMES:			
FUNDRAISING: Collegiate Academies' network office and schools will be well-funded to support the achievement of our mission.			
	Met?	Progress	Help needed
$X raised for Collegiate Academies to fill gaps in current school year's budget.			
$X raised to support expansion in future years.			
An additional $X raised to support new programming (including restorative center)			
REPUTATION: Collegiate Academies will become recognized as the highest performing network of gap-closing high schools in the country.			
	Met?	Progress	Help needed
90% of visitors surveyed rate their tour experience as Excellent.			
REPLICABILITY: Collegiate Academies' future will be in the hands of CA. Funders, educators, and policymakers will support our programming and expansion plans.			
	Met?	Progress	Help needed
Leaders at in target markets will report a desire for CA to grow			
Decide how much money we need to raise annually for the next 5–10 years.			
Identify the biggest social and emotional struggles of a first year school and proactively plan for them.			
Nail down SL Training scope and sequence for 18 months prior to beginning role.			
Create a startup calendar of must-achieves for 12 months leading up to school launch.			
Differentiate SL training scope and sequence for successor (rather than startup) leaders.			

Figure 3.19 Collegiate Academies' Scorecard

I love that this example gives the employee a chance to reflect on his or her own progress regularly. If you find your team members (or you yourself!) are unclear on which goals they own and what they should be accomplishing, the process of scorecard creation can help with this.

FAQ: What if we actually have a point of view about where people *should* spend their time?

Most organizations do operate with at least some goals in mind, but very few express a point of view on where their people can spend time to best achieve them. When you have a number of employees in the same position, it is helpful to clarify where most of their time should go.

Table 3.1 shows one of my favorite examples of high-impact responsibilities, or HIRs, from YES Prep Public Schools. What I love about this example is YES has taken the time to articulate the large buckets of the school director role and then spelled out blocks of activities that can and should be on the school director's calendar in order to meet the organization's goals.

School directors at YES even color-code their Outlook Calendars by HIRs, noting time spent on teacher coaching, leadership team development, and a few other key areas.

Table 3.1 YES Prep School Director High-Impact Responsibilities (HIRs)

Key Word	High-Impact Responsibilities
Vision	Analyze key sources of data to identify school priority areas, invest stakeholders in the school strategy, monitor progress toward identified metrics, and adjust strategies to ensure continued growth.
Culture	Establish, model, and uphold a strong student, staff, and parent culture in which the behaviors of the school's stakeholders represent YES Prep and campus values.
Achievement	Manage progress toward increased student achievement.
Persistence	Manage student persistence that leads to college graduation, focusing on intervention strategies and increasing persistence for all students and subpopulations.
Team	Manage, support, and develop effective school leadership team members and other leaders on campus to develop growth in performance along with consistent coaching and management strategies and leadership succession planning.
Talent	Manage the development and retention of high-caliber teachers and staff and the campus process for recruitment and selection.
Systems	Manage and develop effective school systems and long-term strategy with respect to school sustainability.

When a team member is not on track to meet goals, the head of schools typically first checks on time alignment to understand why and then helps reconnect his or her time to the goals.

Reader Reflection

Consider a person in a particular position in your organization. How are his or her individual goals connected with organization goals?

START STRONG

Let's take a breath. We did some big work in this chapter, really foundational stuff. We got clear on what you and your organization are shooting for, ensured that the organization chart and roles and responsibilities staffed will help you meet your goals, and prompted you to get to a point of view about where you thought your team members should spend their time.

Now you can do the following:

- Define your long-term goals with Yearly Goals.
- Outline your goal-setting time line and cascade process.
- Determine the owner of your organization's goal setting and progress monitoring.
- Lay out your internal and external roles and responsibilities.
- Ensure your organizational charts, job descriptions, and scorecards enable you to achieve your goals.
- Consider outlining an annual activities chart.

But none of this is enough to operate on a day-to-day basis. It is meant to provide us with direction and ground us in a vision. The next step is to break it down. Our next chapter will break your goals into three-month increments. Let's do it!

SEE IT IN ACTION: GOAL SETTING START TO FINISH

Steven Epstein and Emily Schneider-Krzys, superintendent and chief talent officer for KIPP Austin Public Schools, took a thoughtful approach when goal setting and work planning across the organization this year. In this "See It in Action," I will break down KIPP Austin's approach step-by-step to help you thoughtfully implement your own process. Emily and Steven acknowledge that the goal-setting process doesn't look neat, clean, and perfect, and it was highly iterative. Not only is figuring out the actual goals really hard but also is getting the process right in a way that invests and commits others.

1. **Focus on the mission.** Steven and Emily started with what mattered: KIPP Austin's promise to students. It is very easy to get lost in the weeds of a goal-setting process, so Steven started with the mission and let all terms, documents, and processes flow from there (see figure 3.20).

2. **Align process and language.** Steven and Emily knew that the language of goals, priorities, targets, benchmarks, and more could be very confusing. They borrowed heavily from another KIPP region and then started with aligning a common language with their team, including principals and home office leaders. They used terms such as *outcomes* and *initiatives* (see figure 3.21).

3. **Show the flow of events.** Steven and Emily knew the order of events affected investment and buy in from their team, so—after defining terms—they outlined it clearly as a flowchart in figure 3.22.

4. **Took the show on the road.** Steven and his team went to each school and visited the home office to gain insights from each team on what it had accomplished and where it was going (figure 3.23).

5. **Put the team to work.** Steven asked his team to consider their own goals, priorities, and more. He gave clear guidelines along the way (figure 3.24 and figure 3.25).

6. **Set goals for individuals.** After understanding where each team was headed and aligning it to the goals of the organization, Steven and Emily took goal setting down to the individual level (figure 3.26).

7. **Create an overall road map to pressure test the work.** This may be my favorite step. Steven and Emily took all of the work for the year and laid it out across stakeholders and actions needed to accomplish the goals (figure 3.27). They asked themselves if teams were resourced enough, if some months were heavier than others, and were the goals achievable.

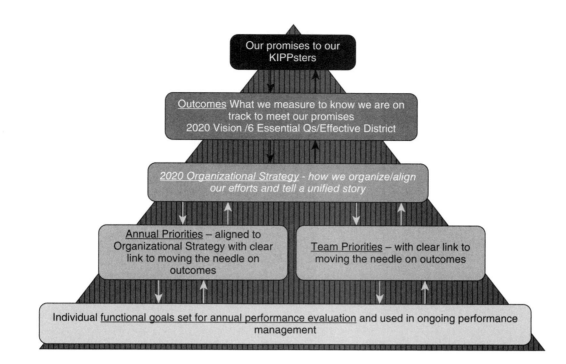

Figure 3.20 Mission and Goals

This year...

1. Outcomes: These are measures of performance that tell us if we are on track to achieve our strategic plan and keep our promises to our KIPPsters. They are directly related to our 2020 Vision, 6 Essential Questions, *or being a stable and effective school district.*

2. 2020 Organizational Strategy: *The focus of our work towards our 2020 vision; there are 4 components – Academics, Talent, Data, Healthy Org – they will last until 2020*

1. WHAT success looks like

3. FY1X Annual Priorities: Major work that occurs in a year to move us toward our outcomes.

4. FY1X Regional Initiatives: Smaller scale work that occurs each year to move us toward our outcomes, often are seeding the work for a future year Regional Priority

5. FY1X Team Priorities: Major theme for a specific school or SST team; contribute to our outcomes.

2. HOW we will achieve it

6. Functional Goals: Individual goals that clarify each team member's part in achieving an Annual Priority or Team Priority

3. WHO contributes what work

Figure 3.21 Aligned Language

What do you mean when you say "priority"?

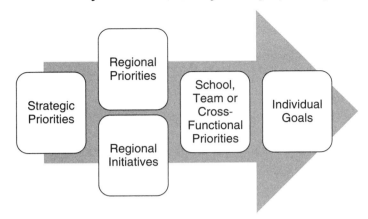

Figure 3.22 Flowchart

Objectives

By the end of the session, KAPS team & family will be able to:

- Restate in their own words the major accomplishments of the KAPS 2020 Plan during this school year
- Determine how they will be interacting with the strategic priority work in the coming school year

Figure 3.23 Objectives

Guardrails

- Priorities
    - 3 is good, 4 is okay, 5 is max, 6 or more is unlikely to stick
    - Must be represented in school leader or director functional goals
    - Will draw from either/both exponential work (regional priorities and regional initiatives) and/or continuous improvement work (6 Essential Questions or Ops Dashboard) depending on the team/school

Figure 3.24 Guardrails

For the team (or teams) you lead, brainstorm the priorities for the next 3 years.

Team	Year 1 (Current Year)	Year 2 (Next Year)	Year 3 (Year after Next)	"Headline of Success"
Recruitment	Building networking skills & habits across the org Efficiency through playlists and decision-making tools	Across the board quality of selection processes What defines "potential"	Shifting the work centrally Quality candidates through a quality candidate experience	KAPS Recruitment Team Nails the "Art and Science" of Building Great Teams

Figure 3.25 Three-Year Priority Map Template

	Topic	Goal	MOY Evaluation	EOY Evaluation
1	STAAR Level II	93% of 7th grade students will earn a Level 2 on the 7th grade math STAAR assessment (predicted at 43%).	1: less than 90% 2: 90–92.9% 3: 93–95.4% 4: 95.5% or greater	1: less than 90% 2: 90–92.9% 3: 93–95.4% 4: 95.5% or greater
2	STAAR Level III	16% of 7th grade students will earn a Level 3 on the 7th grade math STAAR assessment (predicted at 85%).	1: less than 13% 2: 13–15.9% 3: 16–18.4% 4: 18.5% or greater	1: less than 13% 2: 13–15.9% 3: 16–18.4% 4: 18.5% or greater
3	MAP	7th math: 75% of students will meet their college readiness growth target	Not Evaluated at Mid-Year Not Evaluated at Mid-Year Not Evaluated at Mid-Year Not Evaluated at Mid-Year	1: less than 72% 2: 72–74.9% 3: 75–77.4% 4: 77.5% or greater

Figure 3.26 Individual Goals

Stakeholder	Priority work	Implementation action item
School Leaders	TCP/KCP	• Participate in train the trainer for TCP Roll Out sessions and lead 2 sessions for all teachers • Provide feedback on draft functional goals for advancement which are finalized centrally • Review each teacher-manager's portfolio and ensure transfer of knowledge from interview data or past year data • Set all school-specific non-advancement goals
	Elem. Math	• Weekly schedule has 60 minutes (K) and 70 minutes (1st-4th) for English & Spanish math • Attend CGI/Bridges sessions • July 13th-17th: ½ day for SL meeting for Math Q1 expectations, structures and CPG sharing
	Sec. Lit.	• Attend one day of Curriculum Preview and intro to CPG for SLs and APs • Attend curriculum rollout with teachers • (HS) Attend tech/library training with teachers
	R&R	• Communicate changes to school staff • For schools with BMs, outline a clear set of goals/ competencies to demonstrate by Q3 of 15-16 for BMs to transition into AP Ops role
Assistant Principals	TCP/ KCP	• Participate as needed in summer roll out PD • New APs attend intensive calibration training for teacher managers (3 90-minute sessions)
	Elem. Math	• Attend CGI/ Bridges session (2.5 days) • (AP Math) Lead Number Corner PD • Facilitate teachers organizing math resources • July 13th-17th: ½ day for SL meeting for Math Q1 expectations, structures and CPG sharing

Figure 3.27 Overall Goals Road Map

Stakeholder	Priority work	Implementation action item
	Sec. Lit.	• Attend one day of Curriculum Preview and intro to CPG for SLs and APs • Attend curriculum rollout with teachers • (HS) Attend tech/library training with teachers
School-based Operations	TCP/ KCP	• Confirm teacher-student data
	CRF	• Include information about college savings program and family series for students and families at enrollment/registration
	Data	• Train on new SIS
	R&R	• AP Ops/ BM attends training in mid-July
		• Set functional goals based on regional goals

Figure 3.27 Continued

Although goal setting never will feel perfectly smooth, it is helpful to lay out your process for goal setting from start to finish, from organization level down to the individual, and to recognize that the process can dramatically affect the outcomes and investment of your team.

CHAPTER 4

Break Down the Goals
Create a Priority Plan

SEEN AND HEARD

"Priorities that are not as time sensitive get pushed to the back burner until they become emergencies. I need pressure to meet a deadline to get something done."

"I spend time on less important things because I can check them off a list, but bigger stuff builds up and then ends up taking over the weekend or just giving me anxiety and not ever getting done."

"I try to be organized, but I have difficulty putting it into action when unpredictable events occur and are in conflict with what I have prioritized."

OVERVIEW AND OBJECTIVES

Do any of these statements resonate with you? Yes, me, too. Hello, rebranding project I've never gotten around to! Almost all leaders I've coached have found themselves caught in the tyranny of the urgent and failing to make headway on something that really matters to their organization. One of the classic examples is important visionary or planning work. I was coaching a wonderful school leader, Adam Cobb in Brooklyn, and he was an outstanding daily and weekly planner. However, when I asked him what mattered most in the next three months, his answer was clear and definitive. "Set the vision for seventh grade" [the new grade being added at his school in the fall]. We quickly checked his calendar, and indeed, planning time for this priority was nowhere to be found. It's *very* easy to get in this position when you are caught in the day-to-day. Nothing would catch on fire if Adam didn't set the vision and plan for seventh grade, but he knew from experience that he needed to start now or he would feel the burn in the fall. So we created a Priority Plan and mapped out the steps: staff input, parent and family investment, piloting ideas with students, and what to discuss when with his leadership team. Once we broke apart this seventh-grade vision, it felt more doable to Adam. He was easily able to incorporate this topic into some of his standing meeting agendas and work backwards from when he wanted to send information home to families. Adam reflected, "Being forced to step back from my calendar and break down this topic that had become a bit of a psychic mountain made me feel like I was really doing my job as a leader."

With a clear picture of your long-term direction (your Yearly Goals) from the previous chapter, as well as the structures and resources you've aligned to get there (your Organizational Chart, Roles and Responsibilities, and Scorecards), we need to focus now on a shorter period of time. Enter the Priority Plan—a three-month view of your priorities, key actions, and your team's priorities. We'll fit in a little personal planning, too!

In this chapter, you'll learn the purpose of a Priority Plan, follow step-by-step instructions on how to create one, see examples of real-life Priority Plans, and consider concrete suggestions for living out your Priority Plans on a daily basis. As always, examples and templates for your personal use are available on my website (www.thetogethergroup.com).

In this chapter, you will do the following:

- Articulate the purpose of a creating a medium-term plan to achieve your Yearly Goals.

- Follow a step-by-step process to create an effective Priority Plan.

- Determine how you will roll out the planning process to your team.

- Decide how to keep Priority Plans alive and functioning for your team and organization. (See figure 4.1.)

Figure 4.1 The Togetherness Tools

The Model: I Already Have Goals—So Why Do I Need Something Else?

Chapter 3 focused on setting the annual direction for you and your team or organization. But we cannot jump into the daily details of our calendars just yet. First, we need a medium-term view of our work. Here's why. Your list of goals can occasionally feel like an overwhelming Excel spreadsheet that makes your head spin. And typically, it's usually only *some* of those goals that matter during a particular time period.

What we need to do is extract the parts of your goals you will focus on for the next three months only. Then, we can specifically focus on (1) what's most important to achieve in the season ahead and (2) the key actions that you and your team will take to do so. A strong Priority Plan will not only reflect your own To-Dos but also it will address requests you may have of others, input you may need to gather, or decisions you may need to tee up. It will serve as a communication tool between you and your team, and maybe even between you and your manager. *We need a bridge between our annual aspirations and our daily To-Dos to ensure that all of our work is steering us ahead in a unified and correct direction. The Priority Plan is that bridge.*

Definition

A **Priority Plan** is a three-month extraction from your Yearly Goals that names what matters most for you and your team. It also defines the high-level actions needed to arrive at the desired outcomes.

A Priority Plan typically contains the following elements:

- A clear statement of outcomes for the following three months (often drawn from Yearly Goals)

- The key actions required to achieve the outcomes, such as meetings, deliverables, or decisions to be made

- A transparent picture of the priorities of your team members and direct reports so everyone knows who's doing what and how each person is contributing to the overall mission

Your Priority Plan could look something like figure 4.2. Or it might look like figure 4.3.

LEADER | **PRIORITY PLAN** ⏱

Area of Responsibility		Month 1	Month 2	Month 3	Annual Goals
	I support				
	I own				

Figure 4.2 Priority Plan Template 1

LEADER | **PRIORITY PLAN** ⏱

Priorities:

1.

2.

3.

4.

5.

Priority	Month	Month	Month	
Priority #	Key Actions	Key Actions	Key Actions	
Evidence of Effectiveness		Manager Support Needed:		
Priority #	Key Actions	Key Actions	Key Actions	
Evidence of Effectiveness		Manager Support Needed:		

Figure 4.3 Priority Plan Template 2

FAQ: How is a priority different from a goal?

There are literally a million schools of thought on this question—you could easily Google yourself into a rabbit hole trying to find the best answer. Here's my take: you need a long-term view on the expected outcomes for your work; these are your Yearly Goals. Then you need to prioritize certain goals during a period of time, thus your priorities. You also need to map out a high-level path to actually achieve these priorities, and so, enter the Priority Plan. To get a clearer picture of how this works, let's look at some examples.

In this section, I will walk you through two different Priority Plans. One is a nonprofit-based example and the second is for a school-based organization. In both cases, each leader kept an eye on their Yearly Goals to create her Priority Plan.

JEN'S PRIORITY PLAN

Jen Salvador, a manager at Teach For America's Massachusetts region, created the Priority Plan shown in figure 4.4.

Jen followed a simple process to create her Priority Plan:

1. Listed her Yearly Goals in the column on the far right. She also included the benchmark, or where she wanted to be, by the end of January, to show progress toward her goals. For example, the Yearly Goal is "Staff will meet performance goals by 8/1" and the benchmark is "100% of staff will score proficient or exemplary on mid-year performance reviews."

2. Listed her top priorities, such as "staff hiring" and "student instruction."

3. Created key actions to achieve her priorities, such as "prep interviews" within December's staff hiring priority. She also carefully distinguished between what she owned versus what she supported. This helped Jen keep an eye on important work from her team.

4. Spread the actions across a three-month period. Jen signaled the percentage of her time she believed should be spent each month toward each goal. This will be very helpful when we map her priorities into her Comprehensive Calendar.

5. Got personal. Jen also took one more step to outline some personal priorities. She has gotten very specific with exercise, books to read, and relationships to keep kindled.

Reader Reflection

Which pieces of Jen's Priority Plan would help inform your medium-term planning?

Now that you viewed Jen's Priority Plan, let's look at Kari's.

KARI'S PRIORITY PLAN

Meet Kari Thomas, who manages a centralized instructional team and also directly supports school principals at YES Prep Houston. We'll look closely this time at how she includes her team in her Priority Plan.

Figure 4.4 Jen's Priority Plan

		November	December	January	Annual Goals
Staff Hiring (2) (4)	I support	**30%** • Staff hiring project plan • Identify target leads for each role (3) • Interview materials and meetings planned	**30%** • Prep interviews (potentially visit classrooms) including applicant activities, calendars, and interview guides • Staff decisions made	**20%** • Offers made • Make school teams	**Fully hired by 2/1** • XX% of instructional staff will have 3+ years of teaching experience • XX% staff retention from start of first Leadership Conference
	I own	• Identify target leads for operational roles • Returning staff on-boarded	• Interviews scheduled and executed • Staff decisions made	• On-boarding process	
Staff Training & Management	I support	**15%** • Spring scope and sequence project plan created • Meetings with LA, CC, JB, AS	**25%** • Spring scope and sequence materials prepared • Meetings with LA, CC, JB, AS	**20%** • Spring scope and sequence materials distributed to summer staff • Meetings with LA, CC, JB, AS	**Staff will meet performance goals by 8/1** • XX% of staff will score proficient or exemplary on mid-year performance reviews • Staff are Instructional and Cultural leaders (1)
	I own	• Spring scope and sequence project plan created (Ops)	• Spring scope and sequence materials prepared (Ops)	• Spring scope and sequence materials distributed to summer staff (Ops)	
Student Instruction	I own	**25%** • Review IPPs from other regional Institutes • Create Instructional Project Plan with potential partners • Create project plan for ISAT finalization (who, what, when, how – includes start dates for writers, dates for draft submissions, feedback loops for writers, key collaborators, dates to present draft materials with stakeholders for input)	**15%** • Leverage resources and human capital to enact ISAT project - ISAT writers recruited, invested, and trained • Data systems identified • Phase 2: DEI, SPED, ESL	**20%** • ISAT drafting and finalization • Growth goals defined • Instructional materials created, organized, and ready for distribution and spring training	**Students meet performance goals by 7/24** • Academic Growth: XX% of students will meet their individualized growth goal • Personal Growth: XX% of students will make personal growth, measured by a student survey
Personal	I own	**10%** • Get in routine of working out 4 times/week (5) • Write two chapters • Read two books (*The House of the Seven Gables* and *No Struggle, No Progress*) • Dates: So You Think You Can Dance & Wicked	**10%** • Work out 4 times/week • Write two chapters • Read two books (*Multiplication Is for White People* and *The Scarlet Letter*) • Christmas vacation plans – holiday cards, vision boards, gifts	**10%** • Work out 4 times/week • Write two chapters • Read two books • Two dates • Reset annual personal goals	**Happy and Healthy**

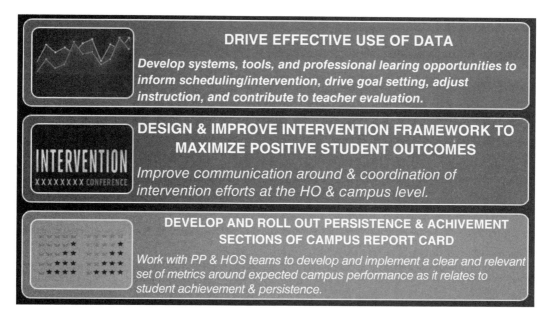

DRIVE EFFECTIVE USE OF DATA

Develop systems, tools, and professional learing opportunities to inform scheduling/intervention, drive goal setting, adjust instruction, and contribute to teacher evaluation.

DESIGN & IMPROVE INTERVENTION FRAMEWORK TO MAXIMIZE POSITIVE STUDENT OUTCOMES

Improve communication around & coordination of intervention efforts at the HO & campus level.

DEVELOP AND ROLL OUT PERSISTENCE & ACHIVEMENT SECTIONS OF CAMPUS REPORT CARD

Work with PP & HOS teams to develop and implement a clear and relevant set of metrics around expected campus performance as it relates to student achievement & persistence.

Figure 4.5 Kari's Yearly Goals

Step 1: Pull Out Your Yearly Goals

In Kari's case (figure 4.5), they are as follows:

1. Drive effective use of data.
2. Design and improve intervention framework to maximize positive student outcomes.
3. Develop and roll out persistence and achievement sections of campus report card.

These goals are motivating and very big picture. In Kari's specific case, many of her goals are more process based because she is in a school-supporting role. This may also happen to you when designing your Yearly Goals and it is okay as long as you can measure the outcome. When Kari gets into the nitty-gritty of planning her days, they could easily fall by the wayside. But a strong Priority Plan will help Kari and her team plan the key actions necessary to making solid progress.

Step 2: Now List Your Top Priorities for the Next Three Months in Five or Six Bullets

In Kari's case, she listed priorities related to her three key programmatic areas: her own management of her team, relationship building, and her personal life, and then she did some further brainstorming:

1. Programmatic campus report card goal. Write Project Plan for the creation of a campus report card related to student achievement and persistence, which is approved for implementation. Complete first semester portions of Project Plan.

2. Programmatic intervention goal. Gather evidence on what works and what doesn't in relation to elements of intervention across the system; use this data to inform upcoming recommendations. Come up with a clear vision of how this evidence informs system-wide recommendations re: master scheduling, staffing, and program.

3. Programmatic team growth and staffing for next school year. Develop comprehensive plan for prioritized team growth for next school year. Reconcile plan with projected budget. Develop and post open positions.

4. Effectively and consistently lead and manage core members of the programmatics team and the team overall in order to meet Yearly Goals and provide excellent service to campuses.

5. Maintain and build positive relationships with key campus stakeholders in order to provide relevant and timely support.

6. Personal.

A full sample of her plan is available on my website (www.thetogethergroup.com).

FAQ

But I do mission-driven work! How on *earth* can you expect me to say one aspect of my job is more important than any other? Well, my friends, at some point, we all have limited resources, whether they be time, money, energy, or staff (or all of the above!). We simply cannot be good at everything all at once. Defining and naming your priorities in advance, seeking alignment with important stakeholders, and then adjusting as necessary help immensely with making the biggest and best changes you can. And isn't that why you got into all of this in the first place?

Step 3: Spell Out the Key Actions Required to Achieve the Priorities

Let's take Kari's intervention priority (number 2): Gather evidence on what works and what doesn't in relation to elements of intervention across the system; use this data to inform upcoming recommendations. She broke it down even further by thinking to herself the following:

- How do I support my team members? *Lean in on school site support.*
- What data do I need? *I need to base my decisions in evidence.*
- Whose investment and support must I gather? *I should schedule a working group meeting.*
- What am I working toward? *An actual staffing plan recommendation.*

Here's Kari's breakdown:

Yearly Goal	Priority	All Key Actions
Design and improve intervention framework to maximize positive student outcomes	Gather evidence on what works and what doesn't in relation to elements of intervention across the system; use this data to inform upcoming recommendations. Come up with a clear vision of how this evidence informs systemwide recommendations re: master scheduling, staffing, and program.	• Gather data on intervention successes and areas of challenge • Intervention working group meeting • Create second semester communication and action step plan • ID and check in with campuses with highest need re: intervention • Support Amy's campus intervention teamwork • Get info to create recommendations by February

Step 4: Spread Out Your Key Actions across a Three-Month Period

Kari sequenced her concrete next steps across the upcoming three months (see figure 4.6). She was very careful to space out the work so that she could be sure to gather the right information to create a strong recommendation for her organization's leadership. This would have been close to impossible if she tried to do it all at once!

Kari did a few wise things in figure 4.6:

Deadlines. She carefully included hard deadlines and also created some where none existed.

Key meetings. Kari noted important meetings well in advance to ensure adequate preparation time.

Repeating priorities. In team support and management, Kari allowed some actions to span across multiple months.

Go ahead, get personal! It should be mentioned that Kari is not a superwoman, but she is a practical and careful planner. She's also the mom of two little ones, one of whom

	October	November	December
Intervention	-support Amy on work with campus intervention teams	-gather data and plan for intervention working group meeting - intervention working group meeting (Nov 15): ID campuses of highest need -schedule December working group meeting - complete action steps coming out of Nov meeting	-plan and hold working group meeting: have info needed to be able to create scheduling-staffing-intervention recommendations in early Feb –hold meetings with campuses of high need re. intervention guidance -create 2nd semester communication and action step plan
Team Support and Management	weekly check ins/ongoing support - once monthly tacticals -monthly strategic -confirm team members have completed IMP process and check ins with their teams -IMP focused check in week of 10/3 -Mid-semester meetings with direct reports week of 10/17 -Assist team members in preparation for their mid-semester meetings (review written feedback before meeting, as necessary) -team luncheon on 10/18	weekly check ins/ongoing support - once monthly tacticals -monthly strategic -sit in on team member MYMs as necessary -November happy hour for team -submit mid-year bonus amounts	-weekly check ins/ongoing support - once monthly tacticals -monthly strategic -IMP focused check in (end of month)
Personal	-pick Lucia up from school 2 days per week -1 or 2 date nights per month -Evie only time -Lu only time -get landscaping quotes -Lu: Doctor Appt on Oct 14 -Evie: schedule check-up for end of the month	-pick Lucia up from school 2 days per week -1 or 2 date nights per month -Evie only time -Lu only time	-pick Lucia up from school 2 days per week -1 or 2 date nights per month -Evie only time -Lu only time -Trip to Austin during break -Christmas shopping

Figure 4.6 Kari's Priority Plan

had a serious medical emergency just while Kari's job was picking up. Having her Priority Plan laid out made it so much easier for Kari to manage her team while also juggling her own work and personal responsibilities. She wanted to make sure she picked up one of her daughters from school at least twice per week. Without the proactive Priority Plan in place, Kari could have easily slipped into crisis mode at work and at home, only thinking one day (or one hour) at a time. In every tool I mention moving ahead, I will push you to include the personal as well as the professional. This is because I want to ensure the same amount of intentionality with your personal life—and often that takes planning to fit in.

Step 5: Articulate Priorities for Direct Reports

Kari then thought about what mattered most with the folks on her team for the next three months by reviewing their Yearly Goals, upcoming large events, and their development needs. She included a variety of topics such as their own goals and career interests (see figure 4.7). By looking at this before each team or individual check-in, Kari could avoid being pulled into the tyranny of urgent emergencies and stay focused on proactive and effective moves forward that were aligned with Yearly Goals.

It took a few hours for Kari to plan ahead so clearly. But once her Priority Plan was in place she could quickly make adjustments and communicate changes in her fast-paced work and personal life. I've said it before and I'll say it again—being more planned actually enables you to be more flexible.

Benefits of Priority Plans

- Enable you to look at your work and ask, "Will this work push us to meet our goals or are things missing?"
- Give you a window into your team's prioritization
- Let you have more time to gather input or feedback
- Permit thoughtful trade-offs when opportunities or emergencies arise
- Help you manage expectations of others
- Prevent collisions of multiple competing priorities across your team
- Enable more proactive delegation

Rick (DRAFT)	Alex	Josh	Annie	Harley	Mora
➤ Communicating the rationale to stakeholders ➤ Identify opportunities for new experiences and opportunities for feedback	➤ Collaboration with stakeholders ➤ Sarah's development ➤ Identifying future opportunities at YES, getting feet wet in those areas	➤ Strategic planning: SpEd student achievement and team goals ➤ Delegating to team members ➤ Time management	➤ The time management > planning > follow-through connection ➤ Team management: check-in structure and communicating clear expectations ➤ Building positive relationships	➤ Establishing positive relationships with SSC managers ➤ Proactively and meaningfully leading the SSCs ➤ Developing SSC programming	➤ Serving as resource to campus deans of students/principals ➤ Identify opportunities for me to provide her with coaching and feedback

Figure 4.7 Priorities for Direct Reports

Build Your Own

Now that you have seen Jen and Kari's examples, it's time to build your own. In this section, we will work backwards from your Yearly Goals to create your Priority Plan, step-by-step.

Step 1: Pull Out Your Yearly Goals

At this point, I hope your Yearly Goals from chapter 3 are in good shape. Pull 'em out, wherever they may be … written on an index card, buried in a crazy Excel sheet, stuck in a board presentation, or stashed in a binder on a shelf. Highlight which of those goals are applicable for the next three months. For example, if I oversee teacher recruitment for a school district, my Yearly Goal, or outcome, might be "source and hire a new director of recruitment." But if it is the fall, it's likely that the goals around building a strong candidate pool are more applicable than the goals around hiring. Sure, they are connected, but right now, I'm focused on building the candidate pool.

If you feel really stuck, ask yourself to complete this sentence: "*The next three months will be successful if _____.*"

Step 2: List Your Top Priorities for the Next Three Months in Five or Six Bullets

Now, use the table in your Reader Reflection Guide and list your top priorities in five or six bullets. You want to be sure they start with verbs and are clear enough that everyone will know (and be able to celebrate!) when success has been achieved. So, don't just write "candidate pool." My priority for the month might be, "*Build a pool of three strong final candidates.*" This priority is clearly derived from my Yearly Goals and defines a clear task.

> **Reader Reflection**
> Look back at the Yearly Goals you wrote in chapter 3. Thinking about the next three months only, what are some key priorities you need to push ahead to achieve each goal?

Step 3: Spell Out the Key Actions Required to Achieve the Priorities

Didn't I just say it? "*Build a pool of three strong final candidates.*" Yes, but that still sounds too much like one of those things we always *need* to do but never find the time to *actually* do. It's too big and too broad to stand on its own. Without more clearly spelling out Key Actions it's easy to just stare at the phrase "build a pool" and get nothing accomplished.

Let's make things easy on ourselves and break our priority down even further. Here are some potential Key Actions, along with things I might realize as I plan (see table 4.1). I'm going to let you in my leader brain and show you my thinking, noted in italics. Then you can pretend I'm right beside you as you draft your own Priority Plan! Lucky you!

Table 4.1 Sample Key Actions

Yearly Goal	Priority	All Key Actions
Hire a new director of recruitment.	Build a pool of three strong candidates.	Write job description.
		Personally send job description to my top thirty connectors.
		Draft interview process start to finish.
		Update interview and performance task materials.
		Schedule interview days with key stakeholders.

- Write job description. *I realize I'm not clear on a couple of pieces of the role and I need to clarify those with my manager.*

- Personally send job description to my top thirty connectors. *I could get lazy and over-rely on typical processes for hiring, so I really need to push myself to do this one.*

- Draft interview process from start to finish. *The team has really messed this up before, so I need to remember to include an overview of the process to manage candidate expectations.*

- Update interview and performance task materials. *This is the kind of chore I tend to avoid, so I need to find quiet work time to get it done.*

- Schedule interview days with key stakeholders. *I am putting this here because it will require planning ahead to account for other people's time.*

Reader Reflection

Select one of your priorities from the list. Brainstorm a list of possible actions you need to make headway.

Step 4: Spread Out Your Key Actions across a Three-Month Period

You can't do it all at once, so let's space things out, shall we? Not every Key Action will fit cleanly in one month. It's okay if some actions roll over from month to month, and it is also fine if some actions are repeated each month (see table 4.2).

Table 4.2 Key Actions Spread across Three Months

Yearly Goal	Priority	January	February	March
Hire a new director of recruitment.	Build a pool of three strong candidates.	• Write job description. • Personally send job description to my top thirty connectors. • Schedule interview days with key stakeholders.	• Draft interview process start to finish. • Update interview and performance task materials.	Conduct interview day.

"*I am doing this one sooner rather than later because it requires the work of others*"

Wait, wait, wait! *In doing this planning work, I realize I just missed something. I will need the help of my operations director in* all of this, *especially with scheduling a finalist interview day. And if I really think about it, she is super talented and has a keen interest in learning how to hire. Could I teach her how to screen résumés? I obviously can't do this last minute, but it would mean huge learning for her—and be a huge help to me. It will just take some planning for us to pull it off. Let me add a Key Action to January to introduce this project to her (see table 4.3).*

Table 4.3 Key Actions with Operations Director Added In

Yearly Goal	Priority	January	February	March
Hire a new director of recruitment.	Build a pool of three strong candidates.	• Write job description. • Personally send job description to my top thirty connectors. • Schedule interview days with key stakeholders. • **Introduce project to operations director and co-screen résumé with her.**	• Draft interview process start to finish. • Update interview and performance task materials.	Conduct interview day.

Repeat across All Rows. Continue to take these steps with each of your top priorities over the next three months. If you find yourself hitting an ambiguous priority that has fallen over and over to the proverbial back burner, this is your opportunity to step back, plan, and make concrete progress. An ambiguous priority, you ask? What does *that* mean? I mean something really vague where the key actions to take aren't immediately clear. It's a thing that has been lurking in the back of your head that you *know* will make your organization or team stronger, but because it's never been done before it's hard to think about how to get it started.

If we go back to Adam's example from the start of the chapter, "Set the vision for seventh grade," it is easy to see why people can get stuck. I mean, that is one big job and it is not easy to figure out where to start. But when we actually plotted the first step, which was "Create a time line of actions with your team," the rest of the steps were easier to outline.

Reader Reflection

Using your Reader Reflection Guide, pause and specify your key actions for each of your priorities for the next three months.

What about the personal stuff?. Many folks find they like to enter a personal priority or two on their Priority Plans. To the extent you are comfortable, I recommend putting those on paper and planning the key actions you will take to make them happen.

Hey, if you've been struggling to take a vacation for years, or you've always wanted to complete a triathlon, or you absolutely want to ensure that you have dinner with your family at least three days per week, why not try a Priority Plan to see if it helps you make some progress?

Reader Reflection

List one or two personal priorities and note the key actions you'll want to take to help you accomplish them.

Step 5: Articulate Priorities for Your Team Members.

Think about each of your team members. What do you care about most in their work? Why do you care about it? Do they proactively know what you value? The point here is to consider what the priorities should be for those you manage and align on them in advance. But before you go issuing to everyone what their priorities are, I suggest you have your team draft their priorities back to you—and you give input.

One of my favorite examples of this comes from Brian Jaffe, a dean of students at YES Prep in Houston, Texas. Brian's principal, Corey Crouch, asked him to create a Priority Plan, and he created the version in figure 4.8.

In addition to carefully outlining deliverables, such as the culture guide, and some key practices, such as "provide individual coaching around systems," Brian did a few very wise things when he drafted his Priority Plan for Corey's review:

- He drafted this himself. Although it could have been tempting for Corey to just tell people their priorities and path to achieve their goals, she asked her team to do it themselves. This is important because as Together Leaders, we ultimately want and need our teams to own their own work.

- He inserted evidence of effectiveness and cited various organizational pieces of data that would help measure and demonstrate success.

- He proactively listed management support needed, which helped Corey know where he needed her input.

Brian explained, "At the end of the previous year, I knew my strengths and where I needed to develop. To continuously improve, I needed help. The year before I was not strategic in getting help or even knowing what help I needed. If I outline what support I think I need from Corey, she and I are both accountable for it."

Brian J's Priority Plan
July – September

Priorities:
1. **Ensure consistent and culturally aligned execution of systems**
2. **Create cohesive, motivated, and collaborative GLC Team and GLTs across the MS**
3. **Build open, trusting, coaching relationships with teachers and teams**
4. **Practice alignment and collaboration between culture and academics**
5. **Personal Priority - Make things happen**

Priority	July	August	September
1	• Complete Culture Guide and invest GLCs such that they can invest teams • Plan in-service sessions, including framing and work in GLTs (how to execute with consistency and with the values in mind) • Framework for pre-term sessions with students • Create year-long cultural calendar (events, values)	• Regular observation of key system execution (personal observation, data review, feedback) • Provide individual coaching around systems • Check-ins with teachers focused on system consistency • Complete student handbook revisions/updates	• Continue observations and data review • Continue individual coaching around systems • Plan A1 State of the Middle School presentation • Check-ins with teachers focused on system consistency

Evidence of Effectiveness:
- Quantitative Data (marks, WS, RISE, suspensions, etc.) demonstrate consistency across Grade Levels
- Quantitative Data through Cultural Walkthrough Form (Hallways: 16/20, Common Areas: 9/10, Restrooms: 7/8, Classrooms: 16/18, TOTAL score at least 80)
- Qualitative Data (personal observations, reflections, conversations with teachers and GLCs around consistency and cultural alignment with vision)

Manager Support Needed:
- Review and provide feedback on Culture Guide; champion the vision with the rest of the Jedi Council and among staff during in-service and throughout A1
- Presence across the Middle School with focused feedback on consistency with regard to systems (holistically as well as individual teachers)
- Feedback when disciplinary decisions are/are not aligned with manager vision
- Feedback around communication regarding disciplinary decisions and culture, generally
- Accountability and review of progress toward goals with use of data as support

Figure 4.8 Brian's Priority Plan

We need alignment and buy in from our teams on which work matters most. As leaders, it's our job to take the time to think not only about our own tasks but also to help our teams name and define their biggest priorities. At the very least you should align with your own manager, or the board, if needed. Using Priority Plans helps focus your meetings on proactive work that matters the most because the topics that are on your Priority Plan should drive the bulk of your meetings.

Reader Reflection

List the top priorities for your team members for the next three months. You may not share it with them yet, but jot out your thoughts.

Recap: Elements of a Priority Plan

- **Bold and clear statement of priorities for the next three months** (or whatever medium-term interval works in your organization), often using language of outcomes

- **Key actions needed to accomplish the priorities,** often include milestones, meetings, or creation of deliverables

- **Includes personal priorities**

- **Outlines priorities for team members**

HOW BIG OR HOW SMALL—ARE THESE GIANT LEAPS OR BABY STEPS?

Your Priority Plan should ideally be an outline of the giant leaps you and your team will make when crossing the bridge between goals and progress. It should not be a detailed diagram of your baby steps. Remember, a good Priority Plan completes the statement, "The next three months will be successful if _____." That said, there are occasions when "regular" work or more specific tasks may find their way onto your Priority Plan. Let's review a few real-life examples.

Regular, Predictable Work—To Include or Not to Include?

Let's say you are a nonprofit human resources manager and running payroll is a regular part of your role. If the team is functioning well and everyone is getting paid accurately and on time, well, then, this predictable task would not need to hit your Priority Plan. It is a part of your work and your team's work that is essentially on autopilot. It would land in the Annual Activities from the previous chapter.

But let's say payroll had been tough recently; perhaps a few deadlines were missed or a few checks were written inaccurately. In that case, I suggest that you *do* put this task on a Priority Plan, either your own or one belonging to a team member you manage. Eventually this job may fade back into the regular To-Do List, but for right now, you know you want to spend *more* of your time on payroll. Including it on a Priority Plan will remind you of this and help you effect real and positive changes.

One way to ensure your Priority Plan provides an overall big-picture view is to limit it in length to two pages. If it gets any longer, then it is a To-Do List. Think forest, not trees. You can find more on To-Do Lists in chapter 7.

The Case for Tiny Detail—Yes or No?

Although we want to maintain reasonably big steps in our Priority Plans, there are a few cases when teeny-tiny details really affect outcomes. We want—we may even *need*—to make sure they happen. For example, let's say you have a board member who absolutely must weigh in on the hiring of a new manager. You noted it in your hiring Project Plan (more on those in chapter 12), but it is simply mission-critical that you get her input. You cannot afford to delay or forget this step. In this case, it is completely okay to have a line in your Priority Plan that says, "Schedule phone meeting with AB to get her input on the candidates." Basically, you can ask yourself this:" If *x* didn't happen, would this priority go straight to you-know-where?" If the answer is yes, you'd better include it.

Common Pitfalls of Priority Plans

- Exceed two pages
- Take more than two hours to draft
- They become the To-Do List
- They're kept on the shelf and forgotten about
- Not aligned to calendars (see chapter 6 on putting priorities in your calendar *first*)

FAQ: How is a Priority Plan different from a To-Do List?
Your Priority Plan is *much shorter* than your To-Do List. It should force you to define what's most important and make choices about resources. This is different from a To-Do List (as described in chapter 7), which covers everything on earth you need to do, from the most minute (ummm … pay parking tickets) to the most fun (book trip to New Orleans) to the most important (draft strategic plan).

THE ROUTINE

It's easy (well, not really) to just think and write about your priorities—and much, much more challenging to live them on a daily basis by making smart choices about your time and resources. In our experience, you need a few rituals or *forcing functions* to compel you to review your goals—and more important, align your time with your priorities. In this section, I will discuss how to use your Priority Plan for yourself, with those you manage, and even with your boss! I also share how Boston's Achievement Network (ANet) uses Priority Plans across the entire organization.

Your Personal Review of Your Priority Plan

At a minimum, take a spin through your Priority Plan at least once per week when preparing for the week ahead. Check to make sure you have time allocated to the following:

- Complete independent work toward priorities.

- Hold or attend necessary meetings aligned with priorities.

- And if something is taking up *major* amounts of time on your calendar that is *not* on your Priority Plan, well, then you have two options:
  1. Your Priority Plan isn't actually correct and you need to add this time-leecher to it *or*

  2. You need to shift that other work that is creeping up; delegate, delay, or defer it; and get back to your priorities!

This sounds silly but keep a printed copy on you in whatever you carry around (more on portability in chapter 14). For some reason, your priorities stay more vibrant when they're written down right there in front of you.

Ashley Martin, an executive director at ANet, describes why Priority Plans are so important to her work: "Creating Priority Plans and reviewing them at the end of every week helps me prioritize the tasks on my ever-expanding weekly To-Do List. I make intentional choices with my limited time that are grounded in the most important stuff. It is so easy to get stuck in the weeds of daily and weekly execution. But my Priority Plan helps me get up on the balcony for a big-picture view and gives me a real sense of my larger purpose."

If you feel like you are drowning in work, creating a Priority Plan can be a great way to take charge of your calendar, cut away any fluff, or delay the work that's less critical. Often, we complain about being overworked. But when we're asked why, we say, "I just have too much to do," not, "I have carefully weighed my priorities and I'm working on what matters most in my role for the betterment of my organization." The reason we don't state the latter is that we usually don't *pause to plan* when we're feeling overstretched; we just keep on going. And that is rarely the right approach.

Update Priority Plans on a Rolling Basis

The instinct of many folks is to just create Priority Plans four times per year for the following three months. But reviewing on a rolling basis is a better habit for a few reasons. First, it is simply less work to do a little each month rather than a lot all at once. But even more important, if you wait until you've wrapped up one quarter before you turn your attention to the next one, you may get smacked with a very large project (or one of those "emergencies") and zero resources in place to accomplish it! You can also set your Priority Plan cycle with one that makes sense for the rhythm of your organization, whether aligned with board meetings, testing schedules, or semesters.

I predict the first Priority Plan will likely take you two to three hours, and after that, you can budget one hour per month to extend your Priority Plan out for the next month. Get in a quiet spot and have your Yearly Goals, your calendar, any Project Plans, and any data you may need to review. Make sure you are in a mental state of reasonably high energy. Perhaps it makes sense to write your Priority Plan at a coffee shop early in the morning, or maybe you want to crank it out late at night in your home office. Either way, you will not fit this in between meetings on a busy day, even if you think you have time. Block out your Priority Planning time as a regular appointment on your calendar. Then you can begin just by extending your existing Priority Plan out another month. If it makes you too uncomfortable to do this on a rolling basis, begin your new Priority Plan early. I also suggest you look backwards each time you update to ensure the past is accurately reflected. This can create a great road map for the next year or someone else in your role in the future. For example, during your reflection, if you noticed you didn't make progress on one priority and another event on your calendar completely dominated that time period, ask yourself these questions:

- Were my priorities the right ones?
- Was my time aligned to my priorities?

Reader Reflection

When and how will you create your Priority Plan? How will you keep it updated and alive?

GETTING A TEAM ONBOARD

Now that you have created your Priority Plan, realized its benefits, and kept it alive, it is time to think about how to bring your team along. In my own experience managing individuals, and later managing people who managed other people, Priority Plans were the number one way I kept a pulse on prioritization across the team. They also helped colleagues connect on similar projects and motivated us all to keep our eyes on the proverbial prize.

I'm a huge fan of shared organizational language around planning because it sets the stage for how people plan and manage time and other resources. If you don't have a common language or cycle, you may have a marketing team planning its year before the recruiting team does, resulting in a huge mess when you realize that one team wants something from another that it's not yet prepared to share. Imagine a world in which you could get a peek at everyone's priorities for the next three months, draw connections, allocate resources, and help the team move along together.

Following are some practical tips on how to engage your team in the Priority Plan process.

Introducing the Concept

Many managers now introduce their expectation for Priority Planning to new hires during the onboarding process. If you did not have that foresight or you're just reading this now, it is never too late (see more thoughts on assessing Togetherness during onboarding in chapter 15). Just sending samples along with a note that says you "have to do this" never works well. Instead, the concept is often best shared at a team meeting or retreat in response to folks feeling overtapped and under-effective or if the team's work is just not getting done. Kari, whose example we reviewed previously, was incredibly thoughtful when she introduced Priority Plans to her team. In table 4.4, you can see the agenda she used to roll out the concept at a recent retreat.

Table 4.4 Kari's Intro to Priority Plans Team Meeting Agenda

Set the stage	• What is a Priority Plan?	10 min
	• Why make a Priority Plan?	
Examples of the end product	• What does a Priority Plan look like?	10 min
	• What questions do we have about the end product?	
Outline of the priority planning process	• Determine key priorities and explore priority killers.	60 min
	• Identify key action steps for each priority.	
	• Identify time required to complete action steps.	
	• Put it all together in a clean, concise format.	
	• Block time to complete action steps and revisit priority plan weekly.	
Key takeaways and next steps	• How can this process make you more effective?	10 min
	• What are your biggest concerns about making this a consistent practice?	
	• Commitment to review Priority Plans during check-ins the week of Jan 22	

Kari's team was excited, though nervous, to begin planning ahead and collaborating with Priority Plans. The end result was a more coordinated team that could react much more effectively in their to dynamic school environments.

FAQ: Should I require my team to create Priority Plans—or any tool?

I generally prefer to start change with a few key colleagues, which usually leads to widespread adoption. Personally, I did require Priority Plans for each of my direct reports, but I was neutral on the actual template, as long as it included the key elements listed previously in the chapter. I can say with confidence that it was my single best move as a leader to align with them (many of whom managed their own large teams) on where their resources were going.

Manage Your Team with Priority Plans

Priority Plans are a great way to lead an entire team. A shared Priority Planning process enables your team to collaborate and communicate without wading in the weeds of Daily Calendars and Project Plans. Melea Nalli, the COO of ANet, describes how her organization uses Priority Plans during meetings: "Teams schedule 'step-back' meetings at the end of each quarter, which typically take a full day (and include culture building and professional development, as well as a reflection against goals and priorities). I see each team's Priority Plan drafts after those team meetings and provide feedback at a check-in, which typically takes about 30 minutes."

As the COO, she is gaining valuable insight into work happening across the many teams she manages. She can then have a clear sense of not only each team's goals but also their planned paths to get there. Melea can also connect her managers to each other, note any capacity issues, and better manage the amount of change in a growing organization.

FAQ: But I thought I was just supposed to manage toward outcomes—not on process? Isn't this micromanagement?

I find that managers who *only* manage toward outcomes often get blindsided by emergencies too late in the process, or they are not fully supporting their teams in the hardest parts of their jobs. It *is* micromanagement if you start meddling in people's detailed business mid-course. If you've started *writing* the Priority Plans for your team, take a step back and let them drive their own work. However, if you are proactively helping your team figure out how to move their work forward on the front end, linking them to resources and colleagues doing similar work and investing early in key constituents—well, then, that is just good supportive management.

Managing Your Meetings with Priority Plans

Once you have Priority Plans up and running, the next step is to *use* them to drive your work. Most leaders spend an extraordinary amount of time in meetings. Therefore, we need to make sure these meetings are focused on the right stuff. Reviewing Priority Plans at meetings with your direct reports is one way to keep priorities alive and kicking. In chapter 5, you will find example agendas that include Priority Plans.

Erica Phillips, formerly a human capital director for Achievement First, a charter management organization, shares how she does it: "My team sends Priority Plans to me via e-mail at the beginning of the month. I go through them and identify the top areas I will work with them on throughout the month. We go over these together at our weekly check-in. During meetings, team members reflect publicly on their priorities and progress toward goals."

FAQ: Should I require a particular Priority Plan template?

I try really hard to be template neutral and requirement heavy. I want folks to write Priority Plans, but I don't care how they do it. If you let your team know what elements to include (refer to "Elements of a Priority Plan" previously in this chapter), then you can care less about the exact format as long as it is straightforward and easy to read. However, if you leave things too open-ended for folks, especially those new to this sort of thinking, the process can feel overwhelming. It's always nice to provide choices. There are several Priority Plan templates available on my website (www.thetogethergroup .com).

You can also reap the benefits of Priority Plans in team meetings, not just regular one-on-one meetings. For example, you could open each weekly team meeting with a whirl around asking everyone to share these points:

- What is one success from your Priority Plan last week?
- What is one challenge you encountered from your Priority Plan?

This gives additional focus to your meeting without falling into the trap of just sharing typical highs and lows because you are forcing people to reflect on progress toward priorities. Additionally, this gives your team valuable insight into each other's work.

Reader Reflection

How will you roll out Priority Plans with your team? Are any team members particularly primed to try Priority Plans? Who may need additional support?

Manage Your Boss with Priority Plans

Most managers I know do not dramatically sweep down from on high and tell you what your priorities should be. Try using your Priority Plan to inform *them* what you see as your priorities. Seek alignment, confirmation, and feedback. Most of us slowly learn over time what our bosses care most about. Here are several ways you can use your Priority Plan with your boss to gather up-front input, align on resources, and course correct when the inevitable emergency pops up.

Just Starting Your Role

Creating a Priority Plan after a few weeks into a new job is a great way to digest what you think your role is *really* all about. To start, write down everything you hear when you ask folks what your priorities should be. Then, narrow your list to ten items. For each one, state the corresponding actions that will help you achieve your goals. Share this draft with your manager, ask for feedback, and see how pleasantly surprised he is that you've proactively sought input.

You can continue to share your Priority Plan with your manager by bringing it to your (ahem) regularly scheduled meeting (request one if necessary!). Bring a printed copy in case she hasn't had a chance to review it in advance. Ask for her input: Do these feel like the right focus areas? Does she see anything missing? Is there anything in particular on which she wishes to be kept updated? Where does she want to give specific input? I don't think you need to do this weekly, but it is a great way to coordinate on a monthly basis.

Aligning Resources

Priority Plans are also an excellent tool to help gather investment on where time and money should be directed. Let's say you are an executive director reporting directly to a board. You might hear a lot of feedback from its members about what's most important. Creating a Priority Plan, perhaps even in a shareable form, such as PowerPoint, can help rally a group of advisors around what matters most. It also demonstrates that their voices have been heard—even if you cannot accomplish it all at once. Boards and senior leaders often align on strategic plans, but too often the actual workload it would take to accomplish said plan is far too much for you to accomplish. Updating your board and boss every three months with your Priority Plan is a great way to get buy in on the steps you've deemed most critical.

Manage Emergencies with Priority Plans

Priority Plans are also a great tool when "emergencies" arise. I say "emergencies" in quotes not to minimize your crises but to remind you that no one's day is filled with emergencies 24-7, even if it feels that way. Let's look at the following classic example.

Let's say you are the head of communications and government affairs for a school district and you get hit with an urgent media request that is going to suck up the remainder of the week. At this moment, before you do *anything* else, take out your Priority Plan and start thinking about what could be delayed, delegated, or simply not done. Check for alignment with your team and manager, and then shift your priorities accordingly. Too many of us start immediately following the crisis. In their book, *Scarcity,* Sendhil Mullainathan and Eldar Shafir aptly name this fire-fighting mentality *tunneling.* Before you go there, take a few minutes to pause, plan, and reprioritize, even if you have to hide to do so. Then, communicate: Let your colleagues know you are "going under" to deal with a crisis, what's happening, and when you will resurface. Without a Priority Plan written ahead of time, it's too easy to spend our days running from one fire to the next.

Reader Reflection

How will you use your Priority Plan with your manager? What is your purpose in doing so?

MY PRIORITY PLAN ISN'T WORKING FOR ME

Here are some of the typical challenges I see with Priority Plans, along with some common causes and solutions.

I'm Just Ticking Things off a List Each Day. If this happens to you, your teeny-tiny To-Dos have crept onto your giant-steps, big-picture Priority Plan. Consider boiling the whole thing down to the size of an index card as an exercise in prioritization and making choices. Look at this card only at the beginning and end of each day. Folks who are super-organized often fall prey to this challenge.

I Am Constantly Interrupted by Humans, Emergencies, Vendors, and My Kids. Me, too! Aren't we all? Consider how you communicate your priorities to others. What language can you can use when focusing on your most important work? I've seen everything from purple feather boas used as do-not-disturb signals to organizations that norm on language to use when people need privacy.

My Priorities Shift Constantly. Why Bother? Indeed. But this is why you work where you do. It's dynamic, interesting, and fast-paced. Still, no one reading this book got into their line of business just to react and put out fires all day long. As Rachel Strauch-Nelson, the director of media and government relations for Madison Metropolitan Public Schools, put it, "My day goes off the rails all the time. You never know when you will be hit with a story that you have to respond to immediately. But if I didn't recalibrate by returning to our key messages [her priorities] and then blocking time to make sure we are getting the positive stories out there too, I wouldn't be doing my job!"

There will always be thousands of things that get in the way of proactive planning to meet goals. But I guarantee that using Priority Plans will help you see more progress, find more time to align to your priorities, and establish a clear sight line into your team's work.

START STRONG

Priority Planning each month will help guarantee that you, your team, and your entire organization align your calendar and energy to the right work. You can plan ahead to get input, delegate well in advance, secure people and resources, and even plan for some respite and fun! If done well, Priority Plans should give you a clear and manageable path to achieve those goals you set in chapter 3.

Time commitment: two hours for your first Priority Plan and one hour per month moving forward.

- Create your *own* Priority Plan for the next three months. Make sure you get input from your board or manager.

- Review your Priority Plan and block necessary time on your calendar.

- Use your Priority Plans to coordinate with your own manager about upcoming events.

- Consider asking a few members of your team to test out creating their own Priority Plans.

- Use your Priority Plans to drive your meetings with your team members and manager.

SEE IT IN ACTION: WRIST, ELBOW, AND SHOULDER

At the beginning of my Priority Plan workshop, I ask people, "How do you determine where and when to get more involved in your team's work?" I frequently hear answers such as, "When something is messed up," "When I know the answers," or "When it is urgent."

But we can and must be more systematic than that so we can lead our teams with clear expectations. It can be hard to determine how and when to get involved. In this "See It in Action," I will feature Shannon Donnelly, an operations leader at Teach For America. Shannon perfectly describes a classic leader dilemma: "I am accountable for everything the team does. However, I simply cannot pay attention to every single detail." To help alleviate this pressure and provide transparency for her team, Shannon took a few steps to articulate her level of involvement.

1. Shannon starts by getting a pulse of the entire workload of the team. Shannon and her team have a clear list of projects connected to priorities. This is stored in a Google Doc shared by the entire team (table 4.5).

Table 4.5 Shannon's Team's Google Doc of Projects

Workstream	Project	Driver
Corps Communication Strategy	Incoming corps member TFANet experience (landing pages, access, training)	April
Corps Communication Strategy	Overall TFANet user strategy (incoming CM representation)	April
F&C—Procurement	Computers	Brennan
F&C—Procurement	Rental cars	Brennan
F&C—Procurement	Copiers	Brennan
F&C—Procurement	Cell phones	Brennan
F&C—Procurement	MiFis/Internet devices	Brennan
F&C—Procurement	Tech supplies (e.g., LCD projectors)	Brennan
F&C—Procurement	Office supplies	Brennan

2. Her second step is to outline how she determines the depth of her involvement. Shannon pauses to articulate why she leans in (figure 4.9).

I choose my level of involvement for each project based on the following factors:

1. Experience and confidence levels of the project owner
2. Layers of management in between me and the project owner
3. My expertise with the project and ability to contribute to it
4. The priority level of the project for our team this year
5. Potential risk to the team and our goals if the project is not successful
6. Budget implications
7. Involvement/investment of other teams and team leaders
8. Personal interest

I tend to be more deeply involved with projects where the owner needs more help, I manage the project owner directly, I have expertise that could be helpful, it's a high priority, there is a high level of risk, there are large budget implications, the team VPs and SVPs are invested in the project, and/or I have a high level of personal interest or investment in the project. Most of the projects where I would like to be deeply involved meet at least 4 of those criteria.

Figure 4.9 Decision-Making Criteria

3. After this, Shannon goes a step further. She spells out how her level of involvement connects to how the team uses meeting times! She labels her levels wrist, elbow, and shoulder, with shoulder-deep signifying her highest level of engagement (figure 4.10).

Category Definitions

For each project, I chose how deep I want to be involved: wrist-deep, elbow-deep, or shoulder-deep. Below are descriptions of what that means for each category. Please note that this is on top of any work I would generally do for projects as a manager on the team, like escalating issues to the VPs and helping with urgent problem solving, which happen for projects at all levels.

Wrist Deep

I generally don't need to know about this project unless something is going wrong.

- Do not need to discuss in check-ins, step-backs, or retreats unless there's an issue (delay or risk ahead). Just keep me posted in the status reports as needed
- I will assume everything is okay unless I hear otherwise
- I will be available for consultation at the request of the project owner, but may not always be able to prioritize it and may direct that person elsewhere

Figure 4.10 Categories of Involvement

Elbow Deep

I need to have a good understanding of what's going on with the project, and be involved more if there are any problems.

- Regularly discuss the project and its status in pre-existing structures (check-ins, step-backs, retreats, etc.)
- Be included in communication updates sent out about the project to stakeholders
- Be available for consultation for the project driver upon request
- Serve as an advocate for the project and what we want to do with it with key stakeholders, team leadership, or other teams in TFA
- Occasionally be involved in feedback loops, especially for new materials or ones that have been changed significantly, or ones where I have a perspective the project owner wants to include

Shoulder Deep

I need to be considered one of the key stakeholders in the project, and not only know about where it stands at all times, but be given opportunities to weigh in and participate regardless of status/risk. These are often also the highest priorities for the team, and therefore the areas where everyone who has these projects under their purview should be focusing lots of time and energy.

- Be involved in initial vision-setting, research, and decision-making processes to weigh in on the overall direction of the project
- Regularly discuss the project and its status in pre-existing structures (check-ins, step-backs, retreats, etc.)
- Meet directly with the project owner (and that person's manager, if I do not directly manage him/her) on a regular basis to discuss the project, either through or in addition to pre-existing structures
- Participate in calls where groups of people get together to discuss the project – I would like to be invited to most and have the option to opt out if my schedule does not allow me to attend
- Be involved in feedback loops for project materials and outputs, with the option to opt out of reviewing and giving feedback if my schedule does not permit it
- Be available for consultation for the project driver upon request
- Serve as an advocate for the project and what we want to do with it with key stakeholders, team leadership, or other teams in TFA

Figure 4.10 Continued

4. Once the work has been initiated, Shannon rolls out this memo to her team: "Every year, after we complete the portfolio of work (from step 1), I go through and add in my level of involvement for every project. After that, I have individual check-ins with my team

members. Last, I circulate the full memo and attached portfolio of work and put the responsibility back on the team to ensure they are involving me at the right level."

5. Shannon makes time to regularly review her depth of involvement during quarterly step-backs: "I ask myself, 'Do I have enough information? Has anything changed?'" She likes to point out that this review really only takes her one hour each quarter or three hours over the course of the year, and often forces an "uh-oh moment" by reminding her of what should be prioritized.

Shannon reiterates why she does all of this when she says to her team, "If I didn't do this, I could not give you support and direction in your roles. It is my job to make you successful and this enables me to differentiate support." Creating these wrist, elbow, and shoulder levels also ensures Shannon's meetings stay focused on what matters the most!

CHAPTER 5

Align Your Meetings
Make a Meeting Matrix

SEEN AND HEARD

"*Long* meetings are not a good use of my time! I feel like meetings should be for collaborating shared priorities and making decisions, not about sharing information that could have been shared via e-mail."

"I have three meetings per week with the same group of people to talk about basically the same things!"

"Sometimes I walk into a meeting to discuss a certain topic and two hours later I walk out—and realize we just spent two hours talking about it, but didn't really decide anything!"

OVERVIEW AND OBJECTIVES

For most leaders, meetings take up a large chunk of calendar real estate. This is not bad, per se, but if those meetings are not an *excellent* use of our time, then we are completely wasting the bulk of our days. For meetings to feel useful, they needed to support our actual priorities. Kimi Kean, the Bay Area superintendent for Aspire Public Schools, described improvements in her meetings over time: "Last year we didn't always prepare or use our meeting time intentionally. Sometimes we would spend check-in time on updates that didn't need discussion. My colleagues and I created a template so that we could (1) align check-ins to the big buckets of work in our shared work plan and (2) spend more of our time together on an in-depth issue rather than just giving quick updates." Whether you are just coming around to the idea of meetings or looking to make a long-term plan for your meetings, what matters most is planning and intentionality.

Most organizations follow a fairly predictable evolution in their feelings and practices about holding and attending meetings. It helps to identify where you and your organization are in your development so that you can determine where to jump in to improve your practice. Let's take a quick quiz to see where you fall on the continuum.

QUIZ
Meeting Development Phases

- **Phase 0:** We do not have meetings; we just grab each other as needed.
- **Phase 1:** I hold regular one-on-one and group meetings; they are never canceled or pushed aside.
- **Phase 2:** Someone creates an agenda for these meetings, often dominated by one person's interests.
- **Phase 3:** The agenda is co-created by multiple parties, occasionally turning into an unprioritized laundry list of topics.
- **Phase 4:** Our meetings focus on key priorities, often using an agreed-on standing meeting agenda; prework is completed in advance.
- **Phase 5:** A predictable Scope and Sequence of meetings for the year is created and published ahead of time.

Reader Reflection
Which meeting phase are you in and why? What is the impact of this phase on your work?

It's no coincidence that this chapter on meetings falls directly after the chapters on Yearly Goals and Priority Plans. I want you to make sure your meetings, similar to the rest of your time, are aligned with what matters most!

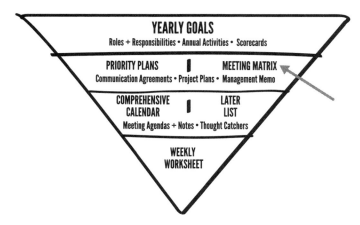

Figure 5.1 The Togetherness Tools

In this chapter, you will do the following:

- Articulate the purpose of a Meeting Matrix.
- Determine whom you meet with, when, and for what purposes.
- Decide on standing agenda items and define meeting-preparation expectations.
- Gain clarity on note-taking methods.
- Plan a Meeting Scope and Sequence if necessary.

Our ultimate goal in this chapter is to build a Meeting Matrix (see figure 5.1).

Definition

The **Meeting Matrix** is an articulation of whom you meet with, when, and for what purpose. This helps shape each meeting's required preparation and standing agenda items.

THE MODEL

The blank Meeting Matrix template in figure 5.2 invites you to envision a world in which your meetings are clearly aligned with your priorities, highly predictable, and require strong preparation and follow-up. There are, of course, opposing schools of thought, especially in "maker" roles, such as software development, that eschew the idea of *any* standing meetings. In so much, as I want to help you lead proactively, avoid fire drills, and plan for the predictable, I'm going to advocate that you map out your meetings. Of course, I'm not opposed to clearing out your calendar certain weeks of the year!

Name of Meeting	Purpose	Facilitator	If Applicable, Meeting Manager	Participants	Timing/ Frequency	Standing Agenda Items	Preparation/ Follow-Up	Goal or Priority Alignment, Scale of 1–3

Figure 5.2 Meeting Matrix Template

Tool-Building Tip:

- If your calendar is currently completely blank because you are starting a new role or at a new organization, now is the perfect time to think about your meeting structures from scratch.

- If your calendar is completely full, note each of your meetings in the matrix. You may find some meetings that keep happening purely out of habit or don't include the right people. Be sure to rank each meeting against your goals and priorities!

Sally's Meeting Matrix

Sally Houston, a school leader in Washington, DC, took time at the beginning of the school year to outline the objectives of her various meetings in a Meeting Matrix (figure 5.3). Each meeting's purpose is clear to her—and to her team! For a full sample, please check out my website (www.thetogethergroup.com).

There are several elements I love in Sally's example:

- The leader of each meeting is clearly named. This can feel small, but sometimes people really don't know who is in charge.

- The data to review at each meeting are listed. This helps everyone know how to prepare and what to expect.

- A full description of each meeting is included. This basically creates a standing agenda to be modified as needed.

Sally also shared this Meeting Matrix with her entire team so that everyone was clear on expectations. When you and your team know that your meetings are purposefully planned, thoughtfully led, and aligned to what actually matters most, you can focus on true problem-solving and proactive work—and let everything else fall around the edges.

DC Prep Benning Middle · Meeting Matrix				
Meeting	**Leader**	**Attendees**	**Data**	**Description**
Academic Team	Julia	• Sally • Julia • MK • Katie • Emily	• F&P • Interim data • Finish Lines • Observation data	• Debrief feedback on PD & prep future PDs • Review upcoming EMC department meetings. • Discuss department goal progress • Discuss and strategize around teacher support • Monthly "retreat" for at least a half day to look at observation feedback to teachers • Reflect on collaboration with EMC

Student Support Team	Sally	• Sally
		• Joshua
		• Deb
		• Becky
		• Julia
		• Danielle
		• Neema
			• ICS data
			• Suspension
			• Grades
			• Homework
			• Any data that is aligned with a student's individual **measurable** goal.
				• Progress monitoring
				• Discuss individual student needs regarding their academic and/or behavioral progress.
				• Potential cycle of meetings:
				   o Academic supports
				   o Behavior supports
				   o Data Dives/observation of implementation of plans
				   o Stage 2 meetings

Figure 5.3 Sally's Meeting Matrix

Melissa's Meeting Matrix

Melissa Rouette, the chief program officer of Citizen Schools, shares another great example of a Meeting Matrix in figure 5.4. She walks through this with her team at the start of each year. This way, everyone understands how the pieces fit together—and most important, how intentional Melissa is trying to be with her team's time.

Similar to Sally, Melissa names each meeting's type, purpose, and standing agenda topics. She also does a few more nifty things:

- Articulates her expectations for the time and frequency of each meeting

- Spells out her standards for meeting prep and follow-up

National Program Department How We Do the Work: Meeting Structures September Team Retreat

Type of Meeting	Purpose	Standing Agenda Items	Preparation/Follow-up Expectations	Time & Frequency
Weekly 1:1s with Direct Reports	• Ask quick questions • Tackle urgent issues • Provide feedback on work	• 5-10 min – Check In & Follow-Up • 25 min – Project Feedback | Deep Dives • 15 min – Priority Review • 5 min – Quick Questions • 5 min – Review Next Steps	• Direct reports prepare agenda and send to Melissa R 48 hours in advance (Melissa R adds agenda items as needed) • Direct reports identify the projects that they need feedback on and send pre-reading 48 hours in advance • To maximize meeting time, Melissa R attempts to answer quick hit questions over e-mail in advance of the meeting • All National Program Dept. supervisors will have 1:1s with direct reports every 1-2 weeks	• Once/week • 60 min (unless otherwise determined individually)

Figure 5.4 Melissa's Meeting Matrix

National Program Department How We Do the Work: Meeting Structures September Team Retreat

Type of Meeting	Purpose	Standing Agenda Items	Preparation/Follow-up Expectations	Time & Frequency
National Program Dept. Directors Meeting	• Get input and feedback on decisions and projects • Tackle larger vision and strategy questions • Share management best practices | questions | concerns • Share organizational decisions (pre-whole team)	• 5 min – Bright spots sharing at the beginning • 80 min – Topics TBD by directors group: a living, breathing scope and sequence will be determined at the Sep Strategy Retreat, but we will always keep a certain amount of time flexible for top of mind topics that are submitted by one or more directors • 5 min – Next Steps review at the end	Standing Expectations • Directors submit agenda topics • Pre-reading is sent 24 hours in advance OR presenter provides reading time in the meeting New Expectations • Directors rotate responsibility for agenda creation and dissemination to group • Directors rotate facilitation of the meeting (including assigning others to certain responsibilities in the meeting)	• Every other week • 90 min

Figure 5.4 Continued

Creating your Meeting Matrix may seem like a lot of up-front work. That's because it is! But I guarantee it will be worse to spend your precious time in bad or ineffective meetings … which just lead to more bad or ineffective meetings … which just lead to … well, you get it. Even if your calendar is already entirely full, it makes sense to pause and create a Meeting Matrix to align your time with your priorities. P.S.: Don't just issue a memo without getting input from your team. I suggest putting forth a draft, getting input, and then adjusting as needed. Are you ready? Let's build your own Meeting Matrix, step-by-step.

Reader Reflection

How will a Meeting Matrix help you better align your time with your priorities?

BUILD YOUR OWN

Let's start here: Why even bother meeting to begin with? If your schedule is crowded with meetings, how will you deal with the emergencies you face every day? When will you have the time to accomplish any follow-up work? Why on earth would you subject anyone else to the kinds of dreaded, boring meetings you have suffered through yourself?

Good questions! Your fears are fair. That said, you are a leader. You manage others, and ultimately, you are accountable for their work. If I were you, I would want a window into that work! To get that window, you're going to need to meet.

Meetings can have several purposes. Following, you can see some of the most typical.

Possible Purposes of Meetings

- Review progress toward goals
- Disseminate information
- Gather input
- Make decisions
- Plan ahead
- Troubleshoot
- Inspire and motivate
- Learn and grow

The problem is that most people try to fit *all* eight categories into *every* single meeting. This is ineffective for different people or groups who need different things, not to mention impossible on everyone's time, including your own. We need to break things up a bit.

Whom do you meet with? Let's start easy and get more complex.

Anyone You Manage. In some organizations, this meeting is called a *check-in,* or *an O3,* or *a one-on-one.* I don't care what you name it, but I want you to have a regular standing meeting with each person you manage, either weekly or biweekly. The main purposes of this meeting are planning ahead, measuring progress toward goals, and information dissemination. You may hit some of the other options mentioned previously as well.

Your Own Supervisor. Even if your manager isn't excited about meeting regularly, push for a regular meeting with your boss. At the very least, you want to keep him or her informed of your progress so you can seek input and guidance through structured discussions.

Leadership Team. If you are very senior or run a big team, you likely have a leadership team composed of other leaders who each oversee various divisions. With this group of people, you need to disseminate information, strategize, and plan ahead.

Project Teams. Maybe you are part of a cross-functional working group (a group that represents various perspectives and teams across your organization) for a new website, and your advice is needed. The project team may operate for a limited period of time. Your meetings would likely focus on project updates, troubleshooting, and looking ahead.

Lateral Colleagues. You may coordinate with other peers in your organization on various projects or initiatives. Some of these projects may be ongoing and some may be discrete. With this group of people, you are likely preparing decisions and proposing recommendations.

Skip-Level Meetings. By skip-level, I mean those members of your organization who work directly for your own team members. You'll want to check in on their performance, happiness, and satisfaction. If you don't, you may lose your pulse on the team and have a retention risk on your hands. At the very least, these people should know you, understand the organization's goals, and feel connected to the mission.

Vendor Meetings. If you manage special projects or hire independent contractors, you may need regular meetings with vendors or consultants. At these meetings, you'll likely focus on progress toward goals, setting expectations, or planning ahead.

Other Constituents. Only you know your role. Maybe you also need meetings with board members, donors, or other important people in your work world.

FAQ: Who should run the meeting?

For each meeting, I also want you to select a leader. This is the person ultimately responsible for creating the agenda and following up each week. And if you select your direct report to be in charge of her own weekly meeting with you (which I hope you do), it doesn't mean you are absolving yourself of any input. It just means that when this meeting happens, you aren't the one facilitating it. Let your people lead the way. This is wise for a number of reasons. First of all, you are building a long-term sustainable organization, and you want your team to feel empowered. Second, think of how much time you'll save by not creating a huge number of agendas yourself each week! You can easily adopt a process by which you agree on a standing agenda (more on that in a minute). Then, your team member can create a draft each week and send it back to you for your input!

Reader Reflection

Let's get your Meeting Matrix started. I assume your calendar is already full of meetings, but let's start from scratch. Consider your Goals and Priorities … With whom do you need to meet regularly? What is the purpose of each meeting? Add your list to the Name of Meeting, Purpose, Facilitator, and Participants columns in the Meeting Matrix table in your Reader Reflection Guide. Be sure to evaluate each meeting on its alignment to your goals and priorities in the last column.

THE MECHANICS OF A REGULAR ONE-ON-ONE MEETING

Now that you are jazzed about regularly and purposefully meeting with people, let's dive into the mechanics of when all this discussion is actually going to happen.

How Often Should You Meet?

This depends on the performance level of the individual, the importance of his or her work to meet your goals, and your own workload. Start with once per week for forty-five to sixty minutes but know that can vary. For example, some leaders check in with direct reports for just thirty minutes each week but hold a two-hour meeting once a month to explore deeper topics and check in on goals.

When Should You Meet?

All too often, organizations stack all meetings on Mondays. I strongly advise against this. Think about how you feel on the Sunday evenings when you glance at your calendar and see a schedule of wall-to-wall meetings to start the week. That's an energy killer right there.

Use Mondays for bigger work, and move meetings to the back end of the week. This move is useful for a few reasons:

- It lets you look backwards and celebrate successes.
- It enables you to preview the next week ahead.
- It can boost energy after a long week.

Once you've decided when each meeting will happen, go ahead and send e-invites for the remainder of the year. These invitations should include a specific location for the meeting, contact info for each person attending, the agenda, and any required materials. This list may feel picky, but we don't want to waste any time wandering into someone else's office when the meeting is about to begin, wondering "Are we meeting?" "Where is the meeting?" or "What should I bring?" Sound familiar? Let's take the guesswork out where we can.

FAQ: Should I have all of my internal meetings on the same day or across different days?

My preference is for internal meetings all on one day, particularly Thursdays. Mondays and Fridays are too frequently killed by holidays or long weekends. The downside is that if you have a weeklong conference or you're out for that one day, it can mean a lot of rescheduling. However, my experience is that this inconvenience is outweighed by the power of getting in the internal mind-set, preparing all at once, and drawing connections between people and teams.

Reader Reflection

What is the right time and frequency for each meeting on your calendar? How will you communicate expectations to those with whom you meet? Add them to the Timing and Frequency columns in the Meeting Matrix table in your Reader Reflection Guide.

FAQ: Should I ever differentiate the content and frequency of my one-on-one meetings?

Absolutely! This will be dependent on the needs of your people and your organization. Sometimes it may be only for a discrete period of time. For example, I often met with brand-new leaders up to three times per week as they settled into their roles, but then dialed back to once per week when they seemed to be getting the hang of things. Given the fast-moving nature of our work, sometimes it made more sense to meet with my assistant for ten minutes each day rather than an hour once a week. I recommend using your Priority Plan as a guide to differentiating your meetings.

FAQ: What about the random meeting request?

I get these a lot too! People asking for career advice, resume review, or to review a business plan. I try to err on the side of both generous *and* ruthless with my time—and you should too. You can take these meetings while strategically multitasking (often I warn people I'm washing dishes or en route to the airport), you can block out Random Days for and dump all of these requests into a few days per year, a practice highlighted by prolific Warton professor Adam Grant in his wonderful blog, or you can create a template or document for frequently asked questions.

Select the Right Setting and Appoint a Meeting Manager

I'm sure you've attended a big meeting only to find someone fiddling with the video feed just as it's *supposed* to start, right? There are countless small decisions required when planning meetings. Though each one is tiny, they add up fast.

- Does the meeting require attendees to prepare? How far in advance do materials need to go out?
- Will your meeting be held all in one room or will there be breakout groups?
- Are some people calling in via phone or video?
- Are handouts needed?
- Who is making the copies?
- Is privacy needed?

Make sure to clearly identify the specifics of place and time, along with any directions needed (driving or dialing in), and preparation required. If you are not the one in charge of these decisions and their execution, appoint a Meeting Manager to handle all of the details in advance.

Definition

A **Meeting Manager** is the person assigned to function as the administrator for the meeting, doing everything from communications to setup to sending the invite to note taking to timekeeping to food ordering.

Reader Reflection

Which of your meetings could be improved with a Meeting Manager? Add them to the Meeting Manager column in the Meeting Matrix table in your Reader Reflection Guide.

FAQ: Why schedule all meetings out for the entire year?

By doing this, you can make sure you plan ahead, let other people know what to expect, make any necessary reservations, or invite special guests. I suggest publishing the meeting calendar at the beginning of your organization's calendar or fiscal year to avoid any last-minute surprises for your team.

NAILING THE CONTENT

Okay, we have tackled the easier part of your Meeting Matrix—whom to meet with and how often. But *what* should you even talk about? Most agendas, if they even exist, look like a laundry list of random ideas instead of what they should be: a summary of steps taken since the last meeting, a focus on priorities and looking ahead, and a little time for info sharing and Quick Questions. You will want to talk about the work, but you'll also need time built in to share information or get input. In this section, I'll discuss how to select the *right* content for your one-on-ones, your group meetings, and your one-offs (not regularly recurring meetings).

Great One-on-One Meetings

Typically, it makes sense to agree on a shared standing agenda, based on the most important parts of the work. Melissa R., met earlier in the chapter, shares one frequently used format in figure 5.5. This agenda typically covers a thirty- to sixty-minute weekly meeting, differentiated by team member.

Melissa specified the framework for her team, and figure 5.6 shows an example of how one colleague filled it in.

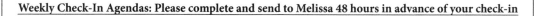

Weekly Check-In Agendas: Please complete and send to Melissa 48 hours in advance of your check-in

I. **Next Steps Review/Status Updates (5 min)**

II. **FYIs (3 min)** *I don't want to take time during our meetings to cover these, but would like to have in writing with your agenda each week just so I am informed.*

III. **Deep Dives and/or Project Feedback (20 min)** *1-3 things that you need us to think together about or work together on and/or that you need me to review in advance and be prepared to give you feedback on.*

IV. **Review of Priorities/Projects for the Next Month (15 min)** *Please distinguish priorities and projects that require the input/assistance of other members of this team and be prepared to describe how you are communicating/collaborating with those team members*

V. **Quick Questions for Each Other (5 min)** *What answers do you need to move forward on a project?*

VI. **Review Next Steps (5 min)**

Figure 5.5 Melissa's One-on-One Agenda

Keely/Melissa 1-1: March 5th

Next Steps Review/Status Updates (5 min)

Next Steps from Last Week	Status Updates This Week
• Revisit Apprenticeship Curriculum Development topics with Rob & Mandy • Brainstorm places/people to find C3 resources	• Rob to move ahead with two new units: Design Thinking and Time to Invent • Mandy to revise In Your Dreams and (tentative) write new Math Secrets & Codes unit • Thinking about reaching out to Grace for 21st Century Skill student work and staff resources assignment

FYIs (3 min)

- My phone is working again. :)
- Sending Priscilla, Joel and Finance team some key milestones on AppEx to work with for a late breaking funder report that needs to go out.

Deep Dives (20 min) 1-3 things that you need us to think together about or work together on:

- AppEx
  - Rough planning timeline found here
  - I'd like to discuss approximate time estimates and major gaps/additions you recommend to this plan
- Review of 4 Ds
  - I'd like to review the Design team specific doc: Design Team 4 Ds. Amy and I have added some notes on projects that have been delegated or downgraded that I want to flag and review with you.

Review of Priorities/Projects for the Next Month (15 min)

- AppEx Pilot–Regional Planning launch
- CPM proposal process development
- Aship curric development
- ID CCSS skills for FY16 focus

Figure 5.6 Melissa and Keely One-on-One Agenda

Quick/Medium Hits for Each Other (5 min)

- When are coaching assignments for next year getting made? What will the process entail and if I have input/questions, should those go to you or Katie?
- All set to move on CPM process for roll out on March 19th MDP call. Do you need me to flag this for Katie or have you already connected with her?
- Were there specific next steps that came out of this week's ED call?

Review Next Steps (5 min)

Next Steps from This Week

- Send Melissa revised AppEx Planning Timeline by Friday for final review
- Reach out to Grace & Tamara for 21st C samples
- Send Krista e-mail about delegated projects (cc Melissa)

Figure 5.6 Continued

Here are some key strengths in Melissa's agenda:

- Next steps from the previous meeting are reviewed at the beginning of the meeting and new actions are recapped at the end of the meeting.
- Quick Questions are toward the end of the meeting. Often, these can consume a whole meeting when they are at the start. This way, the most important stuff gets covered first, and the smaller stuff can be deferred to e-mail if needed.
- There is a clear space reserved to look ahead and get aligned on priorities for the coming months.
- There is real time reserved to troubleshoot.

FAQ: But what if my team members don't put the *right* things on the agenda, and I have no say?

This is why you collaborate up-front about the structure of the standing agenda, request the weekly version in advance, and give input. I recommend a regular cycle such as the following:

- Forty-eight hours before meeting, team member sends agenda to leader.
- Twenty-four hours before meeting, manager reviews agenda and replies with additions and questions.

- Team member updates and finalizes agenda and brings to meeting.
- Team member and manager agree at beginning of meeting what is most important to cover and what could get cut if needed.

The Deep Dive

I'm really in love with this idea of a Deep Dive to ensure interesting work really does happen during meetings. The Deep Dive is the largest section of the meeting. It is focused on what matters the most, often related to goals or priorities. See how all of this is handily connecting to your Priority Plan?! Because our time is so limited, some structure can be helpful.

Running the Deep Dive is empowering for the person leading the meeting (your team member). It also preserves time to actually discuss and debate an issue, ideally resulting in the best possible outcome. If you don't want to read all of this prior to meeting, perhaps you can just share the template and ask your team member to come with these thoughts considered. No more time wasted!

You can also take it a step further and agree on *which* projects you want to review with your team for the next three-month period, clarifying where you want to be involved and why. You can read more about that in the "See It in Action" section about wrist, elbow, shoulder previously in the book.

Reader Reflection

Consider the one-on-one meetings in your Meeting Matrix. What are your standing agenda items? Add them to the Standing Agenda Items column in the Meeting Matrix table in your Reader Reflection Guide.

Great Group Meetings

Once you nail your standing structure for one-on-one meetings, it's time to do the same for group meetings, the recurring ones and the one-offs. In this section, I will share examples of standing leadership team meeting agendas, as well as agendas from larger organizational meetings and conferences. In each, I will indicate where you can see the purpose, efficiency, and follow-up.

A Strong Weekly Team Meeting

Similar to how you meet regularly with each individual member of your team, you should also meet as a group on a consistent basis to share information, collaborate, and plan ahead. Sharon Johnson, a principal at Aspire Public Schools in California, shares her Team Meeting Agenda (figure 5.7) with strong Togetherness practices.

EPACS Leadership Team Meeting Agenda
Week 3
August 20 4:30pm-5:30pm

Lead Team Member	Deliverables from Previous Meeting
Sharon	Create COI calendar template
Sharon & Arlena	Lesson Plan Objectives walkthrough
Leads	Bring back COI calendars from teams
Laura, Stephanie, Arlena	Bring calendars to schedule coverage for observations

Facilitator: *Sharon*   Recorder: *Mari*   Time Keeper: *Margarita*   Participation Leader: *Jen*

Time	Session	Guiding Questions/Goals/Outcomes	How	Aligns With ...
4:30-4:40	Check-in	What are you celebrating? Any needs from you or your team? Any broken windows?	Whip Around	Domain 4
4:40-5:00	COI Calendar	How will we organize cycles of inquiries for the school year? What challenges do we anticipate?	Calendar Review	Domain 4
5:00-5:15	Lesson Plan Feedback	What are the expectations for Lead Team in regards to lesson plan feedback and support? What is the first focus area for lesson plan feedback?	Define Criteria	Domain 1
5:15-5:25	Coverage for Lead Teachers	Who will cover lead teachers to get into their teams' classrooms? How frequently will leads observe?	Calendar Planning	Domain 2 & 3
5:25-5:30	Team Meeting Planning	What information do we need to collect from each team to inform our COI planning in lead team next week? What else is on team meeting agendas?	Agenda Planning	Domain 4

Figure 5.7 Sharon's Team Meeting Agenda

Sharon has created many structures to keep her team on track:

Deliverables and next steps from the last meeting, publicly posted at the top of the agenda to help hold all accountable

Times built into the agenda, with broad topic areas clearly labeled

Guiding questions and goals outlined to help launch and facilitate discussion

Naming how each topic will be discussed

Sharon saves boatloads of time by using a standing template such as this one. She is free to focus on the content of each meeting, rather than its logistics. This is exactly where her leadership brain *should* be focused!

An Organization-Wide Meeting

Let's look at an example from YES Prep Public Schools. This is an agenda from a one-off meeting that pulls people together from different teams across an entire organization (figure 5.8).

There is so much to love about this sample (and the full version is available on my website, www.thetogethergroup.com). Let me highlight a few reasons why I think it is a strong model:

- Times are clearly attached to sections. This doesn't mean you have to be constrained by them, but they do signal priority level and enable you to make adjustments in the moment by acknowledging trade-offs.
- Outcomes are named for each and every section—and they all start with verbs!
- The larger purpose of each time is also articulated.
- Facilitation responsibilities are shared across the team, and the facilitator for each section is clearly named.
- The agenda is distributed in advance.
- There's time built in for transitions.

FAQ: Should we ever have looser meetings?

I remember very clearly when someone I respect hugely said to me, "We have no room for loose meetings here. I wonder if that inhibits our innovation and creativity when identifying issues and solving problems." Sometimes you *will* want and need space for pie-in-the-sky big dreams and goals meetings. My two cents: If you know this is a need, why not just schedule them into your organization's calendar? This way the time for them is blocked and protected in advance.

Reader Reflection

What are your standing agenda items for your group meetings? Add them to the Standing Agenda Items column in the Meeting Matrix table in your Reader Reflection Guide.

Leadership Team Strategic Planning Kick-Off

June 4

Time	Topic	Outcomes / Skills	Purpose	Facilitator
8:00 - 9:00	**Position Specific Pre-Meetings**	Preview the day's agenda and the current year's campus strategic planning process. ****These meetings are required for SDs and OMs.*	Enrollment	HOSs, Recy
8:30 - 9:30	**Breakfast and Warm Up**	8:30-9:10- Breakfast 9:10 to 9:30- Warm Up ****We will start precisely at 9:10am, please arrive by 9:00am if you do not want to have breakfast.*	Team-Building	Jeremy Recy
9:30 - 10:00	**YES Prep Strategic Priorities**	Campus leadership teams will understand the content and purpose of the YES Prep Strategic Priorities.	Enrollment	Mark
10:00 - 10:10	**Transition**			
10:10 - 11:30	**Introduction to the 14-15 Strategic Planning Process**	Campus leadership teams will: • Identify the connection between YES Prep Strategic Priorities, the YES Prep Campus Report Card, SST goals, and SST drivers • Understand the purpose of strategic planning and basing goals/drivers on CRC aligned data • Explore and practice process for creating campus-specific goals and drivers that are aligned with either SST goals and drivers or campus specific needs	Enrollment/ Information	HOS, Recy, Nella, Mark

Figure 5.8 YES Prep Meeting Agenda

Time	Topic	Outcomes / Skills	Purpose	Facilitator
11:30 - 11:45	**Break/Transition**			
11:45 - 1:00	**Campus Work Time: Part One**	Campus leadership teams will: • Review available CRC data from last year • Begin creating campus specific goals and drivers related to talent performance • Brainstorm potential campus goals and drivers related to student achievement/persistence and campus culture performance • Create a summer plan for completing the strategic planning process and required deliverables	Action Required	SDs

Figure 5.8 Continued

THE ROUTINE

So, now that you have thought purposefully about all of your meetings, who attends them, and when to have them, it's time to make sure the expectations for preparation and follow-up are incredibly clear. There are already many, many good books out there about running good meetings. One of my favorites is *Death by Meeting* by Patrick Lencioni. I will concentrate on sharing some specific Together tricks to help facilitation run smoothly.

Prepare

I get it. You are wildly busy. Preparing for a meeting can feel like the last thing you have time to do. But if you don't want to fall into the bad meeting trap, some preparation is necessary. The quantity and quality of this prep really depend on the type of meeting you're having. I know your time is limited, and I don't want you to spend hours preparing. However, if you are asking your people to prepare agendas and complete prework, then it behooves you to read what they send. Nothing deflates people more than doing work and not having it acknowledged. So, let's make sure you and your team have blocked time in your calendars to actually prepare. For example, let's say you communicate to your team that the weekly meeting agenda always comes out on Tuesday mornings. Then you can ask them to keep thirty minutes of preparation time blocked in their Comprehensive Calendars on Wednesday to prepare for the meeting on Thursday morning. Otherwise, if you vary when you send out the agenda, you won't be giving your team a chance to prepare. And let's face it, most meetings need at least a little bit of preparation.

Let's flip back to Melissa's example and look at her expectations for preparation in table 5.1.

Table 5.1 Melissa's Meeting Expectations

Type of Meeting	Preparation and Follow-up Expectations
Weekly one-on-ones with direct reports	• Direct reports prepare agenda and send to Melissa forty-eight hours in advance (Melissa adds agenda items as needed).
	• Direct reports identify the projects that they need feedback on and send prereading forty-eight hours in advance.
	• To maximize meeting time, Melissa attempts to answer quick-hit questions over e-mail in advance of the meeting.
	• All national program department supervisors will have one-on-ones with direct reports every one to two weeks.

Melissa clearly outlines a few important details:

- How far in advance the agenda should be sent.
- Shared responsibility for facilitation.
- Identification of which items can be moved to e-mail.

FAQ

What if the meeting goes off schedule? This is actually fine. The key is to name it explicitly, seek group agreement about the shift, and be clear on the trade-off. For example, it may make more sense to continue to discuss the policy for detention as long as everyone is okay with what will *not* be covered. Remember to make a quick plan for how and when to return to that topic!

> **Technical Tip: Accurate Digital Invitations:**
> Now let's look at a few good examples of meeting invitations, including one I sent while scheduling an interview for this very book (figure 5.9). Gotta practice what I preach! You will notice the dates, times, and phone numbers are included.

We can get even more complex and keep the agenda *in* the invitation. Kendra, my director of operations, sends me meeting invites that are full of juicy details in advance (figure 5.10)!

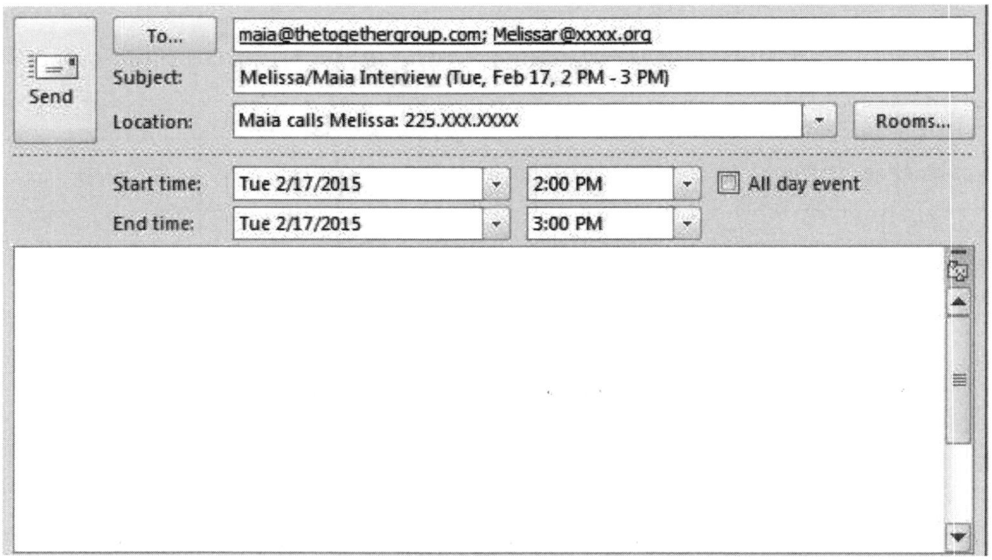

Figure 5.9 Melissa and Maia's Meeting Invite

Subject	Maia & Kendra weekly meeting		
Location	Maia sends Zoom link		
Start time	Mon 2/16/2015	2:45 PM	▾
End time	Mon 2/16/2015	3:15 PM	▾

☐ All day event

<u>Agenda</u>

1. Review QQs/FYIs
   a. <u>QQ</u>: OK to order supplies – more than needed to get the good discount?
   b. <u>QQ</u>: If needed, confirm timing of production steps for Aspire & Rocketship
      i. Leave it as a 2-day cushion
      ii. Adjust Aspire & Rocketship deadlines accordingly
   c. <u>QQ</u>: So tell me more about Cleveland!
   d. <u>QQ</u>: Can we be creative with Baychester's books?
      i. Ship books may arrive right after pending timing

2. Review emails
   a. Email 1: Clarify unique user thing for this one.
      i. Send Gianna both – for webinar videos, and zip files

3. Review EchoSign and confirm which SoW/MSA to delete from the system *(the old unsigned ones)*

4. Review Client Tracker (only as needed)

Figure 5.10 Kendra and Maia's Meeting Invite

Reader Reflection

What's most important for you to include on future meeting invitations?

Assistant Alert

Your assistant can schedule all of these meetings for you once you have aligned with your team members why you are meeting with them.

You may not know at the start of the year what you want folks to bring to a meeting in May or what the agenda items will be, but you can always add this information or modify agendas as the date approaches.

MEETING FOLLOW-UP

What's the purpose of a meeting without follow-up? If you haven't done so already, please block time for meeting follow-up in your calendar! More on that in chapter 6 when I discuss your Comprehensive Calendar. Let's walk through what effective meeting follow-up looks like.

First of all, there should be a commitment to follow up by all attendees. This is easier said than done, but we can solve this by creating what I like to call *forcing functions*—any task, activity, or event that forces you to take action. Someone needs to take notes. However, most groups make the mistake of deciding in the moment who the note taker will be and how he or she will take and format the notes. You may be thinking that as a busy leader you are too important to even consider planning for something so trite. But as the leader, it's your job to know what you want out of the meeting. Do you want a list of next steps? Do you want a chart of rationale for decisions? Name your outcome, and enable it to shape the notes and information you want to walk away with. Otherwise you run the risk of wasting time with minute-by-minute notes that don't mean anything to anyone!

Appoint a Note Taker in Advance (Preferably Not You)

Appoint a note taker in advance, whether it's always your direct report for your one-on-one meeting or your assistant for a big quarterly board meeting. With small-group meetings, the duty can rotate among the members. The note taker should know your norms, such as where he should sit, if technology is welcomed, and if he can interrupt to ask clarifying questions. He should also know your preferences for formatting as previously discussed!

Determine a Format for the Notes in Advance

Here are a few of my favorite ways to keep Together notes:

- A simple who is doing what by when chart (table 5.2) and examples available on my website (www.thetogethergroup.com) sent in an e-mail (and please put the next steps in a chart at the beginning of the e-mail, not buried at the end!)

- A template that documents which decisions were made, what was considered, and the rationale for the final decision
- A meeting-specific template agreed on in advance by the team; for example, if you just need to capture action steps, a simple chart such as the one in table 5.2 is adequate, but if you need to document how decisions are made, then you may want to take notes differently

Then you need to decide where the notes go when the meeting is done. I will share more thoughts on storage options in chapter 14, but some common choices are as follows:

- E-mailed out to the group
- Stored in Dropbox, Google Drive, or some other file-sharing platform
- Stored in a running Excel document

Reader Reflection

Look at each of your meetings. What kind of preparation would make the meeting more effective? What is the plan for follow-up? Add your ideas to the Preparation and Follow-Up columns in the Meeting Matrix table in your Reader Reflection Guide.

Table 5.2 Talent Mansion Short-Term Next-Step Tracker

Owner	Short-Term Next Step	Deadline	Status
Emily	Follow up with Talent Mansion group about follow-up diversity discussion over lunch.	12/2	
Emily	Reach out to Sylvia and Henry to discuss diversity session topics for PD day.	12/2	
Gail	Send Talent Mansion the deck on top three traits we select based on the behavioral study.	12/2	
Maddie	Find out about access to Teacher U video library and follow up with Natalie and Sam.	12/2	
Maddie	Look into whether we have seen a benefit at the schools with intern hires.	12/2	
Mitch	Send job description out to the group for the communications associate position.	12/2	
Mitch	Follow up with Sima on the data to share comments about TCP observations from his focus groups.	12/2	

The Case for Breaking Up with Your Notebook

If you have watched any of the videos that accompany this book on my website (www .thetogethergroup.com), you may have caught several busy leaders say, "I ditched my notebook" or "My notebook and I broke up." In general, I'm going to advise you to follow suit. Why? Well, notebooks are often one more source of hidden next steps and To-Dos. I see many busy leaders take notes on legal pads or in Moleskins, with every intention of going back through the notes. But *no* one ever has time to do this. Additionally, note-books can get pretty heavy and you are basically stuck with not a lot of ability to search, sort, and file. In general, I advise you to take notes digitally, preferably in some sort of digital archive, such as Google Drive, Evernote, or OneNote, so that you can sort and search in the future. And if you *must* take notes by hand, use one of my meeting agenda templates so the thoughts and actions get separated in the moment. And at the end of the week, or after you have memorialized the notes, throw them away, file them if you must for compliance reasons, or scan them!

Okay. Your Meeting Matrix is now done! You've determined whom you need to meet with, when, and why; considered standing agenda items and structures; and thought more about strong before, during, and after practices. Let's go one step further for those of you who *really* want to get ahead.

A LONG-TERM VIEW

Now that you have very clearly laid out whom you meet with, when, and why, there is one more planning step we can take. There are predictable sets of topics you need to discuss with teams or individuals over the course of each year. You may not *think* they are predictable, but I'll bet there are certain data sets, events, or operational cycles that require similar discussion questions annually. For example, I bet your organization has a budget, and I bet the budget needs to be discussed in roughly the same month each year with a predictable group of people. Or, I bet you receive some important data sets, such as employee satisfaction surveys, that you need to talk about with your team, again at the same time each year. With examples like these, it is helpful to sketch out ahead of time what you'll need to discuss when and with whom. This way the time is reserved for your priorities in advance. Remember, we have enough *real* emergencies. Let's not let the predictable stuff take us by surprise!

Reader Reflection

Take a peek at your Meeting Matrix. Asterisk which meetings could benefit from a predictable Scope and Sequence.

Definition

A meeting **Scope and Sequence** is a set of preplanned and well-timed discussion topics for your recurring meetings (see figure 5.11).

In this section, we will look at two different examples of a meeting Scope and Sequence: one is for a series of one-on-one meetings and the other is for a leadership team meeting.

Amy's Scope and Sequence for One-on-Ones

In table 5.3, Amy Christie, a director of college services at Achievement First, shares how she and her manager, Elana Karopkin, align at the beginning of the year on their predictable one-on-one meeting topics.

You will note several things as Amy and Elana plotted out what they needed to discuss when:

- There is a list of things to do repeatedly. These are items that Amy and Elana agreed must be discussed every week.

- There is a set of data tools. These are data that are ready at particular times that help drive decisions and plan ahead.

- There is still room for unique and time-sensitive topics. Some of them Amy already knows, but she can adjust this section as needed.

LEADER | **MEETING SCOPE AND SEQUENCE**

Week/Month	Meeting A	Meeting B	Meeting C	Meeting D

Figure 5.11 Meeting Scope and Sequence Blank Template

Table 5.3 Amy's Meeting Scope and Sequence

S&S?	Qrt	Date	Repeatedly Do	Data Tools	Unique/Time-Sensitive Topics
EK	1	10-Sep	Team leadership Adam coaching DoC coaching		
EK	1	24-Sep	Team leadership Adam coaching DoC coaching	College match report	College list College essay Team college quarterly report ISL #1
EK	1	8-Oct	Team leadership Adam coaching DoC coaching	College match report ISL #1 data/survey results	College list College essay HS DOP #1
EK	1	22-Oct	Team leadership Adam coaching DoC coaching	College match report	College list College essay College application audits ISL #2
EK	2	5-Nov	Team leadership Adam coaching DoC coaching	College match report Naviance quality check HS DOP data/survey results	College list College essay College application audits

Amy describes how this meeting Scope and Sequence helps her stay focused on what matters most: "It helps me be more deliberate when the frenzy and frenetic nature of our work pushing us to deal with every crisis. For example, if one of my huge priorities is 'college list creation,' the only way I can do this proactively is to decide what data I'm looking at with Elana and when. If we don't talk about lists by the last week of September, the ship has sailed. This Scope and Sequence gives me focus and helps me feel confident that I'm aligning time to priorities across the year."

Corey Crouch, the school leader in Houston you met in chapter 3, chose to combine her standing meeting agenda items *and* specific topics to create an annual Scope and Sequence for her leadership team meetings.

Corey's work is incredibly deliberate. Let's walk through her model in figure 5.12:

The Term. She breaks the school year into chunks by term. This helps direct focus to certain points in the year.

The Week. Each week, she's noted which Wednesdays are for staff PD (professional development) and which Fridays are full or early dismissal days. This is key because it affects who can attend what meetings. Rather than be surprised, she'll plan ahead accordingly.

The Notes for This Week. In this section, Corey notes other school events that might affect meetings, topics, or agendas.

The Connections. Corey intentionally puts *two* recurring weekly meetings side by side: the early dismissal staff PD topics and the Jedi Council (her leadership team) topics. She may want to discuss something with the whole staff for input and then follow up with her leadership team or vice versa.

Just because you *say* this is how you want to spend your meeting time does not mean that it always and absolutely must happen this way in practice. But once again, the more planned you are for the predictable stuff, the better you can react to the changing dynamics around you.

If something huge and unavoidable popped up for Corey's team on September 22, she could say, "Hey team, we had planned to review our staff satisfaction data this week. However, this other issue with our student culture really has to take precedence right now because it's an emergency." Everyone is aware of what is being changed and can intentionally refocus on the new topic. Meanwhile, Corey knows she needs to return to the initial priority—staff satisfaction—at a later date. Another way to address the same dilemma is to split the meeting half and half. I want you to think long and hard before you deviate—but when you do, you'll be very confident about why.

FAQ

What if I simply don't know what we should be discussing in the long term? I actually bet you do know and just don't realize it. Ideas about what to discuss probably pop up while walking down the hall, brainstorming in a meeting, or sending an e-mail. As a first step, you can use the Meeting Scope-and-Sequence template from my website (www.thetogethergroup.com) to capture your thoughts as you have them. Just think how much easier it will be to create your agenda when the time comes!

Jedi Council Scope and Sequence

	Week of …	Wed	Fri	Notes for this week	Gulfton Early Release Topics	Jedi Council Topics
Term I	12-Aug	PD	Full	Early Dimissal 8/12 and 8/13	In-Service	First Days with Students (Look-Fors)
	18-Aug	PD	Full		Diff. PD/GLT	Earning the Y Logistics
	25-Aug	PD	Full		GLT/Team Building	Prep 9/3 Data Dive MS Fall Trip Staff Retreat*
	1-Sep	PD	Full	Labor Day this Week	Data Analysis/Power Planning	
	8-Sep	PD	Full	Content Day on Mon	Diff. PD/GLT	
	15-Sep	MH	Full		Mental Health	
	22-Sep	PD	Full	MS Fall Trip	Data Analysis/Power Planning	A1 Survey Analysis
	29-Sep	PD	Full		Diff. PD/GLT	
	6-Oct	Full	Early	College Fair October 8 (Wed)	GLT/Team Building	CA Schedule Review
	13-Oct	PD	Full	Content Day on Mon	Data Analysis/Power Planning	
	20-Oct	PD	Full		Diff. PD/GLT	
Term II	27-Oct	PD	Early/MH	Common Assessments	T- GLT/work time W- Diff. PD/work time Th- Team Building F- Mental Health	

Figure 5.12 Corey's Meeting Scope and Sequence

Assistant Alert

Your assistant can track meeting Scope and Sequences for you! If you are in one meeting and have a thought for another meeting topic four months down the road, pop your assistant a note to insert it in a Scope and Sequence document. Then, when the meeting date nears, your assistant can build a draft of the agenda using the information on topics. You, as the leader, can edit for final adjustments and additions as needed.

Reader Reflection

Which recurring meetings of yours could benefit from a Scope and Sequence? What do you already know you should plug into it?

START STRONG

Getting the purpose and structure of your meetings right on the front end will help make the time you spend with others well worth it! Once your Meeting Matrix is complete, you should share relevant pieces of it with team members and encourage them to make their own. Most leaders update their Meeting Matrix at least once per year or in case of a major role shift. Some leaders also make a public version for their entire organization.

Time commitment: one to two hours to create. Updated annually or as needed.

- Complete your Meeting Matrix.
  - Evaluate your current meetings and see what type of purpose each meeting holds.
  - Decide the right timing and frequency for your meetings.
  - Determine standing agenda topics.
  - Ensure preparation and follow-up expectations are clear.
- Create a Scope and Sequence for recurring meetings over the course of the year.
- If applicable, enlist your assistant to support your meeting planning process.

COMMON CHALLENGE: THE CRISIS

"Karolyn Belcher is the president of a leading education nonprofit, TNTP (formerly known as the The New Teacher Project), which partners with school systems nationwide. As a former head of teacher preparation programs, school principal, nonprofit human resources director and now head of client engagements in more than 30 cities, Karolyn is no stranger to emergencies foiling her best laid plans."

What I am always struck by in my conversations with Karolyn is the discipline with which she manages an emergency. Here's a recent example from when she was in the midst of a high-stakes contract negotiation. Let's get into Karolyn's head to help you think about your own plan for emergencies.

Step 1: She asks herself, "Is this a 'drop-everything-right-now' crisis or a 'get-someone-else-on-it' crisis?"

As a senior leader, Karolyn tries to make sure she is not stuck holding the ball. More often than not, the issue can be capably handled by her team members. In order to determine if she should own the crisis or put someone else on it, she asks herself these questions:

- Is this a key client decision?
- Are there possible legal or media ramifications?
- Are multiple staff members affected?
- Should I serve as the messenger?
- Is this a key strategy decision in which my input will greatly affect the outcome?

Step 2: She steps in to rally organizational resources as needed.

Even if the crisis didn't land in her lap, Karolyn still needs to highlight the challenge to other folks to ensure the person tasked with solving the problem has the resources he or she needs. For example, if Karolyn needs budget information for an immediate contract, she may have to explain the context to the finance team as she interrupts their work on payroll.

Step 3: She assists someone with framing how fast the problem needs to be solved.

Karolyn says that her job is sometimes to actually slow people down. She helps them make a sound plan to get through the crisis, mapping it out step-by-step before they jump in. This results in a time line and action plan that everyone can understand and support.

Step 4: She determines when she wants to be inserted into the crisis.

After making a rough plan with her team member, Karolyn highlights when she wants to be informed or inserted. For example, she may want to review another draft of the contract before it goes back to the client.

And all of this is in the middle of a day when Karolyn is frequently in meetings from 9 AM to 5 PM straight! There are certainly occasions when a crisis requires her to tell another colleague, "I'm going to be fifteen minutes late to our call in order to solve *x*." That is completely fine. What Karolyn wisely doesn't do is *drop* everything immediately. Instead, she is intentional about her decision to pivot or stay the course.

Get Yourself Together

CHAPTER 6

Get Macro
Design a Comprehensive Calendar

SEEN AND HEARD

"I take on more work than I can complete and I don't have a system for holding time to react to things that pop up during the day or week."

"I don't keep track of deadlines very well. I'm not always sure where to put them, or also deciding where I put the prework on my To-Do List."

"I spend so much time on getting little tasks done that aren't necessarily connected to my priorities but are necessary to the team."

OVERVIEW AND OBJECTIVES

You've set your goals, articulated your priorities, and ensured your meetings align with what you are trying to achieve. But how to bring all of this together? And what about everything else you have to do in a given day or week?! What about all that other work that still requires your attention? It's all gotta get done sometime. And somehow!

Enter the Comprehensive Calendar (see figure 6.1)!

Definition

The **Comprehensive Calendar** is a long-term, macro view of your calendar that reflects your priorities.

Figure 6.1 The Togetherness Tools

Most leaders use their calendars only to schedule their meetings. Although you certainly have *tons* of meetings to put on there, there's plenty of other work, too, that needs to get done in a day. This chapter will help you create a picture of your time that goes beyond just meetings.

In this chapter, you will do the following:

- Identify and protect time blocks necessary for Planned Priorities.

- Allocate time to accomplish Standard Stuff.

- Thoughtfully schedule Major Meetings.

- Consolidate all calendars into one master calendar.

- Look ahead at the entire year for long-term calendar planning.

This chapter will help *you* happen to your calendar, before your calendar happens to you. Chapter 8 provides further guidance on how to sequence the work when your schedule inevitably changes over the course of any given week.

CREATE YOUR COMPREHENSIVE CALENDAR

When I talk about creating a macro view of your time, I am not thinking of the calendar you are living and dying by right now. I'm talking about sketching out a clear point of view on your time as it compares against all of your known work, including meetings, priorities, events, projects, e-mails, memos, and calls.

You won't be able to construct a reliable macro view overnight. You may have to look ahead a few months, or tweak and retweak your plan as it begins to take shape and you realize what is and isn't working for you.

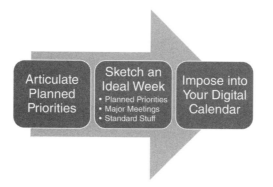

Figure 6.2 Comprehensive Calendar Process

Assistant Alert

To be truly able to effectively delegate scheduling to an assistant, I suggest you invite him into this chapter to help you develop your Comprehensive Calendar.

In this section, I will walk through a three-step process to arrive at your Comprehensive Calendar (see figure 6.2).

ARTICULATE YOUR PRIORITIES

Let's just step way back for a moment. What matters *most* in your world right now? Hint, hint … pull up that Priority Plan and Meeting Matrix.

When I ask this question in workshops, I typically hear comments such as these:

- "My calendar is very aligned on the priorities that involve *other* people, such as project meetings."

- "My calendar is very aligned when one of my priorities has clear and impending deadlines."

- "My calendar is not so aligned if the path forward is not clear."

- "My calendar lacks alignment if only I am involved in the work."

Meet Hannah Lofthus, the CEO of a small group of schools in Kansas City. Hannah was rightfully obsessed with making sure the time in her calendar matched up to her Priority Plan and Meeting Matrix. She and her talented assistant, Maggie Klos, were determined to maximize Hannah's time to the fullest.

Hannah was determined to focus on the following areas:

- Supporting her instructional and noninstructional leaders

- Leading with data and school culture in mind

- Recruiting new staff members
- Remaining nimble enough to be accessible to her staff

Reader Reflection

As you review your Priority Plan, how aligned is your calendar to your priorities?

SKETCH AN IDEAL WEEK

Now that your priorities feel front and center, let's sketch an Ideal Week. How do you think your time *should* be spent? An Ideal Week should include the following:

1. Macro time blocks (to accomplish Priority Plan work)

2. Major meetings (from the Meeting Matrix)

3. Standard stuff (work that just has to get completed) (see figure 6.3)

Back to Hannah! Figure 6.4 shows a blank template of Hannah's week with priorities for each day listed along the top. Let's look closely at how she created an ideal view of her time.

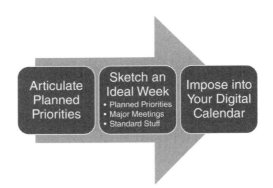

Figure 6.3 Comprehensive Calendar Process

Priorities		Monday	Tuesday	Wednesday	Thursday	Friday
		Instructional	Data & Culture	Recruitment & Noninstructional	Instructional	Flex
Morning	9–11					
Mid-Morning	11–1					
Afternoon	1–3					
Closing	3–5					
Evening						

Figure 6.4 Hannah's Ideal Week Blank Template

Step 1: Planned Priorities

Let's figure out how much time you need for your *most* important work. We will then insert time for this into your calendar as Planned Priority Blocks.

Based on her described priorities, Hanna scheduled her Planned Priorities (from her Priority Plan!) for these activities:

- Her ILT (instructional leadership team)
- Time for one-on-one meetings
- Time for open office hours
- Time for big picture thinking

Figure 6.5 shows these priorities scheduled in.

I'll give you a really personal example. In the two years it took me to write this book, I held ten hours per week for writing in my calendar, in two-hour blocks each morning. These were my Planned Priorities. Then, once per week, I scheduled my Planned Priorities with micro-action steps, such as edit chapter 8 or schedule interview for the vignettes.

It can be hard to figure out how much time to block out for Planned Priorities. Think about it in percentages of time, assuming a day is 20 percent of your time. So, if supporting your instructional leadership team is a big priority, perhaps 20 percent of your time, or one full day (spread out across a week), is the right amount of time. Only you can say how much time you will need.

Reader Reflection

Review each priority and its key actions. How much time do you need to block for each one each week? Record your thoughts in the table in your Reader Reflection Guide.

Priorities		Monday Instructional	Tuesday Data & Culture	Wednesday Recruitment & Noninstructional	Thursday Instructional	Friday Flex
Morning	9–11	① ILT	Big Picture Thinking Time			
Mid-Morning	11–1	Big Picture ④ Thinking Time	1:1's	1:1's	1:1's ②	
Afternoon	1–3	1:1's	Office Hours③			
Closing	3–5					
Evening						

Figure 6.5 Hannah's Ideal Week with Macro Time Blocks

Table 6.1 Time Needed for Priorities

Priority	Hours Needed	Location

Step 2: Major Meetings

You know you need weekly recurring meetings with those you manage, and some time slots are better than others. Take a peek at your Meeting Matrix and ask yourself when you want to schedule those throughout the week. Some leaders prefer them all in one day, and others like to scatter them throughout the week. We discussed benefits and drawbacks of each approach in chapter 5.

Hannah and Maggie, Hannah's assistant, asked themselves when their major meetings ideally would happen. They chose to scatter them throughout the week, often in a mid-morning or early afternoon time slot to help with energy management and the demands of a school schedule (figure 6.6). For example, Hannah made sure that her meetings with her team fell at a time during the day when she could also co-observe in classrooms. If you look closely at Thursday, you can see she has stacked her meetings for the mornings.

Reader Reflection

Consider each of your Major Meetings. Do they fall at the right time of day and week? How do you know?

		Monday	Tuesday	Wednesday	Thursday	Friday
Priorities		Instructional	Data & Culture	Recruitment & Noninstructional	Instructional	Flex
Morning	9–11	ILT	Big Picture Thinking Time		Baker 1:1	
Mid-Morning	11–1	Big Picture Thinking Time	Vavroch 1:1 Daniels 1:1	Potter 1:1 Ben/Klos 1:1	Dolge 1:1	
Afternoon	1–3	Coleman 1:1	Office Hours	Nichols 1:1		
Closing	3–5					
Evening						

Figure 6.6 Hannah's Ideal Week with Meetings

Step 3: Standard Stuff

Hannah and Maggie also blocked time for Standard Stuff:

- Friday professional development time
- Thirty minutes at the end of each day for tasks, e-mail, close-out work, and meeting with her assistant
- Flex time. Hannah knew she needed a certain amount of wiggle room in her schedule for things that came up, so she deliberately left chunks of time open on her calendar (see figure 6.7).

Other leaders may insert predictable work, such as these activities:

- Checking e-mail
- Writing a weekly staff memo
- Returning phone calls
- Completing expense reimbursements

Reader Reflection

What kinds of Standard Stuff do you do on a weekly basis? How long will it take you?

Assistant Alert

Hannah actually created her Ideal Week *with* her assistant, Maggie. This enabled them to align on her priorities, energy levels, and ideals before any appointments were even scheduled. It also gave Maggie more agency over decision making on Hannah's calendar. Because Hannah has clearly communicated her priorities, Maggie can make better decisions about what to plot where, when, and why.

Priorities		Monday Instructional	Tuesday Data & Culture	Wednesday Recruitment & Noninstructional	Thursday Instructional	Friday Flex
Morning	9–11	ILT	Big Picture Thinking Time	Time for Interviews	Baker 1:1	Flex
Mid-Morning	11–1	Big Picture Thinking Time	Vavroch 1:1 Daniels 1:1	Potter 1:1 Ben/Klos 1:1	Dolge 1:1	Flex
Afternoon	1–3	Coleman 1:1	Office Hours	Nichols 1:1		PD
Closing	3–5	30 Minute Tasks, Closing, & MK & HL Check In				
Evening						

Figure 6.7 Hannah's Ideal Week

Get Your Energy Right

Yes, this is a book about productivity, but there are many ways to be productive in addition to list making. Tom Rath, Tony Schwartz, and Steven Covey are three of my favorite authors who research and discuss how renewal relates to our ability to be effective. Here are some common tips for structuring your Ideal Week to match your energy:

- Place your hardest work for when your energy is highest. Save the task-easier items for when your energy is waning.

- Conduct your internal meetings later in the week to boost energy and prep for the week ahead.

- Block out proactive loose time for when you know you need it.

- Build in time for exercise and eating (and preparing food if necessary).

Reader Reflection

Sketch Your Ideal Week and be sure it includes Planned Priorities, Major Meetings, and Standard Stuff. Now glance through the whole week and see if it includes methods to manage energy.

IMPOSE THE IDEAL WEEK ONTO YOUR DIGITAL CALENDAR

Now that you've named your priorities and have thoughtfully outlined an Ideal Week, we have to make this real. The only way to get real is to impose this stuff right onto your digital calendar, thus creating your very own Comprehensive Calendar (see figure 6.8).

Input the work directly into your digital calendar as recurring events for the entire year—or at least the next six months. Hannah and Maggie loaded these Planned Priorities Major Meetings and Standard Stuff from the Ideal Week into Hannah's Outlook Calendar as recurring appointments for the remainder of the academic year. Figure 6.9 shows what Hannah's Comprehensive Calendar looks like!

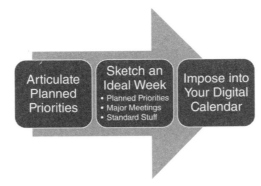

Figure 6.8 Comprehensive Calendar Process

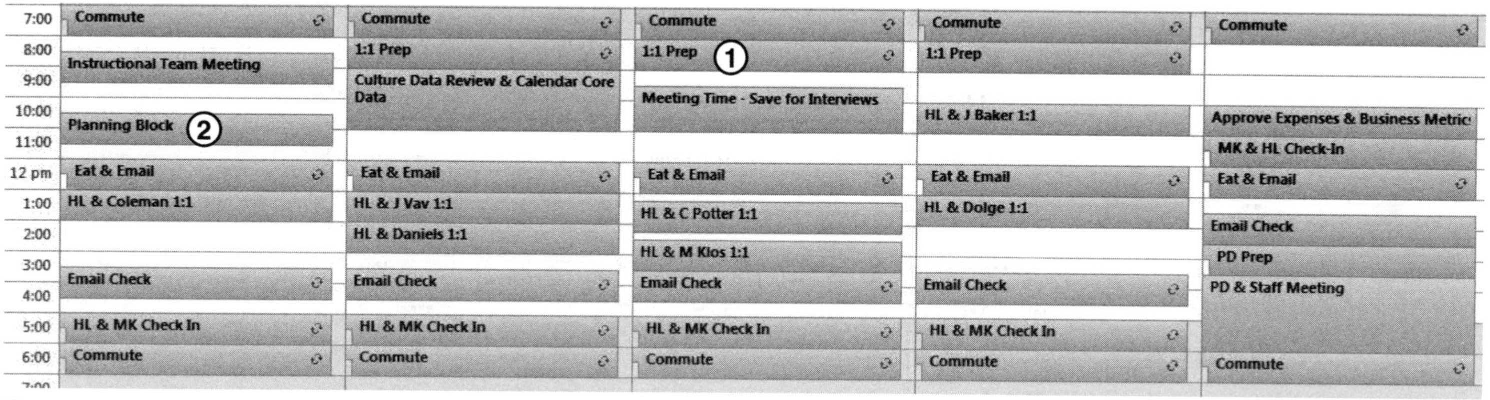

Figure 6.9 Hannah's Weekly Comprehensive Calendar

Time	Day 1	Day 2	Day 3	Day 4	Day 5
7:00	Commute	Commute	Commute	Commute	Commute
8:00	Instructional Team Meeting	1:1 Prep	1:1 Prep ①	1:1 Prep	Approve Expenses & Business Metric
9:00		Culture Data Review & Calendar Core Data	Meeting Time - Save for Interviews	HL & J Baker 1:1	MK & HL Check-In
10:00	Planning Block ②				
11:00					
12 pm	Eat & Email	Eat & Email	Eat & Email	Eat & Email	Eat & Email
1:00	HL & Coleman 1:1	HL & J Vav 1:1	HL & C Potter 1:1	HL & Dolge 1:1	
2:00		HL & Daniels 1:1	HL & M Klos 1:1		Email Check
3:00	Email Check	Email Check	Email Check	Email Check	PD Prep
4:00					PD & Staff Meeting
5:00	HL & MK Check In	HL & MK Check In	HL & MK Check In	HL & MK Check In	
6:00	Commute	Commute	Commute	Commute	Commute

Please, please, please don't be scared. Remember our mantra: the more planned you are, the more flexible you can be. For example, Hannah knew she always wanted to be prepared for meetings (one-on-ones) with her team. Therefore, she blocked time to prepare on Tuesday, Wednesday, and Thursday mornings (item 1 in figure 6.9). If something else comes up, Hannah has the freedom to move that preparation block around. But by putting it on her Comprehensive Calendar, she is not fooling herself into thinking that is white space. The preparation should happen at some point. May as well make your calendar reflect reality, right?

Assistant Alert: Can someone else manage my calendar?

Some of you are fortunate to have someone else manage your calendar for you. If this is the case, I want to make sure he or she is equipped with the knowledge to make good decisions about your time. Typically, two things can go wrong when an assistant manages a leader's calendar. The first is that the manager and assistant both book appointments because the manager hasn't given up full control of scheduling. This results in miscommunications and double-bookings. The second thing that can go wrong is that the manager *over*delegates scheduling to his or her assistant, resulting in time not aligned to the manager's priorities. There are lots more tips on calendar delegation in chapter 13, but the most important thing for now is to make sure that you and your assistant are aligned on your Priority Plan and Meeting Matrix.

Select the Right Tool

Before you go picking any old calendar, I do want you to go digital for this tool. I'm truly neutral on tool choice for the remainder of the book, I promise. But the benefits of sending electronic invites, sharing calendars, and creating conference room booking options are too powerful and efficient to give up! Most likely, your organization probably has Google, Outlook, or iCal up and running already, but if not, do make the move or encourage your organization to get on one calendar system.

FAQ: What if my calendar is *already* too cluttered for me to even think straight?

It's totally fine to start from scratch. You could also start planning for a few months from now, when you hope there's less on your schedule. I recommend you do not jump directly into your organization's digital calendar, because this can clutter your perspective with assumptions about your work. Start with a clean slate, and we'll build up from there.

Input the Work

Start entering those Planned Priorities, Major Meetings, and Standard Stuff times as recurring appointments into your digital calendar. It's fine if some of them seem generic right now. The point here is to get them in there because they can and should take up your time. If you don't reserve it now, who knows what your time will get spent on later! For example, Hannah inserted planning and meetings time in her calendar. We cannot know what kind of longer-term planning work she'll need to do three months from now, but when we take the last step of calendaring in chapter 8, we will plan in detail exactly what work will get done when.

For example, Hannah has reserved a Planning Block on Monday mornings (item 2 in figure 6.9). As she gets closer to the time, she can insert items such as these:

- Plan for board meeting
- Prep for staff retreat

I also want to make sure there is time to plan each day and week. We will talk more about how to best use that time in chapter 9, but for now, let's block off fifteen minutes at the beginning and end of each day and sixty to ninety minutes once per week. There is also the simple life stuff, such as commuting, eating, and traveling, which just needs allocated time in your calendar. If you don't plug those things in, you run the risk of doing them poorly. Or worse, harboring an illusion of time you don't actually have!

FAQ: If my calendar is *this* full, how will people schedule meetings with me?
You have a few options here. You can show your work time as free or tentative within the appointment so that you are shown as available. You can also use various types of technology, such as TimeTrade or Calendly, which can support scheduling. That said, in leadership roles, I'm not a fan of anyone being able to crash into your calendar whenever they see you are available. I'm all for accessibility, but if you have a party crasher culture, that will defeat all the work we just did in this chapter. Consider setting some norms on checking in before scheduling a meeting to ensure purpose is clear and the timing is right.

I find it most useful to share your Ideal Week, such as Hannah's model, with your team. This accomplishes several things. First, it lets your team know your priorities. Second, it lets your team know your preferences. Last, it gives your team permission to set and manage their own boundaries.

Reader Reflection
What are the Planned Priorities, Major Meetings, and Standard Stuff you need to input into your Comprehensive Calendar? What tool will you use?

LET'S GET CONSOLIDATED

Now that your Comprehensive Calendar is completed, I want to make sure you are completely consolidated. In this section, we will beef up your digital Comprehensive Calendar even more by funneling in deadlines, FYIs, and any personal stuff, too!

Get Rid of Calendar Strays

At any given moment, someone is probably sending you one calendar with a performance management cycle, while another shoots you a list of testing release dates. Meanwhile you've got your own grad school deadlines, and somewhere you know an e-mail is lurking that tells you your kid's softball schedule and the date for costume day! Yikes!

In many schools, districts, and nonprofits, different calendars for different issues, topics, work projects, and themes are all running amok. It's hard to find time to cross-reference them, and you shouldn't spend any energy trying to do so! Toss in your personal life and you've got a clear recipe for disaster. We need to take all of our calendar babies and consolidate them into a single calendar of choice (aka the Comprehensive Calendar). Then pitch the rest.

Assistant Alert

You can give your various calendars to your assistant and ask him or her to load the relevant dates into your Comprehensive Calendar. For example, your organization may keep separate calendars of testing dates, Project Plans, or staff birthdays. Or you may receive a copy of your own children's school calendars. Let's take a moment to think of all the calendars in your life and what you need from each one—and if they can be integrated into your Comprehensive Calendar.

Reader Reflection

What calendar strays are floating around in your life? What information do you need from each one?

Get All Deadlines Centrally Located

Now let's get all of your deadlines in one central location. We're going to put them right at the top of your Comprehensive Calendar as "all-day appointments." And while we're at it, let's get the deadlines for your direct reports in there, too! For example, if you sent out a meeting agenda requesting feedback by a particular date, insert that deadline as an all-day appointment in your Comprehensive Calendar. Then, as the deadline gets closer, you can send out friendly reminders. Only if necessary, of course!

Unless the deadline has a specific time associated with it, I recommend keeping it at the top of the day. In some cases, the deadline may trigger you to populate your macro time blocks.

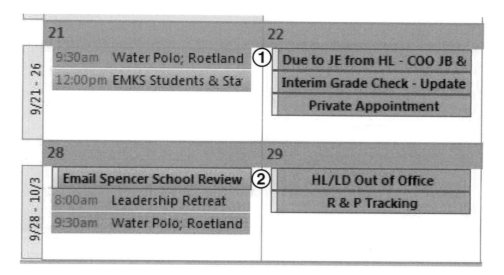

Figure 6.10 Hannah's Monthly Calendar: View 1

For example, in figure 6.10, Hannah's monthly view of her Comprehensive Calendar, you can see she has notes for these events:

1. Due date on September 22. Hannah (HL) owes work to JE.
2. Due date on September 28 e-mail Spencer school review.

Making your deadlines all-day appointments enables you to look at the monthly view of your Comprehensive Calendar and quickly scan ahead to see what's happening in your world. You'll see everything from the big stuff, such as "performance evaluations due," to the smaller tasks, such as "sign time sheets." Each week, when you pause to plan, you can look ahead at what you need to get started on.

Reader Reflection

What are some deadlines you need to record in your Comprehensive Calendar? How about deadlines for other people you manage?

FAQ: Should my calendar be color-coded?

This is truly a matter of personal preference. I've seen some leaders take this a teensy-tiny bit too far, with sixteen different colors for every fifteen-minute increment. If you are inclined toward color-coding, ask yourself your *purpose* for doing so and then operate accordingly. For example, I use just three colors—pretty simple and nothing fancy. I like to color-code my time with family, my time for meetings, and my time to work. Having the visual helps me achieve the correct balance. I can quickly scan my calendar and make sure my priorities are not out of whack.

FYIs Clearly Noted

As a leader, there are lots of things happening in your organization, division, team, or school you may want to know about. Let's go ahead and load these into our calendars now, too, so we're not surprised later on.

Let's go back to Hannah's Comprehensive Calendar, and look at her FYIs in figure 6.11.

1. September 11: Talent Firm visit. Hannah wants a reminder that there will be visitors from an outside group on campus that day.

2. September 15: Colleague out of office. It is always helpful to know when colleagues will be out, in case this affects scheduling.

3. September 24: T. Beshore's birthday! It can never hurt to add important team and relationship-building reminders to your calendar.

Some FYIs that frequently land in leaders' calendars:

- Holidays and building closings
- Colleague birthdays
- Important organization events, such as conferences
- Important happenings in other divisions or buildings, such as school testing
- Other people's meetings that you want to be able to ask them about or occasionally attend

Reader Reflection

What are some FYIs you may need to add into your calendar?

8	9	10	11
		Private Appointment	
		NWEA Assessment	
	Aaron N's Birthday	Board Meeting Notes ①B	Visit to EMKS (Age
15	**16**	**17**	**18**
		STEP Testing	
		Tom in NOLA	
②Ajia Out of Office 9:30-12:00		Due COB: Update Google Doc	Birthday - B. Brown
22	**23**	**24**	**25**
		STEP Testing	
Due to JE from HL - COO JB & Interim Grade Check - Update	A Birthday	③ Birthday - T. Beshore	Anne N Shadowing EMKS

Figure 6.11 Hannah's Monthly Calendar: View 2

It may annoy some of you to see all of this information on your own calendar. One easy fix is to create (or delegate the creation of) a separate calendar for these organization-wide events and FYIs that you can turn on and off as you wish. This is fairly simple to do in Outlook and Google. If your organization does not have an annual calendar that is viewable to all employees in some digital format, now is the time to get this in place.

Go Ahead, Get Personal!

Most of you keep up robust lives outside work. Perhaps you need to see that your son has baseball practice, your mortgage payment is due, or your family reunion is coming up. We are believers in seeing everything represented on one calendar, so you can also easily see if and when these events collide with professional commitments. This section will lead you through calendar personalization.

In Hannah's example, we can see she's scheduled lots of personal stuff (figure 6.12).

1. September 14: Water polo game!

2. Week of September 15: Hannah's boyfriend is out of town. It's always helpful to know the whereabouts of your loved ones. My own husband plans his Netflix consumption around my travel dates!

3. And all of those "private appointments" you see? Those are personal commitments that Hannah wants to see lined up against her work obligations.

Let's think through all of your personal undertakings, the mundane and the wishful, and get them on your calendar. The scheduled stuff is easiest. Some examples are as follows:

- Any regular appointments you have, whether they be to the dentist or your weekly watercolor class

- For those of you with children, kid and school events, such as sports or evening programs

- Bill-due dates and time for household administrative work

- Big events such as weddings, reunions, baby showers, and graduations

Figure 6.12 Hannah's Monthly Calendar: View 3

FAQ

How do I synchronize multiple digital calendars? Some of you may feel strongly about separating your personal and professional calendars. But if you do not combine at some point, there is a real danger of events colliding. Fortunately, there are ways to import Google into Outlook or vice versa, or view all of your calendars using iCal. You can find technology directions on my website (www.thetogethergroup.com).

Don't forget the unscheduled stuff, too. These responsibilities are often our most important and also the hardest to find time for. Together Leaders block time for things they want to prioritize, such as these events:

- A weekly phone call to a cherished relative
- Class times at the gym (list them all and you are guaranteed to get to at least one!)
- Time dedicated to hobbies
- Time to track personal finances
- Time to watch favorite TV shows (I am personally not above putting the season premieres of a few favorites in my own calendar!)

Reader Reflection

What are some personal commitments you need to get into your calendar?

> ### Elements of a Comprehensive Calendar
>
> - Planned Priorities
> - Major Meetings
> - Standard Stuff
> - Rituals and Routines
> - Personal Plans
> - Drop-in Deadlines
> - Complete Consolidation
> - Planned Ambushes
> - Buffer Time

ZOOM OUT TO VIEW A YEAR

Now let's zoom out to take an annual view. This way, we can be sure to include other, more cyclical blocks of time and commitments. Remember, it's all in the name of you keeping in charge of your own time (and not the other way around). In this section, I will lead you through exercises to identify crunch times, block out vacations, and ensure you have adequate recovery after big events.

Identify Crunch Times

I have seen many a great leader get crushed by what I'll affectionately call the "predictable" emergency. You know, such as auditors coming? Or report card time? Or salary publication? In mission-driven settings a predictable emergency may be when certain data sets are released—and there are tons of numbers to slice. In a school context, a predictable emergency may be transportation issues in the first few weeks of school. We *know* there will be issues; we just aren't sure the specific nature of the problems yet. But let's go ahead and block time to deal with them now!

Take a moment to look at your organization's calendar for the entire year. Are there times you can predict something *will* go down, even if you're not quite sure exactly what it is just yet? Why not build a buffer to accommodate this? Literally, block the time now to deal with *whatever*. If it turns out you're pleasantly surprised when nothing goes wrong, then great! I have no doubt you can fill the time with other useful work. But given the 95 percent chance one of those predictable emergencies will arise, why not prepare now? Remember, we are trying to surface *all* possibilities here.

Reader Reflection

What are the predictable emergencies in your world? Think through each season of your role. If you are not sure, ask someone who has been in your role before.

Block Vacation

Vacation? Yes, take it. Those of you working in schools may be limited to certain times of year for vacation. Others may have more flexibility. Regardless, I want you to take your vacations. Consider when it makes the most sense for your workload and your family. I know of one busy team that planned ahead to stagger their vacations during a very busy season at work. Their manager created a chart for team members to choose when they wanted to be out. Additionally, the expectation was also set that the whole team could not be gone in the same week.

Reader Reflection

When will you take a vacation this year? What expectations do you need to set with your team?

Block Time Off

Do you lead a team that operates particularly intensely at certain times, such as when running large conferences or attending retreats? If so, there's benefit to looking ahead on the calendar and blocking paid time off following intense periods. For example, if you run a teacher-training program with a large weekend component, then perhaps you want to pick a day during the subsequent week for the team to take off to accommodate the additional workload.

Reader Reflection

Are there times of year, or particular days, when you should build in comp time?

Block Recovery Time

Even when things are going well, a week out of the office for a conference or vacation can really wreak havoc on your calendar. What was supposed to be relaxing or invigorating becomes another source of stress to manage. To tackle this, look ahead for the entire year. Do you notice times when you may be out of the office? Block time now for recovery and catch-up, typically a half-day on the morning you return. I know that when I fly in from the West Coast on a red-eye, I try to block a few extra hours to sleep in the next morning. But there is no way that can happen unless I plan it well in advance.

Reader Reflection

When are some times of year when you could use a recovery buffer?

START STRONG

Whew, this is quite a chapter, right? Give yourself a gold star for getting through it. I'm sure your brain is pretty full now that we've surfaced all of your known work, planned ahead, and blocked time to deal with emergencies and the mundane. It took time, energy, and focus, but trust me, your Comprehensive Calendar will pay you back when you return to operating day-to-day. There will be time preserved for priorities, time blocked for emergencies, and time to breathe!

- Identify your priorities through review of your Priority Plan.
- Create your Ideal Week that reflects your Planned Priorities, Major Meetings, and Standard Stuff.

- Impose your work onto a digital calendar.
- Ensure all of your calendars are consolidated.
- Brainstorm predictable emergencies by taking an annual view.
- If applicable, schedule a meeting with your assistant to align priorities.

Togetherness Talks: Vince Marigna

Name: Vince Marigna

Title: Chief people officer, KIPP New Jersey

Why Togetherness matters: I need to have all moving pieces organized to keep my head in the game.

Tell me about the mission and scope of your work. What are you most proud of?

Our team handles finding, engaging, and developing the best teachers and leaders for the students we serve in Newark and Camden. I'm proud to have played a role with helping our region grow from three to nine schools in five years.

At 10 AM on any given workday, what might I find you doing?

Reviewing development plans for our leaders, pondering our long-term growth strategy, figuring out the best ways to find teachers, or reading check-in agendas from my direct reports.

What is your favorite Together Tool and why?

Thought Catchers. They help me to capture my ideas or notes for my team so that I can remain focused on what's in front of me.

Tell me how you start and end each day to remain Together.

I begin each morning reviewing the list and seeing if what I've prioritized still makes the most sense. I end each day by printing out my Outlook Calendar and Outlook Tasks for the next day.

What do you proactively do to remain productive?

I start my day with a run or some sort of workout.

What is a challenge you still face with Togetherness?

Continuing to prioritize and reprioritize on a daily basis. When I have competing priorities, it's always challenging to ensure my activities enable me to achieve my goals.

How do you remain focused when the work is swirling around you?

I turn my e-mail to work offline when I really need to focus on a presentation or complete a large task that involves my computer.

What recenters you when the work feels overwhelming?

I spend time in one of our schools and connect with our kids. They are the reason I do what I do.

It's 10 AM on a Saturday morning. What keeps you rejuvenated?

Saturday morning is my workout time. I get a long workout in and it helps rejuvenate me. Also, my wonderful husband, Justin, who is also in this work and is super supportive. He makes sure I get away from the weekly grind and do something outside or with friends and family.

What have you learned to let go?

E-mail response time.

CHAPTER 7

Strategic Procrastination
Design a Later List

SEEN AND HEARD

"I don't have a consistent format for keeping track of my To-Dos. Right now, I toggle between (1) a To-Do List on my phone, (2) a To-Do List on my Google Docs (that enables me to prioritize), and (3) a To-Do List on my online calendar."

"I don't track my To-Dos. I just do!"

"I record my most immediate To-Dos on sticky notes that I stick to the screen of my laptop. For To-Dos that are further into the future, I write them on my desk calendar, but sometimes I end up forgetting about them until the week of."

OVERVIEW AND OBJECTIVES

You've nailed the Comprehensive Calendar. But you may be starting to realize that not everything in your life can fit directly into a time slot. And there are some things you'll want to keep track of beyond just the upcoming week. You know, such as "Get a head start on performance evaluations" or "Check back on so and so's event planning" or "Make sure the reimbursement came in" or "Follow up with that donor."

What to do with these timeless tasks? Enter the Later List! How exactly does this tool work? Let me sketch you a little vignette:

It's the middle of a cool September when Johanna Parkhurst, a busy nonprofit leader in Denver, thinks to herself (in the middle of a meeting), "Ahhhhhhhh, I have to plan out Christmas break!" Johanna knows that making this plan will probably require more than just her own brainpower. She'll need to coordinate with family, look at tickets in advance, and figure out who will take care of her cat!

I guarantee you have these kinds of thoughts constantly. Most of us either write them on this week's list (if we have one) or a sticky note. Or we forget entirely! No longer. Johanna pulls up her Later List (kept in Microsoft OneNote) and jots down to think about it in October (figure 7.1). Now she can refocus on the meeting at hand (see figure 7.2).

Definition

The **Later List** is a long-term and total list of To-Dos, organized and grouped in some logical fashion.

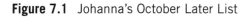

	STRIVE	Personal
August		
September	For 6th grade Unit 3: maybe keep books in the regular class period. Take OUT Freedom Songs. Possibly add Walking to the Busrider Blues (400 or 500 L). Add Civil Rights Movement Choose Your Own Adventure (extension text). Make Mississippi Trial a HIGH book.	
October	Follow up re: Delgado booking for NHD.

Look into STAR conferences (from Blair) | Plan Thanksgiving and Christmas break. ① |

Tabs shown: STRIVE Weekly To-Do List | Writing Weekly To-Do List | Later List | Thought Ca...

Figure 7.1 Johanna's October Later List

Figure 7.2 The Togetherness Tools

In this chapter, you will do the following:

- Ensure your To-Do List fully reflects your entire workload.
- Determine what items on your To-Do List require strategic procrastination.
- Separate your short-term from your long-term To-Dos.
- Figure out what hits your Comprehensive Calendar versus what lands on your Later List.
- Work backwards from deadlines to make progress on larger projects.

As I'm sure you're starting to predict, I will review several examples of leaders' lists and discuss their benefits and drawbacks. After that, I will help you select a format that will work best for you. Then we'll get started on building your very own Later List.

THE MODEL

The thoughts for *beyond* this week pop in your head when you least expect it and often at highly inappropriate or inconvenient moments. In this chapter, we will untangle your short-term and long-term To-Do Lists. From now on, when a thought about the future pops into your brain, I want you to do the following:

- Briefly analyze: "Is this idea for this week or is this idea for the *beyond*?"
- If for the beyond, decide when: "What *month* does it make sense for me to even begin thinking about this?"
- Open up your Later List and dump the thought in the right section (see figure 7.3).

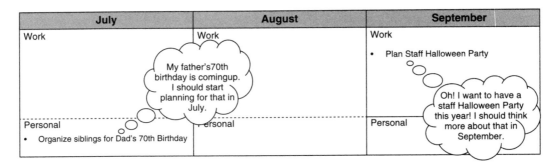

Figure 7.3 Later List Template

Of all the tools in this section of the book, this one will feel most familiar—a To-Do List! But the Later List differs from a typical list for a few reasons:

1. It is for everything you have to do *beyond* this week.

2. It should only be reviewed once a week to identify items to scoop out. Trying to accomplish it all at once would be too overwhelming! And impossible!

3. It is not organized by due date (because those are already in your calendar), but rather by *start* date.

4. It is likely to be digital, though it certainly doesn't have to be.

5. It is never completed. It is an additive and long-term document.

6. It will include items that are aspirational and without due dates.

Now that you get the idea, let's take a peek at how three different leaders approach this process. Some of them like to think in chart form, others in lists. Some are paper-based, and others are more digitally inclined. But the similarity across all of the samples is that they all cover To-Dos for *beyond* the week!

Steve's Later List

Meet Steve Holz-Russell, a busy education technology leader at Strive Prep based in Denver. Steve created his Later List using one of my templates in Microsoft Word (see figure 7.4). He uses it in conjunction with his Google Calendar. Similar to other examples you will see, Steve employs two levels of sorting: (1) by the month he wants to *start* taking action and then (2) by work and home. Let's look at a few specific examples of how Steve keeps track of his To-Dos for the future.

LEADER | **LATER LIST**

November	December	January
Work • Brainstorm fun Ed Tech things • Flipped Classroom • Blended Learning • Gamification • Coding/Programming • Plan for Hour of Code ① • Continue to Revise/Implement PARCC Plan • Connect with John D (Summit Schools) re: blended learning, online assessments and Illuminate	**Work** • Determine budget for pilot projects? • Develop guidance for classroom management in 1:1 environments (e.g. Use of Chromebooks)	**Work** • Review schedule/process for delivering Ed Tech PD • Discuss plan to expand Ed Tech consistent with network growth and network priorities • Field Trips: DSST, Sparkfun • Plan/Advocate for Quest2Learn Field Trip • Think about a Parent Survey for Tech • Investigate Ed Tech related course ③ offerings for MS and HS for Summer/Fall 2015
Personal • Contact Xena re: House assessment and House search • Implement Landscaping Plan • Create house wish list\ • Christmas Presents	**Personal** • Travel Management • Evaluate Eleanor's School Placement • Research Pre-schools ②	**Personal** • Revisit Budget • Revisit Church Tithing

Figure 7.4 Steve's Later List

1. **November/Work:** Steve looked ahead on his calendar and saw a coding event scheduled in December. Therefore, he wrote in November to "plan for hour of code." This kind of backwards planning will ensure nothing sneaks up on Steve.

2. **December/Personal:** Steve knew it was the time of year to "evaluate Eleanor's [his daughter's] school placement." If he waited until too late, there would be no options left to evaluate. This is one of those pesky undeadlined things that's super important but can easily get shoved to the back burner.

3. **January/Work:** Steve noted, "investigate ed tech related course offerings for MS and HS … " Though he'll just be in research mode here, keeping this on his list enables him to coordinate with the rest of the organization as course offerings are being prepared.

Steve described why the Later List worked so well for him: "Being in a new role, I felt like I was kind of flailing around, trying to define the Scope and Sequence of my work. A simple tool like the Later List helped me frame the medium-term and long-term tasks that I anticipated being a part of my job. It's been a great foil to work against as the nature of my position solidifies, and it's been a good tool to drive the discussion around what I'll be doing in the years to come."

Planning ahead at this level enables Steve to see the big picture of his To-Dos across a year, be proactive about his work, plan backwards from deadlines, and shift items around accordingly. For example, if Steve realized that November was an extra-packed work month (and it often is with usually only three full work weeks), he could say, "Well, I better think about holiday gifts in October or just decide that I will rush it in December."

Benefits of a Later List

Now that you've seen one sample, let's step back and discuss the benefits of keeping such a mega-list. Some of you may be scratching your heads and asking, "Seriously, Maia, you are asking me to write every single thing down?!?" Indeed, I am. In one of my favorite recent reads, *The Organized Mind,* author Daniel Levitin (2014, p. 35) explains, "The most fundamental principle of the organized mind, the one more critical to keeping us from forgetting or losing things, is to shift the burden of organizing from our brains to the external world. If we can remove some or all of the process from our brains and put it out into the physical world, we are less likely to make mistakes."

In addition to keeping track of things, your Later List can help you do the following:

Delegate. Although this is not a book on people management, I do believe that many aspects of good leadership require lots of Togetherness. The dirty little secret of delegation is that it requires planning ahead. For example, if you realize that you have to plan a professional development session that's three months from now (because you, your Comprehensive Calendar, and your Later List are in such a committed relationship), you'll be able to delegate well in advance by asking your assistant to pull together the research and prepare handouts.

Manage Expectations (Proactively and Reactively). You get asked to do things all the time. The amazing thing about a Later List is that you can see the heavy workload months coming, and then name this for your colleagues. The classic example is performance evaluation time. Let's say that you've listed in March that you want to start writing performance evals because you know they are all due in April. You even already have the meetings scheduled. When you see Performance Evaluations approaching, doing their death march across your calendar, you can start breaking that enormous task into all of the steps it will take to accomplish, such as draft, read 360-feedbacks, solicit self-evaluations, and so on. You quickly realize there is no way you can get ten written in one single month, so you start to rearrange and spread them out. You can let your team know, "Hey, folks, in planning ahead for the next quarter, I realized there is no way I can realistically have high-quality performance conversations with all ten of you in a month-long period. Attached please find the proposed schedule for spacing the conversations out across a three-month period … "

Plan for Input from Others. Let's say you are leading an organizational process on revamping how knowledge is managed across offices. You've listed the roll-out date of May 1 bright and clear in your calendar, and you've outlined high-level steps your Priority Plan, such as user testing and site mapping. But as you break down your Priority Plan into smaller levels of detail, you may realize there are more levels of input that you need to get along the way. This is where your Later List comes in. Take those big dates and plan out the small steps to reach the goal.

Stay Focused. Inevitably, drifting To-Dos work their way into your head when they are technically not supposed to be there. This is what leads us to distraction and causes us to lose focus. If you realize that it is time to start planning for your father's big birthday and you are in the middle of a meeting with your manager, you can quickly jot that To-Do into your June Later List (for an August birthday) and return to the meeting fully present.

Avoid Ambushing Others. Another benefit of the Later List is that it forces you to plan ahead to avoid last-minute asks of other people. If you see you want to make progress on the website revision process, you may realize in advance that you want to ask one of your teammates to review certain pages before you compile your report for the developer.

Be Flexible. It helps to look ahead and get a sense of which months may be more full than others. If you see a *doozy* coming, you can start to move things around. Remember how Steve could easily shift when to buy holiday gifts? With a clear picture of what's on his plate, he has the freedom to make changes based on the rest of his workload. P.S.: To-Dos can die, too. Sometimes you may have written something down to consider at a later date, but when you eventually get to that date, the To-Do has lost its ooompph. For example, for a long time, I planned to have a wheel repaired on my favorite suitcase. This task hung out on my Later List for about two years … right until I found a new favorite suitcase on sale. So I let this To-Do die. It is perfectly acceptable to ask yourself if the To-Do will still get you the bang for your buck that you originally thought it would. If not, say good-bye.

Be a Thoughtful Human. Some of you may rebel against this line of thinking; if so, you are welcome to skip this bullet. But I would be remiss if I didn't offer some feedback I hear from workshop participants over and over. By planning ahead at this level, gifts can be more thoughtful—and you may save a bit of money in overnight shipping costs to boot! I once heard a participant say, "Oh, my goodness, my wife will be so happy that I actually have a Mother's Day gift." And I know I personally got a special rush of joy the over the holiday season when we planned ahead enough to order my mother-in-law a life-size dog pillow replica of her beloved dog from an artist on Etsy. The Later List helped me accomplish this by triggering me to get started on it in October.

Track the Teeny-Tiny Things. Let's face it, whether personal or professional, there are always some annoying teeny-tiny bits of nonsense you just have to keep track of, such as remembering to use a discount coupon for your holiday cards. Your Later List serves as the place to record the To-Do, and when you revisit your list each week, you can determine if it is time to take action.

A Later List can help you do the following:

- Delegate
- Manage expectations (proactively and reactively)
- Plan for input from others
- Stay focused
- Avoid ambushing others
- Be flexible
- Be a thoughtful human
- Track the teeny-tiny things

Now that I hope I have convinced you of the benefits of keeping a big list, let's preview a few more examples. Heather and Joanna have each gone slightly more high tech than Steve. They've also used additional levels of sorting.

Heather's Later List

Heather Peske is a busy leader in a state education agency in Massachusetts. She's also the mom of two girls under the age of 9, an avid distance runner, and a committed neighbor. Heather has a LOT to do. She has no choice but to keep a long, running list.

Heather keeps her Later List in three simple columns using Microsoft Excel (see figure 7.5).

Project	Task	Start Date	Estimated Time Needed
Book	Proposal to Cassie	February	3 hrs
Program Team	Send update on the week to Monique	February	15 min
Program Team	Co-write expectation email to Program Team	February	2 hrs
Book ①	Proposal and send to Caroline	February	3 hrs
Program Team	Set up once/week 1hour meeting with Corey	March	30 min
Program Team	3 big accomplishments; 3 things working on for next week -->To Anna on Fridays	March	30 min
Book	Contact authors	March	2 hrs
Program Team	Set up a meeting with Anna (1hour): Week in the life of Heide	March	30 min
LA	Review preparation docs for mayor's event	April	2 hrs
Home	copy taxes and mail to accountant	April	1 hr
Home	Call Mary re: Lilly spot in Another Place to Grow	June	15 min
Chicago	Call Lillian Koro re: behavior	April	30 min
Home	buy tix to charlotte	April	30 min
Program Team	Job fit conversation with AB	July	1hr
Program Team	Book time 6 weeks from now with Anna	July	15 min
LA	DESE scope of work	July	2 hrs
Home ②	Set up Google calendar	Rainy Day	1 hr
Program Team	Rethink file labeling system for drive	Rainy Day	45 min
Home	Clean out hall closet	Rainy Day	2 hrs

Figure 7.5 Heather's Later List

The Project. This is the category header for the type of project on which she's focused. It might also be the location of the project, such as home. Heather includes the people she manages as categories as well. Sorting by project (or context) is an idea made popular by David Allen, author of *Getting Things Done*.

The Task. This is simply the To-Do. Heather uses active verbs when writing her To-Dos.

The Start Month. Heather lists her To-Dos by the month she wants to begin working on them. This is how she strategically procrastinates. Just because she thinks of an idea in January doesn't mean that's the right time to start it. But she doesn't want to forget it either. If she doesn't know the month she wants to start something, Heather simply labels it "rainy day." She'll get to it when she can!

Estimated Time Needed. Heather also attempts to predict how long a particular To-Do will take at the time of recording it. This can be helpful to consider when she fits items into her calendar.

I want to highlight a few elements in Heather's sample that demonstrate some benefits to organizing your Later List in this way.

1. Heather has a book proposal due in April, which is noted as a deadline on her Comprehensive Calendar. So, on her Later List, Heather recorded that in February, she needs to "write proposal and send to Caroline." By planning this far ahead, Heather saves herself stress and ensures her colleague will have ample time for input.

2. Let's flip to the personal: Heather wants to set up a Google Calendar for her family, but she is not sure when that will ever happen. For this task, she lists "home" as the category and "rainy day" as the start date.

Although Steve kept his Later List in a Word document turned Google Doc (for accessibility purposes), Heather uses Microsoft Excel, which enables Heather to auto-sort her To-Dos to meet her energy and time allocations. For example, if she's scheduled Planned Priorities in her calendar to work on her book, she can filter her Later List to show only book-related tasks (see figure 7.6). Then, when she plans her week in detail (more on that in chapter 9), she can use this mini-list to populate her macro time blocks with specific tasks (see figure 7.7).

Project	Task	Start Date	Estimated Time Needed
Book	Proposal to Cassie	February	3 hrs
Book	Proposal and send to Caroline	February	3 hrs
Book	Contact authors	March	2 hrs

Figure 7.6 Heather's Later List Filtered for Book Tasks

Book Writing

| 2/9/2015 | 1:00pm | to | 3:00pm | 2/9/2015 | Time zone |

☐ All day ☐ Repeat...

Event details   Find a time

Where   Enter a location

Video call Add video call

Description   Start proposal for Cassie and Caroline

Figure 7.7 Heather's Planned Priority Blocks in her Comprehensive Calendar

FAQ: Why not enter this stuff directly into my calendar to begin with?

Honestly, this is a question I've grappled with for *years*. I have personally tried to skip the Later List for efficiency's sake, but I always end up resurrecting it. When I skip the list, I find I often get things done in the short term, but lose a long-term view of my workload. I also miss opportunities to take advantage of tasks that are dateless. For example, for two years, I have wanted to fix a certain section of my website, but it is truly an undated task and not a huge priority (yet!). I need an external place outside my brain for this idea to live but it cannot be on my calendar until it has a date.

There are a small percentage of people who calendar everything immediately, but you should be aware of these common challenges if you choose to do so:

- You lose sight of the full view of your workload that you can get on one page or one screen. It becomes harder to see the broad sequence of events and manipulate them when needed.

- You fall victim to a lot of fake deadlines. Let's say Heather enters "buy tickets to Charlotte" directly into a thirty-minute slot on April 14 (instead of keeping it here on her Later List). And then April 14 rolls around and Heather has a very busy day because she is scrambling to get her taxes done and take care of a few other last-minute things. So she dismisses the alert about the tickets thinking she'll do it another time—and all of the sudden it is April 16. The task gets stuck in her digital calendar and forgotten about, and Heather is unlikely to review her calendar *backwards*.

Entering Tasks Directly on Your Calendar versus Your Later List

There is no exact rule here, but you should consider the following.

Threshold of Time. I usually recommend that if something will take you more than thirty minutes, enter that To-Do directly into your calendar. For example, let's say you receive a budget process e-mail from your chief financial officer and you know there is a lot of work to review the e-mail, get communications out to your team, and align your budget to your priorities. That one may make sense to get right into your calendar because of the amount of time it will take as well as collaboration with others.

Deadline. If your task has a *real hard bona-fide* deadline, I suggest plopping that deadline directly into your calendar as an all-day appointment. Then work backwards to block off the necessary time in your calendar to prepare. If you are not quite sure of the exact date you want it to happen, store it in your Later List.

Time and Place. By putting To-Dos directly into your calendar, you can consider your physical location, needed materials, and energy level. If there is a natural reason that the To-Do should fall into a particular calendar slot, enter it there directly.

Let's continue exploring approaches for creating and maintaining your Later List.

Johanna's Later List

Back to Johanna from previously in this chapter. Johanna works on the curriculum team of Strive Charter Schools in Denver. She approaches her Later List a little differently than Heather. Similar to Steve, Johanna prefers a chart over a list (see figure 7.8). She slices her To-Dos across a few dimensions:

- By month
- By life bucket (Strive [her employer], medical, financial, writing [she is a young adult author!], and rainy day)

The chart enables Johanna to think chronologically *and* by category. The benefit here is that many of our brains like to *first* brainstorm by bucket and *then* order items chronologically. Johanna's system enables both. Her tool of choice is Microsoft OneNote, which also houses all of her other Together Tools, with the exception of her Comprehensive Calendar. It is synchronized to her various gadgets and devices.

A few examples from Johanna's Later List:

1. **Financial/September**: Johanna notes she wants to get that 401K up and running.
2. **Medical/October:** Johanna reminds herself to set up her annual doctors' appointments.

What I like about Johanna's system is this: All of this stuff would cause her brain a *lot* of stress if it were just sitting around in her head. And there is no way all of it could get done in a single week. Johanna is pacing her work. As she put it herself, "Before my Later List, I was never planning ahead. I was doing everything reactively. This is the first year that I have had a proactive system in place, and it has helped me get ahead, avoid drowning, and respond to requests with data about my time."

Johanna can also use her Later List to look ahead for deadlines and work backwards to break down large projects into pieces. But what you do *not* see on any of the Later Lists are deadlines. Why? I want all hard deadlines in your *calendars* so we can see them all in a calendar format, complete with when weekends, vacations, and your many other deadlines come to play. If you *must*, you can be extra safe and put deadlines on your Later List *and* your calendar, but I prefer to send deadlines to the calendar and keep softer To-Dos on my Later List.

Later List

	STRIVE	Personal	Financial	Medical	Writing	Rainy Day
August						
September	For 6th grade Unit 3: maybe keep books in the regular class period. Take OUT Freedom Songs. Possibly add Walking to the Busrider Blues (400 or 500 L). Add Civil Rights Movement Choose Your Own Adventure (extension text). Make Mississippi Trial a HIGH book.		Set up 401k - begin contributing ①		1 more blog post Write October in ALSOAT For Rad: Write project summary/statement. DUE BY END OF MONTH!	
October	Follow up re: Delgado booking for NHD. Look into STAR conferences (from Blair) Figure out Google Classroom (ask EdTech for help) Email Saira re: meeting prep	Plan Thanksgiving and Christmas break.	Begin saving for next summer's trip (monthly). Transfer money from 403b to 401k	Set up dentist/doctors appointments for either Nov or Dec ②	Finish Stan. Proposal Further requests re: BAS 2 blog posts Write Nov/Dec in ALSOAT	

Figure 7.8 Johanna's Later List

Now that you have seen three examples of Later Lists, I'm sure you have all kinds of ideas about how to organize your own, which tool to select, and then, of course, how to actually *use* it. The remainder of this chapter will focus on building your tool and implementing it with fidelity.

Reader Reflection
How will the Later List support your Togetherness practices?

BUILD YOUR OWN

As you saw in the examples, there are many approaches to making a Later List, but they all have one thing in common: a way to track To-Dos for *beyond* a single week. In this section of the chapter, I will lead you through a process to build your own Later List.

Select Your Categorization Method

Here's a recap of possible ways to group, sort, or layer your list, keeping in mind that many Together Leaders, such as Steve, Heather, and Johanna, actually choose to sort across multiple dimensions.

By Start Month. This is my personal favorite! Steve made this choice (and then he sorted again by personal and professional).

By Job Category. Heather did this. It's often helpful to think through things in categories. You may think about "development," "alumni," or "team management."

By Project. Some people have to think through their work by actual project, such as "website rollout," "alumni gala," and "benefits switch-up."

By Context. This tells where we will be physically located when we work on the task, such as "home," "office," or "car." David Allen, author of *Getting Things Done,* made this way of thinking popular.

By Life Bucket. Johanna did this with her work, writing, medical, and financial needs.

If you're still not sure what will work best, here's how to get started: close your eyes and empty your brain of all the To-Dos it's holding. Efficiency expert David Allen (2001, p. 113) calls this a "mind sweep." As you close your eyes, ask yourself, "How am I thinking about my work? By project? By start month?" Let your natural instincts be your guide. And remember, similar to all of these leaders, you are welcome to have a few levels of sorting. What we do *not* want is just a jumbled long list that takes us two hours to untangle and recopy each week!

I also want you to consider your sorting option *before* you pick a tool because your preference for sorting may dictate one tool over another. For example, if you really want to be able to see across three dimensions, you should pick an option such as Excel that enables you to sort and filter. If you like to think by project first, then perhaps you should select a tool more geared toward project management.

Reader Reflection

How will you sort or categorize your Later List? Do you need multiple dimensions?

Select a Tool

Tool selection for calendars is relatively easy because there are just a few good options and we usually have to get onboard with whatever our entire organization is already using. But tool selection for Later Lists is very challenging. There is an abundance of choices, paper and digital, and it can be hard to find the perfect fit. Steve selected a simple Microsoft Word document to upload to Google Docs. Heather used Microsoft Excel with its powerful sorting and filtering abilities, but it lacks online accessibility—though this could be easily solved with Google Docs or Office To-Go. Johanna chose Microsoft OneNote, which is more accessible but requires manual sorting. I don't want to get into the ins and outs of all the technology, because it's likely to be obsolete by the time you read this book. Current reviews of the many apps, hacks, and platforms are available for reading on my website (www.thetogethergroup .com). But no matter which platform you're considering, there are some consistent questions about your own preferences to keep in mind.

Later List Selection Questions

- How many layers of sorting are you inclined to use?

- Do you gravitate toward technology or paper?

- What kinds of devices do you own and carry?

- Do you like to tinker around and move things manually or do you like automatic sorting?

- Does your organization's culture allow technology use in meetings and hallways?

- Do you like to break items into teeny-tiny details? Or do you prefer a big picture view?

FAQ: Can I mix and match my tools?

Of course! Just because you use a digital calendar for your Comprehensive Calendar, doesn't mean you have to keep a digital Later List. And just because you use Google Calendar similar to Steve doesn't mean you have to use Google Tasks. However, beware of tool proliferation: you don't want a million windows open on the bottom of your screen.

If you are truly unsure about which tool to select, I always recommend starting with a paper option to build the habit. You can add in the technology if it makes sense later. Remember, your Later List can literally be as simple as index cards with the month listed on the top of each one. The important thing is to keep a long-term To-Do List that will help you prepare for each week!

Reader Reflection

What is your Later List tool of choice? Why are you sure this is the tool for you?

FAQ: What is the connection to my Priority Plan?

The Priority Plan should be limited in scope. It articulates for you and communicates to others what is most important. The Later List should be more micro in scale and should flesh out the actions necessary to getting the stuff in the Priority Plan done. Your Later List will be longer and should keep track of *everything*.

Your Priority Plan will definitely drive some of the To-Dos hanging out on your big list, but your Later List is also going to also catch some of the teeny-tiny stuff, such as "switch my seasonal clothes," or "check on the funder prospect." It will be a combined list of priority and standard work.

Once you understand the ultimate purpose of each tool, you are welcome to customize. For example, Ashley, whom you met in chapter 4, combined her Priority Plan and Later List to ensure they were connected. Let's take a look at figure 7.9.

1. Priority Plan and big To-Dos make up her Priority Plan.
2. Little To-Dos and personal are her Later List.

Ashley put everything in one mega-document. The downside is that she loses a simple and clean communication tool about her priorities. But she decided it was worth it to her to keep her Later List aligned with what matters the most. This is why Ashley created the "Priority Plan for quarter 1" list you see at the top of the page.

Complete the Content

Now that you've got ideas from several models, an idea of your own sorting plan, and a tool selected, it's time to get started on your own Later List. Figure 7.10 shows some prompts and examples to help you proactively build your list—keeping in mind, of course, that you can also add to it at any time.

Later List

Priority Plan for Quarter 1

1. Ensure clear practice and performance goals for schools
2. Ensure MDs have clear systems for managing A1 execution
3. Get a clear simple message and communication plan around this perf benchmarking predictive issue
4. Clarify district interactions for the year aligned with school practice goals
5. Clarify learning trajectory for teacher eval

	Big To Do's	Little To Do's	Personal

Sept	☐ Plan the Salem Principals PD
	  ○ Draft the trajectory for the principal P
	  ○ Draft the agenda for the Salem Oct Principal PD
	  ○ Tune with NE Team Meeting and Assign Roles
	
	☐ Draft the purpose of Q1/Q4 quarterly district stepbacks
	  ○ Tune it at an MM Meeting
	  ○ Ensure M is set up with NSA support team
	  ○ Align with Dorie around steps for preparing for Chelsea and Revere
		☐ (Ron) Re-read Salem AIP and report out on key turnaround goals and metrics
		
		☐ Send Melinda's school inter-actions sheet to MDs
		
		☐ Finalize contract with SPS
		
		☐ Read Pei's docs RE teacher eval
		
		☐ Compare admin rubric with three SPS practice focus areas
		
		☐ Review planning tools in MY
		
		☐ Pick priority schools to go observe in the field in Spring-field and have Marg calendar
		
		☐ Week of Sept 3 plan presenta-tion to board RE acct goals
			☐ Find passcodes
			
			☐ Sign up for monthly yoga workshop
			
			☐ Reschedule my Dr. C apt
			
			☐ Calendar all the kids days off
			
			☐ Book time with Orlean
			
			☐ Subscribe to poetry/writing links Beth sent me
			
			☐ Dragon journal write

Figure 7.9 Ashley's Combo Later List and Priority Plan

Assistant Alert

You can most definitely have your assistant maintain your Later List. You might send an e-mail saying, "In May, let's revisit the Scope and Sequence for the team meetings." He or she can capture that on your Later List, and then bring it to your weekly meeting (more on those in chapter 13).

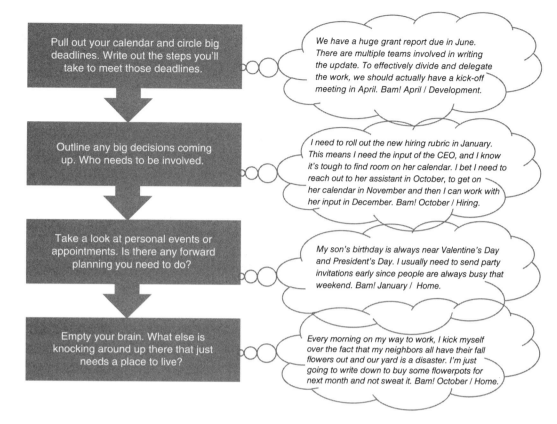

Figure 7.10 Build Your Later List

Reader Reflection

Add at least twenty items to your Later List!

THE ROUTINE

I bet you are now starting to formulate a vision of your very own Later List. But before you enter list-making nirvana, let's pause and discuss how and when to actually *use* this tool. After all, this list is only as good as your commitment to it.

Systematic Weekly Review of Your Later List

Different from some productivity gurus, I actually do not want you to stare at this list any time you have a free moment. Too overwhelming! The reason I strongly prefer it organized by start month is so once per week, you can look three months ahead. Then, each week, you will pull out *just* the items for this week and put the Later List away!

Determine How You Will Keep Your List Accessible

Once you start populating your Later List, I guarantee long-term thoughts will pop up at the most inopportune times. You'll need to get them out of your head and onto a list you can easily and reliably return to later.

- If you decide to use an app to manage your Later List, be sure to have it available on your phone, tablet, and computer. This is especially important if you are using one that requires Internet access. Even when you cannot get to it on your computer, your smartphone may save you!
- If you choose to go paper but still want to view your list digitally sometimes, consider moving a Word document or Excel sheet into Evernote or Google Docs for consistent access.
- If you're only using paper, well, make sure you always carry the list with you!

To make a long story short, I don't want this list scrawled in the back of a random notebook in your backpack or tucked away in a desk drawer. It will be too much of a chore to get to it when you have a flash of brilliance. The tool, and your great idea along with it, will die. Keep your Later List accessible and available, and keep it alive!

Make Sure the To-Dos Don't Get Stuck

Speaking of using this thing, *when* are you supposed to return to it? Given the list's size and scope, it can feel overwhelming. That's why I do not want you to return it to daily—except to add things in. Once a week, systematically spin through the entire list and scoop out the To-Dos for the coming week only. This spin-through will likely take five to fifteen minutes, depending on the length of your Later List. By *scoop out,* I mean one of two things (spoiler alert: this is a preview of chapter 9)!

1. Some of you will simply make a mini-list within your larger Later List. For example, you may add a tab in an Excel sheet for "this week" or create a "this week" tag in whatever app you are using.
2. Some of you will place the To-Dos for the week directly into your calendar, thus filling in those Planned Priorities and Standard Stuff blocks that have been hanging out just waiting to be filled.

START STRONG

For many of you, this chapter may have really changed things. The biggest adjustment for people using the Later List is getting comfortable with the idea that it will *never* be completed and that is okay. Remember, the Later List is a holding ground for your longer term To-Dos.

In my years of coaching and training on Togetherness, people consistently rate the Later List as having a huge positive impact on forward planning, communicating with colleagues, and plain old stress relief. Even if you do not immediately go whole hog, I encourage you to at least carry around a blank template to jot down your thoughts as they arise.

Time commitment: I predict the initial build of your Later List will take you **about one to two hours**. After that, you simply use it when reviewing your Priority Plan each week, as well as to record items that come up for the future.

- Determine the purpose for your Later List.

- Decide how you will sort and group your To-Dos.

- Select a tool to host your Later List.

- Populate your Later List with at least twenty items.

- List how and when you will use your Later List.

- Ensure your Later List is 100 percent accessible.

In the following chapter, we'll craft the To-Do List for this week—called a *Weekly Worksheet*.

COMMON CHALLENGE: THE CALENDAR AND TO-DO LIST COLLIDE

Indrina Kanth, a chief of staff to CEOs in New Orleans, came into our coaching relationship at a very high level of Togetherness. Her Outlook Calendar accurately accounted for all of her meetings, and she maintained a very organized To-Do List (sorted by category) in Excel. Nary a sticky note in sight!

At first glance, it was easy to assume Indrina was already in great shape—and truthfully, she was. Except for one teeny-tiny issue that actually had a huge impact: Her To-Do List and Calendar didn't talk to each other. Indrina had an enormous list of things to do, but no time blocked to actually work through it.

In her words, "I wasn't building enough time in the day to accomplish all I needed to get done. I've always been good at keeping a list of my To-Dos, but I was not as diligent about ensuring I had time in the day to complete my work. I wound up scheduling over my work blocks, so the only time I could get to my To-Do List was late in the evening."

In this epic battle between the Calendar and To-Do List, which tool wins? In Indrina's case, both got equal weight. But here's what we did to reconcile time with tasks:

1. **Inserted Indrina's "standard" work tasks into her Outlook Calendar as recurring events.** For more details on this, please see chapter 6. By blocking time each week for standard work, such as preparing for meetings, answering e-mail, and pausing to plan, Indrina obtained a more accurate picture of how much time she *actually* had.

2. **Upgraded Indrina's To-Do List to indicate priority level and allotted time.** Indrina could fight the urge to just work on smaller, easier work by identifying ahead of time what work mattered most (figure 7.11). She could also make better decisions about how to use small pockets of time.

IK Action Plan

Category	Priority ①	Meeting	Tasks	Start date
i3	X	CREDO	Review impact report - compile with Maggie's and Michael's	21-Sep
Board	X	Investment	Reschedule investment cmte	22-Sep
NGLC		NGLC conf	Print the schedule for convening	22-Sep
NGLC		NGLC conf	Practice presentation	22-Sep
i3	X		Send Jen projected hours on i3 for rest of the month	22-Sep
NGLC		ALU check-in	Edit Learner profile RFP (flight)	24-Sep
Comm		FF	Schedule meeting with SB to add" what's on deck" to newsblast	25-Sep
TT Training		PD	Final count to Maia on 9/25	25-Sep
Comm		FF	Compile exit ticket feedback	25-Sep
Comm		FF	Compile Org calendar feedback	25-Sep
Portfolio	X	DZ check-in	Schedule time with DZ to go over teacher pipeline/facilities work	25-Sep
LT		LT	Schedule HR stepback in October (LT and JK)	25-Sep
TT Training		PD	Check on surveymonkey progress	25-Sep
Board	X	Full board	Send out invite for November 17 meeting (if we have quorum)	25-Sep
Board		Investment	Reschedule October investment cmte (Hunter email)	25-Sep
Perf Mgmt	X	IK/MRS PM convo	Complete upward feedback for Maggie	25-Sep
Onboarding			Reviewi3, NOLA CEF onboarding materials	28-Sep
Perf Mgmt	X	IK/MRS PM convo	Complete upward feedback for Michael	28-Sep
Board		Investment	Reschedule November investment cmte	2-Oct
Board		Investment	Reschedule December investment cmte	2-Nov

Figure 7.11 Indrina's To-Do List

3. **Entered key To-Do's directly into Indrina's calendar.** (Figure 7.13) People ask this question ALL THE TIME. Which should be the driver — my calendar or my To-Do list? In Indrina's case, we chose three types of entries for her calendar:

  ○ **If the To-Do was incredibly high priority and connected to her goals.** For example, for her most important work, like investment decisions, Indrina held these times directly in her calendar.

Category	Priority	Meeting	Tasks	Start date
i3	X	CREDO	Review impact report - compile with Maggie's and Michael's	21-Sep
Board	X	Investment	Reschedule investment cmte	22-Sep
NGLC		NGLC conf	Print the schedule for convening	22-Sep
NGLC		NGLC conf	Practice presentation	22-Sep
i3	X		Send Jen projected hours on i3 for rest of the month	22-Sep
NGLC		ALU check-in	Edit Learner profile RFP (flight)	24-Sep
Comm		FF	Schedule meeting with SB to add "what's on deck" to newsblast	25-Sep
TT Training		PD	Final count to Maia on 9/25	25-Sep
Comm		FF	Compile exit ticket feedback	25-Sep
Comm		FF	Compile Org calendar feedback	25-Sep
Portfolio	X	DZ check-in	Schedule time with DZ to go over teacher pipeline/facilities work	25-Sep
LT		LT	Schedule HR stepback in October (LT and JK)	25-Sep
TT Training		PD	Check on surveymonkey progress	25-Sep
Board	X	Full board	Send out invite for November 17 meeting (if we have quorum)	25-Sep
Board		Investment	Reschedule October investment cmte (Hunter email)	25-Sep
Perf Mgmt	X	IK/MRS PM convo	Complete upward feedback for Maggie	25-Sep
Onboarding			Review i3, NOLA CEF onboarding materials	28-Sep
Perf Mgmt	X	IK/MAS PM convo	Complete upward feedback for Michael	28-Sep
Board		Investment	Reschedule November investment cmte	2-Oct
Board		Investment	Reschedule December investment cmte	2-Nov

Figure 7.12 Indrina's Work Blocks

- **If the To-Do would take her more than an hour.** For example, if Indrina had to review and synthesize headlines from an impact report (Figure 7.13) that would take her several hours. Looking at her calendar, there would be no way to magically "fit" it in, so she'd have to block some time.
- **If the To-Do required being in a particular location.** For example, if Indrina needed to write a grant report and it was easiest to pull data from the server in her office, this may need to go in her calendar.

According to Indrina, "Now that I plug in my work directly into the work blocks, it's much easier for me to assess whether I can schedule over a work block or whether I need to move things around and build more work time."

Don't assume that just because your tools look good, they serve your larger goal! Instead, try making tweaks similar to what Indrina did: develop a calendar that provides you with an accurate picture of your workload and a To-Do List that enables you to quickly prioritize.

CHAPTER 8

Reconcile Your Time and To-Dos
Create Your Weekly Plan

SEEN AND HEARD

"I schedule long chunks of time to do work both on the weekends and evenings but am not always working efficiently the entire time."

"I know *what* I have to do, but I'm not strategic (or disciplined) about *when* I'm going to do it."

"The thirty-minute chunks in-between meetings or observations always feel like the biggest wastes of time because I don't know how to productively use them and never get anything real or meaningful accomplished."

OVERVIEW AND OBJECTIVES

Now that you've created your Comprehensive Calendar and Later List, it's time to craft a very detailed plan for your week ahead. So far, you've imprinted your big priorities, deadlines, and events into one single digital calendar. And you have sorted your To-Dos for the long term into an organized Later List.

Now it's time to zoom in. In my travels, I see leaders typically fall into one of a few camps when they get ready for the week ahead:

- Leaders who have a strong understanding of their calendars for the week, their meetings, and their events, but they do not have a clear plan on what to do with the open space between scheduled items.

- Leaders who start the week with a strong list, maybe even categorized, but they have little sense of whether they have time to accomplish items on the list—and no regard for physical location and energy levels.

Both of those methods are okay, but neither is strong enough to stand alone. We have to sew up your time and your To-Dos into one singular location for the week ahead, thus creating your Weekly or Daily Worksheet (see figure 8.1).

Definition
A **Weekly or Daily Worksheet is** an hour-by-hour view of your time and To-Dos for the week ahead, created *before* the week starts.

In this chapter, you will do the following:

- Master the how and why of getting micro for the week.
- Understand if you are time or task oriented and what that means for how you plan your week.
- Develop ways to get more time back in your day.
- Determine how to put it all together when you are on the move.

Before we engage with the actual tool, let's discuss the process of building it. The next section outlines reasons for how and why to prepare for your week.

Figure 8.1 The Togetherness Tools

THE MODEL

Remember how you have been holding all of those Time Blocks in your Comprehensive Calendar? The ones for Planned Priorities and Standard Stuff? We are now about to break them down. Simply said, I am going to help you specify and break down your work into small little chunks. The point is not to be obsessive and overprogrammed but rather to ensure your work actually fits within a given day or week.

Similar to your other tools, your Weekly Worksheet can take a few different forms. Whichever one you choose, each model forces you to reconcile your time commitments with your To-Do List—and to fit the *right* work in at the *right* times. Here's a brief overview of three of the most common forms of Weekly and Daily Worksheets. Then we'll see a few real-life samples in action.

Option 1. You might create a homemade list for the week, using one of my templates or making your own. This will work for those of you who are mostly nondigital. You can find many variations of the worksheet in figure 8.2 and the resource section of my website (www.thetogethergroup.com).

Option 2. The next option is to use a template similar to the one shown in figure 8.2 but insert your digital calendar right into it. We will see an example of this in the coming section.

Option 3. Instead of writing up a week on one page, you might choose to create five daily pages, often using your digital tools as a starting point. Figure 8.3 shows examples of a Daily Worksheet printed in Outlook and Google's Daily View. The handwriting captures unplanned items that popped up throughout the day.

Whatever tool you select, any good Weekly Worksheet will contain the following:

- Priorities clearly named (don't skip this!). This should flow through from your Priority Plan.

- All meetings and appointments listed, as well as Time Blocks mapped out for Standard Stuff

- All To-Dos spelled out by conducting a sweep of the Priority Plan, Later List, and your in-box

- Enough flexibility to handle the ambush of the week and your ever-changing environment

LEADER | **WEEKLY WORKSHEET**

's Weekly Worksheet, Week of _____

PRIORITIES

X	Y	Personal

SHAPE OF THE WEEK

	M	T	W	R	F	Weekend
Appts						
Deadlines						

Big Work	Emails/Calls (TMTs)	Meeting Notes

Errands/Home/Personal	To Read	Next Week

Figure 8.2 Weekly Worksheet Template

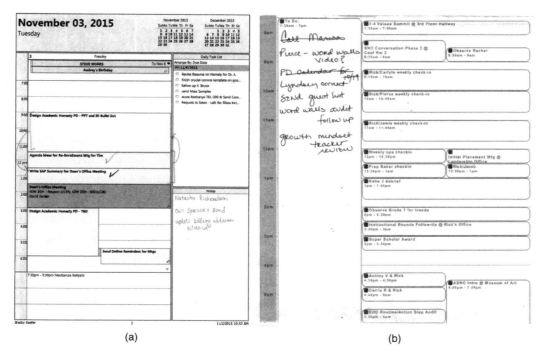

Figure 8.3 Daily Worksheets in Outlook and Google

TASK-DRIVEN, TIME-DRIVEN, OR BLENDED?

As you contemplate the best tool to map out your week, it is first helpful to know if you are driven by tasks (To-Do Lists are your friend) or time (you love your calendar). Let's take a short, unscientific quiz to determine where you land.

QUIZ

Task-Driven, Time-Driven, or Blended?

When you prepare for x big meeting in your work life, you prefer to do which of the following?

A. Add to your list "Prepare for x meeting."
B. Create a calendar appointment called "Prepare for x Meeting" but only if the preparation takes longer than an hour.
C. Automatically create a calendar appointment, "Prepare for x Meeting" from 3:00–3:45 PM Wednesday.

For those of you who raised your hand for option A, you are more driven by completion of the task, no matter how much time it takes. You probably love lists and start the week with a good one. It's likely that you are decently flexible. You may hate to start something because you fear being interrupted, so why bother? The challenge is that you may not have a clear understanding of the actual time you have to complete the items on your list. This may lead to overcommitment, procrastination, or both!

If you fell in the option B camp, you are a blended version. This is me. If a task will take me longer than an hour, I will automatically enter it in my calendar. The reason is that if you asked me to do something that would take an hour this week, I cannot magically squeeze it in. However, I don't want to enter *everything* in my calendar. That feels too constraining.

Option C means you are likely time driven. You probably start each week with a clear sense of your calendar commitments, but no plan for what to do with the white spaces in your days. You get nervous when you see loose To-Dos, and you likely feel comfortable when everything can fit in a week.

One way is no more effective than the other. I know that I prefer to be time-driven during the week, but task-driven on the weekend. The power is in knowing your preference, and using this knowledge to wisely blend your time with your To-Dos on your Weekly or Daily Worksheet. Now that you know your natural inclinations, let's examine several models of different ways effective leaders organize their weeks.

Now let's make it real. In the next section, we will meet several leaders who plan their weeks in very different ways, but they each do so at a high level of detail using a Weekly Worksheet.

Option A: Dave's Homemade, Task-Driven, Weekly Worksheet

Dave Howland, a principal in Atlanta, uses one of my templates to create his Weekly Worksheet in Microsoft Word (figure 8.4). Dave's plan easily meets criteria for naming priorities and listing his To-Dos in an organized fashion. It does not, however, name meetings and appointments. Those are kept separately in Dave's Outlook Calendar. This is a key difference for task-driven models.

You can see that Dave thoughtfully listed out his To-Dos by day, and he made a *key* move that task-driven people often skip. He checked his Outlook Calendar to see how much time he actually had available. For example, on Tuesday, he noted that he had two hours of work time, and planned to "draft agenda for admin retreat" and so on. But on Thursday, he had zero work time. Therefore, no proactive To-Dos were listed.

Dave's Weekly Worksheet, Week of 9/21

ANNUAL BIG ROCKS

Be Present	Be Prepared	Be Sustained
Quarterly Priorities		**Action for this week**
Improve asset-based coaching through PD for LT & Observations with feedback of coaching sessions		Plan out "intro to state of being" for Oct. LT mtg.
Increase capacity of coaches/managers		Mtg. with Shyam/CP re: Root Cause analysis
Thought-partner with RST to increase restorative practice and staff mindset		Action plan in O3/ Champion to join O3

	Work Time Tasks – This Week	A little later list – Sort Into Work Time for Next Week
		GA Tech Teacher Info Docs – Due 10/12
Monday	*1 Hour*	
	File Papers	Homestead Application
	Rik to RST re RJ	Athletic Waiver for KAC
	New staff meet-up each month Sept/Oct/Nov.	Gift for Trae/Wizdom
	PISA Online Survey	Review video from MS on "College for everyone?" – Ted Talk
		Research SLACK as alt. to Email
Tuesday	*2 Hours*	Lou Work Schedule 5% with Sub time
	Draft Agenda for Admin Retreat	Read Maia's chapters on priority setting
	Book Hotel/Flight for Denver Trip	Register for Harvard Course on Education
	Assistant survey to Jefferson – Schedule O3 time – leverage admin guide and adjust	Review KF HS strategies document prior to call
	Review ?s for AFAEE Video	
	Plan for Students with issues with Cheating	
Wednesday	No Work Time	
Thursday	No Work Time	
Friday	*2 Hours*	
	Finalize documents for Admin Q1 Step-back (Add ACT Analysis)	
	Draft Slides for LT Mtg. on 10/15	
	Mini-Grants approval/Feedback	
	Marshmallow Structure test for LT in October	

Don't Compromise your Vision or your Expectations

Figure 8.4 Dave's Weekly Worksheet

Let's recap what Dave did:

- Clear naming of priorities for the week (taken from his Yearly Goals and Priority Plan)
- Time allocation clearly laid out per day
- Deadlines accounted for in the section underneath each day
- Room to deal with the unexpected by having blank spaces remaining

Now let's check for understanding. When Dave sits down to plan his week, where will he

- Get his amount of work time schedule? Why, from his Comprehensive Calendar, of course!
- Get his To-Dos? From his Later List!

And, of course, a whole bunch of other To-Dos come from phone messages, his e-mail in-box, memos from staff, and more.

Reader Reflection

What appeals to you about Dave's approach that you could add to your own practice?

For you visual learners, here's what the weekly planning process looks like in graphic form (figure 8.5). This is when the big picture view of your time gets together with the big picture view of your To-Dos and get married.

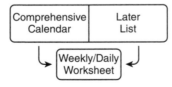

Figure 8.5 CC + LL = WW

So, that is Dave, a more task-oriented leader who creates a homemade Weekly Worksheet. But let's look at other options. What about a slightly more digital leader?

Option B: Lo's Blended Time and Task Weekly Worksheet

Lo Nigrosh is an instructional coach for a Boston-based nonprofit, the Achievement Network. She moves around between schools all day. She is a heavy Google user, but doesn't want to slot every single To-Do in her calendar. She's slightly more motivated by a To-Do List than a calendar. But she does some very creative things to reconcile her time and To-Dos—and have them all with her in one place for when she's on the move (see figure 8.6).

I want to give a huge shout-out here to one of the original time management gurus, the late Steven Covey. Two concepts he made part of the regular vocabulary are

1. **Big Rocks**—Important activities, aligned to one's priorities, that have an outcome leading to the achievement of one's goals
2. **Quadrant 2 Time**—All activities can be classified by their urgency and their importance. Quadrant 2 time is focused on activities that are important, but not urgent, such as planning, prevention, and capability improvement.

This is one of my favorite examples for a number of reasons:

1. **Lo writes out her priorities (big rocks) for the week.** Lo uses her Priority Plan to determine her biggest priorities for the week. I also like how she includes the personal *and* professional.

2. **Lo lists all of her To-Dos for the week**. She gathers them up from multiple locations, such as her Later List, her in-box, meeting notes she has gathered, and so on. And then get this . . . she *groups* her To-Dos by energy level. The bigger brain jobs, such as "Review Kensington IB Materials," are called high-energy tasks, and her low-energy tasks, such as printing a document, are tracked separately. This is a pretty awesome way to think about your To-Dos for the week. That way when you have an energy plummet, you can work the low-energy list.

3. **Lo figures out how it will all fit into the time she has available.** Lo opens her Google Calendar for the week and starts to fill out all of those macro work blocks she has been holding on to. If you look at Monday from 2 PM to 5 PM, she has a big block of time for that higher energy work. Lo populates *most*, but not all, of her major work blocks.

Because she is highly mobile throughout the week, Lo prints her Weekly Worksheet and uses it as a flexible guide—not a rigid script—for her time.

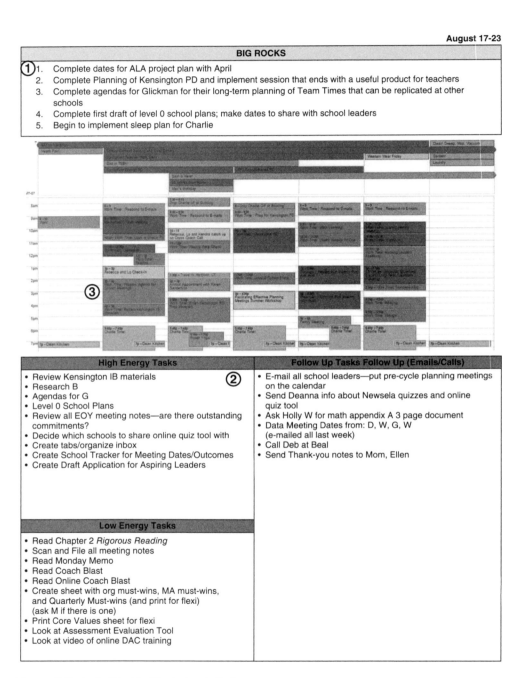

August 17-23

BIG ROCKS

① 1. Complete dates for ALA project plan with April
2. Complete Planning of Kensington PD and implement session that ends with a useful product for teachers
3. Complete agendas for Glickman for their long-term planning of Team Times that can be replicated at other schools
4. Complete first draft of level 0 school plans; make dates to share with school leaders
5. Begin to implement sleep plan for Charlie

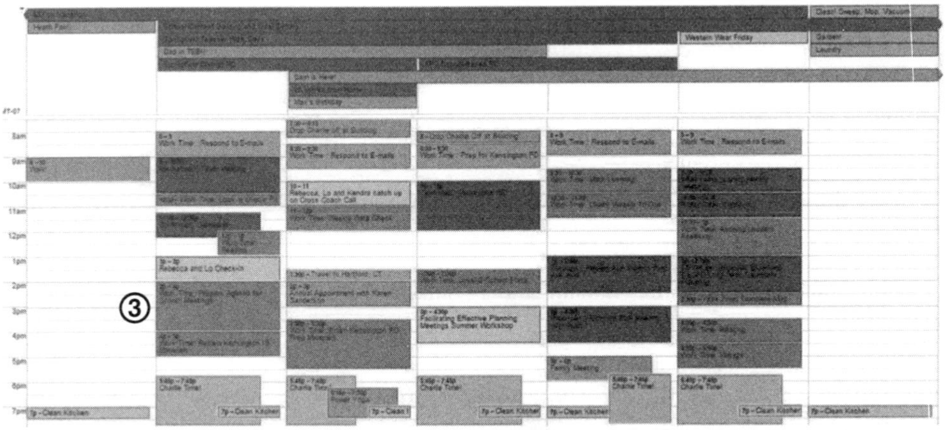

High Energy Tasks ②	Follow Up Tasks Follow Up (Emails/Calls)
• Review Kensington IB materials • Research B • Agendas for G • Level 0 School Plans • Review all EOY meeting notes—are there outstanding commitments? • Decide which schools to share online quiz tool with • Create tabs/organize inbox • Create School Tracker for Meeting Dates/Outcomes • Create Draft Application for Aspiring Leaders	• E-mail all school leaders—put pre-cycle planning meetings on the calendar • Send Deanna info about Newsela quizzes and online quiz tool • Ask Holly W for math appendix A 3 page document • Data Meeting Dates from: D, W, G, W (e-mailed all last week) • Call Deb at Beal • Send Thank-you notes to Mom, Ellen
Low Energy Tasks	
• Read Chapter 2 *Rigorous Reading* • Scan and File all meeting notes • Read Monday Memo • Read Coach Blast • Read Online Coach Blast • Create sheet with org must-wins, MA must-wins, and Quarterly Must-wins (and print for flexi) (ask M if there is one) • Print Core Values sheet for flexi • Look at Assessment Evaluation Tool • Look at video of online DAC training	

Figure 8.6 Lo's Weekly Worksheet: Before

FAQ: What if something *changes* in Lo's schedule?

Things change all the time! In fact, let's look at exactly how much. Figure 8.7 shows Lo's Weekly Worksheet at the end of a week!

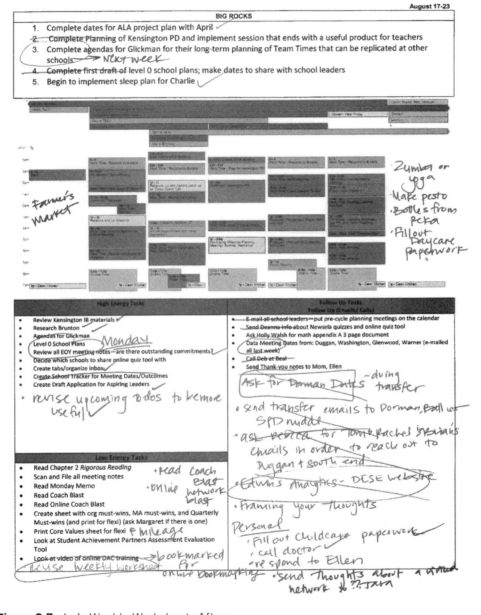

Figure 8.7 Lo's Weekly Worksheet: After

This is a messy, real-deal example here. Good organization tools *should* be messy because that means they are well used and well loved! Lo does this in a few different ways as she goes about her week:

1. She takes meeting notes directly into her Weekly Worksheet. No more notebook full of hidden To-Dos and next steps! One less place to look.

2. She fills in changes to her calendar as they happen.

3. She enters her To-Dos into her open Time Blocks.

4. She is also anticipating her weekend, planning for things such as "farmer's market" and "zumba or yoga."

So, there you have it . . . Lo's half-paper, half-digital approach.

Reader Reflection

What are the benefits of a more blended time and task approach?

Option C: Roslyn's Hybrid Time and To-Do Daily Worksheet

Meet Roslyn, a school leader. Similar to Lo, she's a Google-based person, but different from Lo, Roslyn gets ready for her week using another tool—Daily Worksheets, similar to the models you viewed earlier in this chapter. She still accomplishes the same outcome—an hour-by-hour plan for her time and To-Dos for the week ahead—but does so by planning each individual day, rather than the overall week.

Roslyn prints her already existing Comprehensive Calendar on Google, and then plans more specific tasks within the appointment space (figure 8.8). Because she's printed it in the daily view, it's highly portable and accessible for Roslyn as she moves around her school building.

Take a closer look at Roslyn's Daily Worksheet:

1. Adjustments for changes—A grade-level meeting (GLM) was canceled and replaced quickly by "debrief w/ Dr. Smith."

2. Room to capture—Roslyn did something nifty here. Check out the left-hand side of her Daily Worksheet. She created an appointment called "To-Do" from 8–5. This gives Roslyn a To-Do box where she can capture items as they come up during the day. (Outlook users: this to-do box prints automatically for you.)

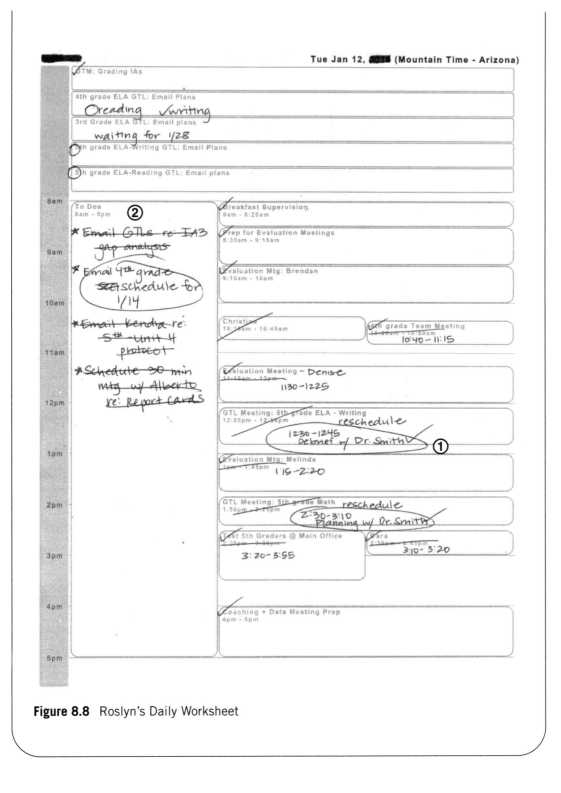

Figure 8.8 Roslyn's Daily Worksheet

FAQ: Do I need *both* a Weekly Worksheet *and* Daily Worksheets?
A resounding *no*. Even if you elect to print just the daily view, I still want you to plan for an entire week at one time. Both push you to do the exact same thing—develop a specific point of view about how you want to spend your week. Those who select the daily route just need to have five pieces of paper but are still planning according to the same principles—the tool just looks different.

Option D: Mark's Digital, Time-Driven Weekly Worksheet

Mark DiBella is the superintendent of YES Prep Public Schools in Houston, Texas. At home, he's strongly committed to spending time with his family, running, attending church, and watching football. Mark does not have any loose tasks in his week; everything is programmed into a time slot (see figure 8.9). Those of you who are more task-driven like Dave or Lo may feel suffocated by this approach, and others might find the structure supportive. Either way is okay—this is an individual journey!

Mark's plan meets Weekly Worksheet criteria in a few ways:

1. **Strategic color-coding.** On my website (www.thetogethergroup.com), you can see how Mark smartly uses colors to scan his calendar to ensure it reflects his priorities. His personal and family commitments are in green, meetings are in blue, travel time is in red, and work time in orange.

2. **Work block specificity.** Similar to most Together Leaders, Mark doesn't wait for work time to magically present itself, nor does he go digging around for hours in his calendar with short notice. Instead, he uses his Later List (kept on paper in his notebook) to populate his prescheduled work blocks with specific tasks for the week. Bonus tech points here: Mark views his Outlook Calendar in appointment preview mode, enabling him to see right away what he's planned for each work block.

3. **Personal and professional.** Talking with his wife, Mark has carefully planned his free time in advance of each week. This enables them both to fit in exercise as well as quality time with each other and their two kids.

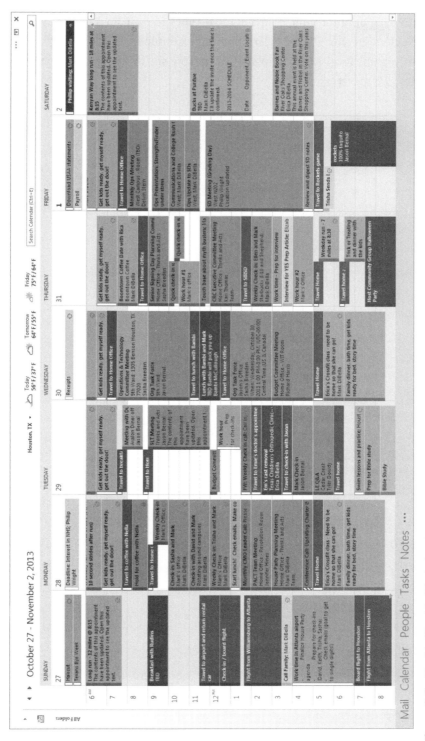

Figure 8.9 Mark's Weekly Worksheet

Within each appointment, Mark literally types in how he plans to spend that time. Lots of leaders do this. Figure 8.10 shows an example from Molly Day, a leader at the nonprofit organization LIFT, who spells out how she'll use the time on an upcoming train ride.

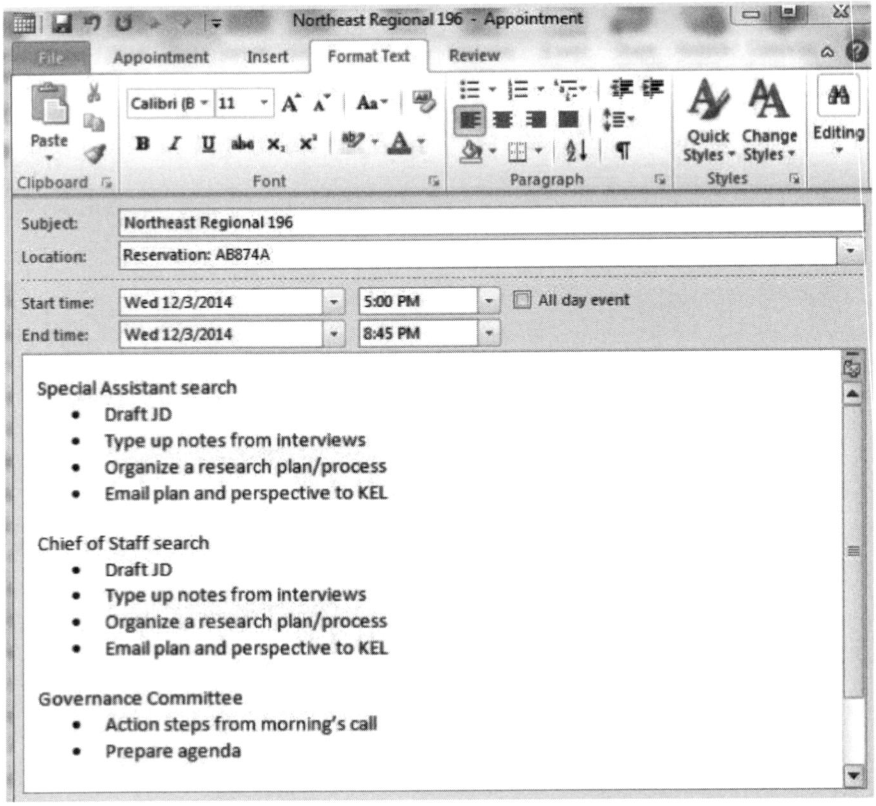

Figure 8.10 Molly's Train Ride Tasks

Now that you've seen four different models (and there are many more on my website, www.thetogethergroup.com), I want you to plan what will work for you. You'll want to carefully consider your own working style as well as the demands of your specific environment.

You are free to choose or create whichever version of a Weekly Worksheet you wish—as long as you reconcile your time and To-Dos before the week actually starts.

Reader Reflection

What elements of the Weekly Worksheet speak to you?

BUILD YOUR OWN

I know you are excited to get started. Let's build your own Weekly Worksheet taking what appealed to you in the various models as well as what works best with your own preferences and work environment.

Once you select the format that works best for you, it's a matter of completing your Weekly Worksheet before the week begins. Let's walk through your steps to get it ready for the week (figure 8.11)!

After you complete these steps (and there will be even more steps you can add in chapter 9), your Weekly Worksheet is done and ready for the week ahead. But let's add a few more things to ensure you can make the most of your time ahead.

Reader Reflection

How did it feel to create your Weekly Worksheet? What did you catch for the week ahead?

Table 8.1   How to Select the Right Weekly Worksheet

If you are . . .	Select this Tool
Prone to procrastination	Select a time-based Weekly Worksheet model, such as Mark's or Roslyn's example.
Occasionally overcommitted	Select a time-based Weekly Worksheet model, such as Mark's or Roslyn's example.
In an organization that shuns technology in meetings and in hallways	Select a digital version, but print it or create a paper-based model such as Dave's.
A self-proclaimed Luddite	Select a paper-based model or even use an old fashioned commercial planner
Full of endless meetings that don't connect to priorities	Select a task-based model, such as Dave's, so at least your open space will be aligned to priorities.

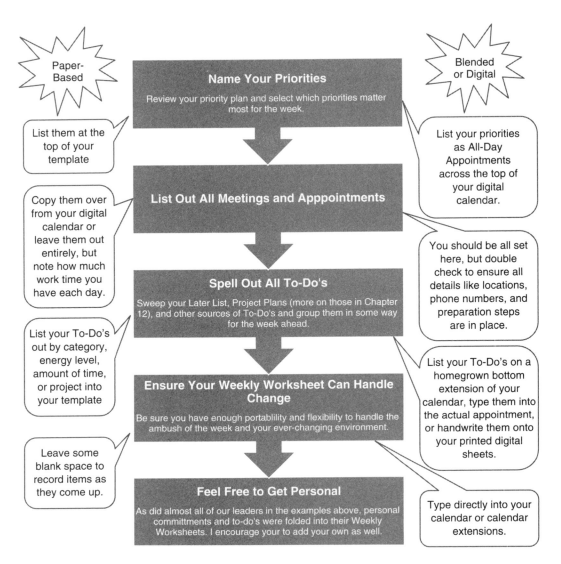

Paper-Based

Name Your Priorities
Review your priority plan and select which priorities matter most for the week.

List them at the top of your template

List Out All Meetings and Appointments

Copy them over from your digital calendar or leave them out entirely, but note how much work time you have each day.

Spell Out All To-Do's
Sweep your Later List, Project Plans (more on those in Chapter 12), and other sources of To-Do's and group them in some way for the week ahead.

List your To-Do's out by category, energy level, amount of time, or project into your template

Ensure Your Weekly Worksheet Can Handle Change
Be sure you have enough portability and flexibility to handle the ambush of the week and your ever-changing environment.

Leave some blank space to record items as they come up.

Feel Free to Get Personal
As did almost all of our leaders in the examples above, personal commitments and to-do's were folded into their Weekly Worksheets. I encourage your to add your own as well.

Blended or Digital

List your priorities as All-Day Appointments across the top of your digital calendar.

You should be all set here, but double check to ensure all details like locations, phone numbers, and preparation steps are in place.

List your To-Do's on a homegrown bottom extension of your calendar, type them into the actual appointment, or handwrite them onto your printed digital sheets.

Type directly into your calendar or calendar extensions.

Figure 8.11 Build Your Own Weekly Worksheet

LITTLE THINGS MAKE A DIFFERENCE

Now that your Weekly Worksheet design is locked down, let's think about some little things that will be helpful to include when you plan your week in more detail.

Time to Eat

This may sound silly, but one of the first things I do when I coach leaders is stock their offices with healthy snacks! I know you're not going out for luxurious lunches (unless you are wooing a funder), but you do have to eat. Whether you order lunch in or bring it from home, you need time to refuel. Even fifteen minutes of silence at your desk can go a long way to boost your endurance on a long day. And if you are prone to not eating because of lack of readily available options, keep food stashes everywhere. I have Ziploc bags in my purse, backpack, and suitcase that always contain something:

- KIND or Larabars
- Nuts
- Dried fruit
- Organic, no-sugar beef or turkey jerky
- Fresh fruit or veggies
- Water bottles

I often preorder huge amounts of healthy snacks from Amazon or stock up at Costco, so I can just grab something and run out the door. You may consider doing what Tom Rath, author of *Eat, Move, Sleep* and *Are You Fully Charged?*, and others advise, which is to "standardize" your lunch each day so you don't even have to think about it.

Time to Move

Yes, yes, yes, this is a professional book. However, the benefits of physical movement are so great, that I would be remiss if I didn't mention blocking out time to exercise. Whenever I ask mission-driven leaders what they wish they had more time for, exercise always tops the list.

And Tom goes on to quote the University of Illinois's Justin Rhodes (2013), "Research shows that when we exercise, blood pressure and blood flow increase everywhere in the body, including the brain. More blood means more energy and oxygen, which makes our brain perform better." Convinced? I got convinced. Looking at your week to find time to move could be done in these ways:

- Reviewing the gym schedule and picking two to three classes that fit in your week (bonus points if you have already entered all relevant classes in to your Comprehensive Calendar!)
- Getting a fitness tracker, such as FitBit or JawBone , to track your steps; most people like to hit ten thousand per day
- Shifting various parts of your commute so you walk part or all of the way
- Getting a standing working desk
- Taking some of your meetings while walking outside

Reader Reflection

Review your Weekly Worksheet for next week. When will you recharge with food and exercise?

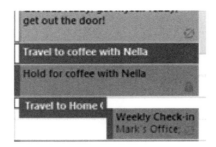

Figure 8.12 Mark's Calendared Travel Time

Time to Travel

Many a leader race from building to building, frantically looking for parking or climbing the stairs two at a time. If you move around frequently, be sure to add these buffers in your calendar for travel:

- Your regular commute to and from work
- Traveling between meeting locations
- Traveling to and from the airport or train station (more on travel in chapter 9)

If you zoom in on Mark's Weekly Worksheet, you see he blocked time for travel to and from his coffee meeting (figure 8.12).

Reader Reflection

Look ahead for one month on your Comprehensive Calendar. When will you need to block travel time?

Although perhaps none of these calendar tricks is rocket science, I do find most leaders I meet say "I don't have time to exercise," or "I'm constantly running behind," or "I just frittered away fifteen minutes on social media." I'm not asking you to be a robot here but rather to make room for things such as eating, sleeping, and exercising that will help you feel and *be* more Together. If we don't schedule them into our calendars, they are less likely to happen.

SOME OTHER SNEAKY CALENDAR TRICKS

Similar to these samples, your Weekly Worksheet should look about 80 to 90 percent full. Depending on how many emergencies tend to arise, you can determine how much time should be unscheduled. Just make sure you also have a plan for what to do if an emergency *doesn't* fill all of the time.

You can also start moving things around to maximize your time even more. In the next section, you will find a consolidated list of tips to make the most of your energy, small pieces of times, and chunks of work.

Managing Energy

I am a huge fan of Tony Schwartz's work at The Energy Project. Once your work is all laid out for the week, you make changes based on your energy levels, mental bandwidth, or brainpower at certain times of day. For example, if you know your energy typically dips around 3 PM, you could reserve this time for signing checks, approving time sheets, or accomplishing the other less mentally taxing things on your list. Or, if you're a morning person who works best without distractions, you might reserve two to three early mornings a week to dive into deeper projects, such as writing memos, creating agendas, or drafting performance evaluations.

Reader Reflection

Review the week ahead. What can you adjust to help you manage your energy?

Managing Organizational Rhythms

The classic case here is the chronic use of Mondays for meetings. All that does is drain everyone of his or her energy at the start of the week and make people dread coming to work. Move internal meetings to the end of the week when everyone needs a nice pick-me-up and can look ahead to the following week. Thursday afternoon and Friday mornings can be great times to have standing internal one-on-one meetings. Leave Mondays for big, important thinking work.

Reader Reflection

Consider the rhythm of your week. What tasks and meetings do or do not need to happen on particular days of the week?

Batch Process

Too many of us do lots of little things all day long. Why not put them all together? For example, if you sign checks, let people know which day and time you'll do this each week and leave them a clear directive on where to put the checks. Then, sign them all at once. You can apply this concept to cooking, answering e-mail, and sending contracts, too. Batch processing can also help if you tend to avoid some boring administrative tasks. And per previous comments on personal health, maybe you can grocery shop or cook all at one time, too. If only exercise worked like that … Gretchen Rubin's recent book, *Better Than Before*, recommended saving an hour per week, called Power Hour, for all of the little annoyances that can linger on a list, such as "fix office chair."

I've recently instituted a "twenty small things to do on Sunday Nights" chunk of time in my calendar. Whenever I generate or acquire a small task during the week, I often dump it into my calendar for Sunday evening. I know I need to get a little work done, but after spending the weekend with my lovely small children, I'm too exhausted to give my attention to anything that requires any degree of thoughtfulness. Tasks such as paying parking tickets, scanning receipts, booking flights, and inputting data land here.

Reader Reflection

What small tasks can you batch process for efficiency? What would you need to communicate to your team to make this system effective?

Using Small Pockets of Time

Be prepared to use those little pockets of time that arise when someone is late to a meeting, your flight is delayed, or you arrive somewhere early. A few tricks I rely on:

- Keep a plastic envelope of thank-you notes and stamps at the ready.
- Carry a folder of articles you may want to read.
- Have a few interesting podcasts preloaded on your smartphone.
- List topics that need brainstorming in a small notebook.
- Keep your To-Do List organized by how much time something will take you, and check off the little things when you can.

Jason Womack details many more options in his book *Your Best Just Got Better.*

Reader Reflection

What preparation do you need to fully use your small pockets of time?

Strategic Multitasking

I'm not talking about the kind of multitasking that involves checking out of a conference call to answer your e-mail. I'm talking about smartly combining activities that meet your goals. As you look at the full view of your week, you may find opportunities to combine some items to accomplish your priorities. For example, you want to foster strong relationships with your team and you clearly need to eat. Can you set aside one meal per week to share with a staff member? Or maybe people often request your career advice, but you still have to make your kids' lunches or wash dishes at night. When I get asked for conversations that just require me to listen deeply but not take notes, I frequently offer time slots when I may be doing other low-level work—and I disclose this to the other person in advance so they don't feel slighted.

Reader Reflection

Review next week's priorities and appointments. Are there opportunities for strategic multitasking?

Now that your Weekly Worksheet is strategically aligned to your energy levels, thoughtfully arranged with organizational rhythms, coordinated for batch processing, and full of a few bits of strategic multitasking, let's get real about all of the things that get in the way of that beautifully constructed week.

BUT, MAIA, WHAT ABOUT THINGS THAT JUST COME UP?

Now that you have your calendar entirely set, let's consider how to protect it. Or, as I say in workshops, "Let's move from ideal to real." On any given day, any number of situations can squash our best-laid plans. Some of these "situations" are actually things we do to *ourselves,* and other times the crushers come from our colleagues, our external landscape, or even our own children!

Internal Crushers

There are just so many crushers we bring on ourselves. I'm no psychologist, but I've seen people fall completely prey to any of the number of situations described in the following, including myself. Some of them will sound familiar. Maybe you've set aside time to work, but then you avoid what you'd planned to work on? Or maybe you woke up early to write a book chapter (ahem) but then just cleaned out your in-box instead? Or maybe you meant to focus on that grant report, but trolled over to *Huffington Post*?

Table 8.2 shows a list of common internal crushers and some possible solutions.

Reader Reflection

Which internal priority crushers do you face? What solutions are you committed to trying?

External Crushers

Of course there are also a whole host of external factors (table 8.3), many of which we have little control over. But we can manage some of them better than we do.

Table 8.2 Common Internal Time Crushers

Common Internal Crushers	Description	Possible Solutions
Lure of the lusty checkmark	You're completely addicted to getting things done but perhaps fall prey to easy wins at the expense of bigger priorities.	• Make a list of two to three most important items to do first thing the morning. • Do the hardest things earliest in the morning. • Save easy stuff for low-energy times.
Procrastination	Enough said.	• Set a timer at the start of the task and tell yourself how much you will have completed by a certain time. • Break your task into small chunks.
Distraction	If you find yourself with ten windows open on your computer and spend a lot of time on social media, this could be you!	• Work offline. • Ask others for help. • Use various technology solutions, such as Rescueme.com that keep you locked out of Internet access.
Perfectionism	If you find yourself spending an excessive amount of time color-coding or formatting documents, you are guilty as charged.	• Force yourself to start with content work and save any formatting for later. • Check with a colleague or your manager on what has to be A level work versus B or C level. • Determine what you can live with as "good enough."
Rapid responder syndrome	You feel compelled to reply to every e-mail, message, or text as *soon* as it comes in, thus killing your ability to focus.	• Normalize with colleagues on response time. • Set and abide by clear windows of time to check and respond to e-mail and other messages. • Consider using other channels of communication, such as Slack.

Table 8.3 Common External Time Crushers

Common External Crushers	Description	Possible Solutions
The ambush, pop-in, or fly-by	Someone or something pops up at your cubicle, turkey necks by your office, or prairie dogs by your desk!	• Humor! Set norms with your team around work time and interruptions. One team in Houston flies the Beast Mode flag (figure 8.13) when they are concentrating. • Say "Can I reply to you later?"
The good idea fairy	This could be you or someone else. Either way, a "good idea" comes up, and you or your team feels compelled to chase it down.	• Check your Priority Plan and see where the idea fits. • If it makes sense, swap something else out. If it doesn't, delay the idea. • Note it in your Thought Catcher for later.
Ambiguity	The path forward is unclear or people have various levels of commitment to the priority.	• Seek constant clarification. • Don't be afraid to put things on paper and get people to agree!
Staff drama	Other people's issues	• Proactively set expectations and practice common workplace interactions; model and practice what you want your staff to do in these situations.
Other people's poor planning	This one is fairly self-evident: when you're the victim (or perpetrator) of a last-minute and urgent request	• Proactively meet with the person or team and ask what they anticipate needing from you in the next six months. • Track the asks and see if there are any patterns, for example, does the IT team hit you with a bunch of inventory requests at a certain time of year? If so, sit down with that team and establish certain drop points when you can proactively provide them with inventory updates.

Figure 8.13 Beast Mode Flag

Both sets of solutions are rooted in three themes:

1. **Systems building.** Yes, it will take time up-front to build a system to prevent chronic interruptions, but it will save you so much in the long run!
2. **Trust.** It can feel hard to have a conversation with a colleague to sort out roles and responsibilities for an ambiguous project. But if you build trust with your team, they will know your intentions are good!
3. **Communication.** It will take some effort to sit with a team and map out how their workload affects you, but it will prevent a lot of last-minute asks and leave room to address proactive work and the real emergencies.

Reader Reflection
Which external priority crushers do you face? What solutions are you committed to trying?

Tracking the Crushers

If you're not sure what kinds of crises you may face in your role, use my Crusher Tracker (available on my website, www.thetogethergroup.com) to analyze what pulls you off task from your ideal schedule. With your team, revisit any patterns that emerge to see what you can proactively put in place to address the issue in the future. What was once a surprise becomes predictable and planned for.

If your entire team or organization is plagued by crushers, I recommend having *everyone* track them. Then categorize them using the Common Crushers buckets from table 8.2 and table 8.3. You can then facilitate strong, data-driven discussions about why the crushers exist and how you might solve them.

Table 8.4 shows us a Crusher Tracker from Hannah Lofthus, the CEO of the Ewing Marion Kauffman School in Kansas City.

Thankfully, Hannah already had work and prep time blocked into her calendar, so there was room in her day to tackle the emergencies. But we also thought together about the following questions:

1. **What could have been delegated?** Although the bus issue could not have been totally delegated, Hannah realized she could have modeled, taught, and coached her team further so that this issue doesn't come immediately to her in the future.

2. **What could have been predicted?** The hiring search was entirely predictable work. Although they couldn't have predicted when the search firm would send candidates, Hannah and her assistant did know the process would consume a certain amount of hours. They can block time for these sorts of happenings in the future.

Table 8.4 Hannah's Crusher Tracker

Crusher	Time Spent on It	Took Away From
Personnel issue re: staff transition	4 hrs	Weekend—personal
Hiring search	2 hrs	Weekend—personal
Emergency at district	20 min	Work time
Personnel issue	30 min	Work time
Emergency personnel issue	5 hrs (over 2 days)	Work time, quadrant 2 time, hiring search prep, doctors appointment
Bus issue	1 hr	Evening—personal /e-mail
Check-ins	2 hr	Prep, work time

3. **What could have been prevented?** Although the personnel issue was not predictable, it was preventable. To address this moving forward, Hannah implemented office hours to hold strategic conversations with various teachers. This will help provide insight into any brewing issues ahead of time.

There are also the truly true emergencies that pop up. Some are exciting, such as earning a grant at the last minute, and others are tragic, such as a school district experiencing the death of a community member. These things will happen, but when you have a great plan and a reliable way of communicating it to others, they are much, *much* easier to deal with.

Reader Reflection

What are the true, unanticipated emergencies you've experienced in the past six months? How did you and your team do at managing them? What could have been predicted or prevented?

KEEP IT ALIVE: THE ROUTINE

You are likely wondering the when and where of creating your Weekly Worksheet. I will go into great detail on this answer in the next chapter on routines. But the short answer is that I want you to take a small chunk of time, about sixty minutes, on Thursday or Friday, and devote it to planning for the following week.

I know an hour can feel like a lot, but it will be so worth it because you will go into each week with such a clear sense of what you want to accomplish and knowledge of how you will get it done. You will print it out, if necessary, or keep highly accessible on your devices. As the week goes on, you will likely prioritize by moving items around, and you will also record new To-Dos as they come flying at you. The key here is you have *one* single place where everything is going for the week.

And once you are finished with a Weekly Worksheet, you can simply transfer any undone To-Dos (and trust me, they will be there) into the appropriate spot and throw the old worksheets away. There is no need to keep them. If you feel nervous pitching them, take a photo or dump them in a box.

START STRONG

In this chapter, we looked at our own preferences for organizing a week, examined models from four different Together Leaders, and added in some time for exercise, eating, and sleep. Although planning a week at this level of detail may feel constraining, I firmly believe it can lead to more flexibility. When the emergency or opportunity arises, you will be completely aware of what you are sacrificing when you pivot to a pop-up. It is all about striking the right balance between systems and spontaneity!

Time commitment: Once you establish your template or tool, this process will likely take you **about sixty minutes per week.**

- Determine whether a task, time, or blended orientation works best for your working style, preferences, and environment.
- Select the right tool for your Weekly Worksheet. Are you going to make a task-driven model such as Dave's, a hybrid such as Lo's, daily pages such as Roslyn's, or go mega-digital such as Mark's?
- Use your Priority Plan and Later List to create your Weekly Worksheet for the coming week.
- Review your Weekly Worksheet to see if there are opportunities for batch processing, strategic multitasking, or using small pockets of time.
- Track your Time Crushers to see where you might be able to get some time back.

COMMON CHALLENGE: TOO MUCH TO DO!

When I first started working with Max Koltuv, a regional superintendent at Achievement First, before he began regularly looking ahead and blocking off work time to address his priorities—which included providing direct school support and participating on a senior management team—we stared together, stumped, at the week of September 22.

"Whoa," I said.

"See, I told you so," he responded.

According to Outlook, it was indeed a very full week. Tuesday, Wednesday, and Thursday were entirely blocked for principal meetings, a school visit, and two days of an executive team retreat. That left Monday and Friday to get out in the field, take phone calls with the schools he couldn't get to, and prep for the big meetings mentioned previously. Oh, yeah, and what about walking his daughter to school three times, hitting the gym twice, observing the Jewish holidays, and attending an evening board meeting? Yep, that was all in there, too.

We were looking at a perfect storm of a week for Max, and even a ninja-like level of personal planning wouldn't have helped. Although I do want you to be able to evaluate each meeting and To-Do to ensure each one is absolutely connected to your goals, the items on his calendar were structural issues over which Max, no matter how senior he was, had very little control. Luckily, this week was a point-in-time situation, not the norm.

We brainstormed five steps to ease the pain of Max's very full week:

1. **Chisel, chisel, chisel.** Review every single meeting in your calendar and ask if it can be canceled, postponed, delegated to a colleague, or completed in half the time. It's not crazy to name your dilemma to others and ask for forgiveness. And then do this proactively moving ahead to ensure only priority meetings take a spot on your calendar.

2. **Post an auto-responder.** Even in today's connected world, people often forget to do this. Max created an out-of-office message that included details about his meeting schedule

and let people know to expect a delay in reply. (There are a few examples of out-of-office replies in other chapters.)

3. **Aggressively manage expectations of those around you.** We drafted an e-mail to Max's assistant, team members, and managers to explain that Max was going under for the week. We asked that they please hold all nonurgent e-mails, draft subject lines carefully, and simply be aware of the crunch he was facing.

4. **Have a plan for e-mail.** Okay, it happens to all of us: you are in a workshop, conference, or retreat for a day, and the e-mails pile up. And yes, you have managed expectations as mentioned previously. But time-sensitive stuff is still going to come in! If you're constantly checking on your smartphone and then aimlessly rechecking again at night, you need a better method to avoid this double processing. Max blocked an appointment called "e-mail" each evening in his calendar and used this time to address anything that *had* to be answered that day. Other stuff was moved to later on his Calendar or his Later List.

5. **Block time next week to unbury.** The next week wasn't *much* better in Max's world, but we were able to proactively block off a couple of hours for him to completely unbury out of the storm. Max triaged his in-box for the messages he'd put on hold, checked in with his team to see if there were any other issues that emerged, and realigned with his assistant.

The trick here is to get ahead of these very full weeks by anticipating them in advance. You will be able to do this if you are in a committed relationship with your Comprehensive Calendar and regularly looking ahead!

CHAPTER 9

Keep It Together
Routines and Checklists

SEEN AND HEARD

"On the rare weeks when I actually sit down and prepare my calendar, schedule, etc., I am *superwoman*. But that doesn't always happen."

"At the end of the day all I want to do is collapse on the couch and watch TV. But then my mornings are always frantic because I don't know what's coming up."

"There are so many weekends when I can't relax because I just feel so anxious about the crazy week I have coming up!"

OVERVIEW AND OBJECTIVES

None of these tools will work without a set of rituals to keep them up and running. You know how the second you write "planning" into your calendar, the time gets sucked up by the issues of the day? We have to make our routines more specific and actionable for you to truly reap the benefits of getting Together. Things change often, but these habits are what will keep us focused *and* nimble.

In this brief chapter, you will do the following:

- Ritualize some of your most important steps of the day.
- Create daily opening and closing routines to assess your workload and reprioritize.
- Build weekly/monthly planning time into your calendar and write an agenda to follow.
- Design checklists to track ongoing projects.
- Automate any other routines so that you can better deal with the unexpected.

If you are interested in more resources on building habits, I highly recommend Charles Duhigg's *The Power of Habit* or Gretchen Rubin's *Better Than Before*. Both discuss the power of rituals and habits and the science behind how to create them. But if you need a quick and dirty plan on getting your day and week supercharged, here it is.

Opening and Closing Routines

Reshma Singh is a busy leader who launched a non-profit and subsequently started a consulting practice in the last two years after working for larger nonprofits. She spelled out her daily routine (figure 9.1) to ensure she thinks about these vital personal and professional items daily.

DAILY

- Meditate for five at least minutes
- On weekdays
    - Print my calendar at the start of the day
    - Each day at the end of the day, identify the three most important things that must be done the following day by highlighting them in yellow
    - If needed, adjust the next day's work and email blocks
    - Ask yourself if there is anything you can delegate
- Exercise for at least **7 minutes** each day and do at least **30 minutes** of cardio on alternate days

Figure 9.1 Reshma's Daily Routine

Reshma includes a blend of health routines, such as meditation and exercise, along with her practical professional routines, such as printing her calendar. During this important time at the start of her day, Reshma asks herself if there is anything she can delegate and adjusts work blocks accordingly.

Riley Kennedy, the chief of staff for Collegiate Academies in New Orleans, got even more granular and logistical in her approach to a daily routine. She created a daily closing routine and pasted the steps into her calendar to ensure she built the habit of preparing for the next day (figure 9.2).

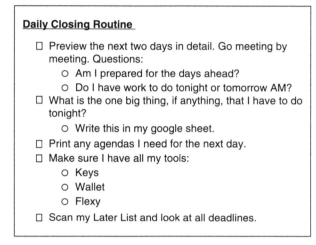

Daily Closing Routine

☐ Preview the next two days in detail. Go meeting by meeting. Questions:
   ○ Am I prepared for the days ahead?
   ○ Do I have work to do tonight or tomorrow AM?
☐ What is the one big thing, if anything, that I have to do tonight?
   ○ Write this in my google sheet.
☐ Print any agendas I need for the next day.
☐ Make sure I have all my tools:
   ○ Keys
   ○ Wallet
   ○ Flexy
☐ Scan my Later List and look at all deadlines.

Figure 9.2 Riley's Daily Closing Routine

Riley is trying to accomplish a few different things with her daily closing routine:

- **Preparation:** "Preview the next two days in detail" and "Print any agendas I need for the next day."

- **Setting boundaries for evening work:** "What is the one big thing, if anything, I have to do tonight?"

- **Looking ahead:** "Scan my Later List and look at all deadlines."

- **Physical assembly:** "Make sure I have all my tools." As someone who is prone to forgetting my keys, this one really resonates with me!

These small routines only have to take five to fifteen minutes at each end of your day. Giving yourself a true opening and closing will help you avoid the wake-up-clutching-smartphone or go-to-sleep-hugging-iPad syndromes that plague a lot of busy leaders!

Reader Reflection

What do you need to include in your opening and closing routines? How much time will they take in your day? Do you need to block it out in your calendar?

WEEKLY ROUTINES: CLEAN UP AND LOOK AHEAD

You probably realized in the previous chapter that creation and maintenance of your Weekly Worksheet will take a bit of time! In short, once per week, it's time to go back into the weeds of your calendar to ensure your time is planned in specific detail. There is real value in a weekly pause to reset and reprioritize.

Enter the Meeting with Myself. Time and task guru David Allen calls this a Weekly Review. In his most recent edition of *Getting Things Done* he states its purpose: "get clear, get current, and get creative. Getting clear will ensure all your collected stuff is processed. Getting current will ensure that all your orienting 'maps' or lists are reviewed and up-to-date. The creative part happens to some degree automatically, as you get clear and current" (Allen, 2015, p. 195).

Definition

The **Meeting with Myself** is a set time of week where you clean up the week behind you and prepare for the week ahead.

When I first met Max Koltuv, the busy manager of principals in Brooklyn featured in the previous Common Challenge, he, similar to many other readers, viewed time to plan as something that would either magically appear or, conversely, felt somewhat indulgent. Leaders of mission-driven work often feel that if they are not *doing* the work, then the time spent is not worth it. However, after some practice, Max realized that this weekly pause to plan was reaping huge benefits—professionally and personally!

Max's Self Meeting

Max describes the power of his weekly ritual: "Having the time blocked out and holding it sacred to get my head up out of the day-to-day and really think about what I should be doing the next week is super helpful. It makes my time more intentional and less driven by what school I am visiting those days or meetings others put on my calendar. It lets me ensure that I am intentionally pushing the really important priorities forward each week. It also provides a structure that ensures that I don't drop small follow-up actions from my day-to-day—going through my notebook, my in-box, and looking ahead at my calendar is really helping me make sure I don't drop any balls."

As we follow Max's Self-Meeting (figure 9.3), we will break it into two portions—cleanup and look ahead—and, all the while, build a version that works for you.

Max's Weekly Meeting with Himself

Clean Up

- Check inbox to make sure no key work is buried with in emails
- Check *Waiting for Reply List*
- Clean off clipboard/notebook for any papers I may have accumulated
- Check Table of School against priority in All Principals Tab
- Read Team Super meeting notes

Look Ahead

- Scan Priority Plan to make sure I have time blocked to meet priorities
- Check Monthly Later List
- Calendar (look ahead for four weeks)
- Empty brain
- Move High Energy/Meaty Things (that haven't made it yet) into the calendar

Figure 9.3 Max's Self Meeting

Cleanup

I hope you have been tidying as you go and don't have much to clean up each week. The trick here is in not getting sucked into *doing* the work. At this point, you want to simply define it.

Over the course of a busy week, it's easy to accumulate a lot of meeting notes, next steps, and small pieces of paper. E-mails inevitably pile up. You want to blitz through this portion but still take a moment to clean up.

Clean Up the Week behind You

- Any papers you have accumulated? Recycle, pass on, scan, or file them.
- Any e-mails that need addressing as high priority next week? Insert them into your calendar or Weekly Worksheet so they don't get lost.
- Review any residual meeting notes to scoop out lingering action steps.
- Straighten up physical space (if this matters to you!).

Reader Reflection

What do you have to do to clean up the week behind you?

Look Ahead

This next section will outline questions to ask yourself as you look ahead at what's upcoming.

Are my priorities reflected? It's time to do a double check. Pull out that Priority Plan and ensure your time is actually dedicated to the right causes.

Can I cluster, consolidate, or cancel any meetings? Are there any meetings you can pack together to get some work time back? For example, maybe you have three thirty-minute meetings in the afternoon scattered at 1:00, 2:30, and 4:00 PM. Can you reach out to the participants in advance to see if you can make this one ninety-minute chunk of meetings? Are there any meetings that could be delegated to others or in which you could make a fifteen-minute appearance?

How will I use Planned Priority blocks? Remember those generic Planned Priority blocks? Work Blocks you have been holding in your digital calendar? Now is the time to fill them in with what you plan to work on during this time. You can type your tasks directly into your appointment. Or, if you like to print your digital tools, you can handwrite on them.

Is every single appointment detail in place? Let's ensure every single detail is in your calendar. I'm talking flight numbers, confirmation numbers, cross streets, addresses, and room numbers for meetings. To illustrate the specificity I'm asking for here, instead of inserting American Airlines Flight 337 at 1:00 to 3:34 PM, I want your calendar to include all of that, plus confirmation number, terminal, and any flight changes noted. This way, you're not searching your Gmail in-box looking for confirmation numbers while juggling a baby on your hip in line at security. Or so I've heard.

Am I waiting on any meeting agendas or other information? As you scan the upcoming meetings, do you see any places where you need additional information from others? If so, write the person an e-mail to get what you need!

Do I need to do any of my own preparation? Maybe you need to prepare for some events yourself. For example, when I looked ahead on my calendar and saw a meeting with my CEO coming up, I knew I needed to ask the VP of recruitment for an update on teacher hiring numbers.

Do I have enough breathing room? Do some of the days look completely jammed? Can you shorten or move any meetings to gain some loose moments? If there were an emergency or crisis this week, what could be removed from your calendar?

> ## Look Ahead at the Upcoming Week
>
> - Are my priorities reflected?
> - Can I cluster, consolidate, or cancel any meetings?
> - How will I use my Planned Priority blocks?
> - Is every single appointment detail in place?
> - Am I waiting on any meeting agendas or other information?
> - Do I need to do any of my own preparation?
> - Do I have enough breathing room?

The ultimate outcome here should be your Weekly Worksheet, in whatever form they may take. See chapter 8 for more models and details on possible tools. But, basically, I'm asking you to go into your week with about 75 to 90 percent of your time mapped out, depending on how reactive you may need to be in your role.

Assistant Alert

The Meeting with Myself can be done with your assistant, especially if he or she does significant preparation in advance to adjust your calendar, identify opportunities to manage energy, and figure out how to maximize your To-Do List. You can also have your assistant analyze if your time is in line with your priorities.

Let's review how this goes one more time by looking at another sample from Diana Halluska, a leader at Relay Graduate School of Education (figure 9.4). Diana built herself a full checklist (you can build your own on my website at www.thetogethergroup.com). Diana describes, "The purpose of the checklist is to stay motivated *and* to spur additional self-reflection. For example, cleaning out my inbox is a task that I didn't complete for two consecutive weeks in the sample. In one respect the checklist me to prioritize tackling the items so I can make the sheet turn pretty colors. In addition, it helps me to prioritize and it encourages me to think about how I am managing my energy on a weekly basis."

Even with the best tools in place, priorities change and issues come up. There is a lot of value to spending an hour per week (less if you can pull it off) walking through your calendar to preview the coming week and month. It helps to click through every single day to make sure the right meetings are in place, at the right times of day, with the right materials prepared ahead of time.

Part 1: Looking Backwards	3/23/2015	3/30/2015	4/6/2015
Review each check-in agenda for each meeting for previous week. Note any follow-up in Comprehensive Calendar or Weekly Worksheet	x	x	x
Review last week's Weekly/Daily Worksheet. Note any additional actions that did not get compeleted and transfer to upcoming Comprehensive Calendar, Weekly Worksheet, Thought Catcher, or Later List.	x	x	x
Review last week's calendar appointments. Do they trigger any additional follow-up items?	x	x	x
Review all Meeting Notes and/or Later Lists. Make sure all action items are processed and throw sheets away.	x	x	x
Clean our your email inbox. Just do this.			x
Clean out any hard copy papers.	x	x	x

Part 2: Looking Ahead	3/23/2015	3/30/2015	4/6/2015
Step back and ask yourself about biggest actions that could push you forward.	x	x	x
Review your Annual Goal's or Priority Plans. Anything you need to activate this week.	x	x	x
Review any Project Plans you are leading or touching. Any actions this week?	x	x	x
Review your Later List. Anything you need to pluck off?	x	x	x
Check your Thought Catchers. Anything to add to 1 : 15 or check in upon?	x	x	x
Review Comprehensive Calendar (for you and the team calendar) for upcoming four weeks. Note deadlines and big action items in Weekly Worksheet - either in priority section or on specific days.	x	x	x
Create your product showing how you will best use your time this week!	x	x	x

Figure 9.4 Diana's Weekly Self-Meeting Checklist

Alan Henry, a popular productivity blogger, describes the mood you may want to be in for your Meeting with Self: "When your weekly review is scheduled to begin, get in the mood. Get up, take a quick walk around your desk or office. Grab a cup of coffee or refill your water bottle. Make sure you're jazzed for it—you're about to close the books on your week, it should be a happy occasion!" (Henry, 2012). So, in addition to considering your agenda, also ponder the ideal where and when of your Round-Up.

Reader Reflection

What steps do you need to take to prepare for the week ahead? What is on your agenda for your Meeting with Self?

ENSURING WEIRD WEEKS DON'T TAKE YOU BY SURPRISE

You know what I mean by *weird weeks,* right? I mean those nonstandard ones when maybe you are at a conference for two days, or maybe there is a Monday holiday, or testing at your school all week, or you have to be out for a half-day at a board retreat. I bet you have at least one nonstandard week each month! The most common leader reactions to these are to (1) not realize they are coming and (2) try to fit everything in anyway. Let's try to avoid both by using the following strategies.

Identify. When you look ahead on your calendar and prepare, check forward for at least one to three months. I know this may feel nuts, but if you can identify the weird weeks in advance, they won't catch you by surprise.

Make a Plan. Remember, time is not an infinite resource! If there are fewer hours in the week, you simply cannot fit everything in. Maybe you have some automatic rules such as if there is a Monday holiday, all check-ins are shortened to forty-five minutes each. Or maybe you determine in advance that you don't send a weekly memo to your staff, and make the week prior a double issue.

Communicate. You probably need to send an e-mail to your team letting them know meetings will be shortened or e-mail replies may be delayed. Figure 9.5 shows an example from Max in which he's previewed his availability and directly named how to be reached.

Reader Reflection

Look one to three months ahead on your calendar. When are your weird weeks? What can you do now to prepare for them?

Keep It Alive: The Routine

Most leaders conduct their Self Meetings on Thursday or Friday. That way, if they carry work into the weekend, they will have a clear sense of what that work actually is. If you clean and prep a little bit each *day* with opening and closing routines, your Meeting with Myself will probably only take thirty minutes. If you let stuff accumulate, it will likely take you sixty to ninety minutes. But either way, I assure you that the peace of mind you'll gain by having a planned week ahead that reflects your priorities and keeps things from falling through the cracks will be well worth it.

From: Max K
Sent: Saturday, September 20 3:45 PM
To: Jabari S, Injy C, Sara I, Stephanie B, Stacey P, Amanda H, Hilary C, Gina R, Colleen M, Katherine B, Stephanie L, Kate C, Kate M, Sorbrique G
Cc: Sarah H
Subject: Email responsitivity next week

Hello folks I work with closely –

Next week, I will be out of pocket for all day meetings three out of five days ☺ and in schools for visits the rest of the week. Because I will have limited desk work time, you may experience a slow down in my response to non urgent email traffic. I will respond to all of it, but if it isn't urgent, it probably won't be until the week of the 29th.

That is not to say I am unavailable to you for more urgent stuff. If your need is more urgent, please note the response time needed in the subject line and send it will a red exclamation point. Since I will have limited email time, if you think your issue can wait, please note it and hold it for our next phone check in.

Thanks!

Max

Figure 9.5 Max's E-mail Availability Preview

Ron Gubitz, a principal in New Orleans, shares the what and the when of his Self Meeting in figure 9.6. He calls his meeting "Ron versus Ron" because Future Ron wrestles with Current Ron to ensure better outcomes for the week ahead!

Ron holds meetings with himself on Fridays, in his office—with great music on his record player—and describes the power of leaving work with just *one* sticky note of his To-Dos for the weekend: "This last weekend—I finished my meeting with myself on Friday, and took a sticky note with the four things I needed to get done. I then scheduled that time with my wife and it was the best weekend I've had because I wasn't anxious or thinking I had all this work to do. I knew exactly what I needed to do, when it would be done, and I hit all four things. I could do this job for five more years or longer at this pace—whereas last year I would have said 'I'm done—just too exhausted.'" This is *exactly* what I want for mission-driven leaders. Yes, we work hard and often because we care deeply about our work. But we also plan intentionally to stay rejuvenated.

You can also take it a step further to get even more ahead for the week. Emily Stainer, a principal in Massachusetts, explains how she does it: "Right after my Meeting with Myself, I prep for my weekly one-on-one meetings with my direct reports. I add things for each person

Ron vs. Ron Weekly Meeting Agenda

Clean Up

1. Clean up my desk

   a. File papers or throw them away.
   b. If there is an action to do, add the action to my calendar with a time block.
   c. Separate receipts into corporate/reimbursement folders
   d. Fill out reimbursement forms ongoing.

2. Clean out my book sack

3. Water plants

Prepare

1. Review the Comprehensive Calendar for the next two weeks.

   a. Look at "All Day" deadlines and events
   b. Add birthdays to morning meeting agendas

2. What are the next week's priorities?

3. Review my comprehensive calendar at least 3 months ahead.

   a. What actions need to happen this upcoming week? When?

4. Review my Later List at least 3 months ahead.

   a. What actions need to happen this upcoming week? When?

5. Review Thought Catchers

   a. Are there things that can/should happen this week? When?

6. Pull Whetstone Action Step report and analyze for trends.

7. Finalize next week's calendar – ARE THESE ON YOUR CALENDAR?

   a. Whole school walkthroughs
   b. Observations
   c. Prep for Debriefs
   d. Debriefs
   e. Prep Check-ins with Tuba Leaders
   f. Email blocks
   g. CMTE agenda reviews
   h. LT PD plan time
   i. RELAY Prep
   j. Sacks/Le/Johnson morning meeting check-in
   k. Two other morning meeting check-ins a week

8. Print out blank organizational tools I need for next week

9. Email Tony my running block each week

10. Email Jennie M any arts stuff going down next week.

11. Tell Leslie about late nights via email

12. Create a yellow post-it of weekend To-Dos

Figure 9.6 Ron's Meeting with Myself Agenda

to their Thought Catchers. This saves me five to ten minutes total per day, and it means I'm ready for my meetings a few days out."

Reader Reflection

When will you conduct your Meeting with Myself? Where will you be situated? How much time will you set aside?

MONTHLY OR QUARTERLY PRACTICES

In addition to daily and weekly routines, you will likely need a longer meeting with yourself to really reflect on how you are personally progressing toward goals, where your time is being spent, and how well you are leading your team. For many of you, this will be the time when you update your Priority Plan for the upcoming three months.

Figure 9.7 shows Reshma's monthly version of her meeting with herself. She keeps focus on the bigger picture, personally and professionally.

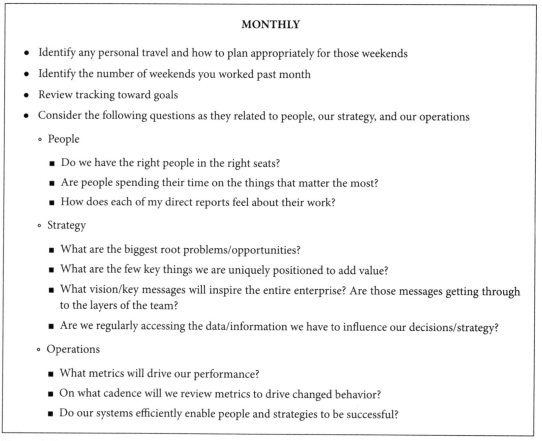

MONTHLY

- Identify any personal travel and how to plan appropriately for those weekends
- Identify the number of weekends you worked past month
- Review tracking toward goals
- Consider the following questions as they related to people, our strategy, and our operations
  - People
    - Do we have the right people in the right seats?
    - Are people spending their time on the things that matter the most?
    - How does each of my direct reports feel about their work?
  - Strategy
    - What are the biggest root problems/opportunities?
    - What are the few key things we are uniquely positioned to add value?
    - What vision/key messages will inspire the entire enterprise? Are those messages getting through to the layers of the team?
    - Are we regularly accessing the data/information we have to influence our decisions/strategy?
  - Operations
    - What metrics will drive our performance?
    - On what cadence will we review metrics to drive changed behavior?
    - Do our systems efficiently enable people and strategies to be successful?

Figure 9.7 Reshma's Monthly Routine

I love how Reshma considers the *most* important buckets of her work: goal tracking, work-life fit, and leading her team with the right people, strategy, and operations. You could schedule a similar routine for a quarterly reflection.

Getting the *when* for this meeting can feel tough, so I often suggest that you just extend your Meeting with Myself to 90 to 120 minutes once a month.

Reader Reflection
When and how will you reflect back on and look ahead for a month or quarter?

OTHER USEFUL CHECKLISTS

Once you have your daily, weekly, and monthly or quarterly routines established and blocked in your calendar, you may find yourself needing some other checklists to make life feel more productive. As Atul Gawande (2009, p. 177) says in his book *The Checklist Manifesto,* "when a checklist is well made … [it] gets the dumb stuff out of the way, the routines your brain shouldn't have to occupy itself with … , and lets it rise above to focus on the hard stuff." In this section, I focus on standardizing some recurring events, such as packing for a trip, preparing for a recurring meeting, and even getting ready for holidays!

Packing Checklists

If you have ever scrambled to pack a suitcase before a flight or realized you forgot your glasses when you arrived somewhere, a standard packing checklist may help you out a lot. As someone who is frequently on the road, I've tried to create routines for travel to make it as predictable and low stress as possible. Figure 9.8 shows a little peek at my travel checklist.

As you can see, I got fairly detailed about remembering everything from my water bottle to my travel pillow. Who wants to be the person on the red-eye flight home with no pillow to catch some zzzs? I keep this checklist in Evernote so I can access it from any device before a trip, but I also print hard copies so I can physically mark off items as I pack the night before.

Of course, there is all kinds of research about decision fatigue and how to minimize it whenever possible. *Decision fatigue* is a recent term coined by sociologist Roy Baumeister that refers to the deteriorating quality of decisions made by an individual after a long session of decision making. The key here is to limit your options whenever possible. I know I try hard to only wear the same outfits when I travel, eat the same breakfast every day, and keep a stocked pantry of healthy snacks.

Meeting Preparation Checklists

Let's say you run some kind of process regularly for your team or organization, such as Indrina Kanth, the chief of staff for New Schools for New Orleans. In her case, it is a bi-monthly board meeting presentation. Previously it had been unclear who owned which steps to prepare for

Maia Personal Packing List (suitcase, backpack and black nylon bag)	Packed?	Notes
Leave cookies for Ada and note for Jack		
Print boarding pass		
Pack healthy food		
Travel Outfit (Leggings, flats, sweater)		
Pajamas/Flipflops/Bathrobe		
Presentation Outfit (Outfit, undergarment, shoes, stockings)		
Toiletries (hair products, deodorant, razor, chap stick, moisturizer, toothbrush/toothpaste)—check each for supply		
Glasses/Contacts into green bag in backpack		
Snacks (granola bars, nuts, Wasa crackers)		
Water bottle		
Stationery		
Fun magazines and decompression activities		
Travel pillow/blanket, if needed		
Cash/Receipt envelopes		
Driver's license		

Maia Workshop Packing	Completed	Notes
Clipboard/Pacing Guide		
Gadgets (iPod, iPad, Kindle) + Power Cords + Air card pouch		
Fanny pack with jump drive / 2 clickers and batteries / WATCH		

Figure 9.8 Maia's Packing List

the meeting and the time line by which items needed to be completed. So, working backwards from the event, Indrina and her team created a meeting preparation checklist (figure 9.9).

There are a few things I love about Indrina's example:

1. **The time line is set** so she and her team can work backwards from each board deadline and enter actual dates into the calendar.

2. **The roles and responsibilities of each person are very clear,** right down to who sends the e-mail reminder, who orders coffee, and who prints materials. Although this may seem too tiny to warrant a checklist, small details make a huge difference.

3. **One person, the assistant to the executive director, is responsible** for managing the entire process each time.

<u>3 Weeks Prior to the Board Meeting</u>

- Development Director meets with Executive Director to determine agenda and materials for meeting
- Deleveopment Director assigns each member on the development team their responsibilities along with the deadline to submit their materials to the Executive Director (cc: Assistant to the Exec. Dir.)
- Executive Director dedicates a portion of the Development Director's check-in to board meeting prep

<u>2 Weeks Prior to the Board Meeting</u>

- Deadline for development team to submit their materials to the Executive Director (cc: Assistant to the Exec. Dir.)
- Assitant to the Exec. Dir. sends e-mail reminder to all regional and advisory board members
- Assitant to the Exec. Dir. receives materials and begins to finalize them for Assistant to the Exec. Dir review
- Executive Director and Assistant to the Exec. Dir. review materials and make any final edits before printing

<u>1 Week Prior to the Board Meeting</u>

- Executive Director reviews e-mail with meeting materials attached before the Assistant to the Exec. Dir. sends it out
- Assistant to the Exec. Dir. sends a RSVP e-mail to all regional and advisory board members with the meeting logistics and agenda. This e-mail should be sent on behalf of the Executive Director.
- Assistant to the Exec. Dir. prints copies of all materials for board members
- Executive Director finalizes talking points

<u>2 Days Before the Board Meeting</u>

- Assistant to the Exec. Dir. calls Eileen A to make sure that Hunter will have the projector set up and that the room will be arranged as necessary

<u>1 Day Before the Board Meeting</u>

- Assistant to the Exec. Dir. orders 2 travel contains of coffee

<u>24 Hours after the Board Meeting</u>

- Assistant to the Exec. Dir. e-mails PPT & action items to board members that result from the board meeting

<u>48 Hours after the Board Meeting</u>

- Director of Development meets with Executive Director to execute any action items that result from the board meeting

Figure 9.9 Indrina's Board Meeting Prep Checklist

Many a board meeting leads to a scramble, and these types of events are entirely predictable and often scheduled a year in advance. Let's save the scrambling for *real* emergencies!

Personal or Family Checklists

Yes, yes, yes, I know, this is a book for professional leaders. But over and over, I hear people say that their personal lives don't get the same effort or pizzazz that they throw into their work—and they *want* to lead a full and joyous life. Well, checklists are not *the* answer for that, but they can certainly ensure you don't end up with a frozen pot roast on your hands. Just for fun, figure 9.10 is a holiday countdown list from Denise Pierce (the mom of Meghan, my book production coordinator, and a systems ninja in her own right).

Reader Reflection

Which regularly occurring events would benefit from a written routine to keep you and others on the same page?

NEED A FEW TRACKERS?

There may also be times you find yourself needing a few trackers for other stuff. In this section, you will see Together Leader trackers for feedback for your team, waiting for items from others, and keeping gratitude front and center. You could also add data to review and meetings to prepare for, so I encourage you to consider your own circumstances.

Tracking Feedback

One of the most important things we can do as leaders is provide great feedback to our teams. It can also become one of the most time-consuming, oh-my-goodness-is-it-that-time-again tasks, especially if you feel like you are starting from scratch.

Chris Hines, the chief operating officer for Crescent City Schools in New Orleans, describes why he keeps track of feedback for his team members, "We do performance reviews three times a year. When I first started doing these for the people I managed, it was a lot of time-consuming work to prepare for them as I had to try to remember—or comb through e-mails and calendar invites to find—everything they had done over the past four months. Then I created this page and incorporated it into my clipboard." You could also incorporate this method into how you format your Thought Catchers. Let's review his page (figure 9.11).

Chris explains how he uses this tracker on the fly: "Going down the left-hand side are abbreviations for our organization's values. Whenever I see a colleague exemplifying one of our values, I jot it down here. I track accomplishments going down the right side of the page.

CHRISTMAS COUNTDOWN

Up to 2 Weeks before Christmas
- Decorate calendar and pick pictures for each month– should be done in October
- Fold luminaria sacks
- Mail all out of state family gifts
- Make menus for all meals served over the holiday
- Start grocery lists

Up to 7-10 days before Christmas
- Finalize menus and start grocery shopping
- Take Betty and Sumner shopping
- Help Betty with Christmas cards and mail
- Mail/give gifts to Frank/Teri/Tina and WM/Recycle/Paper/Mail Carrier

Up to 5-7 Days before Christmas   **Defrost meat for Christmas dinner**
- Figure out the amount of time it will take to defrost all needed frozen items in the refrigerator
- Establish what dishes can be made ahead
- Take calendar to Fed Ex for printing

Up to 3-5 Days before Christmas
- Wash/iron and vacuum/mop
- Clean guest room & make sure electric blanket is on bed
- Finish wrapping gifts
- Fill luminaria sacks with sand & set up on front patio
- Finish shopping for fresh vegetables

Up to 2 Days before Christmas
- Prepare Santa Sacks
- Print menus
- Make ahead as many dishes as possible
- Set table

Christmas Eve
- Set out luminarias & light before leaving for services
- Prepare roast with garlic rub
- Christmas Eve services at 5:00pm

Christmas Day
- Make cinnamon rolls
- Make brunch
- See separate timeline for dinner prep
- Calculate roasting time for the roast beef

Notes:

Figure 9.10 Denise's Christmas Countdown Checklist

Allison

EX	• Staff PD on benefits	**ACCOMPLISHMENTS**
R	• Payroll verifications	• New benefits set up
I	• New WC checklists • Office hours for C Techs	• EE file audit • Benefits enrollment presentation, logistics, execution
T	• Rates chart for PR	• Hired D of DrC
EN	• Sportsketball Cheer	• New York provider
C	• Learning benefits • Setting up urgent care partners	• Termed benefits of termed EEs

Figure 9.11 Chris's Evaluation Tracker

Now, when I prepare for reviews, I only have to refer to this page to come up with a comprehensive list of her accomplishments during the past four months."

Tracking Follow-Up

In chapter 6, we noted that you can put other people's deadlines directly into your calendar so you will be prompted to follow up, if necessary. Because Chris works with a lot of different vendors, he developed a different tracking system for keeping track of outstanding items (figure 9.12).

Chris notes, "In my role I interact with a lot of people outside of the organization. Every time I e-mail or call a person who does not work here and who needs to respond with an answer, a document, a meeting, etc., I write his or her name and a brief note about what I need on this page of my clipboard. Every Tuesday morning, I look at this page and follow up with anyone who has not yet responded."

Frank: Stonehenge & tax credits

Lona: Tubman: Bids in October, Construction in January/February

Mike: Parent handbooks

Coleman: governance committee schedule & LAPCS form &<?xmltex \pgtag{\nobreak}?> COI

James: audit prep

Tickets: A New Brain, Terminator

Doris/Eileen: claim

Jacqueline: eScholar FTP

Mark: Contract

Geizo: Claim

Figure 9.12 Chris's Follow-Up List

Tracking Relationships

It is very easy to become caught in the swirl of the day-to-day and forget to recognize the contributions of our team members, colleagues, and other important people in our work lives. Although some of you may recoil at the idea, I've seen many Together Leaders plan and track their positive recognition of team members. It doesn't mean you are robotic or disingenuous, it just means that you create space or time for something that typically doesn't happen daily.

Even if it's as simple as a chart with all team member names down the left and places to put dates on the right, it sure means a lot to get a positive note from your manager. And in my experience, it is the first thing that goes when we are busy. So why not ritualize it? Here's how Chris does it: "I am not naturally a demonstrably appreciative or 'warm and fuzzy' person. So, I decided to start writing thank-you notes to people I work with. I don't write them every week (though there's a reserved place in my week to decide if I need to do so), but I track the ones I do write and ensure that I get around to everyone with some regularity."

Reader Reflection

What trackers could help you keep it Together?

START STRONG

This could be a very easy chapter to skip or dismiss because it isn't about a new tool or a life-changing app. However, these rituals, routines, and trackers are truly the foundation of Togetherness. At the end of the day, it doesn't matter if your tools are index cards in your front pocket (yup, seen that) or an app'd out iPad mini. What matters is you have time blocked to plan and prioritize on a regular basis, you don't get caught preparing for the same event over and over, and you keep track what's most important.

Time commitment: Opening and closing routines should take **five to ten minutes on the front and back ends of your day.** Your Meeting with Myself will take you sixty minutes per week. And once per month or quarter, take 90 to 120 minutes to do a more detailed look ahead on your calendar.

- Block out time now to complete your opening and closing routines, your Meeting with Myself, and a longer monthly or quarterly look at your calendar.

- Determine which other regularly occurring events or processes could use a standard checklist.

- Consider what items in your work or personal life could use a tracker to improve regularity.

- If applicable, engage your assistant in this entire process.

COMMON CHALLENGE: A NEW JOB

Valerie Evans was humming along as a director at an education nonprofit. She had very tight systems in place and used a combination of Outlook and the Remember the Milk app to keep Together. She also regularly planned ahead by weeks and months. Her organization was fairly large, including many regions and remote workers. There was a strong culture of scheduling meetings only within specific windows of time since colleagues worked across time zones.

And then Valerie switched roles, taking a C-level position with a small charter school organization. It was an exciting move, but it meant some big shifts were in order: She was now working in a school building, full of kids and colleagues (and with them, both welcome and unwelcome interruptions!), and operating from Mac and Google-based systems. In short, everything was different! Valerie describes her biggest shifts, "I was formerly in a position in which, for the most part, I worked from home in a predominately internally facing role. I transitioned to a position that requires much more scheduling around the calendars of both internal and external parties, and I go into an office/school every day. Therefore, my time engaging others has significantly increased, and my concentrated work blocks cannot always happen at the same time each day on my calendar. I needed to create a system that adjusted for an increase in impromptu meetings and conversations and still let me get the work done."

Luckily, Valerie had a strong foundation of Togetherness to fall back on as she regrouped from so many changes at once.

Here's a six-step plan to reset your systems if you move jobs or organizations:

1. **Embrace the new technology.** Valerie says, "I transitioned from being a PC/Outlook guru to becoming a Google Apps/MacBook newbie. And, I'm really starting to hit a stride

with this new-to-me technology. But, that required a need to discover which organizing systems were compatible with the new tools I used on a daily basis. I needed seamless syncing across all devices (personal and professional), and I needed to be able to think of anything at any time, and know that I wouldn't lose the thoughts." The move to Google was somewhat jarring, especially the part about being online all the time. Initially, Valerie tried to re-create Outlook using a Mac version, but it wasn't the same and synchronization got wonky. Plus, everyone else was on Google. Though not preferable, it was ultimately more efficient to convert to Google Calendar and Tasks. And if you use your digital calendar for personal items such as birthdays and appointments, make sure that you are prepared to synchronize your calendar when you leave and then again when you enter your new organization.

2. **Remember the routines matter more than the tools**. Because the tool change was so dramatic, Valerie initially forgot to implement her wonderful planning routines. Once she realized this, Valerie put a Weekly Round-Up back on her calendar, blocked out time to create a Priority Plan, and listed her opening and closing routines for each day.

3. **Create a Priority Plan.** When Valerie first started in her new role, she smartly created a ninety-day plan (check out chapter 5!) but that window of time had since passed. Though she was definitely getting things *done* each day, she realized she was not connecting the tasks with the bigger picture and purpose of her job. Valerie took time to pause, drafted a Priority Plan (for more on this, see chapter 4), and solicited her manager and other content area experts for feedback.

4. **Create a Comprehensive Calendar.** Once Valerie's Priority Plan was ready, she needed to impose it onto her Google Calendar. She knew she had more energy in the mornings to think and produce work, and she preferred to have meetings in the afternoons. However, Valerie didn't always feel she had license to do this in her new role. You may also realize your new role has more or fewer meetings than your last one and that could affect how you structure your time. After some thought, Valerie decided to at least impose the ideal onto her calendar. She could name the trade-offs with her manager when she got ambushed later!

5. **Determine the right folder structure for your in-box and new documents** We'll get into this more in chapter 11 and chapter 14, but less is more when it comes to e-mail folders. At least start with some sort of a game plan to deal with the deluge of information you are receiving, some of which is important for right now and some of which you will definitely need later.

6. **Don't assume what you walk into is how things have to be.** At first, Valerie took for granted that she needed to fit directly into the culture of her new, smaller organization. What she realized later is that she could actually bring some of her habits and discipline to her new colleagues. This *doesn't* mean that Valerie annoyingly started to systemize everything, nor did she dismiss the informalities that made her school hum. What she *did* do was start asking questions such as, "When do you need this by?" and "Is this urgent or can it wait for our meeting?" Small signals like these can add a dose of discipline without crushing the spontaneity that often breeds great ideas and relationships.

CHAPTER 10

Hold That Thought
Save It for Later!

SEEN AND HEARD

"My e-mail is clogged with so many one-off FYIs from people—wading through them is exhausting."

"Often times I'll walk out of a meeting, and remember five minutes later things that I wanted to be sure to tell the person but forgot about."

"Every week, I spend thirty minutes staring at my computer screen trying to remember everything I want to put in my weekly update to my team."

OVERVIEW AND OBJECTIVES

Over the course of any given work—and life—day, millions of thoughts pop in to our heads. The previous chapters covered what to do with deadlines (Comprehensive Calendar), long-term To-Dos (Later List), and short-term To-Dos (Weekly Worksheet). But what about those totally random questions and ideas—the ones you are simply not sure *what* to do with or even if they are worth mentioning? Enter the Thought Catcher, a place where you can grab those thoughts, get them out of your head, and sit on them until a better time (see figure 10.1).

Figure 10.1 The Togetherness Tools

Definition

A **Thought Catcher** is a unified place to record your thoughts for people, teams, or topics to reference at a more appropriate time.

There are many types of Thought Catchers you can put in place. Most leaders typically keep Thought Catchers for people, teams, written communications, and future brainstorms. Paula White, a former school principal, describes the power of using Thought Catchers: "After our graduation event, a parent came up to me with a wonderful idea about placement of the stage during the ceremony. It was a great idea—but it was for a year away! I realized I needed a place to store longer-term thoughts where I could reliably return to them. And the more I thought about it, the more I realized that I actually had a lot of thoughts about how to improve graduation!" Paula wasn't sure she wanted to act on the idea, but she didn't want to lose it, either—she just needed a place to catch it so she could review it later.

In this chapter, you will do the following:

- Identify people and teams for whom you need Thought Catchers.

- Surface long-term topics for which you have brainstorms.

- Use Thought Catchers to effectively capture your ideas.

- Make a plan to regularly review your Thought Catchers.

In the chapter, I will discuss the purpose of each kind of Thought Catcher and give examples. As you read, consider your individual environment, access to technology, and the people with whom you most interact.

Person_____	Person_____	Person_____

Figure 10.2 Thought Catcher Template

THE MODEL

All I'm really asking you to do is create distinct and organized categories for thoughts you know may come your way. If you elect to keep paper-based Thought Catchers, they might look similar to figure 10.2.

You can also go really low-tech here; if you use a notebook, you can title pages in the back for each category of thoughts you want to catch. I just want you to kick the thoughts off of your To-Do Lists once and for all.

And if you wanted to go the digital route for this tool, you can easily set up Thought Catchers as tasks in various apps (more on this later in the chapter) or set up pages in a digital notebook, such as Evernote or OneNote. But before you determine your tool and content, let's see some real-life Thought Catchers at work.

In this section, you will meet a variety of leaders and see what kinds of thoughts they catch, which tools they use, and how they revisit their Thought Catchers. Similar to previous chapters, you will meet people in different roles and see varying uses of technology. As you read, consider what thoughts come your way each day and how you most efficiently record and revisit them.

Mekia's Paper-Based Thought Catcher

Figure 10.3 is a sneak peek at what a final product looks like. This Thought Catcher is shared by Mekia Love, a school principal in Washington, DC.

Mekia keeps Thought Catchers for various team members at her school, as well as for folks in her school district. When Mekia is in the halls of her school during the day and has a thought to discuss with someone, viola, she writes it in the person's box. There it lives until Mekia creates the agenda for an upcoming meeting with that person.

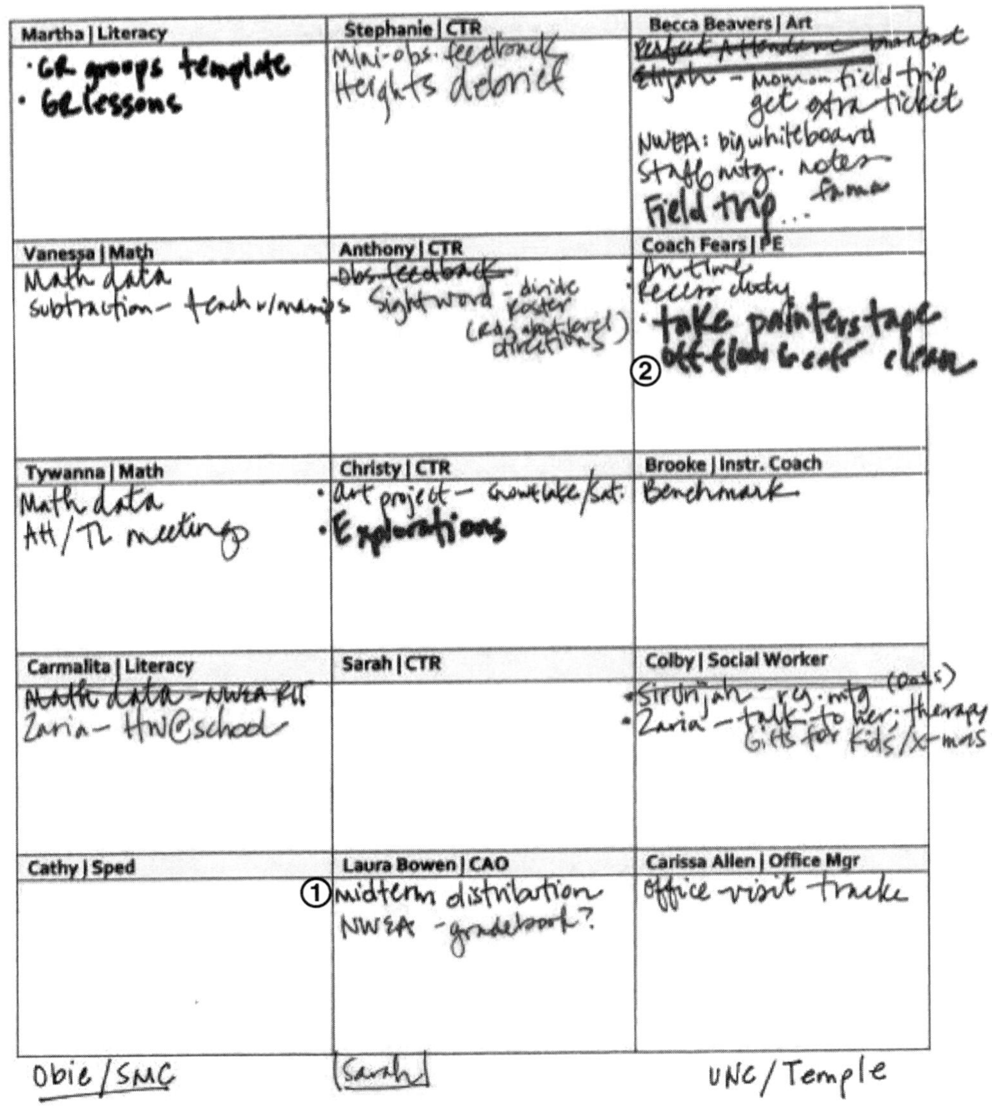

Martha	Literacy	Stephanie	CTR	Becca Beavers	Art
· GR groups template · GR lessons	Mini-obs. feedback Heights debrief	~~Perfect Attendance~~ ~~printout~~ Elijah - mom on field trip get extra ticket NWEA: big whiteboard Staff mtg. notes Field trip... form
Vanessa | Math	**Anthony | CTR**	**Coach Fears | PE**
Math data subtraction - teach w/manips	~~obs. feedback~~ Sightword - divide roster (read about level) directions)	On time recess duty ② ~~take painters tape~~ ~~off floor, keep clean~~
Tywanna | Math	**Christy | CTR**	**Brooke | Instr. Coach**
Math data Att/TL meetings	· Art project - Snowflake/Sat. · Explorations	Benchmark
Carmalita | Literacy	**Sarah | CTR**	**Colby | Social Worker**
~~Math data~~ -NWEA PII Zaria - HW@school		· Strmjah - reg. mtg (Oasis) · Zaria - talk to her; therapy gifts for kids/x-mas
Cathy | Sped	**Laura Bowen | CAO**	**Carissa Allen | Office Mgr**
	① midterm distribution NWEA - gradebook?	Office visit track
Obie/SMG	|Sarah|	UNC/Temple

Figure 10.3 Mekia's Thought Catcher 1

Side note: This means Mekia (and *you!*) should always be carrying your system! Let's see how this plays out with a few examples:

1. As Mekia is talking to one of her assistant principals, she realizes she has a question for the chief academic officer, Laura, about mid-term distribution. But this thought doesn't mean she needs to send an e-mail to Laura right at this moment. Mekia can

hold this thought for a more appropriate time and revisit it in her weekly meeting with Laura.

2. As Mekia roams the halls, she notices painter's tape in a place where she wants it removed. The PE teacher is in charge of that space, so she jots a note for later to remind him to remove it. This is also a good leadership move because she isn't interrupting someone about a small issue.

Mekia also keeps a second page of Thought Catchers for any newsletters or updates she needs to write (figure 10.4).

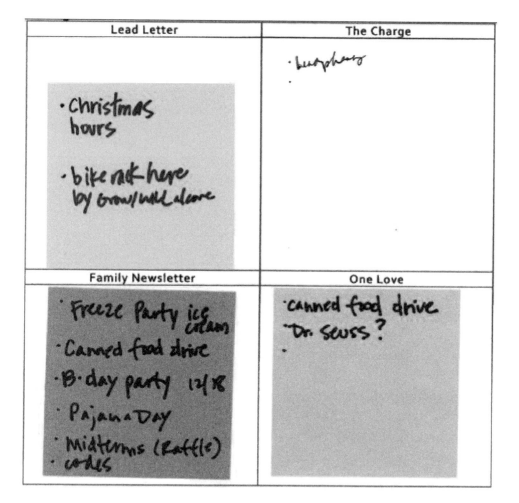

Figure 10.4 Mekia's Thought Catcher 2

For example, she writes a weekly staff newsletter called "Lead Letter." Throughout the week while she moves around her school, ideas or wonderings pop in her head to include. In the week shown in the figure, Mekia realized she needed to add information about "Christmas hours" and provide another update about the bike rack. Storing her ideas here saves Mekia a ton of time—and sticky notes—when she sits to write her actual newsletter. It also saves her from sending a lot of random e-mails to her team!

Mekia keeps a digital calendar but uses paper Thought Catchers because she's constantly on the move. It's not always appropriate to take out her technology in a meeting. It's also just inconvenient to pop open a laptop or tablet in a school hallway.

Now let's look at how other leaders use digital platforms for their Thought Catchers. As you read, start to consider the tool you may want to use for your own Thought Catchers.

Athena's Thought Catchers in Evernote

Athena Mak, at the time working a analyst fellow at Lighthouse Community Charter School in Oakland and currently a leader at Teach For All, uses Evernote to track and store her ideas about many topics. You can read more about Evernote on my website (www.thetogethergroup.com), but here's the skinny: Evernote is a digital notebook that can easily synchronize across all of your devices—and even with a physical notebook. Magical, I know. Let's look at Athena's example in more detail (figure 10.5).

Athena keeps Thought Catchers for these areas:

1. **People and team thoughts:** Discussion topics for the various people with whom she works, such as Steve

2. **Project thoughts:** Feedback for and ideas about the wellness policy or food and meal services

3. **Personal thoughts:** A list of books to read and education organizations to research

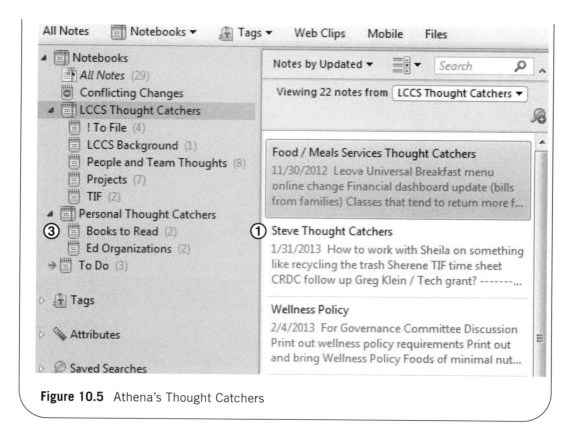

Figure 10.5 Athena's Thought Catchers

FAQ: Should I keep my Thought Catchers in a tool I am already using?

Yes! Beware of tool proliferation. What I mean by that is having too many different systems across too many different platforms. Athena wisely keeps her Later List in another notebook on Evernote. Whatever way you go, you don't want to have a million windows open on your task bar at the same time—your head will explode!

Let's check out one more example.

Johanna's Thought Catchers in Microsoft OneNote

Johanna Parkhurst, a charter school home office leader in Denver, digitally manages her Thought Catchers (along with most of her other Together Leader tools) using Microsoft OneNote (figure 10.6). They are always at her fingertips, whether she is at her laptop or on her iPad or phone.

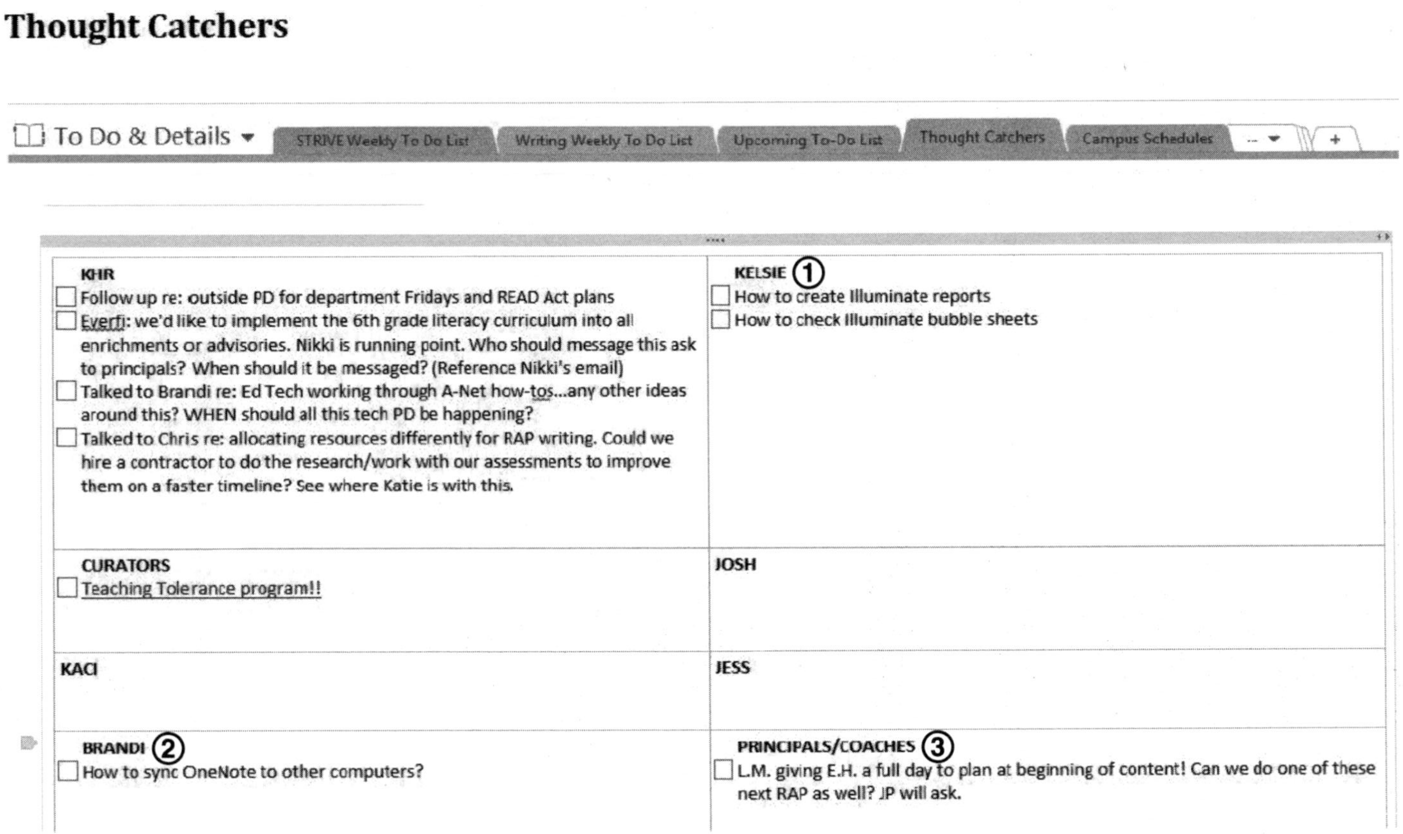

Thought Catchers

KIHR
- ☐ Follow up re: outside PD for department Fridays and READ Act plans
- ☐ Everfi: we'd like to implement the 6th grade literacy curriculum into all enrichments or advisories. Nikki is running point. Who should message this ask to principals? When should it be messaged? (Reference Nikki's email)
- ☐ Talked to Brandi re: Ed Tech working through A-Net how-tos...any other ideas around this? WHEN should all this tech PD be happening?
- ☐ Talked to Chris re: allocating resources differently for RAP writing. Could we hire a contractor to do the research/work with our assessments to improve them on a faster timeline? See where Katie is with this.

CURATORS
- ☐ Teaching Tolerance program!!

KACI

BRANDI ②
- ☐ How to sync OneNote to other computers?

KELSIE ①
- ☐ How to create Illuminate reports
- ☐ How to check Illuminate bubble sheets

JOSH

JESS

PRINCIPALS/COACHES ③
- ☐ L.M. giving E.H. a full day to plan at beginning of content! Can we do one of these next RAP as well? JP will ask.

Figure 10.6 Johanna's Thought Catcher

Johanna keeps Thought Catchers for people she manages, people she reports to, and groups of people she speaks with regularly. Let's walk through some examples.

1. **Her colleagues, Kaci and Kelsie**—When she has a thought or nonurgent request for one of them, such as "How do I create Illuminate reports?" she jots it here in the moment and refocuses on the task at hand. I want to point out here that Johanna is *choosing* to *not* e-mail her colleague about this item; this is a big deal. She is holding the thought for later and will add it to their meeting agenda the following week. This strategy only works if you have an organizational culture and practice of standing meetings. If you do not, please return to chapter 5!

2. **Her managers, Brandi and Josh**—Keeping Thought Catchers for her managers helps Johanna avoid pestering them all day with e-mails, calls, and drop-ins. It also saves her time when she goes to write up the agenda for their meeting—it's already half done!

3. **Content curators and principals or coaches**—These are groups of people with whom she communicates regularly. Johanna doesn't want to bombard the principals in her organization with constant notes, so she saves up her thoughts for groups of people. When she goes to write her weekly memo, the bullets help her get started.

Assistant Alert

You can *definitely* use a trusted assistant to maintain your Thought Catchers—as long as you both review them together during your Meeting with Myself. My former assistant helped me maintain Thought Catchers for my individual team members. I would simply send her an e-mail that said, "Can you please put this on Becca's Thought Catcher?" Then, when I went to prepare for a meeting with Becca, Mila sent me the topics she had collected. This works only if you share a confidential and trusting relationship with your assistant.

Now that you have seen some Thought Catchers in action, let's summarize the benefits and get yours up and running!

> ## Benefits of Thought Catchers
>
> **Maintain Focus.** If you catch your thoughts as they pop up, you can resume your focus on the task at hand much faster.
>
> **Filter Your Thoughts.** Maybe all of your ideas are not as important as they first seem and it would help to noodle on them for a bit.
>
> **Reduce E-mail.** A lot of questions we dash off in e-mails could be held for standing meetings. Instead of sending five different e-mails, you could send one consolidated e-mail.
>
> **Save Time.** When you sit down to plan a meeting agenda, it will already be half-written for you.
>
> **Decrease Ambushes.** I'm not saying don't be friends with your colleagues, but we all need a little focused work time without interruption.
>
> **Capture Feedback.** Ever try to write a performance evaluation with no concrete examples? Me, too. Save up your thoughts here so they're ready to go for when the time comes.

Reader Reflection

How will Thought Catchers benefit you as a leader? How could Thought Catchers benefit your team?

BUILD YOUR OWN

You saw several examples of ways leaders capture different kinds of non-time-sensitive thoughts. Let's take apart the various categories so you can get your Thought Catchers up and running today!

Select the Right Tool

Once you establish all of the specific Thought Catchers you may need, you will want to select the right platform to host them. This will depend on your appetite for technology, existing norms at your organization, and your location throughout the day. Do you sit at a desk? Or are you more mobile?

Digital Thought Catchers

For many of you, I suggest using the same platform for your Thought Catchers as you use for your Later List. For example, if you use Google Tasks for your Later List, add your Thought Catchers right in there in this way:

- Create a new list called Thought Catchers.
- Create a task for each person or team with whom you work.
- Use the notes portion of the task to capture your thoughts.

If you do go digital with your Thought Catchers, please make sure it is always acceptable in your organization to enter information in all kinds of situations. Whatever digital tool you select should be portable, accessible, and 100 percent appropriate to your environment at all times. If not, you will need to carry a paper-based backup for when you are in the field, at a lunch meeting, or roaming a hallway! Just be sure to load the thoughts back into your digital platform during your daily closing routine from chapter 9.

Paper-Based Thought Catchers

You can also go really low-tech similar to Mekia. Options include the following:

- An index card for each Thought Catcher, bound together with a metal ring
- A page in a notebook for each Thought Catcher
- Tabs in a binder
- One of the templates available on my website (www.thetogethergroup.com)

Reader Reflection
Which tool will you use for your Thought Catchers? Why are you making this decision?

Thought Catchers for Individuals

Now that your tool is up and running, it's time to populate the content. The easiest Thought Catchers to get in place are for all the people with whom you interact: your direct reports, manager, vendors, and any other people or groups of stakeholders with whom you have regular, standing meetings.

FAQ: How are Thought Catchers different from my Later List or Priority Plan?
Thought Catchers are simply *thoughts*. They are not To-Dos. They may graduate to To-Do status at some point, but for now they are just thoughts. Some of them may get removed once you cross them off the list (remove tape on floors), and some may hang out for a while (provide the board with a particular data set next spring).

Outside of people with whom I meet with regularly, I personally keep Thought Catchers for my husband, my accountant, and my bookkeeper. When I have questions for them in the middle of the day, I stockpile them in my digital Thought Catchers (housed in Evernote) and save them for a better time. No one wants a life ruled by e-mail, and everyone wants some uninterrupted time. It's likely that you can also get a better result if you save up these thoughts for when folks are more primed to receive them—such as in an anticipated meeting.

Reader Reflection
For whom do you need Thought Catchers?

As with any Togetherness tool, you can go simple or you can get a little more complex.

Option A—Keep it simple: If you are new to catching your thoughts, I suggest just keeping a bulleted list. Don't go crazy with formatting or anything complicated. Mekia or Joanna's models will serve you just fine.

Option B—A little more complex: At some point, once you start separating your Thoughts from your To-Dos, your Thought Catchers will expand to laundry list size. This is because you have very big jobs with lots of moving pieces! So, let's look at a way to organize your Thought Catchers to help establish some order. My favorite outline, which may look familiar because it follows roughly the same sequence of a strong one-on-one meeting, is as follows:

- Goals and priorities
- Professional development areas
- **FYIs.** This is stuff you only need to *tell* someone else. Many items sent via e-mail could actually just be written into the agenda of the meeting. A bonus of many digital Thought Catchers is the option to drag all the e-mails over so they can be addressed during the meeting.
- **Discussion Topics.** These are items that pop into your head throughout the day, as you are in meetings, reading your e-mail, and otherwise going about your business.

The trick here is that not *all* of these items can be discussed in one week, but guess what?! You can space them out.

- **Tracking To-Dos.** I hope most of your people will not need this, but in the rare case when you are worried about someone else's follow-through, it can be helpful to track what you've asked them to do and if they are doing it. Use this section wisely.

- **Feedback.** Have you ever gone to write a performance evaluation only to get completely stymied when trying to think of something concrete to say? Picture this instead: keep a section on each team member's Thought Catcher to record positive and constructive examples you can refer back to when you write their performance evaluations. You can read more about details in chapter 9 on routines.

Advanced Thought Catcher Formatting for One-on-Ones

- Goals and Priorities
- Professional development areas
- FYIs
- Discussion topics
- Tracking To-Dos
- Feedback

FAQ

Why wouldn't I just keep these thoughts in my digital calendar appointment for my standing meeting with that person or team? This may seem the most efficient method, but in my experience there are a few challenges. First, this list can become very long. Second, and perhaps more important, you may not want your colleague or direct report to see every single thought you have. Remember, your Thought Catchers are designed to force you to filter! Yet another technical reason for not inserting your thoughts right into the calendar appointment is that many organizations, especially those running on Outlook, delete appointments after six months.

Here are some other Thought Catchers you can add in if you're feeling up to the challenge.

Thought Catchers for Teams

The next set of Thought Catchers to get in place is for teams of folks with whom you meet regularly. This could be grade-level teams; functional teams such as HR, IT, or Finance; or special project teams. It might also be groups of stakeholders, such as a parent committee or a board of directors. Basically, if you have a regular meeting with some kind of committee or task force, then you'll want to have a Thought Catcher for it.

The same process applies as when you write a Thought Catcher for an individual. You are going about your business when you realize you have something you want to bring up in an upcoming meeting. Simply jot it down and return to the Thought Catcher at the appropriate time (likely when you are prepping for the meeting). In some cases, you may find you are generating enough ideas to create a Scope and Sequence for particular sets of meetings. Curious to learn more about this? See chapter 5.

Reader Reflection

What groups and teams require Thought Catchers?

> **Caution:** Remember that Thought Catchers are not your To-Dos; they are simply your thoughts to be delivered at a later date. We already have two places to record your short- and long-term thoughts.

QUIZ
What Goes Where?

Where would you put ... ?

1. Share newsletter templates with Joe.

2. Call Joe to ensure distribution list is up-to-date before newsletter goes out.

3. Research switching vendors for newsletter distribution.
   Answers are in table 10.1!

Table 10.1 Thought Catchers Quiz Answers

Later List	Weekly Worksheet	Thought Catcher
Research switching vendors for the newsletter distribution.	**Call Joe to ensure distribution list is up-to-date before newsletter goes out.**	**Share newsletter templates with Joe.**
Rationale: This is a long-term thought for next year. It may eventually make it on Joe's list, but you want to do some more thinking about it first.	*Rationale:* This is an immediate task and you are worried there may be an error.	*Rationale:* This doesn't require a separate e-mail and is not time sensitive. I should save it up for a regular standing meeting.

FAQ: And why, oh, why, do you want us to separate this all out? Isn't it simpler to keep it all in one place?

As a workshop participant recently shared with me, "Maia, I realized I was mixing up all of my thoughts into my To-Do Lists and they were jumbled and too hard to sort through!" I am trying to help you avoid the mega-list. You know, the one where it's impossible to tell what is for today versus what is for this month and what you have to do yourself versus what you have to communicate with others. We are breaking up the mega-list of yesteryear into distinct sections.

Thought Catchers for Written Communications

How often have you gone to write a regular memo to your staff, board, or another group, only to forget what exactly you meant to write, resulting in a one-off e-mail later? Like when you get that Friday memo out to your team with the updates for the next week but then you have just *one more thought* about an upcoming event and so you have to send another e-mail right after … and should it get a new subject line or do you reissue the whole darn thing?!

This is why it also helps to make Thought Catchers for any communication you regularly write. For example, if you are a school principal who writes a weekly memo to your staff, wouldn't it be grand to keep a list of topics as they came into your head or in-box? Or if you are the executive director of a nonprofit and you write a quarterly update to the board? Let's say you were out in the field and you snapped a picture of one of your regional sites, and at that very moment you thought to yourself "That would be an *awesome* visual in my upcoming newsletter." How nifty would it be if you could just jot down that idea in a reliable location and return to it when you sit down to write? You can! Using your Thought Catcher!

Reader Reflection

What written communications could benefit from having Thought Catchers?

Thought Catchers for Future Brainstorms

As leaders, we are plagued by the visionary swirl of good ideas for our organization that occur to us late at night. As you start to more consciously monitor what pops into your head, I guarantee you will start to see patterns and categories. Enter, you guessed it, the Thought Catcher.

Work Brainstorms

In my own life, I keep brainstorm Thought Catchers for blog ideas, website improvements, and workshop topics. You might have ideas about how to improve your newsletter, revamp student orientation, or revise your organization structure. Similar to Paula, who wanted to hold on to that idea about student graduation at the start of the chapter, there is likely a set of activities for which you have brainstorms.

Fun Brainstorms

- Gift ideas
- Movies
- Books
- Service recommendations (dentists, plumbers, etc.)

Reader Reflection

How could Thought Catchers help you categorize your many brainstorms?

THE ROUTINE

You cannot put any good idea away without having a trigger to return to it. Often, these occur naturally in the course of your day:

- Your Meeting with Myself! You should review all Thought Catchers weekly (if you go back to chapter 9, you can see Thought Catchers in Max's agenda).
- A standing one-on-one meeting
- A standing group meeting
- An ad hoc meeting
- Something you have to write, such as a newsletter or memo
- Something you have to do, such as purchase holiday gifts

Before you head to your meeting or prepare to complete the task, refer back to your nifty Thought Catchers to give you a boost. Picture how incredible it will feel to write a board update and have the successes section already started! Rather than sitting in front of a blank screen and trying to recall some positives from the last three months, you can just copy and paste.

Reader Reflection

What will push you back to your Thought Catchers?

FAQ: How many Thought Catchers should I keep?

As leaders, you may honestly keep anywhere from ten to twenty Thought Catchers, depending on how many people you manage and teams you touch. I did not come up with this number via any super scientific method but more from watching leaders and understanding general numbers of direct reports and constituents. The large number is why I will gently nudge you to select a digital tool for your Thought Catchers. It's just too much to keep track of on paper. Plus, the ability to search quickly for a name or topic will save you a lot of time. Of course, I would try to avoid having too many Thought Catchers (such as more than fifty).

START STRONG

So, why do I keep a Thought Catcher for my husband? Well, if I have a thought, er, suggestion, for him in the middle of the day, it benefits *everyone* for me to hold it for a more appropriate time. Trust me … I bet you are ready to build your own, so let's get started.

Time commitment: This will take **fifteen to thirty minutes to create; skim daily to maintain.**

- Select a tool for your Thought Catchers, being mindful of which platforms you have in place already.
- Name the individuals, teams, projects, and communications for which you may need to capture ideas.
- Preload lists of topics about which you want to brainstorm.
- Start recording and revisiting.

SEE IT IN ACTION: WHAT SHOULD I CARRY?

Many readers of this book are what I call *mobile leaders,* meaning they are not behind their desks all day. They often move between desks or buildings, or even fly between states! In this "See It in Action," I'll profile Ron Gubitz, a school principal in New Orleans, and his total system. I'll also share some ways to ensure your system is Together enough for work on the go.

Ron uses a clipboard (figure 10.7) because "I need things visually in front of my face or I forget them. I am also deeply impatient. Looking through digital tools feels far away and my phone does distract me. I liked the tabbed part of the five-tabbed report cover, but I didn't like having to open the cover. And I was still carrying my clipboard anyway."

Let's take a look at Ron's table of contents, tab by tab:

Daily Worksheet Ron prints his Google Calendar using the daily view.

Communicate Ron modified a Thought Catcher to include the four conduits he uses to communicate with his team (figure 10.8):

> **Weekly Memo**
>
> He keeps a running list of topics all week long.
>
> **Morning Meeting**
>
> People must submit a text or e-mail before 6:50 AM if they'd like to make an announcement; he then adds their name to the agenda here.

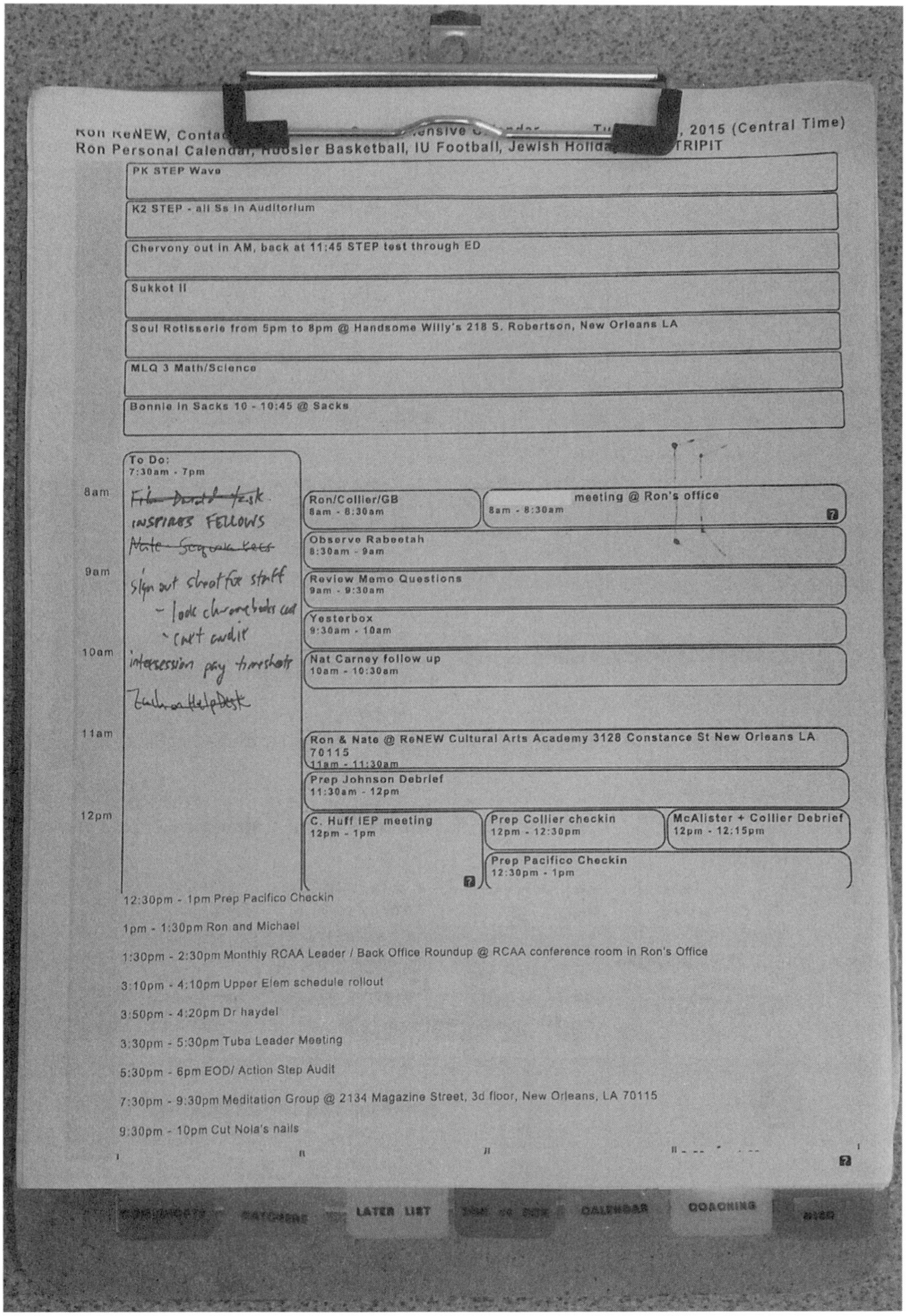

Figure 10.7 Ron's Clipboard

Weekly Memo Items	EODz
	Monday Report Cards — GoALS need lst week para Read GHOSTS **Tuesday** — GOALS Read Ghosts **Wednesday** — GOALS Read Ghosts **Thursday** Performance — GoALS Parent conference **Friday**

Tuba Leader PD	Morning Meeting Agendas
- long view of action steps - PD plan for 10/19 - duty posts changeup - Refresh plan? - PD cul after intersession PC cal 1 culture PD/month cult smaller sessions content What are some of the ghosts parents could be in. You bring? What are implications for us @ parent conferences	**Monday** Report Cards — Big week - with STEP Duty / Committees **Tuesday** STEP — foster — MY shoutouts — Pacific ALGS — Sacks — Antone / Collier upper elem sched rtg **Wednesday** STEP — BANKS Bday — Collier - Ricket — Pacific — Lunch menus — MY shoutouts **Thursday** Collier out ✓ — Super sousaphone — R+F check out form ✓ — Oct 1 attendance — Pacific — SMASH GHOSTS Qs - T+ Talk **Friday** Parker Bday — Different times of work to email GHOSTS — SAT: MOORE BDAY

RESOURCES: template

© 2013 The Together Group, LLC

Figure 10.8 Ron's Thought Catcher

Tuba Leader PD

That's Ron's leadership team name (his school logo is a tuba). This is where he catches all quick hits and other thinking notes he has for their skill development.

EOD (End of Day)

Ron sends one end-of-day e-mail to his entire staff that is a compilation of things such as the absence report and reminders on deadlines. Stuff he wants to send in those e-mails goes here.

Thought Catchers. Ron keeps one for each person he coaches or manages, as well as other folks he meets with regularly, such as the arts integration coordinator for the district.

Later List. Ron sorts his Later List by the month he wants to *start* doing work (my recommended method) and then by work, family, and self (figure 10.9). Way to keep the balance! And good luck with the half-marathon!

September	October
Work	**Work**
• Book RELAY December flight *(struck through)*	• Holidays plan – celebration for staff?
• 20% time order for Intersession *(struck through)*	• Hiring planning work – prep out the project plan
• Opportunity Cost PD? – talk to Pacifico	• Schedule November Togetherness Refresher
• Leadership team Stepback on vision/priorities	• Clean up gmail filters
• *(handwritten)* put deadlines for PD	• BOOK RELAY DEC FLIGHT *(handwritten)*
(handwritten)	• Read GHGR *(handwritten)*
	• thinking wall in office *(handwritten)*
Family	**Family**
• Plan Thanksgiving Break *(struck through)*	• Plan winter break
	• PLAN TDAY *(handwritten)*
Self	**Self**
• Choose ½ marathon *(struck through)*	• Maia executive coaching follow up
Halloween costume planning	

Figure 10.9 Ron's Later List

Meeting with Myself. This is Ron's agenda for his weekly meeting with himself to plan the following week.

Calendars. Ron keeps printed copies of schedules and calendars on hand for reference. He checks this tab frequently to find teachers, see what block is being taught, or remind himself when the next benchmark exam is taking place.

Coaching. This is for all the resources Ron gets from his graduate school program: six steps of feedback one-pagers, rookie teacher Scope and Sequences, and so on.

Miscellaneous. More reference here: floor plans, duty schedules, and the staff manual. Ron also keeps a few personal touches on hand: a picture of Homer Simpson (to remind him to see the world with a kid's eyes) and a drawing of Bob Marley (so that he's always bringing love and music with him wherever he goes).

A clipboard system is really easy (and cheap!) to execute. Originally, Ron told me, "I was just going to wait to do this when I got to a big table, with all sorts of supplies, and have time to 'get it perfect.' But getting started now and making it better along the way was just what I needed to do!"

So, if you follow my theory that your system must be portable and accessible 100 percent of the time, the question becomes, "What do I carry?" You have a few options, but the actual tool matters less than the fact that you consistently have it on your person.

As you consider the various options available (many are listed on my website, www .thetogethergroup.com), ask yourself these questions:

- Do I prefer paper or digital tools?

- What am I most likely to carry with me?

- How often do I need to input information on the fly?

- How receptive is my environment to digital tools?

- Do I need regular access to a printer?

Options for Together Leader Systems

Smartphone and/or Tablet. If you are *entirely* paperless, this is likely your best option. If this is your system, you must ensure that your environment and culture are completely welcoming of technology. By this, I mean that there are always places to charge your gadgets, and people don't mind if you have a screen up during a meeting. And if you do carry your phone, you may need a fanny pack or lanyard if you do not always have pockets. If you go this route, make sure your gadgets are always charged and every tool is synchronized.

Folder with Sections. A folder is useful if you use a blend of digital and paper tools and typically carry fewer than thirty sheets of paper. For example, if you print your Outlook or Google Calendars, but use a paper-based To-Do system, you may want some sort of small binder or accordion file. Don't forget your pen or pencil!

Clipboard. If you need to actively write in your system at all times and are highly mobile, you may want to carry a clipboard. Beware, though: clipboards can quickly become a dumping ground unless you add tabs on the sides or bottom similar to what Ron did.

Arc or Levenger. If you carry *a lot* of paper and prefer taking notes by hand, you may want to purchase an Arc from Staples or a Circa Levenger. Both have special hole punchers, tab options, various pencil pouches, and more.

You notice that I'm *not* mentioning the following: notebooks, wall calendars, or dry-erase boards. Notebooks quickly become a hodgepodge of To-Dos for now, To-Dos for later, and thoughts for other people. It is also impossible to sort or file them. Wall calendars and dry-erase boards are neither portable nor accessible. They are stuck in one location, but your To-Dos come at you all the time!

Togetherness Talks: Shawn Stover

Name: Shawn Stover

Title: Instructional superintendent, District of Columbia Public Schools

Why Togetherness matters: Being Together helps to minimize the urgent so that you can service the important.

Tell me about the mission and scope of your work. What are you most proud of?

My mission is to support and coach principals to ensure our nearly 4,600 students experience the immediate impact of teachers and staff members who work incredibly hard, hold high expectations, deliver well-planned and well-executed instruction, and provide targeted support. I am most proud of the intentionality with which the principals approach their work. They understand the importance of taking a "fifty-foot view" so that they can continually assess and proactively tweak the actions that will help them realize their vision for the school.

At 10 AM on any given workday, what might I find you doing?

Planning meetings and trainings for administrative staff, working with principals on their coaching plans, and problem solving with principals about myriad challenging situations they encounter.

What is your favorite Together Tool and why?

The Priority Plan for sure! Having a quarterly Priority Plan enables me to build a bridge between my vision of success and my day-to-day to work, especially when I pair it with my Meeting with Myself.

Tell me how you start each day to remain Together.

I start each day by scanning the online versions of the *Washington Post, Dallas News,* and *Charlotte Observer* to learn what is happening in the last three places I have lived. I check my calendar to see what's upcoming for the day and think about what I want to accomplish by the end of each item. I stand on my balcony that faces the Potomac River to center myself, meditate, and realize how lucky I am.

What do you proactively do to remain productive?

I am at my best when I am physically active, so I take advantage of living in DC and ride a bike or walk whenever I can. I also try to play squash at least twice a week.

How do you remain focused when the work is swirling around you?

I find someplace quiet where I can be alone and spend ten minutes thinking about what I want to accomplish and how I will do so. Then I dive right in.

What happens when you get interrupted or ambushed?

I know interruptions are inevitable so I build in time toward the end of the workday to catch up or refocus. To allow for the unexpected, I try to never have more than 75 percent of my day calendared out.

What recenters you when the work feels overwhelming?

When I am good, meditating. When I am not so good, playing Bejeweled Blitz or Cookie Crunch.

What have you learned to let go?

Almost all work on the weekends. That time is reserved for my family and my personal passions.

Get Your Team and Organization Together

CHAPTER 11

Keep E-mail in Its Place

SEEN AND HEARD

"I feel e-mail shame! Like, a good e-mailer has everything in folders or deleted and I don't!"

"I wish we could just talk out issues and not send out long elaborate e-mails that take forever to close out."

"Logging into e-mail seems to suck my time dry. I think I'm only going to spend a few minutes, and hours later, I'm in deep."

OVERVIEW AND OBJECTIVES

We have all been on the receiving end of that 11 PM e-mail from a colleague that gently buzzes at us from our smartphone on the bedside table. Do we peek? And if we peek, do we answer? What happens if we don't? If we do?

This chapter will not set hard and fast e-mail rules for you such as "only check two times per day" or "don't check e-mail in the mornings." If you happen to have a perfectly healthy relationship to e-mail and your smartphone, feel free to skip this chapter. But in my experience coaching leaders, e-mail is killing us all. Daniel Levitin confirmed the real science behind getting seduced by e-mail in his book *The Organized Mind*: "Multi-tasking has been found to increase the production of the stress hormone cortisol as well as the fight-or-flight hormone adrenaline, which can overstimulate your brain and cause mental fog or scrambled thinking.... We answer the phone, look up something on the Internet, check our e-mail, send a [text], and each of these things tweaks the novelty-seeking, reward-seeking centers of the brain, causing a burst of endogenous opioids … It is the ultimate empty-caloried brain candy" (Levitin, 2014, p. 96).

I myself have had a varied relationship with e-mail over the years. When I really focus on practicing disciplined habits that keep e-mail a tool to support my work, I just *feel* better. As my friend and former colleague, Kelly Harris Perrin, says, "E-mail is a *tool* to do your job; e-mail is *not* your job." Although it may *feel* like your job on some days, not one single person reading this book has a job description that says "answer all e-mail all day long." We got into this work to serve the greater good, so let's keep e-mail in its rightful place.

This chapter asks you to consider what outcomes you want for your work and then to create and communicate these accordingly. Do you want to be responsive? Get more focused and uninterrupted work time? So, let's start here.

 Reader Reflection
What are your intentions for e-mail?

If it helps you, here are *my* current intentions:

- I want to be considered reliably responsive, but not immediately responsive.
- I want focused work times that are not interrupted by e-mails.
- I do not want to look at e-mails twice. I should not read on my phone *and* then again on my computer. Therefore, I will try not to check during transitions.

In this chapter, you will do the following:

- Identify the root cause of your e-mail challenge.
- Clear clutter to set up your in-box for success.
- Model straightforward e-mail writing to set up your colleagues for success.
- Efficiently process incoming e-mail using STAR-D.
- Set routines and rituals for when and how you check e-mail.
- Determine what shared agreements your team or organization may need.

CONDUCT AN E-MAIL AUDIT

Why even bother to tackle the e-mail challenge? Shouldn't we be as responsive as possible to our tons of constituents? Yes, but there is a big difference between being "reliably responsive" and "immediately responsive." If we are always immediately responsive as leaders, we may unintentionally create a culture that promotes people gluing themselves to their gadgets when they should be focused in meetings, and tethering themselves to their computers when they should be out in the field. Colleagues may send off half-baked responses before giving them full thought (resulting in about ten more e-mails to actually get clear)!

Before we try to solve our e-mail issues, we first need to try to identify the root cause of the problem. To do this, I encourage you to conduct a E-mail Audit:

- Who sends me the most e-mails?

- To whom do I send the most e-mails?

- What time of day do I receive most e-mails?

- How many e-mails require immediate replies?

Indrina's E-mail Audit

I recently asked Indrina Kanth, the chief of staff at New Schools for New Orleans, to monitor what came through her in-box over a three-day period.

Indrina was curious about a few different things:

- Who sent her the most e-mails

- If she was the primary "to" line or just a "cc." This was interesting to Indrina because it could mean her team was over- or underinforming her.

- The connection to goals and priorities. This matters because we *hope* most of our communications are related to our most important work.

- The type of e-mail, for example, action required, meeting needed, or FYI. This was important because it showed her if Indrina's organization was using e-mail for the right types of topics.

- Density (meaning how many lines of prose-like text were in the e-mail)—I love this one because it focuses on the quality of the actual writing.

Here was the outcome of Indrina's e-mail audit:

- Most frequent senders:
  - Direct reports—needing immediate info
  - External contractors—needing decisions or background information
  - Her managers— CC'ing her on various things

- Volume: 814 e-mails over ten working days, ranging from 50 to 75 e-mails per day
- Quality: long e-mails from some externals, shorter e-mails internally, lots of requests for meetings, phone calls, and time

My questions on reviewing the data:

- Why were Indrina's direct reports sending her the most e-mails?
- Was Indrina's role clear when she was cc'd into conversations?
- Was there a more efficient way to deal with scheduling, such as TimeTrade or another software that can be synchronized with Outlook or Google?

I'll get to some solutions later in the chapter. For now, let's just take stock of your current situation. I cannot tell you how many e-mails are too many to receive in a week, but I will continue to push you to make sure your time is aligned with your priorities.

So, what happened to Indrina? Well, after we reviewed this data together, we created a short list of takeaways to share with the team:

- Save more FYIs for standing meetings.
- Articulate when Indrina wants to be cc'd and why.

And if Indrina or others ever wanted, you could take it a step further by making some structural changes. For example:

- Push some items from e-mail to Twitter, Slack, Gmail Chat, or other real-time methods (you can read more about options on my blog at www.thetogethergroup.com).
- Set up TimeTrade to enable people to directly schedule with her, without opening up all of her Outlook Calendar.

Assistant Alert

You certainly could ask a trusted assistant to conduct the E-mail Audit for you and then discuss the results together. Remember to alert people that your assistant sees your in-box, in case folks are e-mailing you with confidential information.

Table 11.1 E-mail Audit Agenda

Question	Reflection
How many e-mails, texts, chats do you receive per week?	
Who, teams and individuals, sends you the most?	
To whom do you send the most communications? Why?	
What percentage of your e-mail is FYI versus you must answer?	
How many times did you enter an e-mail conversation, meaning pinging back and forth?	
Is the writing dense or easily bulleted?	
How often did you reply to e-mail? From which devices?	

Reader Reflection

Review a week's worth of communications and ask yourself the questions in the E-mail Audit Agenda (table 11.1). What trends do you see in your e-mail data? How might you address these?

GET YOUR IN-BOX SET UP FOR SUCCESS

Before you even get started in your quest for a life in which e-mail is simply a useful communication tool, not a burden or a stress, we have to make sure your systems are set up for success! In this section, I will discuss ways to get your in-box in line on the front end!

Declare Bankruptcy

If you have ten thousand e-mails in your in-box right now and dream of one day having enough time to sit around filing them, I need to gently burst your bubble. You will *never* have enough time to file the e-mail. Ever. And if you did, I would advise you to find something more interesting to do! Right now, please turn on your computer and drag every single thing that's older than one month over to a folder called "Bankruptcy." It's not deleted, so don't panic, but it is out of your way.

Sync Successfully

We want to be sure you are not double processing your e-mail by checking it on your phone before meetings and then having to check again at your computer later in the day.

If you do check often on your phone, make sure that when you delete items, they also delete from your server. Get those gadgets on the same page.

Disable Pop-Ups, Beeps, and Buzzers

It happens to all of us. You are in a face-to-face meeting or on a conference call, and out of the corner of your eye, you see that floating bubble with a subject line dash across the bottom of your screen. Or the table buzzes. Or your pocket beeps. You get distracted and lose focus on the meeting. But you can't respond to the e-mail, either. So you're neither here nor there. Turn 'em off.

FAQ

What if someone needs me immediately? Great question. We suggest a conversation with your manager about why you need to unglue from your e-mail and focus on key organizational priorities. Share your plan to reply to all e-mails from him or her in twenty-four or forty-eight hours. In the case of a true emergency, he or she should call you. Remember calling? You know, on the phone? Very effective. We have tried this strategy with a number of folks, even the most unwilling, and everyone gets on board eventually. If your manager is unconvinced, then try sharing one of the articles about what getting interrupted does to the quality of our work. You can find a great list of these on my website, www.thetogethergroup.com.

Get a Watch, and an Alarm Clock, for That Matter!

Admit it. Do you cuddle up with your smartphone before bed? Is it the first thing you glance at in the morning as you rub sleep out of your eyes? As Nick Bilton (2014) explains in his *New York Times* blog post, "Sleep researchers say that looking at a blue light, which is produced by smartphone and tablet screens, sets off brain receptors that are designed to keep us awake and interferes with circadian sleep patterns."

Even if you only use your phone as an alarm clock, I suggest getting the phone out of your bedroom so that you can sleep better, set your own priorities, and be efficient. And for all the same reasons, consider resurrecting the watch. Many of us peek at our smartphones to check the time and inadvertently get distracted by incoming e-mails, texts, or Facebook alerts.

Set Up an Efficient Signature

How many times have you had to ask someone for the best phone number to reach them? Let's get more efficient by ensuring your e-mail signature lists your phone number. Better yet, make your e-mail signature say, "For all phone calls, dial this phone number!" Or write, "Please refer to my e-mail signature for the best number to reach me." Or provide the contact info for your assistant.

Jail the Junk

Ever order anything online? Sign up for e-mail alerts or digests? Consider setting up a separate account for the "junk" to funnel into. This means you will not have to dig through paperless post promotions, Gap sales, or reminders from your realtor when you're trying to focus on your most important priorities.

Unsubscribe

Still getting fitness reminders from the gym you joined five years ago? Take a moment to unsubscribe.

Auto Respond Wisely

A good out-of-office message can go a long way toward protecting your time and focus. In figure 11.1, I like how Jon Schwartz, a vice president of finance at Achievement First, lets people know

- The time frame he will be out of office
- How to reach him in an emergency
- Whom to contact in his absence

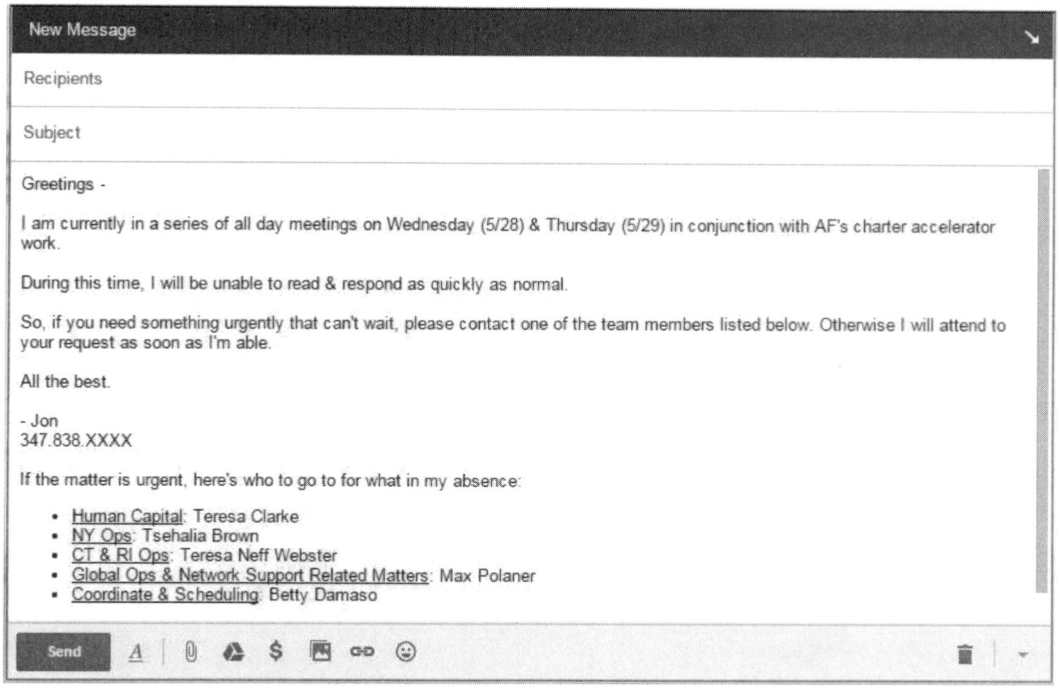

New Message

Recipients

Subject

Greetings -

I am currently in a series of all day meetings on Wednesday (5/28) & Thursday (5/29) in conjunction with AF's charter accelerator work.

During this time, I will be unable to read & respond as quickly as normal.

So, if you need something urgently that can't wait, please contact one of the team members listed below. Otherwise I will attend to your request as soon as I'm able.

All the best,

- Jon
347.838.XXXX

If the matter is urgent, here's who to go to for what in my absence:

- Human Capital: Teresa Clarke
- NY Ops: Tsehalia Brown
- CT & RI Ops: Teresa Neff Webster
- Global Ops & Network Support Related Matters: Max Polaner
- Coordinate & Scheduling: Betty Damaso

Figure 11.1 Jon's Auto Response

You can pre-populate your auto responders so you do not have to rewrite one each time you are out. Additionally, some organizations have norms around how much detail to provide, how often to post an out-of-office message, and more. If you are not sure what to do, ask! If you are the one who should spell these things out, take the time to get clear.

Set Your In-box Up for Success

☐ Declare bankruptcy.

☐ Sync successfully.

☐ Disable pop-ups, beeps, and buzzers.

☐ Get a watch, and an alarm clock, for that matter!

☐ Set up an efficient signature.

☐ Jail the junk.

☐ Unsubscribe.

☐ Auto respond wisely.

Reader Reflection

Which setup for success steps do you most need to enact? How will they help?

Okay, feel better? Now we can *really* get started.

WRITE CLEARLY AND EFFICIENTLY

We can all get a little teeny-tiny bit sloppy when initiating or replying to e-mails, especially if we are multitasking while we write. What's the downside of this? Perhaps something that should have taken one clean reply instead requires ten transactions to accomplish, thus taking up much more of your precious time than it deserves.

Let's look at an example of a typical e-mail that circulates in any organization.

Uggg, right?! What would you do if you saw this e-mail? Close it? Attempt to reread it every day for a week? And as a manager, would I really get the type of response that I wanted? Doubtful. Let's do a rewrite.

From: Maia
Sent: November 3
To: Carrie, Frank, Amanda, Sarah
Subject: Review and Confirm Budget Meeting Notes, Reply by Nov 8

Hi, Budget Team! (FYI Sarah)

Thank you so much for your input at today's budget meeting! Following please find a list of next steps that we discussed.

Who	What	When
Carrie	• Ask Michael if we can adjust our supply order list per school.	• Nov 12—Send answer to Maia or update on when an answer will be available.
Frank	• Check on any changes in permit fees.	• Dec 10—Send list of changes to budget team group (Th before next budget mtg).
Amanda	• Confer with each principal on enrollment.	• Nov 20—Send list to Maia (or update on when info will be available).

Please review these notes and reply to this e-mail to confirm that all looks right by Nov 8!

Thanks so much! Have a wonderful rest of your Wednesday!

Maia

Reader Reflection

What do you notice about the rewrite of the budget meeting e-mail?

FAQ: Won't I sound too bossy, bureaucratic, and formal?

This is certainly a risk, especially if you make a sharp shift from your usual style without explaining why. Start by having your whole team perform a Communications Audit and then use that data to facilitate discussions and agreements on norms for writing and sending. In the following section, I will discuss some of the most common writing improvement norms on which teams agree.

Use Clear Subject Lines

Most leaders get upwards of one hundred e-mails per day from a wide variety of people. If you need to triage your in-box, getting others to write to you with clear subject lines is key. Here are a few recommended subject lines:

- FYI Only

- Action Requested

- QQ (Quick Question)

You can't control the e-mails you receive from outside funders, vendors, or other constituents. However, you can model the type of reply you want to receive, and if it is someone you are paying for services, such as a search firm, you could express a preference with a strong rationale. I don't want people to think you are being picky, but I do want them to see how you're trying to be as effective as possible. On your own team, however, there is no reason you cannot have a simple conversation about subject lines to get everyone on the same page!

FAQ: What's your opinion on that red priority arrow in Outlook?
I think it can be handy *if* it is used wisely and sparingly. Once it's overused, people will quickly begin to ignore it. Similar to many e-mail tips and tricks, it will work best if there is an up-front conversation with your team around its usage. And don't forget the pleasant low-hanging blue arrow, as well!

Use Clear Salutations with To: and CC:

I'm glad you caught this. Yes, the formal old-fashioned salutation may feel funny in an e-mail, but let me tell you, it makes you really consider what you write. At first, I was put off by the e-mail formality at my former employer, Achievement First, but over time I came to appreciate it for many reasons. It was always clear who was the recipient of the e-mail and who was only copied. You knew without guessing if you were supposed to reply, take action, or just listen in.

Let's refer to the example looked at previously.

See how it says, "Hi, Budget Team! (FYI Sarah)"? This enables Maia to signal a few things to Sarah:

- That the task was completed by Maia (therefore Sarah can cross it off her psychic To-Do List)

- That the budget team is on the hook for the reply

Try it. I even do it with my personal e-mails now!

There are other methods to keep folks in the loop without using CC:

- Save the info for an upcoming standing meeting. Use your Thought Catchers. Hint, hint.

- Forward the e-mail to the other people who need to be in the know. Take the extra step of changing the subject line so they know it is FYI only.

- BCC (blind carbon copy): This is a potentially dangerous feature of e-mail, because it makes it hard to keep track of who knows what and who is supposed to know what. Try to avoid the BCC except to proactively remove someone from an e-mail chain. For example, when people e-mailed me and my former boss, the co-CEO of Achievement First, I would reply to the sender to save my boss an e-mail. In the salutation, I'd say, "Dear Jim (FYI Dacia, I'm moving you to BCC to take you off the chain)." That way, Dacia knew I was on top of it, but wouldn't be burdened by the back-and-forth responses. Because she'd been BCC'd, she would not receive Jim's reply.

Clear Up the Prose

Half the people in the world care about context and the other half does not give a flying fig newton. Most people read e-mail just to see what they have to do and by when.

I recommend you clearly put the action in the subject line and in the earlier part of the e-mail and move context to the bottom. Let's look at a before and after sample.

Reader Reflection

What can be improved in the before e-mail? How would you rewrite it?

From: Maia

Sent: January 18

To: Helmer

Re: DRAFT of our step-back agenda (for your modifications by Tuesday Close of Business)

Hi, Helmer!

Good to hear your voice this morning. I miss you too!

I'm attaching a *draft* of our step back agenda for next Wednesday (annual review forthcoming by Tuesday). Please note that I am calling this a draft only so you can feel free to adjust/modify anything on here to really meet your needs and what you want to get out of our time together. Go ahead and make any changes and just send back to me. If you can bring copies of this to our check-in, along with your goals (which I am attaching the almost-final version of our whole shared operations services team goals, plus individuals that I am hoping you can just plug back into the doc you created with your goals/core values/prof development, etc. sheet). I'm also forwarded, as FYI only, something Shannon created during our last annual review that we used as a reflection point yesterday, and it was incredibly helpful she said. I'll send it on to see if you want to do something similar.

Looking forward to talking,

Maia

From: Maia

Sent: January 18

To: Helmer

Re: DRAFT of our step-back agenda (act req by Tuesday Close of Business)

Hi Helmer!

Good to hear your voice this morning. I miss you too! I'm excited for our step back on Tuesday and have a few steps that I'd like you to take beforehand:

Action required:

1. Please make any modifications to the attached agenda for our Tuesday step back that will help meet your needs and maximize our time together. Please send back to me by <u>close of business Tuesday</u>.

2. <u>By our check-in on Friday</u> please plug the goals from the attached doc into your personal goals/core values/professional development sheet that you sent me in December.

3. Please bring copies of the following to <u>our check-in Friday</u>:

    a. Attached agenda
    b. Your revised personal goals sheet (see above)

Optional action:

Review the attached template from Shannon and see if you would like to use something similar in the coming weeks. She found it very helpful.

FYI only

I will be sending your annual review by close of business Tuesday so we can discuss in our mtg.

Looking forward to talking,

Maia

Great, you caught almost everything:

- Effective use of numbers and bullets

- Clear deadlines and rationale

- Leading with the action; context to follow

- Nondistracting use of pleasantries

- Signals to the recipient which steps in the happened previously and which steps are yet to come ("I will be sending your annual review by … ")

Although paying attention to your writing will not solve every e-mail challenge, it certainly can eliminate a lot of clarifying follow-up e-mails and enable people to move forward right away.

Format Matters: Bulleting, Bolding, and Spacing

Perhaps the biggest issue with my two bad e-mails to the budget team and to Helmer was how they were formatted. If you ever find yourself sending an e-mail with more than three lines of straight text, halt! No one wants to wade through that kind of density. Consider using bulleting, bolding, and spacing to get the reader's attention and help her parse out the information clearly.

FAQ: What if I receive a lot of unclear e-mails?

You may occasionally exercise the option to return to sender. You have to use this option carefully, but there will times when you receive an e-mail that is literally undecipherable. In this case, it can sometimes be appropriate to say something like, "I really want to be able to reply to your e-mail, but it is hard for me to figure out what you need answered. Is it possible to bullet out the questions for me?" Some of you may be running for the hills on that one and asking me if I'm trying to get you fired or make people dislike you. But consider it an option in your toolkit!

FAQ: Should I consolidate my e-mails or send people lots of little short e-mails?

Ask the recipient about his or her preference. Many people, myself included, like separate threads about separate issues. This makes an issue easier to respond to and track. One of my pet peeves is when bigger meatier questions get buried in with short little questions. However, other people prefer fewer e-mails with lots of bullets. So, ask.

Reader Reflection

What are at least three practices you will try to make your e-mails more clear?

PROCESS EFFICIENTLY

There are a few reasons it makes sense to get stuff out of your in-box, the biggest of which is your own sanity. I don't want you to have to search your in-box to figure out whom to get back to, where your To-Dos are that you e-mailed yourself (guilty anyone?!), or how to find that budget attachment for a report that is due in three hours. An overflowing in-box causes psychic stress because you *know* there is work buried in there somewhere, if you can just find it. This section describes what to *do* when you actually check e-mail, and address that hot button topic of how many folders, files, or e-mail labels you really need.

I share some original ideas, and also borrow from Michael Linenberger and Charlie Gilkey over at Productive Flourishing (http://www.productiveflourishing.com/). The acronym I'm going to use throughout is STAR-D, which stands for scan, trash, archive, respond, delete.

Scan

Every time you check your e-mail, start with a scan of the subject lines to see what you need to prioritize. If your team has normed on communication expectations (more on this later in the chapter), subject lines should be clear enough to scan for red exclamation marks, same-day reply, or urgent messages. I recommend scanning for any places you see emergencies, when you may be holding up a process, or someone is a VIP and deserves immediate replies. For example, when I do an e-mail scan, I look for anything from my babysitter, husband, or coaching clients.

Trash

In my experience, you can truly trash 10 to 20 percent of your e-mail. Meaning delete. As in make go away forever. I promise you. Such as that all-call for bagels? Or the student dismissal notice? Delete, trash, delete, trash. See? Everything is okay!

Archive

Or file, or label, or whatever you want to call it. This is stuff you actually want to store in an organized fashion. Most leaders either have too few folders or too many folders. I want you to hit a middle ground of just a right amount of folders.

Jesse Rector, a dean at a Relay Graduate School of Education, was a classic case of too many, too rarely used folders. Jesse's folders were organized in Outlook's default alphabetical order (figure 11.2). Some were active folders, for projects currently in the works, such as Alia/Jesse Check-ins. Some were reference folders, such as Marshall Memo and HR. Regardless, this surplus of folders was sending him into an unnecessary tailspin about what, where, and when to file.

You are dying to see the "After" version, right? I won't hold it back any longer (figure 11.3).

Jesse reported, "I love the new filing system. It has really streamlined my e-mail. I am faithfully deleting and filing! This has saved me *tons* of time!"

Jesse created the following folders to get his in-box Together:

Processed. Eighty percent of your e-mail can probably go in this processed folder. The definition here is "stuff you are too scared to delete but is not worth your time to file."

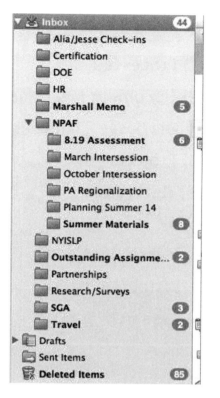

Figure 11.2 Jesse's In-box, the Before Version

Upcoming Meetings. Here's where you put agendas and materials that people send you if they do not include them as part of the digital invitation. Then, when you have time blocked to prepare for a meeting, you scoot right over to this folder and pluck out the information you need!

Projects. Remember those old-fashioned file folders that used to live on your desk? I want you to create e-mail folders for your *active* projects. Jesse can scoot right over to these folders when he needs to work on a project in a protected work block. Once a project is over, you can move the whole project folder into processed.

Reference. This set of folders includes items Jesse may need to reference at some point, such as key HR e-mails or particular sets of research and surveys.

Travel. This is where Jesse dumps any e-mails related to travel that he is unable to enter into his calendar. So, if he received a flight confirmation number, it would go into his calendar. But if he received a longer agenda for an upcoming conference, he may just want to save it here for reference.

After this, we put the folders in the order in which Jesse most frequently used them. We did this by labeling them with a number. I wanted the folders Jesse referenced or used the most often at the top. The default order is alphabetical, which really doesn't make sense for most people.

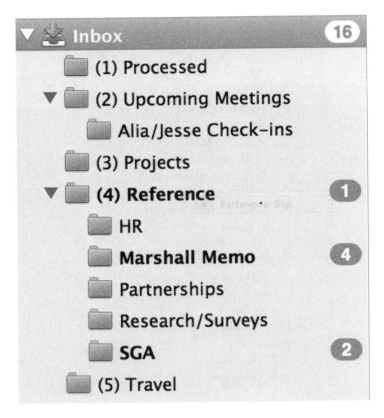

Figure 11.3 Jesse's In-box, the After Version

Table 11.2 Trash, Process, Folder

Trash	Processed	Folder/Label
10 percent	80 percent	10 percent

Let's recap the e-mail situation in table 11.2. Roughly.

Respond

This one is easy. You are probably already good at it. Reply. Write clearly. Be the person to propose the next action!

Assistant Alert: Can my assistant help me with my e-mail?

Yes, *if* you take the time to get clear with him on the purpose of his support. Is it to triage? Answer on your behalf? File? The best examples I have seen are when the assistant and manager sit together each day and work through the manager's in-box to talk about what is needed for each e-mail. And don't forget to make sure all of your team members know that someone else reads your e-mail!

Defer

This is the hardest step—deferral. This is what happens to e-mails you cannot immediately answer in one of your work blocks. You have a few choices here:

- Use the flag or star in your e-mail platform.
- Delegate the reply to someone else.
- Mark it as unread so you are guaranteed to return to it.
- Verbally dictate your reply and have your assistant draft it for you.
- Drag it into your Calendar (Outlook only).
- Turn it into an Outlook or Google Task.
- Use Boomerang or Outlook's delayed send to get the e-mail sent back to you at a time you know you are ready to deal with it.
- Leave it in your in-box—and write it on a To-Do List with a deadline.

Honestly, none of these options is foolproof. They each require some level of discipline and consistency.

FAQ: What if I have serious e-mail storage limitations?
Many organizations do limit server space per person in a pretty serious way. In this case, you may need to auto archive each day or get in the habit of downloading documents to your (very organized) hard drive. You can also make good friends with the IT team and plead your case for more storage space.

Reader Reflection
What is one new e-mail-processing habit you will add to your routine? What impact do you think it will have?

CREATING ROUTINES: WHEN DO YOU CHECK YOUR E-MAIL?

I routinely ask leaders, "How often do you check your e-mail?" The most popular reply: "Constantly." I truly get why this happens. You want to be available to people around you, you don't want to miss out on that e-mail from your boss, and you want to weigh in on important matters. And maybe, just maybe, you are occasionally bored in a meeting, and it is fun to take a spin through your Android or peruse Facebook on your iPhone.

In this section, I'm going to build a case for checking your e-mail only at certain points in the day—to be determined by *you,* based on your role.

Daily Habits

We want to first establish times of day when you check (and reply!) to e-mail. I cannot tell you how many times this should be, but in my experience working with leaders, I typically see that in disciplined organizations with clear communication norms, three to four checks per day suffice. Nothing explodes. This is when you do the STAR-D each time.

The Morning Scan

Most people roll out of bed to check their smartphones (see earlier: *get an alarm clock!*) or check their computers first thing at work and then get sucked in for an hour. I want to make the case for checking only when you are ready to work, not scanning on your smartphone while hitting brew on the coffee pot and getting your blood pressure up! Simply scan and reply only in situations in which you may be bottlenecking something that's critical or there is truly a crisis. Defer everything else.

Complete this morning scan in fifteen minutes or less. Reply to any quick, nonurgent messages at this time as well because they've already entered your mind space anyway! Just as long as you don't spend two hours doing this.

The Late Morning Reply

Now that your organization is fired up and into the thick of the work day, most leaders need a substantive chunk of time to answer those deferred e-mails from earlier in the morning and deal with any other communications.

- Scan
- Trash
- Archive
- Reply from the *bottom* of your in-box up, not the newest stuff first. The rationale here is that today's e-mail may resolve itself if you wait a moment, and I want you to address the older issues first. You may just find that decisions can be made well without you! There are also very few situations that *must* have a same-day reply, so this also trains your staff not to expect immediate replies. Tony Hsieh, the CEO of Zappos, names this method Yesterbox (http://www.yesterbox.com): "We're all guilty of procrastinating and looking for the easy e-mails to respond to first. By forcing yourself to [reply to] … yesterday's e-mails (and not allowing yourself to read any new e-mails that come in today until you do …), it's a lot easier to power through the annoying or harder ones … " (Hsieh, 2013).

- Defer longer replies until later (either later in the same day, or if the replies will really take a while, save time to work on it directly as a calendar appointment).

Complete this phase in thirty minutes or less, and, yes, please block it into your calendar.

> **Caution:** Beware the overflag or overstar for e-mail deferral. You don't want the in-box with fifty stars, so then your stars need stars and you lose the meaning of prioritization. Both Google and Outlook enable you to turn e-mails into Tasks (Google) and into Tasks and Calendar appointments (Outlook). Consider this method overstarring or -flagging to ensure that the longer budget e-mail really gets the time it deserves.

The Afternoon Response

Now your energy is likely flagging a bit, and maybe your opinions are even toned down, so let's get down to business. I recommend going offline to avoid real-time e-mail conversations.

- Scan
- Trash
- Archive
- Reply from the *bottom* up. This is the time to tackle those longer e-mails you have deferred.
- If there is anything you still cannot reply to, please either turn it into a To-Do or defer it with a star or flag.

Block forty-five to sixty minutes to be offline replying.

The Late Afternoon or Evening Closeout

Depending on your own personal and professional rhythms, you'll usually need one more big check to make sure everything is dealt with and no one is left hanging. Take forty-five to sixty minutes to conduct this last check period offline. Some leaders do this before they leave the office; others tackle it at home in the evenings. The trick here is to not get stuck replying to e-mail on your smartphone all night long. Instead, you want to give yourself a well-defined burst of work time when you follow the same routine previously established.

- Scan
- Trash
- Archive

- Respond from bottom up
- Defer carefully—Ask yourself: Can this wait until an upcoming work block in my calendar? Is this a priority for me? Am I holding anyone up here?

FAQ: Why are you so big on working offline?

Focus, pure and simple. There are many folks wiser than I am who have done legitimate scientific studies on distraction, interruption, and recovery time. Outlook makes it very easy to work offline, as do Evernote and Dropbox. You know that feeling on an airplane when you plow through your in-box and then sync up later? Well, that feeling is rare these days given Internet access is widely available on planes and trains, but try to recall it. You were answering stuff without *new stuff* coming in. How freeing! By going offline, you avoid everyone noting, "Oh, Maia is online now, I better shoot her some e-mails in the chance I will get them answered!" Try it. This is easier to do on Outlook than Gmail, but there is a Gmail lab I have successfully downloaded that enabled me to answer e-mail on the subway!

Sample Daily E-mail Checks

- The morning scan
- The late morning reply
- The afternoon response
- The late afternoon or evening closeout

Reader Reflection

When will you check your e-mail? On which device? For how long? When will you *not* check your e-mail?

Weekly Habits

At some point in your week, you will have an all-day meeting or an evening event or something that will cause a backlog of e-mails. This happens. I recommend reserving 60 to 120 minutes per week to "Get to twenty-five e-mails or fewer," which is my alternative to the wonderful, but highly unattainable to us mortals, "Inbox Zero" movement made popular by Merlin Mann (http://whatis.techtarget.com/definition/inbox-zero). If you can do zero, more power to you.

Most leaders do this weekly cleanout on Fridays or at some point over the weekend. If you can unbury during the week, it will feel better than having e-mails flying all weekend.

Will Eden, a school leader for Alpha Public Schools in the Bay Area, created a Wednesday afternoon ninety-minute slot for his deferred longer e-mails and his once-per-week cleanout. Gotta get unburied before the next week begins!

The Power of the Delayed Send

Our e-mail footprints say a lot about us as leaders. Are you glued to your smartphone? Routinely answering e-mails after midnight? Replying all weekend long? The Harvard Business Review article *Are Your Late Night Emails Hurting Your Team* documents the multiple impacts of this practice. I highly recommend using the "delay send" feature in Outlook and Gmail (via the Boomerang app.) Delay your sent messages for a few reasons. First of all, the minute you are immediately responsive, people *always* expect you to be immediately responsive. Second, you may not want to enter a thrice-daily back-and-forth conversation with a vendor who wants your attention; maybe he or she can wait a week!

MANAGING COMMUNICATIONS AS AN ORGANIZATION

Unlike To-Do Lists, e-mail involves other people, so let's tackle that challenge as well. This last section of the chapter outlines the power of communication norms and the role of the e-mail blast.

Communication Rules, Agreements, Norms, or Whatever You Want to Call Them

At some point in an organization's life cycle, whether a school, district, CMO, or nonprofit, you will need to establish some norms for communication. Now, as my old boss would say, "No one ever goes checking a PowerPoint for rules before sending an e-mail," so I would encourage you to lead with an ethos before setting too many rules.

Let's take apart two good examples. As you review the samples, look for expectations, clarity, and rationale.

An Informal School Example

This example (figure 11.4) is from The MATCH Community Day School in Boston. Kate Carpenter Bernier, a school leader at MATCH, introduced this document at the beginning of the year during staff training, got suggestions for feedback, and then lived it alongside her staff.

What I like about this example from MATCH:

- The purpose of the agreements is clear.
- It spells out the various forms of communication the school uses and for what.
- It is more of an ethos than a set of rules.

Communication Norms

MCD has five primary vehicles for communication. Email is LAST – please use it in accordance with the guidance listed below this paragraph.

1. Person to person. Most ideas and questions can be addressed in 1:1 meetings, grade team meetings, and faculty meetings. Put the question or idea in your thought catcher when you have it, then notify the meeting convener to add it to the agenda. Discuss in person.

2. Text. Use for quick questions or immediate needs, ie. "Please bring tissues to my classroom." Texts are also good for saying, "You're awesome, superstar!"

3. Walkie talkie. Every classroom is equipped with a walkie that is connected to one at the front desk and ones on the person of every administrator. Walkies are both used for immediate operations needs (as texts can be) and for medical or behavioral situations requiring immediate assistance. Teachers are responsible for ensuring homeroom walkie talkies are present in their rooms, charged, and functional.

4. Phone call. Remember when phones were used for *talking*? If the matter is urgent – you need to express yourself or need an immediate response – just dial your phone or have a doorway chat with the person who can help.

5. Email. We have found email to be both a giant time suck and a non-optimal way for humans to connect, relate, create, and problem-solve. Thus, we promote low usage of email – while understanding that team communication overall should remain high.

One way to think about communication at MCD is

- if the person needs to know about it by next week, save for your 1:1 or group meeting;
- if the person needs to know about it within the hour, text, or you need immediate response, use the walkie;
- if they need to know right away, call or flag down in person; and finally;
- if you're thinking email, well—consider the above options first.

Note: concerns about child safety are always urgent and should be brought to Kate C.B., Dani M., or Katharine N immediately in person.

Email Details

The technical vehicle is Outlook or MatchEducation Gmail.

- Use meeting requests to set up meetings with others.
- Respond to calendar requests from meeting organizers within 24 hours.
- Keep your calendar updated at all times to make requesting meetings efficient for all.

The two required times to check email are as follows:

- AM: Before school starts at 7:15.
- PM: After dismissal in the afternoon or evening

Figure 11.4 MATCH Community Day Communication Expectations

Figure 11.4 Continued

FAQ: What happens when October strikes and e-mails fly around like crazy?

I hope you built in time for a quick reminder, but also remember to empower your staff to give gentle reminders to each other!

A More Formal Nonprofit Example

The next example (figure 11.5) is from Education Pioneers, a national education nonprofit headquartered in Oakland, California. Please find a full version on my website (www .thetogethergroup.com). Unlike the example from The MATCH Community Day School, Education Pioneers has employees working out of multiple national locations, some from offices and some from home.

Education Pioneers Communication Norms

Why? Part of strengthening our team, partner, and fellow relationships, increasing our efficiency, and improving communication is deciding when to use what form of communication.

Goals:

- We know what method of communication is best for every situation.

- We keep communication over email, text and calls concise and organized so that we can put most of our energy into "face-time" with each other and our partners, fellows, and alumni.

- We don't feel glued to our gadgets (laptops, iPhones).

Communication Mode	When to Use	Guidelines of Use
Email	Use email when you would like to communicate re: issues that are 1) non-controversial and 2) non-urgent (urgent is defined here as needing a response within an hour or two).	1. Do not overuse the high priority option. This option should be used when you need a response from someone as soon as possible to move forward a critical project. 2. Do not overuse Reply to All. If you only have a question/comment for one person, email only that person. 　　○ An example: If you want to welcome a new employee in response to a welcome email, send the email to that person only. 3. Use the CC: field sparingly. 　　○ It's okay to take people off of CC in the middle of the email chain. 　　○ You can use BCC to let people know it has been followed up on but then they do not get included on rest of email chain. 4. Be purposeful with attachments 　　○ Copy/pasting the relevant text into the body of the email allows people to more easily view the text on a smart phone. 　　○ If you want people to be ale to make edits to your version, do include an attachment. 5. When possible, do not use email to schedule meetings (back and forth). Instead, try the following: 　　○ Use meeting invitations and Outlook calendar viewing capabilities for scheduling.

Figure 11.5 Education Pioneers Communication Norms

Communication Mode	When to Use	Guidelines of Use
		○ If you are scheduling with people outside of EP, try to look at other EP employee's calendars to send one email with availability. <u>Doodle</u> is also a great tool for trying to coordinate with a lot of people who don't share calendars.
		6. As a recipient: Drag the email into your calendar for a few days before the due date – an inbox is not a to-do list ☺.
		7. Re-read the email before you send it, checking for clarity and conciseness.
		8. Use the tips outlined below to write high quality email communications.
Phone	It's best to use the phone when: • you want to have a discussion with someone • you might be discussing a sensitive issue • something could cause great difference of opinion, is a big change, is complex, or requires significant rationale to understand.	• Be on time for phone call meetings. If for some reason you are going to be late, send a text message or email to alert the person/people you are meeting with including information on how late you will be. • When scheduling meetings, indicate call-in numbers or who will call who. Include phone numbers in the location information. • Check your voicemail daily and return voicemails within 24 hours if follow-up is requested. <u>When possible, ask ahead (via Skype or email) if you are marking an unscheduled call to confirm whether the timing is convenient.</u> • If you are on a conference call, please put your phone on mute while you are not talking.
Skype	Skype is a great option when you have a quick question or want to see if someone is available.	• If you do not like Skype/you feel that it interrupts your work too much, please feel free to turn it off. You can also use status (busy, etc.) to show that you are not available. • Pleas respect others' "busy" status and do not contact them during this time. • Please also remember that even if someone does not have a busy status up, it is courteous to ask them if it is an okay time to interrupt them, similarly to how you would when walking up to someone's desk.

Figure 11.5 Continued

Communication Mode	When to Use	Guidelines of Use
Chatter	Review Chatter regularly – it's the greatest tool for keeping up to date on what people are doing throughout Education Pioneers	<ul><li>Keep it brief – using abbreviations and shorter sentences makes it easier for people to skim.</li><li>Select the appropriate audience – share with the full team, site staff, or a specific department via "Chatter Groups"</li><li>Posts may be personal or professional – fun chatter posts are encouraged, just nothing you wouldn't want your dad to see</li><li>A few example uses include:<ul><li>Sharing interesting articles</li><li>Posting an update on something exciting for your team</li><li>Reminding people to complete a task</li><li>Sending an update from an event/meeting</li><li>Letting people know what you are working on</li></ul></li></ul>

SOME TIPS FOR ESTABLISHING EFFECTIVE RELATIONSHIPS THROUGH COMMUNICATION

- Ask people you work with regularly for their preferred approach to communication and share your own preferences.
- When possible, group your questions for colleagues – plan ahead so you interrupt them once for several quick questions instead of regularly throughout the day for one question at a time.
- When asking for information outline the details and parameters of your request, confirm the resources you consulted before sending the request, and specify any associated deadlines/time constraints.

SOME TIPS FOR WRITING HIGH QUALITY EMAILS

1. **Put actions at the beginning and context at the end.** All your reader really cares about is what he or she needs to do and by when. Put the actions at the top of the email and offer greater context later. Make it REALLY easy for the reader to do what you want them to do.
2. **Avoid text-heavy, prose-like emails.** Emails are not meant to be novels or creative outlets. Use spaces, bullets, and other signposts to help your reader determine what is important. A common error is to embed many questions within one paragraph; what often happens is you will get a reply but only to your last question. If you really want to get clear replies to your questions, bullet them.

Figure 11.5 Continued

3. **Give or request a timeline or indicate urgency.** Use clear subject lines to help your reader determine when they need to reply.

4. **Answer all questions in emails, and pre-empt further questions or back-and-forth emails.** When writing emails, make sure questions are in bullets (and preferably bolded) so they don't get lost in paragraphs.

5. **Use the subject line to let people know what your email requires without opening the email.**

   a. Never leave the subject line blank
   b. If you change the topic of your email but continue with an existing thread, then change the subject line accordingly
   c. Make it concise – it's ok in your subject line to remove articles, prepositions, etc.
   d. If you write regular emails about a single subject to the same regular contacts try to use a consistent format in your subject line. Add info on action items indicated by a bracket (e.g., NLT update email <Action requested by 4/2>)

SAMPLE EMAIL SUBJECT LINES AND EXAMPLES
The below table is provided by Maia Heyck-Merlin and is copyrighted information for internal staff use only.

Type of Subject Line	Definition
<FYI>	This is *For Your Information*, meaning the reader should be kept in the loop of the email's subject but DOES NOT HAVE TO RESPOND.
<Action Requested by X date>	This is when you request for someone else to do something, but do not need a reply.
<Response Requested by X date>	This means you are expecting a reply from your respondent. Now, you cannot go around saying "Reply requested ASAP" because that approach is simply unfair to your reader. Your team should establish norms for response times so you can be clear what is expected of you.
<Quick Question>	This subject heading would be reserved for items that are TRULY quick questions, meaning the refeiver can giave a "yes" or "no" answer to the question. The general expectation here is 12 – 24 hours of response time for quick questions.
<Urgent>	Use this one wisely. This likely means you need a reply in less than 24 hours, and you should follow up with a phone call to signal your urgency. If you feel yourself compelled into the world of red exclamation points, remember that most people with whom you work are NOT in front of their computers all day, therefore a phone call or text MAY be more appropriate.

Figure 11.5 Continued

This is a much more formal sample but another one I really like for its overall clarity. Some of my favorite things:

- It spells out expectations for which type of communications to use when.
- It makes expectations for response time clear.
- It provides sample subject lines to use.

The key here is to remember why you may need to establish norms and how far you want to go—erring on the side of following principles over obeying exact orders. One organization, New Orleans College Prep, went so far as to turn off e-mail at 7 PM each night, but also implemented the use of Slack, a real-time chatter channel with different live threads, such as #joy, for ongoing communications.

Reader Reflection

Does your team or organization need written agreements? Do you need alternate channels of communication? If so, when and how will you create them? What input do you need from others? What could the roll-out process look like? When will you touch base again?

START STRONG

Although many e-mail challenges feel insurmountable because of organizational culture or unspoken rules, keep in mind that we can only start with our own behavior. And if you are nervous about going offline for those macro work blocks, start a conversation with your manager or team about why you are nervous, and the impact that constant e-mail checking has on everyone's ability to focus. I've never met someone not open to this conversation. Chances are, they have the same challenge. And if you are in a senior leadership role, be aware the unintentional signaling you are doing by replying immediately, sending late-night e-mails, or taking too long to respond to e-mail. Better yet, have a conversation about e-mail challenges and expectations with your whole team!

- Conduct an E-mail Audit using the tools provided in this chapter.
- Get set up for success by unsubscribing, removing alerts, and more.
- Write clearly by using bullets, headers, and short sentences.
- Process efficiently by using STAR-D (scan, trash, archive, reply, defer).
- Establish routines by setting up times of day to check and reply to e-mail.
- Create organization or team Communication Agreements.

COMMON CHALLENGE: E-MAIL EMERGENCY

"I can't keep up!" Ahnna told me. "I mean, *look at my in-box!*"

Ahnna Smith, an executive director of a DC-based nonprofit, had an e-mail in-box that was incredibly full and filling more by the minute. It was bloated with messages already read and addressed, and also with others marked unread in an attempt to prioritize. Then there were the messages with articles attached she may want to read someday, a few flagged ones to return to, and a whole set of drafts started but not yet sent.

Ahnna checks her e-mail constantly from her various smartphones and laptops. Though this keeps her up-to-date in one sense, it also means she's never able to intake the information in a systematic way. Things gets worse when Ahnna is in all-day meetings; the e-mails pile up, and when she doesn't reply immediately as folks have become accustomed to, they write her again! Sometimes they even follow her down the hall to ask, "Did you get that e-mail I sent fifteen minutes ago?!?"

Yes, Ahnna could stand to improve some habits. *And* her team could also benefit from agreeing to some communication norms (which you can learn more about in chapter 11).

Here's what to do if you find yourself in a similar position. I like to call it *Operation Unbury*:

1. **Consider declaring a one-time bankruptcy.** I wouldn't do this often, but the initial cleanup solution may require you to just delete or drag anything older than a month over to a folder called "Bankruptcy." Then, let your colleagues know you did this, so they can (using discretion) bring anything urgent or important to your attention that may be lurking in there.

2. **Unsubscribe or filter any unnecessary e-mails.** If you currently receive a million policy briefings, online sale notices, or you're on every single organizational mail list out there, please consider unsubscribing or creating filters to route the nonessential reads to a separate folder—which you may or may not ever look at!

3. **Turn off any message indicators.** If you are conditioned to check your in-box whenever an unread message indicator dings on your smartphone, or you find yourself constantly distracted during meetings when that darn e-mail pop-up bubble floats across the bottom of your screen, try turning them off. Check your e-mail on *your* terms.

4. **Decide how many times per day you will check and *reply* to e-mail. Block this time in your calendar.** At first, this feels truly crazy to many people. But there are enough studies at this point on the impact of distraction on the quality of your work that you should believe me here! Let your colleagues know you are trying this—they might want to join you! Blocking the time will help you get more work done during work time and actually be more responsive—because you now have a clear system!

5. **Try to send fewer e-mails.** My good friend Allie Rogovin likes to remind people, "The more e-mails you send, the more you get back!" Consider using other channels, such as the phone or popping by people's desks, to eliminate some of the e-mail traffic. You can also set up alternatives such as Slack, like an instant messaging service, for ongoing threads.

6. **Use subject lines and turnaround time to get clear on expectations with others.** Too many organizations, such as Ahnna's, leave figuring out communication expectations to chance! You don't have to create a massive memo, but facilitating a simple discussion about response times, quality of writing, using headings and bullets, and when and how to use the cc: can go a long way. There are examples of some organizations' norms on my website (www.thetogethergroup.com).

7. **Create a simple filing system.** Searching is faster than filing. Most people have too few or too many e-mail folders and labels. See chapter 11 for a great example of a folder revamp.

CHAPTER 12

Project Design, Planning, and Communication
More Than Just Spreadsheets!

SEEN AND HEARD

"I am guilty of leaving big projects to the last minute probably because getting started overwhelms me."

"I tend to put off more vague, ambiguous planning type projects because they're not concrete and can't be checked off."

"People who are in a committed relationship with their Project Plans amaze me. I'm pretty good at making the plan, not so good at actually using it."

"I can never figure out how to involve the *right* people at the *right* time to provide the *right* input."

OVERVIEW AND OBJECTIVES

Lige Shao, the director of strategy and scalability for Rocketship Education in the Bay Area, described the challenge of opening multiple new schools each year:

"Opening new schools is a highly cross-functional, long-term, and complex effort. Like most charter schools, Rocketship teams operated independently, frequently on an ad hoc basis, to open new schools. Like most charter schools, this worked when we were just a few schools in San Jose with a small team sitting in the same room. But as we have grown into other regions, expansion has become an increasingly complex process. We recognized the need to clarify roles and responsibilities for expanding teams and coordinate across functions more deliberately to avoid risky delays and additional costs." She went on to detail the bumps, overlaps, and collisions that can happen—even when a smart group of people is working hard toward the same outcome.

The term *Project Plan* gets tossed around all the time. But I use *Project Plan* to describe a strategy for a discrete project that requires multiple people and more than ten steps to accomplish. In chapter 4, I discussed the need for Priority Plans; Project Plans are about adding more detail. Priority Plans help us define what is most important, whereas Project Plans help us execute it.

Most people think writing a Project Plan is only a matter of banging out a few steps on an Excel spreadsheet. What they miss is the need to also account for team investment, communication, and decision making. Leaders, after all, need to manage their own work *and* manage the work of their people. The focus here on delivery and clarity is what sets this chapter—and this book—apart from many of the project management tools already out there. That Excel sheet should be the *very last* step of an involved planning process. Good leadership requires good systems. And we need systems and tools for projects.

Lige's project-planning process has since improved: "Our leadership team pushed to codify our school start-up work into a single system supported by centralized project management [using the software Wrike]. A single system will allow us to better manage consistent milestones and create visibility into progress on the plane. By establishing a single system, we are able to streamline communication, clarify ownership across teams, and more easily improve upon the work for the next year" (see figure 12.1).

Figure 12.1 The Togetherness Tools

Definition

A **Project Plan** is a step-by-step work plan to achieve desired outcomes on cross-functional projects.

In this chapter, you will do the following:

- Articulate different versions of your Project Plan that vary by audience.
- Identify stakeholders and clearly define roles.
- Invest a team through Project Kick-Offs and regular status updates.
- Predict decisions and create conditions to move projects forward efficiently.
- Debrief projects and improve outcomes in the future.

SET THE STAGE

This chapter will outline twelve steps to manage projects. For simplicity's sake, I will assume the point of view that you are managing your own projects—and that you may also manage other people on their projects. For example, Tracy, a senior leader, may manage others on new staff training and curriculum integration, but she may also directly oversee principal training herself. I will also share tools and habits to help ensure projects are kept alive and kicking. Ideally, your team members are leading the process through these twelve steps. Similar to several other chapters, I will follow one example through from start to finish.

This entire chapter will focus on Kate McCabe, an academic operations team leader, who was responsible for overseeing several weeks of a large-scale summer training for hundreds of new teachers across three states and twenty-six schools. We will call her the Project Owner. Tracy Epp is Kate's manager. Tracy oversees Kate's work, in addition to the work of a number of other direct reports. We will call Tracy the Project Approver.

The Project

Tracy asked Kate to tackle the summer training project despite knowing she already had a very full workload. Logistics had not been fully thought out and whoever was put in charge would have to pull together a plan and a team of peers very quickly. Tracy selected Kate because of her detail orientation, demonstrated planning ability, past experience, and deep knowledge of the organization. Given the project's complexity, Tracy chose to present it to Kate in a weekly one-on-one meeting.

You will get the most out of this chapter if you consider, as you read, an actual project that you are about to start. Or, you might think through someone else's project that you are managing them on. Whichever project you choose, try running it through the steps in figure 12.2 as you go. Working through your own example will help you pressure test your existing plan. And if you currently have no plan, then this chapter will help you build one.

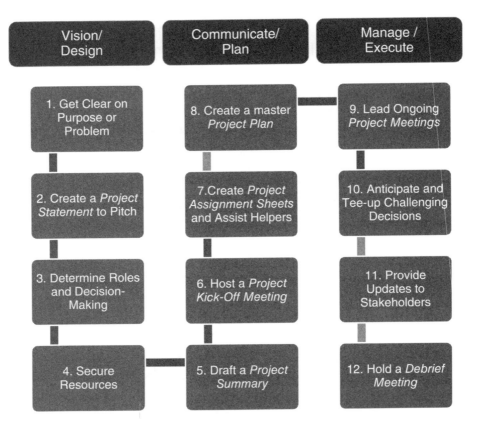

Figure 12.2 Project Management Steps

Step 1: Get Clear on Purpose or Problem

Kate's first step was to get clear on the purpose of her project. What big goals and priorities would drive the training? Why was it so important to get it right? After conversing with Tracy, Kate was able to articulate the following: "The professional development operations for summer training are of huge importance to the organization because they have implications for the instructional training of hundreds of new teachers. It is also symbolically meaningful as many people's first introduction to the entire organization."

Kate's wheels began turning. She immediately asked Tracy, her manager and the project approver, the following questions:

- How is this different from last year?

- Are any other organizations doing something similar?

- Have the resources (people) to help been identified? Are they excited to be involved?

- What is the budget?

- What are key deadlines?

- What are your biggest priorities? Worries? What are the priorities and worries of other important stakeholders?

- How does this fit into our organization's priorities?

- Who are the key decision makers?

Sometimes our instinct is to just dive headfirst into a project without even testing to see if it should exist in the first place! Kate wisely asked a ton of questions and even started a list of other ongoing questions. These helped Kate push for clarity on the project she was taking on and better understand the positives and pitfalls before beginning. Being prompted like this also helped Tracy specify where she did and did not have strong opinions. Tracy was able to proactively weigh in on the front end, which saved her from having to respond and react to issues later on.

Reader Reflection

What is the problem or challenge your project is trying to address? List five questions you should ask your manager about the project.

Step 2: Create a Project Statement

You notice Kate hasn't started the Project Plan yet, right? We will get there, I promise. So, back to our story …

After Kate completely understood the purpose of the project at hand, she and Tracy decided she needed a Project Statement to communicate the high-level time line and required resources to the organization's executive team—for information-sharing and investment purposes.

Definition

A **Project Statement** is a one-page, often visual summary of a project that includes one to two sentences of purpose, a list of high-level actions, a rough time line, a portfolio of key players, and the final outcome.

We need to write a Project Statement before developing a detailed plan. This is because projects require a big-picture summary of their purpose, actions, time line, and players. A manager such as Tracy can circulate the Project Statement to his or her own managers and colleagues. Additionally, the Project Statement can help inform other key organizational players, such as those in charge of budgets, facilities, or fund-raising. It may feel like an extra step, but this tool will pay you back later in hours of not having to answer repeated questions or explain twice.

Kate's Project Statement (figure 12.3), made in PowerPoint, shows the visual progression of the task at hand. I like how she lists these topics:

- A bold statement of purpose
- A high-level time line
- Big picture action steps
- Possible participants

Big Steps Summer Operations
Where are we now?

Smooth logistics and operations will allow our teachers and leaders to stay laser-focused on the content that will help them drive breakthrough student achievement in the upcoming school year

Lay the Foundations
- Secure Resources
- Launch Team
- Establish Milestones

New Leader Training
- Execute
- Capture Learnings for All Leader Training

All Leader Training & Curriculum Summit
- Major execution push while finalizing details for NTT

New Teacher Training
- Major execution push while finalizing details for All Teacher Training & Opt-ins

All Teacher Training
- Execute
- Celebrate

Timing & Participants	April	May	June	July	August
	Project Team	Project Team + More Help	Project Team + More Help	Project Team + More Help	Project Team + More Help

Figure 12.3 Kate's Project Statement

FAQ: How do I use a Project Statement as a manager?

If you are looking at multiple Project Statements from multiple staffers, it helps to think about resource allocation, budgeting, and staffing across them all. I like to keep all Project Statements in one folder and review them weekly, considering the important decisions in the upcoming month, where and how I can best support the team, and connections people have to each other. I ask myself questions such as these:

- Will this statement of purpose motivate others?
- Do I agree with the time line?
- Are there organizational staffing resources I can help secure?
- What are connections or conflicts for other parts of the organization?
- What else is happening in our organization during this time period?
- Are there decisions I can help push forward to clear the path?

Reader Reflection

How could a Project Statement help you? Who would your primary audience be?

Step 3: Determine Roles and Decision Making

Decision time! Now that Kate is secure in her purpose and rallying cry, she needs to clearly define who is doing what. This is particularly important because this project spans outside of her immediate team and will also require the cooperation of facilities, finance, information technology, and even marketing! To ensure that everyone knows what is expected of him or her well in advance, Kate created a Roles Overview and a Decision-Making Matrix.

Roles Overview

Kate started with a Roles Overview so she could figure out what kind of help she would need to successfully facilitate summer PD. A Roles Overview is just a fancy way of saying who will do what. She outlined the overall buckets of work, and within them, the specific bulleted responsibilities of a given role. Kate notes, "I took the time to spell out the responsibilities for all of the roles. Everyone read the overviews of every role, not just their own. This was very helpful for ensuring role clarity amongst the team." (figure 12.4).

Roles Overview

Role	The Details
Owner – Kate	Manages the planning and execution teams Owns overall Project plan Get needed answers from Tracy and other key approvers Proactively builds team morale
Residential Ops – Alex	Hotels, Food
Transportation – Sarah	Transportation plan & guides
Community Building – Sarah H.	Team building, evening activities
Look and Feel – Sarah H	Signage/ Programs/ Schedules, PPTs, Logo, SWAG AF-ing" the space. Ensure key messages & theme filter throughout
Office Ops & Technology TBD (tentative)	Order supplies & facilitator materials Copying plan, copier contracts Supply Distribution & Room Set-up
Communication Kate & Marissa	K: When people (school leaders, teachers, facilitators, the net) find out logistics information and how Marissa: Triage and distribute questions and pro-active communication about who answers which questions Write SLMs, send invites, respond to Questions. Own Many Minds logistics site
Many Minds – Emile	Execution on Many Minds-based communication tactics : session review, materials capture, logistics information sharing
People Ops – Marissa	Manpower: schedule of who is going to be @ what events; their role; communication with these folks
PD Design & Sharing System – Rachel K	Partner with CIO to get key info from Laurie Manage people to get their work in & determine how final docs are shared with participants Registration
Facilities – Alex	Find external and internal session space and hotel space for all trainings
Finance – Alex	Manage Budget & ensure clear guidelines on reimbursements Ensure we sign up with outside vendors (e.g., Wilson), pay them and communicate with schools about any payments

Figure 12.4 Kate's Roles Overview

Next, Kate shared the Roles Overview with her colleagues and their managers. This enabled everyone to be clear on their responsibilities and see how their actions fit into the larger picture of the overall project.

Decision-Making Matrix

Kate drafted the following Decision-Making Matrix and then asked for input from her manager, Tracy, at their weekly one-on-one meeting. A Decision-Making Matrix is used to clarify who makes which decisions—before the project even starts! Done well, it will keep the project moving. After finalizing it, she shared it with her project team.

When organizations fail to plan decision-making structures in advance, it's easy to get stuck or bottlenecked as various people stumble into various issues. Even worse, Project Managers can lose the flexibility to deal with real emergencies because they are playing catch-up to figure out who is involved in which decisions. These issues are entirely predictable and can be dealt with proactively using a Decision-Making Matrix.

Mocha Model

Source: The Management Center (http://www.managementcenter.org/).

M = Manager (assigns responsibility and holds owner accountable)

O = Owner (has overall responsibility for the success or failure of the project; ensures that all the work gets done and that others are involved appropriately)

C = Consulted (should be asked for input and needs to be kept in the loop)

H = Helper (available to help do part of the work)

A = Approver (signs off on decisions before they're final)

The MOCHA model helps Project Managers clearly articulate who should play what role throughout the project. This helps the team generate better results. This is critically important. No one wants a decision dropped on him or her in the last minute. The more clear you are on the front end, the better you can deal with the inevitable unexpected issues that will arise.

In Kate's case, table 12.1 shows what the MOCHA would look like.

Table 12.1 Kate's MOCHA Model

Role	Description	Who?
Manager	Signs off on decisions before they are final. May be the same person as the Owner, though doesn't have to be.	Tracy is the Manager of this project. She also happens to be Kate's direct manager, but it doesn't always have to be this way.
Owner	Has overall responsibility for the success or failure of the project. Ensures that all the work gets done and others are involved appropriately.	Kate is the Owner of the project from start to finish.
Consulted	Should be asked for input on the work and needs to be invested	Kate knows she needs to consult with the following people: • The regional superintendent team because they will facilitate workshops • The facilities team because they will oversee housing • The school leadership team because they will provide follow-up training at school sites
Helpers	Available to do part of the work	• CEO assistant • Team teaching and learning coordinator • Team chief of staff coordinator
Approver	May need to sign off on particular decisions.	• Tracy for most timing decisions • Doug for most content decisions

FAQ: What's the difference between an Owner and a Manager?

The Owner is the person in charge of the project; he or she moves the ball down the court by ensuring that the process is coordinated, decisions are being made, and communication is thoughtful. The Manager is the person who has ultimate approval over most, if not all, aspects of the project.

Reader Reflection

How clear are roles and responsibilities on your project team? What could be made more clear? Complete your MOCHA chart.

Step 4: Secure Resources

There are two types of resources needed for projects—people and money. By making a Project Plan and selling it to the right people, you will find it easier to line up the resources you need. Although I am mostly focused on people, I will also briefly touch on money.

Create a Job Description to Secure the People

With her MOCHA chart in place, Kate now needs to figure out how to get people on board as helpers. Sometimes resources are placed in your lap and sometimes you have to go out to collect them yourself. In Kate's case, some people were already assigned to help with her project, but she also knew she'd need to solicit more to join her cause. This is not ideal, but it can help to ask a few other senior team members to advocate for you if needed.

However, before Kate could go about securing committed helpers, she needed a clear understanding of exactly what folks would do, the time commitment that would be required of them, the relationships they'd need to secure to get things done, and what it would take to motivate them.

Lining all of this up is not easy! But it was so important for Kate to clearly articulate her requests and desired outcomes to people joining her project team. People want to feel crystal clear on what is being asked of them before they commit to joining. The more information you can offer up-front, the more likely others are to be helpful.

In Kate's case, she knew one big work stream of her project would be residential operations—figuring out where all the people were going to eat, sleep, and live during summer training—so, Kate took the time to spell out the work of the residential operations lead (figure 12.5).

Kate did several smart things here:

- **Set outcomes.** Kate said things like "child-care policy is established, 100 percent legally compliant," and so on. Kate did *not* say what the child care policy should be, but she did name the outcome up-front.

- **Highlighted points of intersection with other groups.** This is wise because it is not always obvious where collaboration should happen if you own just one body of work. Kate advises, "Partner with team HC [human capital]" for the child-care bucket.

- **Notes key deliverables.** When an actual deliverable was required that Kate knew of in advance, she let people know. For example, in the session meals and snacks bullet, Kate points out that the meal plans for each training are required documents.

Yes, this took Kate more work on the front end, but taking this job description to the people who helped her staff the project and to the introductory conversations with the helpers themselves gave her team a clear idea of what they signed up for!

Residential Ops

The Residential Ops Leader ensures that our teachers and schools leaders are informed about, comfortable in and energized by the spaces they live and learn in throughout Summer PD.

Key Responsibilities:

- **Communication with Hotels and Session Host:** Once the contract is signed, own all communication around specifics of rooms with hotels (confirming exact # of types of rooms, break out space, where child care will be, where the fun events will be)

- **Communication with Attendees:** (In partnership with Marissa and Emile for Many Minds) Communicate all information about where people need to be & when, what they should bring (this role will need to clarify the fuzzy line with TTL), who they will room with, if they can bring family. (*this is the starter list*)

- **Data Collection & Transfer:** Partner with Registration owner to ensure all info for residential ops is collected by when we need it (ex: single vs. double room requests, dietary need info, roommate preferences) and that that info is communicated to the vendor and to attendees

- **Session Meals and Snacks:** Ensure people have satisfying, diverse, healthy food for B/L/D & snacks on a financially responsible budget. Ensure variety of options for people with special dietary needs. Ensure food is served in an efficient way (set-up to allow for smooth traffic lines, clear signage). Clarify decision on if and when to serve alcohol. Key Deliverable: Meal (what) and serving (how and who) plans for each training.

- **Child Care:** Partner with Team HC to ensure child care policy is established, communicated, 100% legally compliant, and that the child care execution is logistically seamless.

- **Safety:** Partner with Team HC to determine what medical care options we can offer and we are our emergency protocols. Clarify and communicate policy and liability about staff traveling in cars together.

- **Quality Control:** Ensure that People Ops has a role for on-the-ground data control; specify the responsibilities of that role

---

Figure 12.5 Kate's Residential Ops Lead Job Description

As you think about your project, table 12.2 may help you consider what kind of support you will need on your team. This template can also be found in the Reader Reflection Guide. You could use it as a brainstorming tool to think about how to ask for help, or you could use it to eventually write job descriptions similar to how Kate did.

Reader Reflection

Who is responsible for which tasks on your project team?

FAQ: What if you don't even know what your resources will have to do?

Kate knew she needed IT support at all of the professional development events. But beyond this, she was unclear on the details of exactly what was needed and the work required to accomplish it! This is a very common scenario, especially if the project is new to you or the organization. To gather a better sense of this, Kate scheduled a brainstorming meeting with the VP of IT at her organization. The VP appreciated this opportunity, because it enabled her to choose the right person on her team to help with Kate's project and also consider if outsourcing for more people or equipment would be necessary.

Money

A good question to figure out in advance of any project is how much it will cost. Many projects often are also born from particular grants or funding streams that require certain types of reporting. To gain clarity on her budget, Kate asked Tracy these questions:

- What is the total budget for summer training?
- Does the funding come from one source or from multiple sources?
- If we are using other people's budgets, are they aware of the costs?
- What happens if we go over?
- Is there a threshold at which you want me to check in?
- Are there any restrictions on spending, for example, no alcohol at social events?
- Is there budget-tracking support?
- Are there per-diem rates we need to honor?

Reader Reflection

What is your total budget? What other resources do you need?

Table 12.2 Job Description Planning

Work Stream	Responsibilities	Time Commitment	Skills and Experience	Key Relationship	Team or Person Responsible	How to Invest Him or Her?
	What tasks is this person expected to perform? What meetings or documents will she be expected to attend or maintain?	*How many hours over how many weeks? Which weeks?*	*What skills will this person need to complete his tasks? What's required and what's preferred?*	*Who does this person need to know or have access to in order to complete her tasks?*	*What team do you need support from for this work stream? How junior or senior? Is there a specific person or position?*	*Does this person need to be invested? If so, how will you do this?*

Step 5: Draft a Project Summary

The team is in place, the vision is clear, now it is time to get to work. What's next is a more detailed articulation of the project. I call this a Project Summary.

Definition

A **Project Summary** is a two-page or ten-slide-or-fewer document explaining the purpose, players, time line, milestones, and roles of the project. This can be used to help align the team and manage toward deadlines. It is written by the Project Owner and shared with the project team.

This differs from a Project Statement because it is not designed for broad circulation but rather just for the people directly involved in the project. Again, I know I'm asking you to do a lot of work *before* the actual Project Plan, but let's hear Kate remind us of why this is so important: "Project summaries are hugely helpful in two big ways—first, they force you to step back and articulate the big goals and deadlines of the work. Second, they are a great communication tool for sharing that info with and rallying your team when you launch the project." Kate needs to write the Project Summary using all the research she has gathered to date and as a way to rally the project team when they first assemble. Let's take a peek (see figure 12.6).

Elements of a Project Summary

- **The challenge:** Motivate the team by making the challenge inspiring!
- **The vision:** Be sure to share what the ideal looks like!
- **The goals:** Spell out how success will be measured.
- **Key deliverables:** Which documents are essential?
- **The team:** Lay out who is playing which role.
- **Time line:** What are the big dates and deadlines that affect others?

You can find more examples of Project Summaries on my website (www .thetogethergroup.com).

Summer Ops – Project Overview

The Challenge: Teaching teachers and leaders to be great at what they do is a fundamental part of how we will fulfill our mission of preparing our students for college. However, it is impossible for them to be fully focused on their learning if operations and logistics don't run smoothly. Our mission is to take the rocks off the road so our teachers, leaders and facilitators can focus 100% on the content and learning that will help them drive breakthrough student achievement this coming school year.

Our Vision

For All: I knew where to be and when because I received clear agendas and room signage is clear. I knew how to access my pre-work, was easily able to do so and felt capable of completing it. I had all the materials (hard or soft copy) I needed at sessions. I knew all of my hotel & transportation information. I knew who to go to if I had questions.

For Facilitators: I knew what was due when, how to turn it in and get feedback, and how to submit my copy & materials requests. My room had all the A/V and materials I needed, and my copies were perfect. I knew how to access my session feedback data so I could apply it the very next day. I knew all the information I needed about my session (#s of people, people names).

Goals

- 90% Respondents reply Very Good or Excellent to Operations and Logistics Questions on End of Summer Survey

Key Deliverables

- Summer Training Website (calendar, pre-work upload)
- Summer Training Communication Plan
- Copy, Materials, Signage Needs Assessment
- Hotel Contracts & Agreements

The Team

- Kate – Special Projects Manager
- Alex – Residential Ops, Facilities, Finance
- Sarah – Transportation, Community Building, Look & Feel
- Marissa – Communication, People Ops
- Rachel – PD Design & Sharing

Timeline

- April – Secure Resources, Launch Team, Establish Milestones
- May – Execute New Leader Training, Capture Learnings for All Leader Training
- June – Execute All Leader Training, Finalize Details for New Teacher Training
- July – Execute New Teacher Training, Finalize Details for All Teacher Training
- August – Execute All Teacher Training

Figure 12.6 Kate's Project Summary

FAQ: How do I use a Project Summary as a manager?
Simply reviewing Project Summaries each week to discuss successes and challenges with Project Owners is hugely helpful. It gives you good insight into progress and enables you to provide support and draw connections. Kate's manager, Tracy, may review the Project Summary each week as part of their regular one-on-one meeting.

Reader Reflection
How could a Project Summary be helpful to your project? Who is your primary audience?

At this point, you may feel like I'm asking you to spend a lot of time just *planning* and not *doing*. That can feel frustrating. All in all, I'm asking you to spend two to three hours laying the groundwork for your project so you don't hit unplanned stuff later. Of course, you want to match the complexity of your project to the right amount of steps here. You are always welcome—and encouraged—to find shortcuts wherever you can!

Step 6: Host a Project a Kick-Off Meeting

After a Project Summary is in place, it is finally time for Kate to assemble her team. Most projects require a Kick-Off Meeting.

Definition
A **Project Kick-Off Meeting** is an initial meeting to communicate the purpose, resources, and time line of the project. This meeting is hosted by the Project Manager.

It is first helpful to consider who you want to attend, what you want participants to learn, and how you want them to *feel*. Yes, you heard me right, *feel*.

Kate thoughtfully noted that the Kick-Off Meeting for her project needed to be held in person or by video because she was asking people to take on a huge chunk of work—in addition to their regular jobs. This happens a lot in mission-driven organizations, because you cannot afford to add full-time employees for events or special projects. She was also aware that many people assigned to help with her project were not necessarily excited by the prospect of additional work, so getting the *why* right was a huge focus.

No one should find out his or her role in the project *at* the Kick-Off Meeting. It may require meeting with project team members in advance to review their roles, responsibilities, and even time commitments. In this case, Kate took the step to meet with each project team member individually to review the Project Summary and the roles and responsibilities before the Kick-Off Meeting.

Let's look at Kate's Kick-Off agenda in table 12.3. You can also find a template on my website (www.thetogethergroup.com).

Kate not only focuses on collaboration and outcomes but also she focuses on a strong tone for how the group will communicate and interact—right down to a team slogan!

Kate's team had a fruitful meeting, resulting in great products such as the list of open questions per bucket of work in figure 12.7. Kate's team had the opportunity to get answers for all of their questions before they built out their own time lines.

Table 12.3 Kate's Kick-Off Agenda

Agenda Item	Outcome	Time
Intros		15
Where we are and where we are going	We understand the general arc of the next six months.	5
Roles and responsibilities	At a high level we understand what we are each on the hook for.	15
Hopes, fears, and mind-sets	Name the mind-sets now that will help us down the road.	10
Set the vision	Collectively create the vison of what success will look like.	15
Planning and knowledge management tools	We know where to park milestones, see dependencies, and find information.	10
What do we need to touch base on every time we are together?	Provide input on the agenda for our team check-ins.	10
Next steps and flex time	Clarity on what happens next.	10

Figure 12.7 Kate's Team's List of Questions

Elements of a Kick-Off Agenda

- Focuses on purpose
- Spells out roles and responsibilities
- Identifies big barriers and roadblocks
- Provides time to brainstorm possible solutions
- Develops team agreements on communication norms and meeting structures
- Considers a team name or project slogan

Before you jump into scheduling your own Kick-Off Meeting, be sure to watch out for these common pitfalls.

Caution: Common pitfalls of Project Kick-Off Meetings

- Team members learning about their roles and responsibilities for the first time
- Just focusing on the work—not the *why* or the impact
- Shutting down concerns about workload
- Not allowing questions

A skilled Project Owner can handle each of those challenges by striking the right balance between planning and flexibility. By opening up the floor for questions, such as Kate did with her charts, or previewing their roles in advance, such as Kate did with her roles and responsibilities chart, you set the team up for greater ownership!

Reader Reflection

Who should join your Project Kick-Off Meeting? When and where should it be held? What do you want your participants to walk away knowing and feeling?

Step 7: Create Project Assignment Sheets and Assist Helpers

The team is assembled, excited, and chomping at the bit to get started. In some cases, it may not be incredibly clear what they need to do to make progress toward their aspect of the project. In these cases, it can be helpful to create a Project Assignment sheet to clarify roles.

Definition

A **Project Assignment Sheet** is clear, up-front directions outlined by the Project Owner to make it easier for the Project Helpers to create their own plans.

Although Kate had spelled out each team member's role and major deadlines prior to the Kick-Off Meeting, the plans were far from built. After the Kick-Off Meeting, Kate met with each team member again to discuss their specific challenges, questions, and responsibilities. Kate's goal was for each colleague to understand and be invested in how his or her individual work contributed to and fit with the larger puzzle of the project. Yes, it took her a few hours of extra time, but as Kate reflected, "Getting the roles clear before the work starts is absolutely necessary for successful projects. Role clarity ensures that people feel ownership and responsibility for their bodies of work. Clear roles also save massive amounts of time because people don't get lost in e-mail exchanges or conversations trying to determine who is responsible for gray areas of work. In short, clear roles equal clear ownership, and clear ownership is fundamental to a project's success."

Let's look at how Kate created a Project Assignment Sheet for folks working on materials and copies (figure 12.8).

A Project Assignment Sheet should include this information:

- The performer's mission
- Key milestones
- Roles and responsibilities
- Recommendations based on past data
- Questions to solve

You can also find a more examples and a blank template on my website (www.thetogethergroup.com).

Materials and Copies Team

Overview & Mission: The Materials and Copies Team is responsible for all signage, copies and supplies for each session. The goal is that all facilitators know how to turn in their materials and copy requests, and that their supplies and copies are perfect when they arrive. All facilitators have all the materials they need to be successful during sessions, and that all participants know where to go at all times because of clear and well-placed signage.

Big Milestones & Key Deliverables:

- Inventory of supply, copy and signage needs for each event – May 12
- Delivery plan for supplies and copies to all locations. – June 1
- Tracking System for processing of copy requests. – June 1

Responsibilities & Recommendations:

- Determine general supply needs for each event.
- Determine specific facilitator-requested supplies for each event.
- Coordinate transportation and delivery of supplies to each event location. (**Rec - > Reserve three handtrucks)**
- Create and execute plan to distribute supplies on site (**Rec -> Set up Facilitator Packs near Help Desk)**
- Manage Supply Room/Area (**Rec -> Make piles organized by room floor to ease delivery trips)**
- Coordinate retrieval of supplies and transportation back to Network Support locations
- Work with copy vendors to provide materials for each session.
- Ensure copies and signage are accurate and delivered in a timely manner.
- Track event dates, facilitator submission deadlines, vendor submission deadlines (**Rec -> Make Google Doc)**

Questions to Answer:

- File format and lead time requirements from copy vendors
- Pricing options for sign vendors -> need a new one this year
- Budget range for supplies for different tiers of events

Figure 12.8 Kate's Project Assignment Sheet

Reader Reflection

When might Project Assignment Sheets be helpful? If so, who is your audience? When will you meet with them?

Step 8: Create a Master Project Plan

You have been wondering when I would actually say this, right? Well, now it is time to create the Project Plan as most people think about Project Plans. We have waited until now and done all of this other work so that the Project Plan itself is easy to write and simply a summary of the work done to date.

Tip: Select your Project Plan format wisely. Don't overcomplicate things.

- If your project is ten steps or fewer, don't even make a Project Plan. Just send a bulleted e-mail.

- If your project is more complex, it probably requires a Project Plan hosted in Excel, Basecamp, Wrike, Smartsheet, Asana, MS Project, or other project management software. You can read reviews of many of these products on my website (www .thetogethergroup.com).

- If your project is incredibly complex, use a Gantt chart or work-stream map to build your Project Plan.

You can find more examples of Project Plans on my website (www.thetogethergroup .com).

Reader Reflection
Which tool will you use to host your Project Plan? Why have you selected this one?

Identify Dependencies on a Bigger Picture Calendar

But wait, don't just start typing all the steps into Excel cells! You will get lost, I promise. Start with the big stuff. Take all those milestones and plot them on an organizational calendar first. This is important because when you just start writing in Excel, you tend to forget organizational events, vacations, and holidays that can affect your planning.

Definition
Project Dependencies are steps within your project that are dependent on other steps happening first.

Kate's people also collectively wrapped their heads around a big-picture view of the calendar, resulting in the time line in figure 12.9. Kate could have mapped this out and handed her team an exact time line, but she is not omniscient. By doing this together, Kate and her

Figure 12.9 Kate's Project Time Line

team can collectively identify dependencies and other important collaboration points. For example, Kate's team could not send out communication to the new teachers until they had hotel and transportation secured and approved.

Other ways that your team could create a Project Timeline include:

- Print out a monthly view of an organizational calendar and hang it on the wall.
- Work directly within Outlook or Google as a separate calendar.
- Create a Work Stream Map, such as the example in table 12.4.

Kate's food person couldn't very well order the food without having a final count of registrants, right? Before Kate's team goes away and creates detailed individual Project Plans, they need to synch up with each other! You can find a Work Stream Map template on my website (www.thetogethergroup.com).

This exercise will also help you realize that before things can progress information needs to be communicated to various parties and perhaps some of it can be consolidated. For example, principals should know about which of their people will be out of building during the summer training period so they can arrange their local trainings accordingly. Therefore, the principals need to know very early who is participating in the training on which days.

Finally, Finally, Break It Down into a Project Plan

As you write up your steps, make sure they are all bite-sized and start with verbs. Don't just write "Food" into your Project Plan. You will never be clear about what to do! Instead, write, "Call three caterers and obtain pricing for July 17 event." And if you are managing others in this process, have them break down their own steps and insert them into your Master Plan (table 12.5).

Table 12.4 Example Work Stream Map

Time Frame	Work Stream 1 [Transportation]	Work Stream 2 [Food]	Work Stream 3 [Housing]	Work Stream 4 [Communications]
April			Secure vendor in each city.	
May	Order buses to transport from hotel.			
June				
July				

Table 12.5 Kate's Project Time Line

Work Stream	Owner	Action	Deadline
Network teams	Kate	Connect Amanda Pinto with team recruit.	2/18
Agenda finalization	Kate	Update agenda finalization template to include NLT and ALT and final Elm City info.	2/21
Venues/food/hotels/AV	Kate	Confirm ALT school	2/21
Ops performer mapping	Kate	Finish the ops owner performer map.	2/21
Network teams	Amy	Connect with Tracy to link with team HC site for payroll, finger printing, etc.	2/27
Venues/food/hotels/AV	Chandler	Sign ALT hotel contract.	2/27
Venues/food/hotels/AV	Chandler	Sign all external venue contracts.	2/27
Agenda finalization	Rachel	Finalize special rooms: how many breakouts for their days?	3/6
PD design and review	Rachel	Create master skeleton for ATT session.	3/12

Good examples of tasks include these:

- Write communication to facilitators on AV needs.
- Call AV vendor to confirm all deliveries.
- Finalize budget quote from printing vendor.

Not so good examples are these:

- Facilitator note on AV.
- Make sure deliveries are on track.
- Budget.

There are a few reasons that I want your steps to be so specific:

- It will help you and your team build plans for the future.
- It will help you ensure that actions are on track and connections are being made.
- It will help you manage *yourself* in the midst of juggling multiple projects.

DETOUR: DON'T FORGET TO MERGE WITH YOUR PERSONAL ORGANIZATION SYSTEM!

The plan is in place, it makes sense with your organization's calendar, and people are ready to roll—if not started already. But how on earth should you incorporate managing this project into your *own* personal organization system along with all of your other work and deadlines?

Enter Two Weeks of High-Level Deadlines Directly into Your Calendar as All-Day Appointments

Things will change as you go, so don't import every single date for the entire project. But it's worth getting at least two weeks' worth of deadlines from the project copied into your calendar because inevitably, your various projects will collide with your own schedule—or each other. Someone may ask you to review a key document on a day you had paid time off. You might realize you need *four* different things from the CEO all on the same day. To plan ahead for these inevitable overlaps, start by loading the first two weeks of dates and all high-level milestones. Then, review your plan in detail each week and make adjustments as needed. More on that in the next section.

Start a Weekly Project Plan Review, Potentially as Part of Your Meeting with Myself

Shannon Donnelly, one of the best project managers I have ever met (especially because she once sent me cookies after I worked on her project team!), conducted a Meeting with Herself review each and every week as she conducted her Self Meeting. In some cases, she sent written requests for action items to each of her team members or provided a written update to her manager. Having been on the receiving end of Shannon's weekly e-mails, I appreciated her keeping me on track amidst all of the other work I was juggling!

Reader Reflection

Where and when will you review all of your various Project Plans? And if you are the manager of multiple managers of plans, when and how will you review?

Step 9: Lead Ongoing Project Meetings

The project is kicked off, people know their roles, and now you need to get moving on execution. Typically, that requires some kind of regular communication among the members of the project team. To make things more efficient and effective, Kate worked with her team to create a standing Project Check-in Agenda. Kate decided frequency was more important than length, so her team met weekly for thirty minutes. But if you were working with a non-time-sensitive or slower-moving project, you could meet less frequently for longer periods of time. Adjust the intensity to match the flow of the project. Together project teams meet regularly to find efficiencies, prevent collisions, and keep roles and responsibilities clear.

Let's jump into Kate's example in table 12.6. You don't need all of these elements all of the time, but having a predictable, set agenda helped her plan ahead and collaborate with her team.

Table 12.6 Kate's Project Meeting Agenda

What	Who	How Long
Celebrations	Everyone	5 min
Here is what is most important now	Kate	1 min
Sharing communications map and final pressure testing	Marissa	15 min
FYI on agendas for operations Kick-Off Meetings with event owners	Kate	10 min
Weekly summer PD e-mail update	Kate	5 min
Updates and reminders (due by 8 PM Tuesday—we all review beforehand)	Kate and Marissa	5 min
Determine who owns these hot potatoes; tell the group if you know who does	Kate	5 min
Problem solving	Alex and Marissa	5 min
Help requests	Marissa	3 min
Communications CI: problems and solutions	Everyone	2 min
next step check-in and whirl around	Everyone	4 min

The predictable aspect includes the weekly summer PD e-mail update and an updates and reminders section created by Kate; there is also a heavy collaborative aspect. The problem solving and help requests sections are cocreated by the team. I especially love the help requests and problem solving to prevent people from operating in silos. Kate also chose to store her agendas as Google Docs so the team could add items in throughout the week.

Reader Reflection

When and how do you need to meet with your project team? What are your standing agenda items?

Step 10: Anticipate and Tee-up Challenging Decisions

One of the most important roles a Project Owner can play is to anticipate and tee-up challenging decisions. Often the Project Owner can see decisions looming ahead. In Kate's case, she spotted about whether materials should be distributed digitally or in binders. Kate could foresee many members of the project team—and others with interest—having strong feelings on this topic. She also could see the budget, hardware distribution, Internet needs, and preparation implications of any decision.

Convene the stakeholders: She then convened a group of stakeholders, such as finance, information technology, recruiters, and program people, in one room for a meeting and helped them agree on a set of criteria to make the decision.

Identify criteria for decision making: Some of the criteria was participant usability, budget implications, and lead time for document submission deadlines.

Lay out options and benefits/drawbacks: Although Kate did have her own point of view, she wisely laid out possible options (binders, build a website, distribute flash drives, etc.). Because this topic was discussed early enough on in the process, the team was able to solve much of the materials issue through digital distribution.

If Kate had not had the foresight to anticipate the implications of the decision and gotten the right people together to discuss it, the team would have been left with fewer options.

Reader Reflection

What decisions can you anticipate in your project? How can you get ahead on them?

Step 11: Provide Updates to Stakeholders

At some point in your project, people are going to want to know specific pieces of information. In fact, *different* groups of people will want to know *different pieces* of information. In other words, this challenge can't be solved by sending a single e-mail blast to everyone containing all the information. In Kate's case, she was dealing with many factions:

- New teachers (attending the training)
- Principals

- Directors of operations
- Senior leadership team members
- Session facilitators

She paused and tried to put herself in her stakeholders' shoes and realized the session facilitators would need to know these things:

- What participants were asked to bring
- Which sessions the participants were in before and after
- Which grade levels the participants were assigned to teach

Kate also had to think about the ideal frequency and method to communicate this information. She decided that facilitators could get a monthly bulletin in the spring, and she would move to weekly updates in the busy summer season. But she didn't just start issuing the communications! She paused and asked the facilitators what would work best for them … but she gave them a limited set of options.

FAQ: Just *how* much do I tailor communications per stakeholder group?
Issuing fifty different updates each week is obviously unsustainable. I recommend tailoring communications to most effectively get the job done. For example, if you know a stakeholder is notorious for not reading her e-mail, it might be best to find time to give her a ten-minute verbal update via phone!

Reader Reflection
Complete the Stakeholder Communication Chart in your Reader Reflection.

Step 12: Hold a Debrief Meeting

Yayyy! Your project is successfully executed. But don't stop now! We need a real debrief, from your stakeholders and your project team, after reviewing your project results and data.

Capture Ongoing Project Learnings in Real Time

Kate set up an e-mail address to collect feedback in the moment, and any member of the project team—or even a user—could e-mail the address. There was no expectation of response, but the method enabled the team to access, review, and analyze live data. They weren't sitting around a week later trying to remember, "So, how did this project go? What worked? What didn't?"

Survey Your Stakeholders and Examine Your Data

Presumably, you have some data you gathered along the way. In Kate's case, she had a fair amount:

- Results of teacher logistics surveys, usually given right after events
- Results of facilitator's surveys
- Her own and her team's observations

She gathered this info along the way through SurveyMonkey and paper-based surveys when the data would be fresh in people's minds, such as right after a training session.

Lead the Meeting

Kate planned a Debrief Meeting with all members of her immediate Project Team and planned a collaborative agenda using the real-time learnings and stakeholder surveys mentioned previously. Figure 12.10 is a snapshot of her Debrief Agenda.

Outcomes	Agenda
• Align toward a collective view of successes and challenges	• 5 – Timeline overview: where we've been, where we are headed
• Identification of any other questions to answer for debrief	• 15 – Alignment on successes and challenges & clarification on the questions for debrief
• Gather initial input on recommendations for next summer	• 25 – Recommendations
• Gather OAPICs clarity on key decisions	• 10 – Approvers and Resources
	• 5 – Next steps
	Pre-Reading:
	• Criteria for Ops Success
	• Challenges
	• Financial Analysis

Figure 12.10 Kate's Debrief Agenda

A few things I love about Kate's sample:

- Thoughtful attention to prereading
- Focus on the past and the future
- Celebrations via alignment on successes

Kate was really deliberate in how she pushed her team to focus on their outcomes. Figure 12.11 from her Debrief Meeting Materials shows how she shared the data.

(Pre-reading) Criteria for Ops Success

Criterion	How did we do?	How do we know?
Teacher & Leader Experience	Green	*93% respondents agree or strongly agree that "the logistics were clearly communicated and smoothly executed which allowed me to focus entirely on the training and/or work time."
School Ops partnership	Green	*9 out of 11 DSOs gave a 4 or a 5 rating of their hosting experience.
Facilitator experience	Green	100% respondents agree or strongly agree that Team Summer Ops took the "rocks off the road" so that I could focus entirely on leading great adult PD
Team experience & sustainability	Red	*0% agree or strongly agree they would want to be a part of Summer Ops next year
Finances	Yellow	*Not including AV rentals, we came in under cost projections. Including rentals, we came in ~100K over projections. (AV rentals are separated here because they weren't an anticipated need when costs were projected).

Figure 12.11 Kate's Debrief Meeting Materials: Excerpt 1

You can find a full version of Kate's Debrief Meeting Materials on my website (www.thetogethergroup.com).

Codify Your Learnings

Just debriefing is not enough. I want you to codify your learnings for the future. Kate spent half of her Debrief Meeting naming challenges and brainstorming plans for the future (figure 12.12). She pulled from one set of trends one challenge of "not enough people" from all of the feedback, and then created a list of recommendations and rationale for discussion in the debrief. And Kate took it a step further. She started to think about decision makers and time lines needed for certain decisions. This is helpful for activities that require advance planning.

Reader Reflection

How and when will you debrief your project?

START STRONG

Whew. This is quite a chapter. You will not take *all* of these steps in every project you manage or supervise. However, some predictable project management path should be followed in order to keep the entire project Together. There is power in creating a common language and expectations for your organization. I deliberately chose to give you steps for the most complex project out there. Feel free to pick and choose which steps *your* project needs.

- Write a Project Statement.
- Define roles and responsibilities.
- Create a Project Summary.
- Create a Kick-Off Agenda.
- Integrate project reviews into your personal systems.
- Communicate with your stakeholders.
- Debrief and codify your learnings.

Challenge #2:
Not enough people to be at all places @ all times.

Recommendation	Rationale for Recommendation
Determine needs of and R/Rs of work from other Network teams by Dec 15 – esp. facilities, data, recruitment, sys tech/IT. Ensure this work is built into folks' workflows.	Teams need time to plan for our asks. People will be invested if the work is built into their workflows and aligned with development goals.
Figure out ask of other teams for their people by Dec 15: Run a recruitment process, give teams choice on sharing their people	We want people who WANT to do this work. We want teams who feel good about sharing their people.
Larger team with unique roles: functional, ops owner, team of interns. 12-16 (depending on # of locations) interns, 8 functional people, 4-6 ops owners.	It was NOT sustainable to have Ops team members with multiple roles. The different roles also work for diff strengths and interests. On the ground support doesn't require experience –interns would be perfect.
Create a cohort of interns instead of as-needed temps.	Interns are cost-effective and weare able to hire them for specific amounts of time which suits the seasonal nature of the work. They would also be a talent pipeline.
Compensation for Ops team: *Time: 5-15 comp days, depending on role. Or, *Stipend: 2-6K, depending on role (would norm w. team HC) *Some combination	Very long days ask people to make personal trade-offs and work more hours than the AF norm. Compensation for extra time will help get people excited to be on the team.

Key Decision	Approver	Inputters	Resources	Decision Deadline
*What is the Ops team structure?	Tracy?	Kate		11/15
*What is the compensation plan?	Tracy	Kate, Team Human Capital		12/1
*What are the R/R of other network teams (esp. IT, data strategy, facilities, finance, external relations) and available capacity of other people to join team?	Dacia? Doug?	Cabinet, Team Leads		12/15
*Can we hire a team of interns?		Tracy		12/1

Figure 12.12 Kate's Debrief Meeting Materials: Excerpt 2

Togetherness Talks: Erica Phillips

Name: Erica Phillips

Title: Southern Connecticut Director & VP Business Development, All Our Kin

Why Togetherness matters: I lead All Our Kin's operations in southern Connecticut, supporting two hundred caregivers who care for twelve hundred children. If I were not Together, I could not provide the kind of support they rely upon.

At 10 AM on any given workday, what might I find you doing?

I may review a grant for our organization, coach one of my team members, or help a caregiver who has been evicted.

What is your favorite Together Tool and why?

My MS OneNote has a notebook that lists priorities by team member. Throughout the week, I add items to a page for each person so that I know what we need to discuss during our next check-in. It also enables me to keep track of previous conversations.

Tell me how you start and end each day to remain Together.

The night before I review my task list in Remember the Milk and make sure that the highest priority items are at the top. If my day is incredibly busy, I will add key tasks to my calendar so I make sure to get to them during the day. I don't do much in the morning other than getting to my first meeting because I've already planned the night before.

What do you proactively do to remain productive?

Sleep is very important. I try to get at least seven hours of sleep per night. And I really try to get into the office early so I have a few minutes to breathe and connect with my team members before the craziness of each day.

How do you remain focused when the work is swirling around you?

I consistently look ahead at my schedule so I know when I have pockets of free time. I move anything not urgent to these down times, which helps me focus on the most important things. Additionally, I really like working in fast-paced environments—I would probably be bored if a little work wasn't swirling around me.

What recenters you when the work feels overwhelming?

Seeing our childcare providers energizes me. They work from 7 AM to 6 PM caring for small children often by themselves. After these long days, they come out to our professional development with so much joy and energy … it's really inspiring and I am motivated by them.

What is your definition of balanced?

I rarely take home work on weekends—which was really helpful since we just finished a 10-month renovation on our new house. I was able to work on our house most weekends! Additionally, I really value enough time with friends and family and getting a good night's sleep.

What have you learned to let go?

Being involved in everything!

CHAPTER 13

Become a Dynamic Duo
Maximize Your Assistant

SEEN AND HEARD

"I'm not very organized myself, so it's hard to delegate well to my assistant."

"My assistant and I text, talk, and e-mail back and forth all day long. We only schedule formal meetings when there is a lot to discuss."

"My assistant helps with eliminating office management work, but I would like her to help more with my calendar and try to find a system to relay action steps from meetings I attend without her."

"My work with my assistant is great when I'm in town, but when I travel, our communication is less effective."

OVERVIEW AND OBJECTIVES

I have seen many mission-driven leaders loudly proclaim that they do not need assistants. It feels frivolous, and besides, they can handle every detail themselves. Although I don't doubt their competence or yours, I do want you to ask yourself the following questions:

- How much time do I spend managing my calendar and scheduling?
- How often do I find myself managing processes over content?

- Have I ever scrambled to prepare for an event or hit a deadline?

- Am I positive my time is aligned with my priorities?

- Do I have all information I need right at my fingertips?

- Is my team consistently prepared for our meetings?

If you found yourself nodding or running to your calendar scrambling to calculate how much time you've spent managing it, there is a chance an assistant could be useful to you. And even if you cannot afford to hire a full-time support person, perhaps there are certain aspects of your role that you are not uniquely qualified to do and could be outsourced. For example, Adam Cobb, a talented principal in Brooklyn, audited his calendar and discovered the high percentage of time he spent directly scheduling teaching candidates and moving people through a hiring time line. Adam's rationale was that he wanted to keep in personal touch with people he may be about to hire! That made total sense to me, but there is a way to split the difference here. After some brainstorming, Adam and I determined that he could make the initial contact with the potential candidate, but his director of operations could manage moving people through the process and communicate with teachers about which classrooms they would visit. We got Adam about ninety minutes back per week during busy hiring season.

If you are lucky enough to have administrative support, let's make sure you are using it wisely. If you do not have administrative support, you may want to skip this chapter. A word on terminology—you may call the person who supports you or your team your *assistant, executive assistant, coordinator, secretary,* or some other name. For the sake of simplicity, I will use the term *assistant* throughout the chapter and for ease, I'm going to stick to the pronouns *he* and *him*.

In this chapter, you will do the following:

- Clarify the roles and responsibilities of your assistant.

- Learn how to hire and train an effective assistant who will help you maximize your time.

- Get clear on the when, how, and what of communicating with your assistant.

- Support your assistant in managing and communicating his workload.

EVALUATE YOUR CURRENT RELATIONSHIP

First, take a quick quiz (table 13.1) to see where your relationship with your assistant currently stands. If you don't have an assistant but are considering hiring one, take the quiz to help develop your vision for the partnership. If you do have an assistant, take it separately and compare answers.

QUIZ

Consider Your Current Partnership

Evaluate the degree to which your current practice meets the descriptions.

5 = awesome, 4 = good, 3 = so-so, 2 = some gaps, 1 = big gaps

Table 13.1 Assistant and Manager Quiz

	Rating
1. We understand each other's professional and personal priorities.	
2. The assistant is able to focus on proactive projects without getting interrupted by last-minute requests.	
3. We have a solid understanding of each other's workloads for the next three months.	
4. The manager's calendar is mechanically perfect (locations, times, etc.).	
5. The assistant serves as a strategic calendar thought partner.	
6. We meet consistently on a daily, weekly, and monthly basis.	
7. Our check-in meetings focus on the most important topics.	
8. The manager clearly delegates projects and tasks.	
9. The assistant is able to own complex projects start to finish.	

Reader Reflection

Where do you have strengths and gaps? Does your assistant agree?

Don't be discouraged if you and your assistant have different rankings. This is where the important conversations happen! I've seen everything from assistants who only manage calendars to assistants who feed their boss's cats and everything in between. The first step is to make sure it is clear to you both what role your assistant plays. Does he simply execute tasks? Are you asking him to be your gatekeeper? Is he in charge of scheduling for your entire team? What else does your assistant own?

HIRE THE RIGHT PERSON

It all starts with the right person in the job. The work of the assistant often falls into one of the five following buckets listed, ordered from least to most complex. Some assistants enter a role at one level and then move along the spectrum, gaining more responsibility as they go. Others play dual roles. Your job is to get clear on what you want and compare this against the skill of the person you have in the role. In my own nonprofit career, I've tried to find assistants who can play all the parts listed in the next section. This often meant they transitioned to other roles in two to three years, but I felt like it was worth it because of their sheer horsepower in their duration. The choice is yours; what's important is that you are clear with yourself, your assistant, and your team.

Assistant Categories

The Do-er: Manages Your Calendar. This assistant deals with scheduling, processing paperwork, and sending communications. You delegate tasks, and he executes them. This person may or may not also do personal tasks, such as order lunch and drop off your dry cleaning.

The Manager: Aligns Your To-Dos and Priorities. This assistant helps you match your time and meetings with your Priority Plan. He might tell you, "I'm not sure this meeting request aligns with what you want to spend time on this month. Can I push it off?" Additionally, this assistant often helps you manage your Later List as work flows in.

The Coordinator: Supports Your Team. You can often find this assistant distributing and collecting information to and from your team, such as the organization calendar or roles and responsibilities chart. This person may manage Leadership team meeting agenda development or board meeting planning. He may even help you write performance evaluations by collecting feedback throughout the year.

The Project Manager: Runs the Show. In organizations that hold many events or projects, one person is often needed to oversee the entire process from start to finish. He can be seen managing a parent night, volunteer training, or an anniversary celebration. He is comfortable interacting with vendors and acting as a peer to his colleagues.

The Problem-Solver: Develops and Shares Recommendations. These are my favorite assistants. I frequently hired people with strong critical thinking skills who could make recommendations to solve big problems. You can often hear this assistant saying, "I reviewed the past five years of what we have done with the family engagement survey, as well as what other peer organizations do with theirs, and I recommend we _____."

Throughout this chapter, I will feature many examples from my own past assistants, with a special focus on Mila Singh, who was with me for two years before she started business school. Mila now sets the standard for anyone I work with or coach on how to maximize a leader's impact. Am I allowed to dedicate a chapter? I guess it is my book, so Mila, this chapter is dedicated to you!

Reader Reflection

What level is your current assistant? Does it match the demands of the role?

Design the Role

To a certain extent, everyone wants their assistants to possess different types of skills. But in my experience hiring and directly managing assistants—and coaching *many* senior leaders through their own processes of doing so—I have seen a few key talents set the right person apart. In this section, I will guide you through how to write up the right buckets of responsibilities and articulate the skills your assistant will need to accomplish them. Next, we'll look at ways to screen candidates. If you already have a wonderful assistant in place, feel free to skim.

Get the Responsibilities Right

Too many assistants are underused. The work is thought of as discrete administrative tasks and not tied back to the bigger picture of supporting the leader in being more Together so organizational goals are achieved.

Instead of only thinking about the assistant's tasks, consider first what buckets of work he will own. Then spell out the actual associated To-Dos. Some of it may not feel all that glamorous to you, but remember that different people are motivated by different things. In the portion of the job description shared in figure 13.1 (full version available on my website, www.thetogethergroup.com), I like how Collegiate Academies organized the buckets of work into "complex scheduling," "written communication," and more.

Collegiate Academies thought about the assistant's work categories in terms of their specific connections to the CEO's Togetherness. I like how Ben Marcovitz, the founder and CEO of Collegiate Academies in New Orleans, created a thoughtful role by doing the following:

- Gets very clear on the large buckets of work
- Is unafraid to be detailed and specific (e.g. "Make sure CEO is 100 percent reliable …")
- States with whom the assistant will work closely, internally and externally

Reader Reflection

What are the buckets of work your assistant will handle? How will they support your Togetherness?

This person's main goal is to maximize CEO's ability to accomplish our organizational goals. This person must operate in lockstep with the CEO to meet his needs, anticipate his needs, execute on his behalf, and take on extra projects that will support the mission of Collegiate Academies. This person will also work closely with key staff at Collegiate Academies: the Chief Operating Officer, Chief Academic Officer, President, and Chief Talent Officer, along with their teams. Duties include, but are not limited to:

Direct Support to the CEO

- Complex Scheduling – Manage the CEO's calendar. Ensure he is present and prepared for his daily responsibilities: meetings, work time, communication, travel, and personal needs around which to schedule work. Prepare the CEO for upcoming events that require his attention beforehand.

- Constituent Management – Manage all daily phone and email communication on the CEO's behalf. Communicate directly with partner organizations on special projects, including leaders at the Louisiana Department of Education, the Recovery School District, charter operators around the city and beyond, Leading Educators, and other influential organizations within education. Ensure his direct reports, teammates, and collaborators outside of CA hear from him within 24 hours. Keep sensitive correspondence and information confidential.

- Written Communication – Manage all follow up and follow through needed from email correspondence or meetings. Ensure the CEO is 100% reliable in following through on his next steps.

- Document Preparation – Prepare documents (written responses, PowerPoint presentations) for events and special projects.

- Administrative Support – Provide administrative support as needed: manage reimbursements, support him real time during his travel, and other tasks as needed.

Figure 13.1 Collegiate Academies' Assistant Job Description Part 1

Skills Required in a Strong Executive Assistant

Everyone's assistant has a slightly different job description, but there are universal traits that set apart great assistants from the average or below-average folks. None of this is rocket science, but it can be helpful to see the skills as a set.

- Impeccable and reliable follow-through
- Proactive planning with a strong systems orientation
- Outstanding writing and clear communication
- Willingness to break through walls to get to the right outcome
- Ability to juggle short-term tasks with longer projects

In Collegiate's job description, Ben listed the skills shown in figure 13.2.

I really love how Ben's first bullet is a "deeply held belief in the mission of Collegiate Academies." Many candidates for this role will be first drawn to your mission, and you

Additional Qualifications

- Deeply held belief in the mission of Collegiate Academies.

- Fiercely organized and execution-oriented; experience managing many moving parts and consistently delivering on time.

- Acute attention to the smallest details to ensure smooth, predictable, and effective outcomes.

- Exemplary communication skills (written and oral) and the ability to communicate with a wide range of clients and constituents, including scholars, parents, vendors, teachers and teaching candidates, national education reform groups, and donors.

- Superior initiative; anticipates potential snags and plans for them. Takes instruction well, but does not wait for it.

- Focus on delivering quality internal and external client service.

- Ability to work in a fast-paced, high-performing and sometimes unpredictable environment.

- Maturity, humility, strong work ethic, sense of humor, and a roll-up-my-sleeves and "whatever it takes" attitude.

Figure 13.2 Collegiate Academies' Assistant Job Description Part 2

want them to lead with that over all else—after all, most of their work will be in service to that mission.

Reader Reflection

What skills do you need your assistant to possess? What must be in place already? What are you willing to train?

Screening Candidates

This is not a book about hiring. For that, please read Geoff Smart and Randy Street's *Who: The A Method for Hiring* or Daniel Coyle's *The Talent Code* (for a full list of books I recommend, please visit my website, www.thetogethergroup.com). However, I have found most books on hiring focus more on either very senior people or very junior—and this assistant role, if done correctly, really falls in the middle. Although your assistant may not manage other people, you want him to wield great influence in your organization.

Two skills are especially essential for helping busy leaders juggle their work: prioritization and speed. Both of these can be tested with behavior-based interviewing. One of my favorite exercises is a timed and written prioritization exercise, given before an in-person interview is granted. Figure 13.3 is what I sent Mila after speaking to her via phone.

And figure 13.4 shows what she delivered, with a full version available on my website (www .thetogethergroup.com).

Assistant/Associate Prioritization Activity

You have the below tasks on your list of things to complete this week—among other things!

Maia Heyck-Merlin, AF's Chief Operating Officer, and Dacia Toll, the network's Co-CEO/President, are the two managers that you are directly supporting. Maia's team consists of five additional staff members to whom you also provide some support.

Instructions:

- Make a list of the key additional questions you would need answered about each item in order to proceed.
- Write your initial thinking about how you would prioritize this list and include your rationale.
- This activity should take you **approximately 50 minutes**.
- Please return your work in a separate document.

TASKS TO BE COMPLETED THIS WEEK:

- Make travel arrangements for Dacia's trip to Brooklyn for the Strategy Committee meeting next week
- Research how other charter management organizations (CMOs) compensate and reward their outstanding teachers to prepare a comparison report for Maia
- Plan logistics/operations for 2-day Principal Interview Weekend for all 15 principal candidates coming from local sites and out-of-state locations (including communicating logistics info to all attendees and arranging the location)
- Proofread 2 chapters of the SUNY charter application
- Order flowers for the Director of Team Recruit's year of service ($30-40 range)
- Review recruitment data from last season and prepare a report showing where we should invest the highest levels of our advertising money
- Book travel for Maia's 2 day site visit to the New School Venture Fund's annual retreat in Los Angeles. It must coordinate with the Dacia's site visit.

Figure 13.3 Assistant Prioritization Activity

Mila's response stood out for a few reasons:

1. She demonstrated that she would see a task through until the end. For example, after sending an e-mail, she would follow up with a phone call.
2. She understood the importance of coordinating schedules, and she prioritized the most senior members of the organization.
3. She organized her thoughts into columns and bullets, which showed she would present information to me in an organized fashion.

Tasks To Be Completed This Week (5/10)

Task (ordered by priority)	Additional Questions	Priority Rationale
Schedule 2nd round interviews for 3 internal Academic Dean applicants and forward Dacia all of their first round interview notes and resumes so she can prepare for the interviews	For the applicants (reach out to them individually): What interview times fit best with your schedule? Dacia (check her calendar or personally ask her): What interview times fit best into your	I prioritized this task as the first because recruitment efforts must be timely since we strive to attract and retain the best talent. It is important to continue the interview process along for these candidates, especially since it is a second round
Schedule a 3-hour stepback with Maia, Dacia, Doug McCurry (AF's Co-CEO and Superintendent) to discuss Talent Development's progress toward our goals/projects	Maia, Dacia, Doug (check calendar or personally ask): What three hour time fits best in each person's schedule? Is this an in-person meeting or can it be scheduled over a conference call. Any additional resources needed? Example:	I selected this task next because it requires a significant amount of time on three different people's calendars. So I will coordinate with all three individuals to make sure I can block out a three hour time period for this step-back. Since this is a discussion about the Talent Development group's
Schedule 90-minute progress review meetings with Maia, the Director of Team Recruit, and each of the 5 Recruiters (five separate meetings)	Maia: Is this an in-person progress review or a conference call? What times work best for these individual meetings? (check calendar) Each Recruiter (call or email): What time best works for this progress review meeting?	Again, because this task requires time on Maia's calendar, I prioritize this task as high. It requires coordination with 5 different people for 5 different meetings, so I would like to ensure enough time to touch base with each individual and make sure the times work.

Figure 13.4 Mila's Response for Prioritization Activity

As you review your assistant hiring process, consider which skills you need the most and figure out how to gain some real-time data on your candidates. This can be especially helpful when you are comparing finalists.

Reader Reflection

How will you assess your assistant's skills using real-life performance tasks?

TRAIN YOUR ASSISTANT WELL

Now that you have attracted, recruited, and hired the right person, it's time to train him well. Many of you work in organizations that do not have orientation periods for all positions, so there may be some work you or a delegate will have to prepare to set up your new hire for success. In Mila's case, I knew I had to be prepared because (1) she expected it and (2) I was just returning from maternity leave after the birth of my first child. I had to keep my head on straight.

I started by thinking through skills I wanted Mila to acquire, when she would learn them, and what materials she would need to do. So, I developed a plan for "What You Will Learn," "Month-to-Month Responsibilities," and "Immediate Independent Work."

Figure 13.5 shows what I came up with (full version available on my website, www .thetogethergroup.com).

Then, I had to think through the entire year and overall roles and responsibilities (figure 13.6).

And finally, I had to help Mila prioritize all of this info and plan out her own time (figure 13.7).

This Onboarding Overview will take a little bit of time up-front, but remember that you can use it for the rest of your career. You can also have your outgoing assistant really contribute to, or even own, a big portion of this. The front-end investment in training your assistant and leveraging others to help will set up you *and* your new assistant for success.

What You Will Learn

Knowledge or Skill	When Learned	Supplemental Materials
AF REACH and Core Values	Onboarding with Emily	Core and REACH Values Overview
AF Working Agreements	Onboarding with Emily	Working Agreements
AF Mission, Vision, History	Onboarding with Emily	The New York Times Magazine and Yale SOM Articles
AF Organizational Structure	Onboarding with Emily	AF Team Overviews
Benefits and Payroll	New Team Member Orientation	
Establishing Communications Systems	Onboarding with Emily	
Calendar Maintenance and Scheduling	Onboarding with Emily	Scheduling Excellence Document

Figure 13.5 Mila's Onboarding What You Will Learn

Month-to-Month Responsibilities

Month	Big Projects	Reoccurring Monthly Work	Reoccurring Weekly Work
JULY	• Master Calendar Excellence • Scrub Maia's Fall Calendar • Executive Assistant Interview Training	• Doug/Talent/Ops Time • Reimbursement Collection • Monthly Map Collection	• Prepare Weekly Worksheet for MHM Review • 2-Week Calendar Scrub • Prepare MHM Weekly Check-in Agenda • Review CMS with MHM
AUGUST	• Serve as New Staff Training Captain • Organize AF-NY Picnic Assist MHM with the following: • Transition Meetings with Direct Reports • New Staff Training Personal Organization Session		
SEPTEMBER			
OCTOBER			
NOVEMBER	• Prep for Talent Mansion Stepback		

Figure 13.6 Mila's Month-to-Month Responsibilities

After the initial set-up and onboarding, you can transition to Daily-Weekly-Monthly Checklists to stay aligned on how your assistant spends his time. I don't want your assistant to lose sight of the administrative details amid the special project work he is likely to take on.

Figure 13.7 Mila's Immediate Independent Work

FAQ: Won't this be perceived as oh-so-bossy?

It's a good worry to have, but I think if truly done in the spirit of "I deeply want you to be successful in your role, I know the stumbling blocks around here, and I am investing all of this time up-front to help you be very independent later on," assistants feel incredibly grateful and honored that a busy leader understands their role to be so important.

Reader Reflection

What skills and knowledge does your assistant need? What do the first two weeks on the job look like?

USE YOUR ASSISTANT TO MANAGE MORE THAN YOUR SCHEDULING

Having someone manage your calendar is a tremendous time-saver, but once the mechanics of scheduling are mastered, you can take it to the next level and use your assistant as a *time buddy*. By *time buddy* (a term coined by a CEO I was coaching), I mean someone who pushes you to align your calendar with your priorities, points out patterns, notices when you disproportionately spend time on a specific person or topic, and helps you manage your energy. In sum, I want someone who totally focuses on your Togetherness. In this section, we will make sure your preferences are articulated, your calendar matches your priorities, and your energy levels remain well protected!

Aligning Your Assistant with Your Calendar

I bet you have preferences you don't even know you have! Window or aisle seat? See, I told you so. You do have preferences, but how clearly have you articulated them to the person who manages your schedule? It is helpful to articulate them to set your assistant up for success. I recommend you choose some to articulate up-front, and then also encourage your assistant to observe and note them as you continue to work together. Do you prefer just two hours of back-to-back meetings before you need a break? Only interview people in the afternoon? Take a quick nap at 2 PM? Use the following handy-dandy Manager Preferences Interview to get you and your assistant to calendar clarity. I suggest you give the interview to your assistant and ask him to schedule time with you to review your answers.

Manage the Mechanics: Calendar Preferences Interview Level 1

First things first. Let's make sure the mechanics of scheduling are mastered, right down to the teeniest-tiniest details, such as travel time between meetings. As Mila used to say, "To make sure *every single* detail was in your calendar, I would try to picture you [Maia] wandering around an unknown city with no idea where to go."

When I travel now (which I do weekly), I need to open my Outlook invite and see everything from the hotel's cross street (in case the taxi driver asks me!) to the distance between locations to the phone numbers of points of contact. Let's take a peek at a recent example from a trip to Aspire Public Schools in California (figure 13.8).

I want all of these details in your calendar, so you are not wasting precious minutes digging up addresses, searching for a phone charger, or getting lost in a building! Fundamentally, your assistant's role is to increase your Togetherness, and these small touches help.

If you are a school superintendent out on school visits, you may want your assistant to list in the meeting appointment the top teachers at that school, any special people you should say hello to in the front office, and the most recent attendance and student achievement reports so you can scan them *right* before you walk in.

Figure 13.8 Workshop Calendar Entry for Aspire

If you are not sure if your assistant has mastered the mechanics of your calendar, again, share this Manager Preferences Interview and have him sit down and interview you with your calendar in hand. It can be helpful if you consider your answers beforehand and have specific examples in mind.

FAQ: What if I want to reboard my assistant using some of these practices?
If you are pondering how to reset with your assistant, the Manager Preferences Interview is a great place to start. You can get totally aligned on your calendar expectations. After that, I would use a Daily-Weekly-Monthly Checklist to align on recurring tasks and determine how they align with special projects. In my experience, these two exercises are incredibly empowering to the assistant.

QUIZ
Manager Preferences Interview—Level 1
Ask your assistant to interview you on the level 1 questions in table 13.2, coming with his own observations in advance; you consider your answers as well!

Table 13.2 Manager Preferences Interview—Level 1: Master the Mechanics

Questions	My Notes
Are all meetings in calendar with locations, dates, times, addresses?	
Is all travel time blocked off in calendar and parking locations?	
Do all flights, trains, hotels, and so on have confirmation numbers and all relevant details?	
Have we ensured only the assistant receives invites?	
Are all meeting holds blocked off?	
Are meetings scheduled in a timely fashion?	
Do I control all calendar invites sent out?	
Are all attachments within agenda appointments?	
Do I have enough insight into personal commitments?	
Do you prefer any kind of calendar color-coding?	

FAQ: Should my assistant manage my e-mail?

I'll be honest. I'm torn on this one. I have rarely seen this done well without a very clear flow of events determined in advance. At the very worst, an assistant and manager are both in the manager's in-box all day and they cross wires. At the very best, the assistant is in the manager's in-box at set times of day, answering e-mails that can be dealt with and triaging e-mails for his manager to answer later. I think the best way to make this work is to set thirty minutes per day for a co-review of e-mails so the manager can clearly delegate what is being answered by whom. And, of course, if your assistant is helping with your in-box, make sure your team is aware of this in advance.

Manage Your Energy and Tasks: Calendar Preferences Interview Level 2

Once the mechanics are mastered, you and your assistant can move up a level to more advanced work. Most leaders stop at level 1, but that is a waste of your assistant's brainpower. Your assistant can play a key role in ensuring your day is set up to maximize your energy and help you get your most important work accomplished.

As I worked with Eric Gordon, the CEO of Cleveland Metropolitan School District and his scheduler, they would meet weekly to help him figure out how to maximize his work time in his calendar. Eric and Shirrell Greene, who managed his calendar, would meet weekly to help Eric figure out how to maximize the work time in his calendar. Eric decided he needed two two-hour chunks of time each week to get bigger work done. He explained it like this: "If I see white space in my calendar and I only have thirty minutes between meetings, by the time I figure out what I have to do, the time will be gone. So Shirrell and I sit down at our weekly meeting and enter in *exactly* which tasks I will do when, right down to embedding the actual attachments or work products into the appointment."

QUIZ

Manager Preferences Interview—Level 2

Ask your assistant to interview you on the level 2 questions in table 13.3, coming with his own observations in advance; you consider your answers as well!

Table 13.3 Manager Preferences Interview—Level 2: Manage Your Energy and Tasks

Questions	My Notes
What is your preferred spacing between meetings?	
Do you need time to eat? Do you need lunch ordered?	
Do I need to push back on people requesting time, if needed? Which people?	
How much work time do you need per week? When should this ideally happen?	
Do you need set times to answer e-mail per day? Do you want me to preview your e-mail?	
Are there certain types of people you prefer to speak with at different times of day?	
Which materials do you need with you at which meetings?	
Are there agendas I can draft on your behalf?	
What kind of meeting preparation is required by other people? Do you want me to play a role in previewing their agenda?	

Manage Your Priorities and Projects: Calendar Preferences Interview Level 3

Believe it or not, there is one more level of calendar support your assistant can provide—helping you manage your priorities and projects. Start by ensuring that your assistant knows what your priorities are (here is a good plug for sharing your Priority Plan!). Then work with your assistant to map each type of meeting to your priorities. Where are you spending too much time? Not enough?

Let's say you are a school superintendent, and your top priorities are as follows:

1. Team development
2. Teaching and learning
3. Staffing for next year

You look through your calendar and start connecting your meetings back to your priorities.

- "Oh, yes, the chiefs meeting and those one-on-ones clearly map to priority 1."
- "The two times per week school visits definitely match to priority 2."
- "I'm seeing nothing on my calendar that aligns with staffing for next year … Uh, oh! Can we block off some time for me to do some proactive recruiting?"

As you discover meetings that do *not* align with your priorities, think about shortening them or creating a strategic time for you to just pop in.

QUIZ
Manager Preferences Interview—Level 3
Ask your assistant to interview you on level 3 questions (table 13.4). As always, consider your own answers in advance.

Table 13.4 Manager Preferences Interview—Level 3: Manage Your Plans and Priorities

Questions	My Notes
Does time align to priorities? If not, what can be adjusted?	
During weird weeks, what can be shortened or canceled?	
Do all meetings have clear purpose and agendas?	
Are there meetings that can be shortened?	
Are there meetings that can be canceled?	
Are there meetings that can be delegated?	
Are there projects to work backwards from that require work blocks?	

As a way to sum up all of the calendar preferences, many assistants to create a Calendar Checklist to ensure that a week represents priorities and countless other details to make sure things stay Together. Figure 13.9 is an example that Maggie Klos, partner to Hannah

Lofthus met previously, created to ensure she and Hannah were aligned on what a Together Week looked like. You can find a full version on my website, www.thetogethergroup.com. What I love about this model is that Maggie took the initiative to summarize everything learned in her conversations and observations with Hannah. Maggie says, "To ensure we are aligned on best practices, I use the Calendar Checklist to ensure I am catching everything. It also pushes me to make sure activities are aligned, so that the CEO [Hannah] will be spending her time where it is most important." They then aligned on when and how the calendar was *scrubbed* and give this time in their weekly meeting. By *scrubbed*, I mean the conflicts are cleared, the details are in place, and the priorities are well placed. Maggie knew what to do when meetings were off-site, what materials Hannah needed for each meeting, and how much time Hannah needed to be prepared—in short, exactly what Hannah needed to be Together!

CHECKLIST: CALENDAR SCRUB

PURPOSE: Operationalize calendar rules and preferences to ensure there are no calendar issues and CEO is set up for success.

- Is there a **daily one hour block for 30 minute tasks & e-mail?**
- Is there a daily **call scheduled with SPM** for 15 minutes before first morning meeting?
- Is there a **weekly round-up** blocked?
- For all invites, does HL have **what she needs?**
- Are there **no overlapping** invites?
- Is there at least **10 minutes** between invites and **no back to backs?**
- Are all invites **confirmed (not a hold or block)?**
- Are all **blocks** removed?
- Is there **a location** on 100% of invites?
- Is **TK** to any meetings past 5:00 pm or on weekend?
- Are there upcoming **LLI or NPAF** deadlines?
  - MK identifies time to film
  - MK blocks HL task time to review and take notes on videos
- Is there a **call or external meeting?**
  - Block time for FU directly after
  - Add FU to task list

Figure 13.9 Maggie's Calendar Scrub Checklist

Reader Reflection

How will you and your assistant codify your calendar preferences?

The Week at a Glance

Whether or not your assistant manages your calendar, it can be helpful to receive an overview of your week ahead to help you manage deadlines and upcoming work. Ask your assistant to give you a preview of meetings, deadlines, and events so you can see the big picture of the week. At the very least, it may be useful to get a heads-up on these times:

- Key meetings, especially those that require preparation or prework

- Key deadlines, especially those that take multiple days to accomplish

- Any other organizational events that may affect your work

Figure 13.10 shows the weekly summary my assistant prepared for me. This gave me a big picture overview of my week and helped raise me out of the weeds of my detailed Outlook Calendar. Even small flags, such as evening phone calls, and previews of spacing (how frequently certain meetings fall) were hugely helpful to my preparation and communication with colleagues. This summary can be incredibly helpful as you meet with yourself each week to plan out your time as discussed in chapter 8.

This summary also helped me check in on personal balance to make sure I had some fun built in (dinner with friends) or see which days would require more stamina (a full day of meetings on Tuesday).

Reader Reflection

How would a Week at a Glance help you? What information do you need?

The Pending Meetings Tracker

Your assistant can be an amazing thought partner about how to spend your time—as long as you discuss more than scheduling. Not that scheduling is not important. Most assistants are wonderful at reactive scheduling, but how about *proactive* scheduling? By proactive scheduling, I mean those meetings you want to have at the right opportunity but do not immediately need to be calendared. For example, if you are headed to California for an upcoming conference and you look through the participant list, and there is someone you have been meaning to connect with for networking purposes, *that* is proactive scheduling. Enter the Pending Meeting Tracker.

Here's a glance at your upcoming week –

- **Monday (home)** *Flag – evening call*
  - Call with Tony S
  - Josh
  - Ed Pioneers Webinar
  - Lesley
  - Check in call with Amy/Chi
  - Nicole

- **Tuesday (Waverly) – Valentine's Day!**
  - Tentative 25 minutes with Becca – she will pull it off on Monday if she doesn't need it
  - Check in with Mel
  - Check in with Erica
  - Check in with Sarah
  - Check in with Tracy E
  - Mtg with Chastity/Harris/Max on assistant headcount planning

- **Wednesday (Court J)**
  - Jury Duty
  - WoMoWiBiJo dinner

- **Thursday (Waverly)**
  - Check in with Laura
  - Check in with Mila
  - Meeting with Chi to discuss school transitions
  - NS Cabinet Mtg
  - 3PM car pick up. Travel to Milwaukee

- **Friday (Milwaukee)**
  - Workshops

Big Picture Calendar Spacing:

- Week of Feb 13th (upcoming): You have fewer check ins this upcoming week because you gave the option to your direct reports to cancel. Sara cancelled for this week. Becca has a tentative 15 minutes still on the calendar in case she needs it.
- Week of Feb 20th: You have stepbacks with your directs.
- Week of Feb 27th: You are traveling M-W to Maine, so check ins fall on a Thursday
- Week of Mar 5th: Check ins fall on a Wednesday.

Thanks!
Mila

Figure 13.10 Weekly Summary

Assistants are often juggling multiple meeting requests, going out and coming in. It can be hard for anyone to keep their head on straight. The most successful assistants have systems for keeping track of these requests and for finding opportunities to hold other meetings that help you accomplish your goals and priorities.

Definition

A **Pending Meeting Tracker** is an organized list of all meeting requests (requests made by the manager and meetings requested by others).

The Pending Meeting Tracker is usually just an Excel or Google spreadsheet that lists facts such as these:

- Date request was made (from the manager or the requester)
- Date the meeting should be on the books
- Meeting title
- Meeting participants
- Meeting priority level (which often influences the time of day it will be held)
- In-person, video, or conference call
- Preferred length of meeting
- Any prework needed

This tool was particularly helpful when I wanted to have a meeting with someone but did not yet have a set date or time. For example, I knew I wanted to meet Edna N. for lunch the next time I was in New Haven (item 1 in figure 13.11). I didn't need to create a separate trip to New Haven for Edna, but I did want this meeting to happen at some point. Without Mila keeping it alive on the Pending Meetings Tracker, I would have lost sight of this important networking opportunity. You and your assistant can spin through your Pending Meetings Tracker once a week to give you a sense of what is (and is not) getting on your schedule. This tool also creates the added benefit of forcing you to be clear with your assistant on all details of the desired meeting! If you think your partnership could benefit from a Pending Meetings Tracker, there are free examples and templates on my website (www.thetogethergroup.com).

Reader Reflection

How can you help your assistant be proactive with scheduling opportunities?

MHM Pending Meetings Tracker

NAME	DAY/TIME	Internal/External	STATUS	NOTES
Lunch with Mayme H, Teacher U	Manhattan day, tuesdays	EXTERNAL	Pending, for a Manhattan day	City; Lunch/Coffee. Spent some time shadowing Maia, wants to get together for lunch. She is in manhattan- can do coffee.
Lunch with Matt K	TBD	EXTERNAL	Reschedule with Jennie	Assistant- jennifer.h@xxxx.org
Jeff L (Executive Director of TFA- New York) - lunch	Reschedule	EXTERNAL	Reschedule…assistant Craig	
Coffee with Betsy in New Haven (betsy@xxxx.com)	TBD	EXTERNAL	Pending	Former assistant to Maia. Her friend Teri N is applying to AF as Operations Associate. She would like to vouch for her.
Lunch with Edna N ①	TBD	EXTERNAL		In CT. Her assistant- Micaelas@xxxx.org

Figure 13.11 Maia's Pending Meeting Tracker

LEADER AND ASSISTANT COMMUNICATION STRUCTURES

Of course, to make all of this stuff actually work, we need … drum roll please … *systems!* No surprise there, right?! As you read on, please bear in mind that you don't need to use *all* of these structures, but having *some* distinct methods to communicate with your assistant will help you maximize this valuable resource. Some of these might feel micromanagey at first, but I assure you that the time invested in communication to stay on the same page will be well worth it. All too often, we hold hidden or unstated expectations of our assistants and end up frustrated. These structures are intended to clear the path for them to do their work, prioritize their tasks, and not get held up waiting on input from you. In this section, I will discuss the sacred weekly check-in, ideas for daily communication, and monthly step back. We'll also look at ways you can help your assistant manage his or her own workflow.

The Daily Update

You and your assistant may also need some kind of scheduled daily communication to ensure you are not bottlenecking him from getting what he needs. This is also a great way to communicate any real-time changes, such a shortened or canceled meeting.

Typically, the Daily Update takes the form of an end-of-day e-mail written by your assistant to you that updates you on the following areas:

- Accomplishments
- Priorities for the next day
- Quick Questions

Figure 13.12 is an example from Sarah Hogarty, a Director of School Operations, to her manager, the co-CEO. It shows how simple and quick these daily e-mails should be.

Many leaders then answer via e-mail at night or hold a ten-minute phone call or in-person huddle the next morning to ensure the assistant is not delayed.

Instead of a daily written communication, you could also select a verbal option. Erica Perez, the coordinator at Collegiate Academies, who partners with Riley Kennedy, keeps a shared Google Doc with her daily fifteen-minute verbal check-in items (figure 13.13).

Erica and Riley have a dedicated fifteen minutes each morning to review Quick Questions, what Erica needs, new issues, and calendar conflicts. Erica adds to this document throughout the day, and similar to during the quick, informal meeting, Erica takes notes directly into the Google Doc and then adds them to her own lists.

Reader Reflection

What kind of daily communication do you need with your assistant? In writing? In person?

To... Doug

Cc...

Subject: COB 4.21 (one QQ)

Question

- Tracy would like another hour to check in with you tomorrow – **is it okay to do this from 2-3 pm?**

Updates!

- Call with Robert T -> he accepted your invite to talk tomorrow night at 8:15 pm
- Zoho: I made edits based on our earlier conversations and tightened up the reporting pages so that you can see most things on one page. We can look at the pages in a future check in to see if you want to make any further changes.
- D&I mentor sessions with Joshua: I am working scheduling both sessions #3 and #4 – the date we had originally picked out for #3 ended up not working for him. I will try to schedule session #3 for May and session #4 for June.

Thanks,
Sarah

Figure 13.12 Sarah's Daily E-mail

FAQ: What if your assistant supports multiple people or teams?

The need for clear and reliable systems becomes even greater—both to get you the resources you need and to prevent your assistant from getting crushed! This is a huge plug to have your assistant make his or her own Priority Plan to catch and codify the work coming in from multiple directions. Examples of this are available on my website (www .thetogethergroup.com). If you have a secret hunch that your assistant is getting crunched (lots of late night e-mails are usually a big hint!), tell him your worry and ask him to track his time so you can get a sense of the work on his plate. Be careful this is not said in a punitive way; your goal is to support him, so he can support you!

The Weekly Check-In

Similar to how you meet regularly with your direct reports, you will want to meet with your assistant weekly. You can read more about meeting structures in chapter 5. In my experience, assistants are the *least* likely to get time with their managers because they always bump themselves off the schedule. Michelle Hays, assistant to Mark DiBella at YES Prep in Houston, describes her overall approach:

> My strategy for this year has been to schedule *three* meetings for us each week. One is a placeholder that is usually canceled because of other meetings. When I had to cancel

Time Frame	Agenda Items	Information	Action Steps/Notes	Deadline	Completed
1 Min	Hellos				
3 Min	Quick Questions	1. Attendance tracker 2. Order Business Cards (vistaprint?) 3. Sent you messages for two hotels that have rooms available for next week.	1. n/a 2. Do today 3. Call about parking	1. n/a 2. 9/29 3. 9/29	2. Done 3. Done
2 Min	What EP Needs				
3 Min	New Issues	1. Standing Desk: Haven't had time to show me, but will figure out this weekend. 2. Signs for Meeting Rooms: Run by REK 3. Side Roads: No meeting space available at Fontainbleu Park, will call last year's retreat place today.	1. Do it 2. Change CST for Prep 3. Irene (985) XXX-XXXX	1. 10/5 2. 9/30 3. 10/2	1. 2. 3.
3 Min	Calendar Issues	1. Today: back to back meetings. Do you need lunch? 2. 10/13: LAPCS should/can I go?	1. Yes 2. No	n/a	
3 Min	Keep Items	1. Payment Processing 2. REK's Keep	1. n/a 2. Communication Tree: look at Sci's 3. Sped Tours: DFO meeting/ something I would shadow	1. na 2. 10/5 3. 10/2	2. 3.

Figure 13.13 Erica's Daily Check-In Tracker

9/21 Mark & Michelle Check-in

Calendar
- Board prep time for October
- HISD site visits with Jason
- Did you connect with Travis?
- Do you need work time for finalizing ELT agenda & PPT with Kari (you have no check-in with her this week)
- Move Evan call on Friday due to Ann worktime?
- Is there any work time I am regularly missing on your calendar? Anything you want to change?

QQ
- Send LCP an "all-in kid" picture and 2-3 sentences about "I'm all in for this kid because … "
- 8/28 New Leaders team feedback from Recy.
- Do you need a flight to Advocacy day? Hotel?
- Did you hear back from Don?

College Rush

Notes from Graham
- Money for buses
- MD will ask Phil to talk to SDs about this possibility.

Fuel Ed

Notes from Megan:
- Soft copy of one-pager that we can send around?
- Add as agenda item - pre-work - bring a list of invites for who would be good for this.

ELT agenda
- Invite Ann, Robert, Nicole if they would like to attend
- Request to move from WG agenda to ELT meeting agenda: Give update on TEA academic accountability
- Methodology (how they determined the ratings) & Biggest watch areas for this year
- How much time would you need on future agenda in order to answer these questions? Plug into second half of meeting.

Figure 13.14 Mark and Michelle's Check-In Agenda

one last year, it really messed me up for the week, so I made a "freebie" for myself this year and give it back to him as work time if we don't need it. The second is a regular check-in and the third is shared work time for final executive team meeting prep. Having at least two in-person touchpoints each week means that I rarely have to e-mail him.

Whatever your frequency, weekly meetings between you and your assistant should be held sacred. It is one of the most valuable hours you spend all week, because it is explicitly designed to help you make the most of your own time.

Figure 13.14 shows an example of a weekly check-in between Michelle and Mark. She created the agenda in advance of their meeting using their shared OneNote list and took the lead in facilitating the discussion:

- Calendar alignment
- Quick Questions
- Status checks on various projects
- Co-planning important organizational meetings

FAQ: How long should it take my assistant to prepare? What should I do to prepare? This meeting will likely take your assistant thirty to sixty minutes to prep materials and lay out questions. You should not have to do a ton to prepare if you and your assistant have set up the standing agenda together.

The weekly check-in most often contains these categories:

QQs or Quick Questions. This is a time when you and the assistant can ask key questions of each other.

Calendar Preview and Alignment. Walk through your digital calendar on a screen for the next four weeks. Ask your assistant to come to your meeting with ideas about what could be canceled, consolidated, or clustered to help maximize your time. This is also the time your assistant should flag any preparation work for the meetings the next week or track down agendas for upcoming meetings to ensure you can prepare.

To-Do List Review. If you have been using your assistant to manage your Later List, this the time when he boomerangs items back to you. For example, if you forwarded an e-mail to your assistant about registering for a conference, but just couldn't think about it yet, you could ask your assistant to resurrect it in a month when you were ready to make a decision.

Pending Meeting Tracker Scan. This is when the manager and assistant review all pending proactive meetings to ensure scheduling opportunities happen.

Updates on Project Work. This is provided by assistant on his specific project work.

Real-Time Work. Eric Gordon, the CEO mentioned previously, liked to call this *study hall time*. He asked his assistant to ensure he signed checks, got thank-you notes out, and followed up on specific e-mails that needed attention.

Michelle Hays talks about the weekly check-in in this way: "Our weekly meeting is crucial in getting my questions answered so I can move projects and calendar items forward. Meeting in person and having an actual conversation also allows me to get a read on what's on his mind, so I can better align his calendar and my work to where he is mentally. We both dump items into our shared OneNote throughout the week and I spend about thirty minutes filtering and prioritizing them into an agenda the day before we check in."

Reader Reflection

When will you meet with your assistant? What are your standing agenda topics? Who will lead the meeting?

In addition to proactive planning, your assistant can also communicate to various managers via a weekly e-mail. One example that Mila would send out each Friday is shown in figure 13.15. Look closely at how she mapped out her priorities, how many hours she anticipated each would take, and how she indicated which manager she'd work with on each project.

This e-mail accomplished a few important things:

- It gave Mila's various managers insight into her workload (and forced us to duke it out if we needed to)!

- It enabled Mila to have a conversation with us about her capacity, if needed.

- It permitted us to weigh in if we thought Mila's time estimates were off.

Maia, Erica, and Sarah,

Here are my weekly priorities for the upcoming week. Please let me know if you have any questions or feedback!

Thanks,
Mila

Weekly Priorities for Week of 1/10	Hrs Allotted	Manager
May Retreat Initial Project Planning - Kick off meeting. Come prepared with suggestions for the logistics team (me and Leslie). Edit my own project plan.	2 hr	Sarah
FCP follow up with Sarah. Discuss and plan for next steps.	1 hr	Sarah
Talent Snapshot Analysis and Slides - Edit charts and tables. Take out operations people. Try using pivot tables.	3 hr	Erica
Calendar- Block specific PGP editing times. Give Maia table of due dates for direct reports (self-reflection, 360 feedback, etc.)	30 min	Maia
Prep for Mgt Tune Up - look at more examples of adult learning, create interactive handout. Update deck and flesh out notes. Indicate which parts we each facilitate. Focus on I do, We do, and You do. Send Maia draft deck by Jan. 12	4 hr	Maia
Help Maia edit Jan. Blog	30 min	Maia
Office Responsibilities - Conference room upkeep	2 hr	All

Figure 13.15 Mila's Weekly Priorities E-mail

Perhaps most important, this e-mail let Mila own her own work rather than feel put on by a million managers and projects.

Reader Reflection

How will your assistant manage his own workload? What insight do you need into his other projects?

The Monthly Step Back

There is one more level of structure to consider when planning meetings with your assistant: the monthly or quarterly meeting, called a *step back*. I did not invent this concept, but I cannot figure out who did! This big-picture meeting is for you and your assistant to review priorities

---

March Step Back Meeting Mila and Maia

Preparation (team member brings printed copies):

- Agenda (Maia)

- Keeping the PGP alive (Mila)

- Looking forward the next three months (Mila)

- Learning and development plan (Mila)

- 2 × 2 feedback for each other (both)
  - Two areas in which each person is doing well (with examples)
  - Two areas in which each person could improve (with examples)

- Reflections on questions listed below (Mila)

Agenda:

- **Check-In (Both)**
  - Informal Catch up / Check-in
  - Purpose of meeting
  - Agenda adjustment

- **Priorities from now through May**
  - What is most important from now through May?
  - Walk through each project

- **Learning and Development**
  - Agree on PGP goals …
  - Review your revised learning and development plan steps taken
  - Look ahead to see what learning and development opportunities steps can be taken forward

- **Mutual Two-Way Feedback (Both)—***may come out in the reflection on the past two months*
  - Each person comes prepared to verbally discuss the following questions *in relation to working relationship*
    - Two areas YOU are doing well? Two areas in which each person is doing well? (with examples)
    - Two areas YOU could do better? Two areas in which each person could improve? (with examples)

Figure 13.16 Mila and Maia's Monthly Step Back

for the coming months (use that Priority Plan!), touch base on your assistant's professional growth, and share mutual feedback. Figure 13.16 is a step-back sample agenda from a meeting I had with Mila—the full version can be found on my website (www.thetogethergroup.com).

You may be thinking that there is *no* way you can invest this kind of time in your assistant (and yes, these step backs can be helpful with others you manage, too!), but I promise you that this time is crucial to the success of your partnership, your workload, and your assistant's happiness. And I'm really just asking you for sixty to ninety minutes every few months or so.

Reader Reflection

When and where will you hold step backs with your assistant?

Special Project Meetings

If you have an assistant who manages more than your calendar, it can also be useful to hold special project meetings as needed. When you try to squeeze that work into your weekly meetings, too much other stuff gets crowded out. When I worked with assistants on large projects, such as trainings or communications, we would proactively schedule an extra fifteen- to thirty-minute meeting to brainstorm challenging questions or review materials together. For example, when we were working on a training to help principals and assistants create stronger partnerships, we had regular weekly meetings about *just* that topic to keep us focused and engaged.

Reader Reflection

As a summary, in your Reader Reflection Guide complete table 13.5 with your assistant to think about when and how you will best communicate to support each other's work!

Table 13.5 Our Communication Plan

Details	Daily	Weekly	Monthly (or some other quarterly interval)
Topics			
Amount of time and location			
Who prepares agenda?			
Who leads meeting?			
Who takes notes?			

Even More Tools and Habits

In addition to the communication structures list in the table, the tools identified in the following categories can also positively affect your assistant's success. I recommend reading this section *with* your actual assistant to see where there are possible places to expand his role.

Briefings Folder. If you still like things hard copy, ask your assistant to create a daily or weekly Briefings Folder for you that includes a printout of your digital calendar, any agendas you need, travel itineraries, meeting support materials, and documents that require your review. I love this briefings folder (figure 13.17) that Katie Nedelcovych in Nashville uses with her manager, Elissa Kim, at Teach For America.

Katie prints out Elissa's daily Outlook Calendar, plus all accompanying materials, and puts them in a binder for the week. There is a clear tab for each day, so Elissa has all of her materials at her fingertips if she cannot get to her iPad. Elissa also takes notes on her daily Outlook sheets, and returns them to Katie at the end of the day (figure 13.18). Katie then enters these To-Dos into Elissa's Weekly Worksheet and Later Lists. What a great example of using your assistant to help you manage your time, your To-Dos, and your stuff!

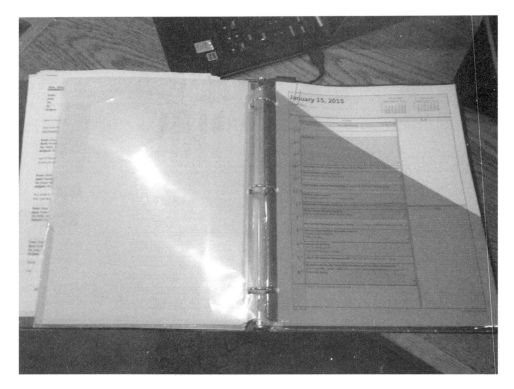

Figure 13.17 Katie and Elissa's Briefings Folder

Figure 13.18 Elissa's Notes for Katie

Reader Reflection

How could your assistant support you in the collection and distribution of To-Dos?

Meeting Scope and Sequences. We learned about the power of a Meeting Scope and Sequence early in the book. Guess what? Your assistant can help you with this entire process. Michelle of YES Prep in Houston describes how she supports Mark in being Together for one of his key priorities, "Mark's executive team is one of his top priorities this year. This means that some of my top priorities this year are creating a Scope and Sequence for our meetings, drafting/finalizing agendas, sending agendas/prework/action items on time, and drafting/finalizing the meeting PowerPoint. This year we never sit down in a check-in and say 'what should we talk about at the next meeting?'; I try to always have a draft ready for him to review and articulate changes that I then go and make. Two days before the meeting we have shared work time to finalize the PowerPoint and last-minute changes. The process has become so much smoother for both of us!"

Stock E-mail Responses. Do you find yourself answering the same e-mail over and over? When I was the chief talent officer for Achievement First, I frequently received questions about the structure of my team, our goals, and our roles and responsibilities. And then

I would rewrite my answers over and over. Once I realized the madness of this situation, I worked with Mila to create a template response including documents to address the issues that were most often requested. We actually created a folder for her with the key documents that I was often asked for. Eventually, I just forwarded the e-mails to her, and she replied directly on my behalf. I deliberately chose to have her send the replies from her own e-mail account for a few reasons. The first reason is that I wanted constituents to see *her* as a valuable resource. The second is that I didn't want follow-up questions to come back to me.

Receipt and Expense Tracking. If you need to turn in regular receipts or track reimbursements, ask your assistant to purchase a brightly colored plastic folder to keep in your bag for receipt storage. Then he should request those from you monthly—and hold you to turning them in.

Batch Process. Getting chased down to sign checks? Approve orders? Ask your assistant to set up a system in which he collects items once per week and then turns them over to you to sign.

Reader Reflection
What else can your assistant handle for you?

START STRONG

One of the biggest transitions when moving from individual worker to leader is learning how to actually *use* the resources at your disposal. Doing so takes up-front planning, a commitment to ongoing communication, and a true investment of time. Consider your assistant to be one of your most powerful tools to meet the goals of your team or organization—and help you stay Together.

- Decide if you need an assistant or any part-time administrative support.
- Determine the roles and responsibilities of your assistant.
- Design a hiring process that reflects the skills you'll need your assistant to have.
- Set up a training plan for the short and long term.
- Articulate your calendar needs for scheduling, To-Dos, and energy levels.
- Create daily, weekly, and monthly communication structures.
- Brainstorm additional systems or tasks your assistant could manage for you.

SEE IT IN ACTION: THE MANAGEMENT MEMO

So now that you have all these great systems for your To-Dos, your meetings, and your calendar, what's the impact on the people you manage? All too often, people learn what their managers want from them via osmosis, observation, and copying their peers. But the best Together Leaders take the time to spell out their expectations at least once per year, often at the beginning of the fiscal or onboarding cycle. They thoughtfully name in advance their expectations for preparation, design, and follow-up. If this feels micromanagey to you, I understand. However, I encourage you to expand your perspective: being clear and enabling other people to meet your expectations frees them up to focus on the content of their work.

Articulate Your Expectations with a Management Memo

Definition

A **Management Memo** is an articulation of how you will manage your team. It will typically spell out expectations for goal setting, meeting structures, planning, and team interactions.

Let's walk through this example from Harris Ferrell, the chief operating officer for Achievement First. As Harris explains it, "I needed to organize my own thinking so that I could communicate my expectations to my team members. It's particularly helpful when bringing on a new hire to lay out the different ways I will spend my time with him or her and for what purpose. It provides a road map to ensure we stay disciplined on discussing important topics (e.g., talent management, learning, and development) and not just on urgent, tactical issues." You can see a full version of his Management Memo on my website (www.thetogethergroup.com).

1. **State the purpose.** Look at Harris's overview letter in figure 13.19. He clearly invites input, states how he plans to manage the team, and shares why he's making the choices he does. The leadership statement and description of how Harris wants his team to feel at the end of their year is very powerful.

2. **Let your team know *how* you will engage with them.** In figure 13.20, Harris deliberately spells out the large buckets of his responsibilities: accountability, support, talent management, and professional growth. This ensures there is no guessing about why Harris joins meetings, asks about how team members are doing, or asks for evidence of progress toward outcomes.

```
┌─────────────────────────────────────────────────────────────────────┐
│                                                                       │
│  **Management Memo – Harris Ferrell**                                 │
│                                                                       │
│  *Purpose of this document*                                          │
│  To provide clarity on how I want to focus our time together over the │
│  course of the year to be an effective manager to you.               │
│                                                                       │
│  *Leadership statement*                                              │
│  My job as a leader is to cultivate a strong team that spikes in      │
│  trust, candor, accountability, and delivering results. My job as     │
│  your manager is to set high expectations with a clear bar for        │
│  excellence and provide you with coaching and support that enables    │
│  you to realize your potential, develop your own leadership, and      │
│  bring your full, authentic self to this work.                       │
│                                                                       │
│  As a result of our time together over the course of a year, I want   │
│  you to be able to look back and be able to say with conviction:      │
│                                                                       │
│  1. I became a stronger manager and have a stronger team             │
│  2. I became a more impactful organizational leader at AF            │
│  3. I stayed focused on the right priorities                         │
│  4. My team hit our goals, and I see how we helped AF achieved its    │
│     goals and move closer to achieving our mission                   │
│  5. I want to keep doing this important work and growing at AF        │
│                                                                       │
└─────────────────────────────────────────────────────────────────────┘
```

Figure 13.19 Harris's Management Memo

3. **Name meeting structures and expectations.** This is simply an extraction from your Meeting Matrix from chapter 5. In figure 13.21, for each meeting, Harris names the following:

- Purpose
- Process
- Standing agenda topics
- Timing and frequency

Of course things will change and be adjusted, but isn't it nice to be so very clear on why you meet with your boss when you do?

4. **Outline long-term topics.** In this section of his Management Memo (see figure 13.22), Harris articulates what he will focus on in his Deep Dives with his team. This is based on some Scope and Sequence work from chapter 5. Harris's Deep Dives are predictable and based on organizational events and cycles. His team knows what to expect in advance.

This forces Harris to keep his meetings focused on priority items, such as talent retention, budgeting, staffing, and organizational health.

5. **Spell out the reference documents.** In the next section of his memo, Harris explains the standard documents he requires of his direct reports (figure 13.23). He is unapologetic about wanting the following:

- Performance goals
- Development plans
- Monthly or three-month Priority Plans

Dimensions on how I engage with you as your manager

1. **Accountability**: ensuring that you and your team deliver against commitments you make and vetting that the commitments you make align to what the organization needs you and your team to deliver. The two corner stones of accountability are 1) clarifying what are the outcomes/deliverables/milestones that your team will achieve and 2) providing recurring updates on status of what is on-track/off-track so that we can determine when/if corrective intervention is necessary.

2. **Support (problem solving)**: leveraging my organizational judgment, perspective, and experience to help you craft a path forward, unstick murky problems, and solve problems. This is most effectively done as a dialog (usually verbally, but can happen via back-and-forth in email/documents). You most often will have more specific context than I will have on a given situation in your team; I use the update mechanisms below as my means of having sufficient context of situations to a) engage at the right level of the problem with you (without spending a lot of time on back story) and b) to vet your judgment that you are escalating the right types of issues on which we engage.

3. **Talent management**: building the depth of your team (from recruitment through retention) and ensuring that they are engaged, motivated, and connected to the work/organization. We are a human enterprise, and the success of our talent is the single biggest driver of the success of the organization. I need to understand the strengths and areas of development of your team members and how you are developing/managing/leading them in order to a) ensure their growth/engagement is on the larger organizational radar and b) I can help you become a stronger leader of people.

4. **Learning & development**: building your skill happens across all of these dimensions. My charge is to help you grow professionally in the areas that will be most impactful to your organizational leadership and trajectory by being intentional on *how* you are leading/managing, not just *what* you are leading/managing. Most of the L&D occurs "in the work" but it requires us to a) name explicitly the areas on which we should focus over a period of time and b) have recurring reflection points (2×2 plus informal feedback) to assess your progress

Figure 13.20 Harris's Buckets of Responsibility

Primary Meeting Structures

The meeting structures below are set up to enable us to be intentional on how we spend our time across the different management dimensions.

Meeting	Purpose	Process	Agenda Topics	Timing
Weekly tactical check-in	These are our regular weekly tactical meetings. They primarily are for me to provide you support (problem solving), although depending on the topics, we can go deep in talent management issues and L&D. These are preferably done in person, but occasionally over the phone/Webex.	• Agendas driven by team members and sent at least a full 24 hours in advance (48 hours if there are written materials to review). *This will ensure I have time to prepare for you and can also send you my agenda items to incorporate* • Group all issues of the week that are not urgent and all documents to review in ONE clear email with the agenda. This will reduce our email traffic to each other. • System in place for next step capture in a way that works for both of us • You can also invite members of your team into the check-ins to go deep on an area to problem solve in which they are particularly engaged (this is both a support and talent management benefit)	• Quick questions • Deep dive topics for problem solving (vet your proposed solutions) • By providing me short (1-2 bullets) on the agenda topics, it will make our time more efficient to dive into the problem-solving itself rather than having the time used on updates/providing context.	60 min every week

Figure 13.21 Harris's Meeting Matrix

Meeting	Purpose	Process	Agenda Topics	Timing
Monthly step-back	Focus on progress towards big goals and looking ahead to major work of the next month. Extra time for deep dive topics and 2×2 feedback. This time blends all 4 management dimensions, where we can look ahead (accountability), where we will spend time problem solving, how to align to your L&D, and diving into your talent management.	• Materials sent at least 2-business days before meeting • Anticipated prep is 90-120 minutes for monthly map, 2×2, and deep dive topic	• See table below for cycle of deep dive topics • Monthly map review • 2×2 (every other month)	Monthly: 90 min, usually the <u>last week of the month</u> (this time replaces the weekly tactical for that week)

Figure 13.21 (*continued*)

Harris is neutral about templates but hard-core on outcomes. In cases when there is an exact requirement, such as a network report card measure, he explains why. Harris is *not* trying to micromanage his team but rather set them up for success from the onset by being clear about expectations.

Why put in all of this time up-front? Yes, this may have taken Harris (a *very* busy COO) a few hours at the beginning of the year, but it saves him from getting updated on the wrong things, ignoring priority issues, and losing sight of goals. It gives his team a clear sense of what to expect from him and what he cares about most.

Reader Reflection

How clear are your expectations? How do you know? What content do you need in your Management Memo? Draft yours now using the template in the Reader Reflection Guide.

Deep dive topics for Monthly Step Backs

Month	Step-back deep dive topics (60 min)
ALL STEP-BACKS	Block out time to prepare and send materials 2 business-days in advance of the step-back so that I will time to review prior to our time together. Based on past experience, you should plan to allocate 90-120 minutes of preparation time for these materials • **Upcoming Monthly map:** look ahead to next month's deliverables and key risks, organized by your major work streams. Highlight your top priorities for the month. • Written update of the key work-streams, state of risk (sunny, partly cloudy, cloudy, stormy), notes (barriers, successes, key risks), and next steps. This is the bi-weekly long-form update and weather map
July	• Review your individual development priorities for the upcoming school year • Review of previous year's final results against FCP • 2×2 aligned to your learning and development goals
August	• Pressure test key FCP outcomes (Big Wins) and how you are organizing the work for your team achieve the results
September	• TALENT: Review of your team members learning and development plans and your approach to support them. How motivated, engaged, and invested are each of your team members (what motivates them and demotivates them)? • 2×2 aligned to your learning and development goals
October	• TALENT: review state of team culture – what is strong, what is concerning, what are you doing to strengthen it; how are you cultivating diversity and inclusiveness mindsets in your team? • PGP cycle II (60 min convo scheduled in addition to 90 min step back)

Figure 13.22 Harris's Deep-Dive Topics

Reference Documents

Document	Description/purpose	Example
Monthly Map	This should be sent to me during the last full week of the month looking ahead to the upcoming month for me to review prior to our monthly step back time. My primary purpose with the map is to:	HF monthly map (page 1 is the map).

1. For big priorities, milestones, and goals for the month, I pressure test if we have sufficient time to engage, review, discuss during the month (e.g., are check-ins sufficient or will we need more time to go deep).

2. Stay informed on the key work streams so I can determine when/how you may need to engage me on problem solving/support (e.g., are there areas that we haven't discussed that should be put onto the agenda). These updates also help me provide air cover and org context to others (e.g., Dacia and cabinet)

3. Ensure that we are staying accountable to our wins and commitments – that we are keeping the trains running on time and making the progress we need to make to hit our big goals

I'm relatively agnostic on template, but I want to understand the following:

- Your top 3 priorities for the month

- Your team's annual goals/priorities and the associated work streams so that we can see how the specific month's activities connect to the bigger picture work

- The overall on-track status for that area of work (e.g., sunny, partly cloudy, cloudy, stormy)

- Updates of consequence relating to the work, including any key risks you are managing for that each work stream

- Flag any deliverables/milestones that were anticipated being completed the prior month that are being rolled over into the upcoming month

- Specific items in the map should be framed as milestone, decision, or deliverable that will be completed rather than just work that will be underway. It should answer the question, "What will be produced as a result of this work"

Example (continued): Sample Map from Amber Follow this link

Figure 13.23 Harris's Required Reference Documents

SECTION 5

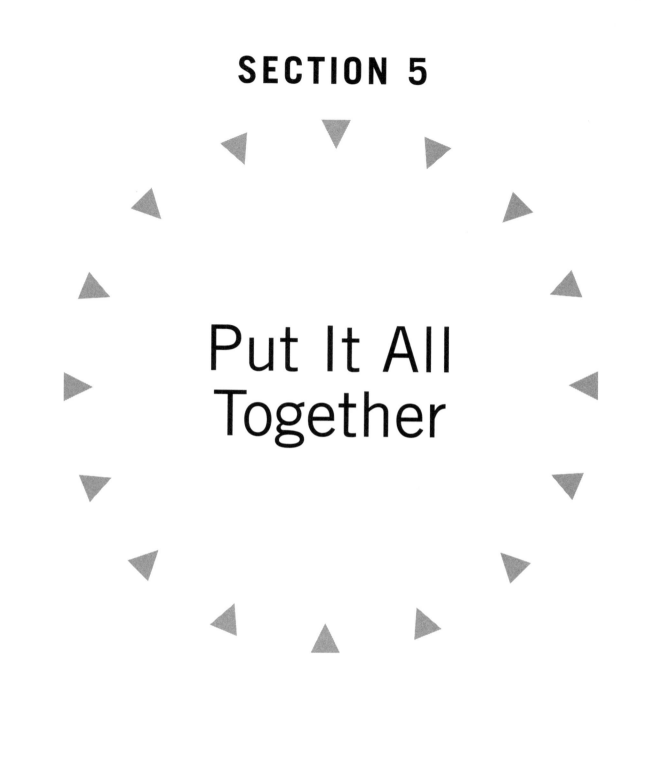

Put It All Together

CHAPTER 14

Keep Track of Stuff, Space, and Knowledge

SEEN AND HEARD

"I start with a clean desk each day. By the end of the day it is piled with stuff."

"We struggle with not having assigned desks. We are consistently packing our bags (that's our portable office) and lose papers, or leave them in another room, so we spend a lot of time just trying to get organized for the next meeting, etc."

"I realize that my open door policy enables me to be interrupted so often I get little done. It makes me feel good to be available to my team to meet their needs, but it also gets in the way of my efficiency. Everyone says, 'Can I have a minute?' but it's never a minute."

OVERVIEW AND OBJECTIVES

We've tackled your time and your team's systems. In this chapter, we'll dabble with your stuff, your space, and your knowledge. At first, these topics can seem trivial; what does it matter if you have to walk down the hall to retrieve paper for the copier? But as your organization grows, it becomes imperative to create systems. Without them, time, money, and focus are lost. How you manage your stuff, space, and knowledge will vary based on compliance requirements, software capacity, and organizational culture. But everyone needs some kinds of systems for their stuff!

In this chapter, you will do the following:

- Decide what to transport and what stays put.

- Manage your organization's stuff, such as technology, books, and other resources.

- Learn best practices for setting up your team's office and other physical space.

- Organize your knowledge: Project Plans, important files, and organizational learnings.

DEAL WITH YOUR OWN STUFF

Even the most organized among us can become quickly buried in an avalanche of articles, receipts, and business cards. After several years of working entirely remotely and several more in an office, including over a decade of heavy travel and multiple moves, I'm ready to help you tackle your *stuff* issues, whatever they may be. In this section, I will cover what to carry, what should stay put, and how to deal with travel!

Set Up Your Stationary Space

Many of us do not have desks anymore. Even if we do, we spend very little time at them. I've also worked in organizations that frequently rearranged office setups to accommodate growth; at one, I moved five times in five years! That alone forced me to try and get my possessions down to just one box. In general, I want you to get as paperless as possible. Seriously, think about the last time you dug in a pile of folders for something. And now think about how many times you searched your hard drive. Even if you don't want to get rid of every single piece of paper, you may want to invest in a shredder!

Let's get inspired by taking a look at the spaces of two different leaders: Sharon Johnson, a principal in the Bay Area, and Sarah Stern, a data manager at a middle school in New Orleans (figure 14.1 through figure 14.5). Now there are many books, blogs, and Pinterest boards about perfectly organized, color-coded desks. But that's not what I'm about. I'm about what *works* well so you can have more time for the important stuff.

FAQ

FAQ: What if I work from home?
Some of you have the ability to work from home or a coffee shop now and again, and some of you even work from home full-time. If you are like me, occasionally you may just set up camp at the dining room table (I wrote a lot of this book under a blanket on our comfy basement couch). But your family may not appreciate seeing the remnants of your work life littered about the house—and you'll want to be able to close the door on your work space, too. You will need some at-home version of the pictured office elements, such as standing files and general office supplies. In addition, the items listed in the following are also pretty darn helpful. Find out what your organization will fund and what they will not.

Figure 14.1 Sharon Uses These Vertical Standing Folders to Catch Papers on Current Projects That She Wants to Have Readily Available

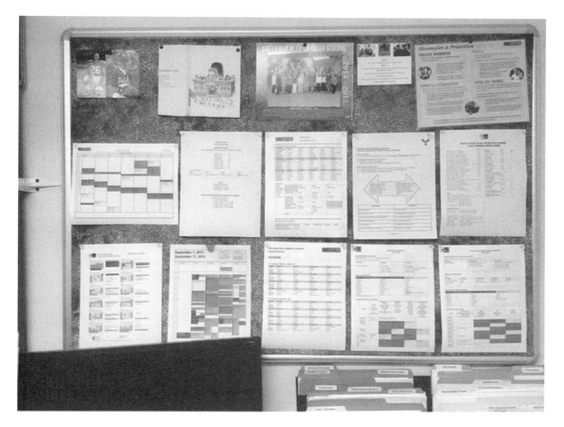

Figure 14.2 Sharon's Reference Wall of Important Schedules and Other Key Information

Figure 14.3 Sarah Maintains Clearly Labeled Reference Materials— Binders of Past Projects If You *Must* Keep Hard Copies (but Consider a Binder Purge or a Scanning Party!)

Recommended for the Remote Worker

- Reliable high-speed Internet
- High-quality headset
- Decently comfortable office chair
- Printer
- Desktop scanner
- Cord container

Whether you work at a desk, on the move, or at home, you will need some place for work materials, reference items, and professional resources. Whether you need a small portable work station or you need to spread out across a huge office, the goal here is to find what you need quickly and not waste a precious minute.

Figure 14.4 Sarah Keeps Pens, Markers, Pencils, Scissors, and Supplies Handy

 Reader Reflection

List two to three adjustments you plan to make to your physical workspace. How will each one help you stay Together?

What to Carry

Now that I have talked about your stationary space, it's time to move into what to carry with you. Many of us are not in one place for an entire day. More often than not, we're on the move between multiple locations—offices, classrooms, coffee shops, trains, planes, and cars. This creates many logistical challenges, such as accessing favorite apps that don't function offline, taking notes in meetings where laptops are discouraged, and getting an e-mail sent while on an airplane! First things first: you must select the right bag, know how to pack it, and know when to empty it! It may sound silly to think about bag selection, but if it saves you from spending your time digging for a pen at the bottom of a grocery bag, then it is well worth it!

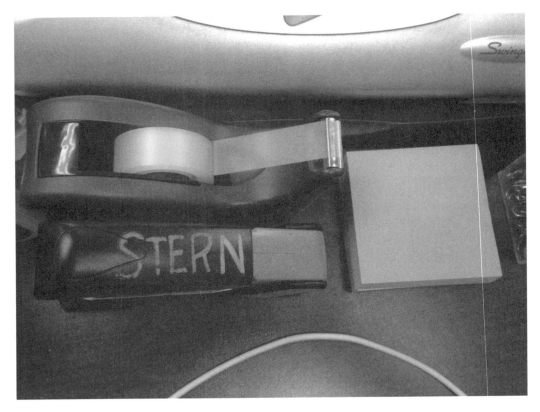

Figure 14.5 Extra Bonus for Clearly Labeling Your Stuff Similar to How Sarah Does

The Right Bag

I'm a huge fan of backpacks simply for health reasons, though I am aware of the fashion hit I take. I particularly like the model from Timbuk2 with a flap for your laptop so you don't have to take it out in airport security lines. You can see the model I like on my website, www .thetogethergroup.com. Bag selection is entirely personal and depends on how professional you need to look, how many pockets you like to have (I actually like to limit pockets or I get confused!), how strong you are, and how much you need to carry.

What I *don't* want you to carry is a plastic grocery bag with your lunch falling out or an old NPR tote complete with stains and one large pocket. You will spend too long rummaging through it for what you need, and this will not convey the sense of Togetherness you wish to demonstrate!

Reader Reflection
What will you select as your work bag?

Getting the Contents Right

Once you have selected the right bag, you need to pack it. Following is a list of items that most leaders need at the ready:

- Laptop or tablet

- Wallet or small purse with cash, credit cards, and ID

- Clear plastic envelope for reimbursement receipts

- Clear plastic folders with room for your Togetherness tools

- Other possible folders (or sections of one simple accordion file):

  - Meeting agendas

  - Travel

  - Action

  - File

  - Read

- Notebook, though see chapter 5 for my thoughts on notebooks

- Thank-you notes, return address labels, and stamps

- Container for chargers and cords (though whenever possible, try to have a duplicate set that can stay put)

  There are also a few bonus items you could add to your bag:

- Pencil case

- Snack sack filled with nuts, granola bars, and other healthy treats

- Pouch with aspirin, contact solution, lip balm, tissues, or any other hygiene products you may need

FAQ: What if my bag is a huge jumbled mess right now? Where do I even start?
I've seen it all. You are not alone. Get cozy with that bag right now, and empty its *entire* contents out on a table. Check out Sherdren's challenge at the end of this chapter for more details. Don't be afraid: I've done this before with many leaders. Once you see everything on the table, sort it into four piles:

After that, use the recommended folders to sort everything else into the categories, and then put it all back in your bag. Remember, you don't want to be the person in the meeting who's excavating piles of agendas and receipts for a pen!

And for all the stuff that is *not* paper-related, sort it into various pouches or pockets that you can easily transfer from bag to bag.

Reader Reflection
What do you need to add *or* subtract from your bag?

Out and About at Conferences, Events, and Galas

Now that we've solidified what you carry on a regular basis and how to access your digital documents, let's hit those tricky situations. What if you are at a gala where you cannot haul around a backpack? Many of you also attend various events with boards, other colleagues, or families. Here, too, you are on the move, often in the spotlight, and under a lot of stress as the leader. These are the times when we are *most* prone to being ambushed and losing track of valuable information. This section will help you create a proactive plan for what to do at those events. Of course, if you are the president of the United States or something (hey, POTUS, are you reading my book?!), you can hire someone to follow you around and keep track of all your information. But most of us are not that person.

Know in Advance What You Can and Will Carry

As you look ahead on your calendar (hint, hint), think about key events, what kind of information you expect to acquire at them, and what you will need to do with it. In the following I've listed some examples and possible solutions:

The Formal Event. Are you attending a huge fund-raising gala in black tie attire? If so, I don't think that backpack is going with you! This may be a time when your smartphone and an index card in your pocket, a super tiny notebook, or small purse will have to do. The trick here is remembering to transfer all that information back into your other systems the next day.

The Conference with Opportunity for Networking. In this case, you may need to do some work in advance, similar to what Michael Stone and Maggie Runyan-Shefa, the co-CEOs of New Schools for New Orleans, did before an education conference. Preview the list of attendees, perhaps even with an assistant, and send individual e-mails to set up breakfast, lunch, coffee, and the like. Select which sessions you want to attend, and consider if and how you will take notes. And, of course, before you get on that airplane home, throw away (or donate!) as much as possible. I love mugs and T-shirts as much as the next person but my house and office are much too small to deal with any accumulation.

The Event Where Everyone Will Want to Ask You Questions. This could be a school event when you're approached by every parent imaginable or a board meeting where members hang around afterwards to ask you questions or offer feedback. If you know you will be barraged, come equipped with a template to log questions that you can follow up on from the office the next day. Legal pads get messy pretty quickly. A table where you can note name, question, and contact information could save you a lot of follow-up headaches. Bringing it back to the office to delegate replies or answer right away is good for your credibility as a leader, too!

Reader Reflection

List three upcoming events. What information do you expect to collect and how you will you follow up?

FAQ: What do you do when someone hands you a business card?

Usually, I input the data into my contacts in my phone in the moment. If I receive a lot of business cards from people I truly want to follow up with, I take a picture of all of them and e-mail them to my assistant to enter into Outlook, using the Notes feature to record when I met them and how they might be useful (see figure 14.6). If I'm less interested in connecting, then I provide my own contact information and encourage the person to follow up with me with specifics. The goal here is to leave with no paper!

Figure 14.6 Sample Outlook Contact from a Business Card

Set Up Your Soft Copies

Not only do we have physical items to keep track of but also there are millions of digital documents that need some semblance of order. I'm not going to dwell on perfection here because, similar to e-mail, searching is faster than filing. However, searches are only as good as document naming. Perhaps this goes without saying, but please make sure your sacred documents are backed up *somewhere,* whether as Google Docs, in Dropbox, or on your organization's server. In this section, I'll share some file organization tips from Emily Frietag, the founder of D2D, an organization that provides academic support to small school systems.

Set Up High-Level Folders

Emily's first layer of folders is her major life buckets, professional and personal, such as "Work," "Personal," and "Archives." She numbers her folders so that the folders she uses most often, such as "Plans," are at the top (see figure 14.7).

Set up Subfolders Underneath Each Main Line Folder

Emily sets up subfolders for frequently used categories and numbers them so the ones she uses most frequently are at the top (figure 14.2). For example, in her Work folder, she keeps subfolders for "Overview Strategy," "Team Culture," "Budget," and so on.

Emily also has a few loose folders. Here's why: "I have a meeting next Tuesday that I have been doing a lot of work to prepare for. I created a folder called 'September.29.meeting' and it is under work but not filed below that so I can get to it easily."

Name the Documents Clearly

Mary Clare Reilley, director of marketing for the KIPP Foundation, takes a detailed approach to document naming: "I always include a pretty long descriptive name, the initials of the last

Figure 14.7 Emily's High-Level Folders

01.WORK.D2D
    00.OVERVIEW.STRATEGY
    01.TEAM.CULTURE
    02.BUDGET.PRICING
    03.SERVICES
    04.NAME.BRANDING
    05.BOARD.FEEDBACK
    06.CONSULTING
    07.ARCHIVES
    Sept.29th.Launch

Figure 14.8 Emily's Subfolders

Documents library
Match Matters

Name

Match Matters post draft 3-25-15(MCR)v1.docx
Match Matters post draft_4-1-15(MCR)v2.docx
Match Matters post draft_4-2-15 (MCR)v3.docx
Match Matters post draft_4-3-15(SC)v4.docx

Figure 14.9 Mary Clare's File Names

person who made edits (in parentheses), the date, and the version number. Version number goes up every time the doc gets opened and touched." Let's peek at figure 14.9 to see her example.

Reader Reflection

What is the current state of your digital documents? How might you begin to improve their effectiveness?

MAKE THE MOST OF SHARED OFFICE SPACE

Office space is much like your home—you share it with many people and spend a significant amount of time there. In fact, you may even spend more time at your office than in your actual house! And although it may feel silly to incorporate homey touches, clear systems, and high expectations, in the end your office is a *shared* space. It must encourage people to be excited to come to work! This section will share tips for focusing in the midst of an open work environment, setting expectations for shared materials, and ensuring your space stays clean (fridge clean-out parties, anyone?!).

Stay Focused in Open Office Settings

Open office spaces appear to be the in thing these days. Although I love the intended spirit of collaboration and community, I hear over and over, especially from people who work in or near schools where quiet is hard to come by, that open offices prevent them from being able to truly focus. In my travels, I've seen individuals and teams employ the following small touches when they need to lock down and produce.

A Visual Cue

Although most people pop in headphones to tacitly prevent interruptions, you could take your visual a step further by posting thoughtful door signs or a humorous desk flag. A few ideas are shown in figure 14.10 and figure 14.11. Each of these systems requires an up-front conversation about the challenge of open office spaces and the need to focus—and then getting everyone on board.

A Separate Designated Area

If you have enough space, you could designate a conference room or specific location as the "study hall" or "library," where people can go to work when they need dead silence.

A Humorous Visual Cue, Such as a Crown or Feather Boa!

Never underestimate the power of humor when communicating your needs.

Reader Reflection

How does your office space help or hurt people's ability to focus? How could you be more explicit with expectations?

Sign-Up Procedures for Meeting Rooms

Nothing is worse than showing up to a conference room only to find people already lurking in it, and then roaming around with your laptop in hand as you look for another private space, all the while losing thirty minutes of your actual meeting just trying to find a place to sit down.

How to solve for this? You could go low or high tech, as long as you have a system:

- Calendars posted outside each conference room in a weekly view. Typically, this is managed by an office manager, assistant, or secretary.

- Setting up a calendar in Outlook or Google for each conference room so people can sign up for the space.

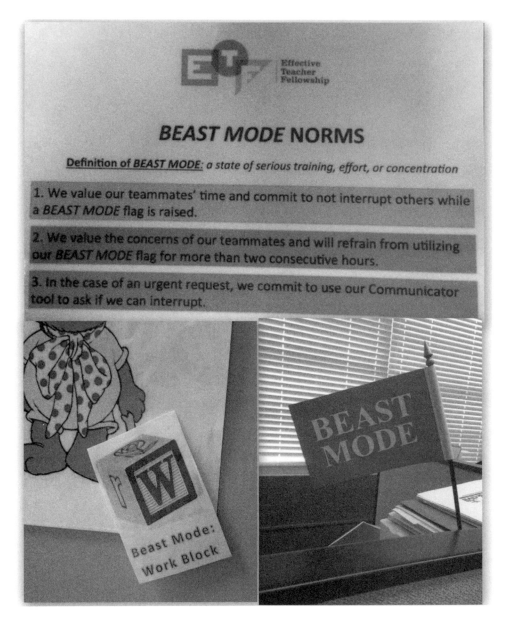

Figure 14.10 Beast Mode Signs

Typically, this process is managed by an operations person, office assistant, or secretary. If your organization has none of these, consider rotating among various staff members.

Reader Reflection

How do people sign up to use conference rooms and other shared spaces? Who is responsible for managing your system?

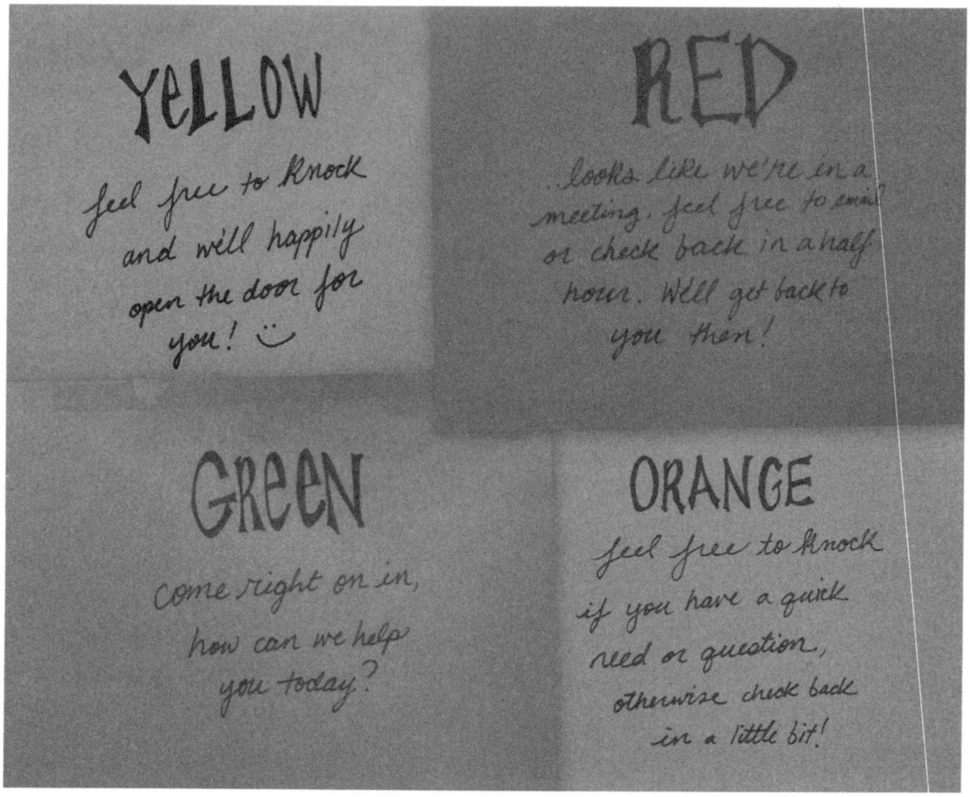

YELLOW
feel free to knock and we'll happily open the door for you! :)

RED
...looks like we're in a meeting. feel free to email or check back in a half hour. We'll get back to you then!

GREEN
come right on in, how can we help you today?

ORANGE
feel free to knock if you have a quick need or question, otherwise check back in a little bit!

Figure 14.11 Door Signs

Expectations for Physical Space

You know that yucky feeling when you walk into a conference room with a trustee and have to spend an embarrassing moment wiping crumbs from the table before you sit down together? Me, too! All too often, offices, hallways, conference rooms, and storage closets become dumping grounds for extra inventory, shipments, leftover papers, and last week's board lunch leftovers. And my guess is that you do not have a cleaning service coming in every minute to tidy up after you! The only way to keep things neat is to set rules for everyone, train on them up-front, and keep them alive through signs and reinforcement! Your definition of *neat and tidy* may not match your colleagues', so spelling things out really matters.

Several real-life examples of physical space expectations are included in the pages that follow.

Set Up-Front Expectations, Document Them, and Train People on Them

Achievement First shares a PowerPoint titled "Working Agreements" with each new employee to explain kitchenette and copy center etiquette (see figure 14.12 and figure 14.13), where to

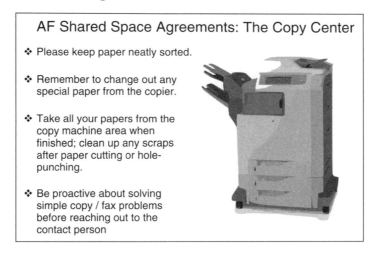

AF Shared Space Agreements: The Kitchenette

✓ The fridge is cleaned out at the end of the day every Friday. Anything that is left in the fridge will be discarded!

✓ Clean spills immediately

✓ When using dishes, wash, dry, and return them immediately

✓ You are responsible for replacing water cooler bottles when they run empty. Ask for help if you need it!

Figure 14.12 AF Kitchenette Agreements

AF Shared Space Agreements: The Copy Center

❖ Please keep paper neatly sorted.

❖ Remember to change out any special paper from the copier.

❖ Take all your papers from the copy machine area when finished; clean up any scraps after paper cutting or hole-punching.

❖ Be proactive about solving simple copy / fax problems before reaching out to the contact person

Figure 14.13 AF Copy Center Agreements

find supplies, and how to reset a conference room after use. You can find the entire PowerPoint on my website, www.thetogethergroup.com.

Reinforce Your Rules with Physical Reminders at Potential Crime Scenes

Everyone forgets that initial training, so if you really want to keep your physical space intact, specific and strategically placed signage can help. The examples in figure 14.14 and figure 14.15 from Teach For America's New Orleans office are crystal clear on what should be removed and replaced after using a conference room.

Figure 14.14 TFA Conference Room Signs

Figure 14.15 TFA Conference Room Signs

Shared spaces are one of those topics we like to ignore until they annoy us with constant interruptions, unfilled water coolers, or messy conference rooms. It makes sense to get clear on the front end to avoid clean up later.

Reader Reflection

How could you or a team member make a shared space more Together?

TRACK THE INVENTORY

Jason Tavarez, the head of IT for Achievement First, explains the need to keep a tight control on inventory: "When we have a huge snowstorm or events like Hurricane Sandy, we run the risk of damaging thousands of dollars in equipment. We need to ensure that our inventory is up-to-date in case of a power outage or flood. If we cannot get the system back up and running as soon as possible, it's harder to reach our goals." When AF was just five schools, it was easy enough to use Excel to track most things. But now with over thirty schools and one thousand employees, it is vital to have a more sophisticated system. Here are some more useful tips from Jason on inventory:

1. Do any inventory management completely and correctly from the start. It's hard to go back after.
2. Make inventory management an explicit and ongoing responsibility of the job. Ensure you have one clear owner of any technology solutions.
3. Invest in some bar code scanners. It will save tons of time later!

I know this is not a sexy topic, but as Jason notes, "The last thing we want is our entire hardware wiped out through a flood and then not have our serial numbers on hand to submit to insurance." Right on, Jason. Spreadsheets of inventory, naming conventions, and conference room–sharing procedures are *not* what our work is made of.

Reader Reflection

Do you have any key pieces of inventory that need an explicit ordering or tracking process?

MANAGE THE KNOWLEDGE

There are tons of ways to manage your organization's knowledge, from the incredibly fancy and expensive to the homegrown Google Drive setup. By managing the "knowledge," I mean the documents, data, and debriefs that inform your organization's work and make it stronger over time. No one wants to re-create an organizational satisfaction survey each year. And we certainly don't want people in new positions to start from scratch every time. For the purposes of this book, I am going to assume you have a little bit of time and human capital to dedicate to knowledge management, but you are not seeking to build a state-of-the-art-system. I'm not going to focus heavily on the technology, because this stuff changes constantly. Instead, we'll look at the purpose, content, and maintenance of systems that can help you and your organization manage your knowledge in efficient and deliberate ways. What more detail? There are entire books on knowledge management, such as *Mastering Organizational Knowledge Flow* by Frank Leistner or *The New Edge in Knowledge* by Carla O'Dell and Cindy Hubert.

A Tour: TNTP's Wiki

TNTP (formerly The New Teacher Project, now just called *TNTP*) was kind enough to describe for me how and why they built their organization's internal wiki. It is helpful to note that TNTP's staff are spread out, working side-by-side with schools and teachers across the country.

Definition

A wiki is an application, typically web-based, which enables collaborative modification, extension, or deletion of its content and structure. The popular blog *Lifehacker* uses layperson terms to describe a wiki: "Any time you're writing a piece of communication that's not just applicable to the person you're e-mailing, but to everyone on your e-mail list—hell, even everyone who may end up working with you in the future—it belongs in your workplace Wiki."

Since almost everything happens virtually at TNTP, they have invested deeply in a virtual infrastructure, so an employee in Denver is just as plugged in to TNTP's latest thinking as one sitting in Brooklyn. Emma Bonnami, Chief of Staff, describes, "Our most significant investment was TNTP's custom-built internal wiki, the nexus of our virtual organization. Launched in 2011, the robust, living platform is the source of almost all information at TNTP: daily news updates via internal blogs, active project hubs for all TNTP contracts, communities for staff to connect. Staff can access years of accumulated knowledge and participate in dozens of conversations each day, fostering innovation and reducing the chance that teams reinvent the wheel. More than 30,000 pages exist on the wiki, and TNTP staff view 1,800 pages each day." Knowledge management is actually built into the job descriptions for a handful of staff on different teams. Here are the purposes of TNTP's wiki:

- To convey current news and updates
- To share work-related resources
- To leverage the past experiences of other team members
- To support project management
- To create a social water cooler

Let's look now at examples of how each purpose drives specific content on the wiki.

To Convey Current News and Updates

The CEO and President, Karolyn Belcher, writes periodic blog posts and updates about the organization's work, as do other members of the management team. CEO, Dan Weisberg, encourages staff members to read the updates by telling them to expense a cup of coffee on the organization while keeping up-to-date (see figure 14.16).

To Share Work-Related Resources

There are so many times when you or someone you manage may begin a project wondering "Where do I begin? How do people collect data in my organization? Are there any best practices on surveying?" One important part of TNTP's wiki is its common resources. Anyone can access these at any time, especially when there is a need for frequently occurring events or topics, such as benefits, off-boarding, or project management support!

Figure 14.17 is an example of how TNTP organizes their resource sharing for client work. Let's say you were jumping into a new district project. You could search by stakeholder or by content area.

To Leverage the Past Experience of Other Team Members

Have you ever started a project or activity and wondered if a colleague had some background knowledge that could help you? Maybe even someone you didn't know? TNTP helps initiate these conversations by creating a public space on the wiki for people to pose questions and offer support. In figure 14.18, a team member can post what he/she is looking for across the

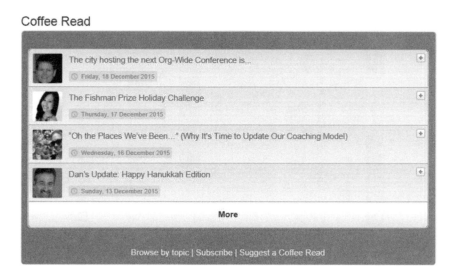

Figure 14.16 Coffee Read

Figure 14.17 Knowledge Base

I'm Looking For

Active Interventions 2.0, Using Video in Coaching Convos?
Friday, 18 December 2015

Conditional Formatting in Mail Merge
Friday, 18 December 2015

Content experts in K-8 P.E. and/or Health
Wednesday, 16 December 2015

More

Enter a post here | Label your post *looking* | Answer a post with a comment

Figure 14.18 Client Inquiry

organization. Whether it is content related, like P.E. and Health resources or technical, like figuring out a mail merge, there are people to support!

To Support Project Management

TNTP's wiki provides real-time technology to delegate work, communicate status, and drive next steps. Most striking is the transparency that this process promotes. Everyone can see where projects are in process. In figure 14.19, a communications team names a common goal and determines steps, owners, and target dates—as well as update status.

To Create a Social Water Cooler

TNTP also uses their wiki to promote social and virtual interactions. The wiki hosts various subgroups based on common interests, such as ones for fitness lovers and working parents, with a dose of old-fashioned humor built in. Figure 14.20 captures TNTP's showcase of the animal employees that keep their remote workers cozy and comfy during the workday.

Reader Reflection

What are the strengths and weaknesses of your current knowledge management systems?

Tech Tips: For those interested, Emma B. notes the technical side of the Wiki, "We use Atlassian Confluence, an enterprise platform that integrates with our system for tracking staff support requests. Staff with questions submit a ticket through the wiki, which is tracked and routed to the best department (e.g., HR). As usage grows, we've moved to increasingly powerful hosting platforms, and we upgrade Confluence as needed (usually twice each year). We test all upgrades extensively in a separate wiki environment. We roll out updates with extensive staff training, and offer both self-guided wiki orientation modules for new staff and monthly 'Wiki 101' trainings for all staff."

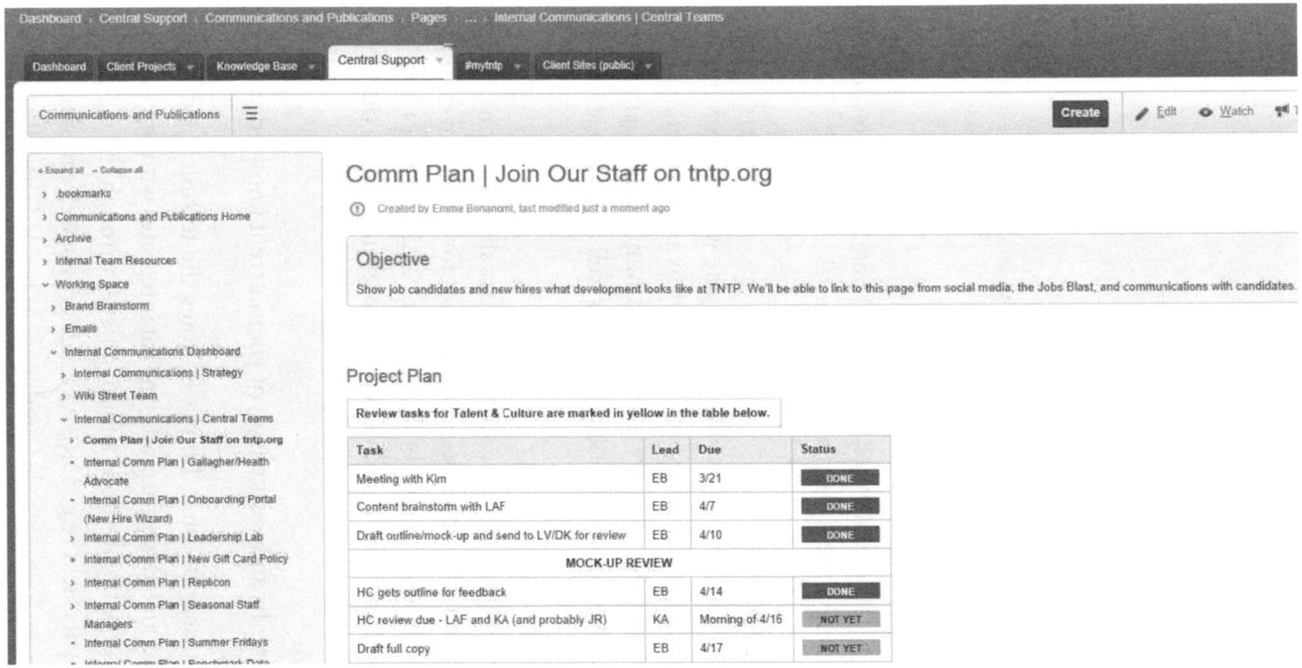

Figure 14.19 Communications Team Project Status

Figure 14.20 Animal Employees

START STRONG

This chapter provides nuts-and-bolts ideas of stuff, documents, and office space. In my experience coaching leaders, the absence of plans for these items can be felt deeply and result in wasted time, stress, and frustration. So, let's do this!

- Maximize your physical office space for efficiency and comfort.
- Determine what you use to carry your own stuff.
- Get your digital files in order.
- Review your current office space to ensure it is maximized.
- Ensure your organization has an inventory distribution, tracking, and collection system in place.
- Determine when and how knowledge management will be routinized.

COMMON CHALLENGE: ON-THE-GO OFFICE

I remember when I met Sherdren Burnside, an awesome leader at College Track in New Orleans. She sheepishly opened her tote bag, backpack, and then her purse. An explosion of papers, books, clipboards, receipts, power cords, pamphlets, business cards, and snacks boomed forth.

"Whoa," I said.

"Help!" she cried.

It's no wonder and it happens often. Sherdren is what I call an *on-the-go* leader, meaning she's rarely at a desk, has no dedicated place to work, and often moves between sites, none of which are fully equipped for her. Add to that her three children, a big busy role as a mission-driven leader, and significant responsibilities at her church, and it's easy to see how being mobile creates a big strain on her job and life—and her bag.

We got started on cleanup with a recycling bin and some file folders. Our goal was to ensure Sherdren had (and could easily find!) the work and personal materials she needed to function more effectively in the field.

Here are the steps we followed:

1. **Identify what to purge, recycle, or trash.** Call it whatever you want, but just get rid of it! We threw away handouts from conferences held over a year ago, data sets from past meetings, business cards that had already been entered in her contacts, and lots of little notebooks.

2. **Clarify what to save and store it elsewhere.** Sherdren identified what she wanted to keep: agendas from a great meeting, a team member's performance evaluation, and budget materials. After a big nudge from yours truly to not save paper copies of items that also

existed digitally, we whittled this pile down to something quite small and manageable. Last, we scanned what was left so Sherdren could archive it digitally.

3. **Figure out what you need with you at all times.** Sherdren needed one notebook, a set of folders to sort incoming papers, writing implements, power cords, and her laptop.

We could work with this! We sorted this final stuff Sherdren truly required into more piles and tamed the mess even further. We prepped these items:

1. **A hardbound folder** to carry her Together Leader tools

2. **Five folders** to sort papers:
   a. **Action:** To hold the items that Sherdren has to actually *do* something with
   b. **Meeting materials:** To contain anything Sherdren prints for upcoming meetings
   c. **File:** For the stuff Sherdren collects that needs to be filed elsewhere
   d. **Others:** To stockpile the articles and flyers she picks up and intends to pass on to her team
   e. **Read:** To catch articles she can read while commuting between sites or sitting on an airplane

3. **Writing instruments.** We tossed all unusable pens, pencils, and markers and added a small pencil bag to hold the survivors.

4. **Power cords.** We reeled them in using a small zipped pouch.

5. **Snacks.** We tossed in a little baggie to store nuts, granola bars, and other on-the-go snacks.

6. **Personal hygiene items.** Yet another bag was filled with deodorant, mints, cough drops, lipstick, and floss.

Last but not least, we ordered a new bag with more pockets so the tote did not default to dumping ground status!

We did this in an hour flat—and you can too!

CHAPTER 15

Create a Culture of Togetherness

SEEN AND HEARD

"I *thought* my new team member was super Together. He really seemed like it in the interview process. But now he is missing deadlines left and right."

"We had a good start as a team, but when things got really busy, all of our Togetherness went out the window!"

"I'm trying really hard to be Together, but my entire organization is a bit of a mess."

OVERVIEW AND OBJECTIVES

Now that you, your team, and your entire organization agree that Togetherness really counts, it's a matter of baking, or codifying, it into your culture to create a shared language. Many organizations *say* they value Togetherness and actually penalize people for not being Together. But rarely do leaders interview for, train on, support, and evaluate Togetherness. And although content knowledge, values fit, and being a team player count for a *lot*, nothing, simply *nothing* moves forward if it's not in the care of someone with a strong organizational system. Remember, I don't care what the system is … I only care that it is defined, intentional, and deliberate.

In this chapter, you will do the following:

- Define what Togetherness means in your particular context.
- Integrate Togetherness in hiring and onboarding new staff.

- Determine how to measure Togetherness.

- Make a plan to keep Togetherness practices alive.

- Plan an approach for when you or the team veers away from Togetherness.

DEFINE TOGETHERNESS IN YOUR ORGANIZATION

You've already decided Togetherness is important. Now you need to define it. Typically, Together skills are often plopped into the bucket of professionalism: dressing appropriately, arriving to work on time, and so forth. Though the two concepts are certainly related, merging them often means Togetherness does not get any real focus, training, or support. For this reason, I encourage you to name it as its own category of performance, with sections devoted to planning, operating, and executing. You don't have to go crazy here; resist the temptation to get caught up in splitting hairs on how quickly people should respond to e-mail. The point is to get clear on what you expect, so you can then support and evaluate. Let's look at two different examples of how this can be done.

Articulate It

Figure 15.1 shows a simple, yet powerful, organizational definition of *Togetherness*. At TNTP, they call this *strategic prioritization*. TNTP is not simply saying "get to meetings on time" or "track deadlines," because rules alone just aren't enough. They've instead outlined a larger, more proactive focus on prioritization, anticipation, and problem solving.

Although these broad competencies apply to all employees, TNTP took their definition a step further and specified what each one should look like for *each* level of employee. This

---

TNTP Leadership Competencies

Strategic Prioritization

- Develops a clear vision and purposeful strategy to advance our work

- Understands and prioritizes larger organizational goals and perspective

- Anticipates challenges and opportunities and adapts as necessary

- Develops a long term view without sacrificing progress in the short term

- Confidently reimagines work even while solving complex problems

- Makes timely, effective decisions and understands how deeply to engage in the decision making of others

Figure 15.1 TNTP's Strategic Prioritization Definition

Vice President Level Success Profile

As a strategic leader of the organization, Vice Presidents are directly accountable for setting strategy and goals that advance TNTP's mission and meet client needs, driving attainment of new business, and building a strong inclusive culture within TNTP that fosters staff success, engagement and retention.

Competency	Competency Description	Behaviors (at meeting expectations)
Strategic Prioritization	Shapes long term vision and drives corresponding strategy for advancing TNTP's core priorities	• Has a deep understanding of organizational and each group's priorities, theory of action, and goals • Has a deep understanding of the larger field of educational reform (history, current research, emerging topics) and relevance to TNTP's work • Provides strategic vision and leadership on group's long-term plans and goals • Anticipates challenges and opportunities (both within department and across the organization) and adapts strategy as necessary • Shows excellent judgment and can effectively weigh the needs of the larger organization, business unit, and individuals in decision making • Proactively tackles complex challenges that don't have easy solutions

Figure 15.2 VP-Level Definition of Strategic Prioritization

acknowledges the Together learning trajectory. Figure 15.2 is an example of how TNTP has defined Togetherness at the vice president level.

There are a few things to call out here. To start, I really like the focus on a leader's responsibility to name team and organization needs, solve complex problems, and understand other people's priorities. TNTP designed their competencies using observable behaviors, such as "proactively tackles complex challenges that don't have easy solutions" and "shows excellent judgment." Karolyn B., President at TNTP, explains how they arrived at their benchmarks: "We used to have a competency around productivity—which was basically about planning well and meeting commitments, but in some ways it was a minimum standard to get work done. You had to be organized enough to be reliable and deliver on deadlines. But the strategic prioritization is the real issue—are you spending your time on the right priorities to get to the endgame?" TNTP knows that these are the actions that lead to strong outcomes for the individual, team, and organization. Naming the outcomes up-front helps ensure their organization is recruiting the right people and supporting them well.

Skill	Narrative	Strands	Level A	Level B	Level C	Level D
Organization	The ability to maximize your productivity, manage your work, and create a high-quality, error-free final product by planning, executing, and prioritizing effectively and consistently.	**Organization: Planning**	Plan tasks effectively and consistently within a project	Plan independent projects effectively and consistently	Plan multiple, concurrent projects effectively and consistently	Plan a set of inter-related projects effectively and consistently
		Organization: Execution	Execute tasks effectively and consistently within a project	Execute independent projects effectively and consistently	Execute multiple, concurrent projects effectively and consistently	Execute a set of inter-related projects effectively and consistently
		Organization: Prioritization	Prioritize time effectively and consistently within a project	Prioritize time effectively and consistently within independent projects	Prioritize multiple, concurrent projects effectively and consistently	Prioritize a set of inter-related projects effectively and consistently

Figure 15.3 RGSE Leveled Rubric

Rubricize Togetherness

Now let's get a little more complex. Figure 15.3 is a great model of a leveled rubric from the Relay Graduate School of Education (RGSE) in New York that spells out varying levels of Togetherness across different career stages.

Relay has split Togetherness into three categories: planning, execution, and prioritization. This is a great place to start because each of these skills is distinct. Remember, Togetherness is not a "you have it or you don't" kind of skill. You could be great at planning but terrible at execution. You might prioritize but fail to deliver. A rubric such as this really defines the various aspects of Togetherness and provides an organization with a foundation for hiring, training, and evaluating.

Let's look a little more closely at figure 15.4.

After distinguishing the three categories of Togetherness, Relay divided employees into four different levels (A, B, C, and D).

- Level A is for the most junior employees whereas Level D covers the most senior people.

- Then, they identified what behaviors demonstrate foundational, proficient, and exemplary performance for each level of employee.

Skill	Narrative	Strands	Level C		
			Foundational	**Proficient**	**Exemplary**
Organization	The ability to maximize your productivity, manage your work, and create a high-quality, error-free final product by planning, executing, and prioritizing effectively and consistently.	**Organization: Planning** Defining Factors Level to level: scope	**Plan multiple, concurrent projects effectively and consistently**		
			Struggle to plan effectively and consistently	Plan effectively and consistently	Excel at planning effectively and consistently
		Organization: Execution Defining Factors Level to level: scope	**Execute multiple, concurrent projects effectively and consistently**		
			Struggle to execute effectively and consistently	Execute effectively and consistently	Excel at executing effectively and consistently
		Organization: Prioritization Defining Factors Level to level: scope	**Prioritize multiple, concurrent projects effectively and consistently**		
			Struggle to prioritize effectively and consistently	Prioritize effectively and consistently	Excel at prioritizing time effectively and consistently

Figure 15.4 RGSE Rubric: Level C

I like this rubric because it shows the full picture of how and where you can grow over time. It treats Togetherness similar to any other skill people can learn, practice, and master!

Reader Reflection

What is your organization's current definition of Togetherness? If one doesn't exist, where could you start? If you feel stuck, ask yourself what pieces of Togetherness you care about most. You can use the Self-Assessment in chapter 2 as a starting point. At a minimum, you'll want to include indicators for planning, prioritization, execution, and follow-through.

SELECT THE RIGHT PEOPLE

Now that you have your own working definition of Togetherness, let's think next about your interview process and what to look for in prospective hires. Before you jump in, you'll want to determine how much Togetherness really matters in the particular role for which you're hiring. When I'm hiring executive assistants, it *really* matters a lot. As you saw in chapter 13, folks in assistant roles are juggling proactive and reactive work, small tasks plus large projects, and all at an incredibly high volume. But when I'm hiring someone more senior, who may even have administrative support, I might care a little less. What I'll try to find out here is how well the person can articulate his or her vision and priorities as well as proactively and systematically delegate work to others. In this section, I will share some ideas for interview tasks and other observational data you can gather.

Interview Tasks

The very first thing you want to think about is how candidates can demonstrate evidence of Togetherness during the interview process. In this section, I cover how to observe for Togetherness, questions you can ask, and tasks you can assign (see table 15.1).

As you interview, you also want to look for the following:

Other Observable Togetherness Behavior

- *Anticipation*: If he or she has extra copies of résumés or other important papers
- *Preparation*: If questions are prepared or a website has been reviewed
- *Timeliness*: If he or she arrives on time (or early) to the interview and submits materials on time (or early)
- *Physical organization*: How well organized is her physical bag? Does he have writing implements on hand?
- *Follow-up*: How does the person follow up? Is communication timely and professional?

As mentioned in the introduction, being Together is not an indicator of effectiveness. In fact, it is very easy for strong Togetherness to mask another deficiency with the candidate. Make sure you don't get seduced by fancy To-Do Lists. Get into the heart of prioritization. What you really want in your new hires is the ability to set and reach your important goals; Togetherness is part of the process to get there.

Reader Reflection

How will you adjust or create a hiring process that includes Togetherness as a selection criterion?

Table 15.1 Interviewing for Togetherness

Test Togetherness	Listen and Look For	Take Heed
Show and tell	Ask candidates to simply *show* you how they stay Together. Ask them open their computers, smartphones, or dig a planner out of their bags. I personally like this more than any hypothetical prioritization situation.	How do they articulate their own systems? Ask follow-up questions about prioritization, tracking deadlines, and following through. I know this may feel silly and awkward with really senior people, but you want to hire someone who can explain how he or she works—even if that means heavy reliance on an assistant!	Be careful about hiring people who are very good at checking things off the list but don't focus on what is most important. If I see heavy color-coding or *too* many systems, I often jot a note to follow this through the interview process. These folks often get caught up in the process and lose sight of the goal.
Ask questions	"How do you decide what to do when you get to work in the morning?" "Tell me about a time you had something important and last-minute thrown at you. What did you do?" Their answers will give you evidence about prioritization, flexibility, and decision making.	You want to hear people tell you things such as "When I arrive at work, I first tackle the most important thing that I identified before I left yesterday. After that, I tackle some shorter-term immediate items. Then I prepare for meetings for the following day." The *exact* content matters less than discerning if the person has a systems orientation and a sense of his or her priorities. You also want to see if he or she can manage him- or herself toward outcomes. You want to probe for specific situations.	What you *don't* want is to hire someone who panics or shifts priorities at the drop of a hat.

(continued)

Table 15.1 Continued

Test Togetherness	Listen and Look For	Take Heed
Give hypotheticals Ask your candidate to respond to a role-based hypothetical prioritization or organization scenario that helps you understand how he or she makes decisions, such as in these examples: • It is the night before the annual fund-raising gala and you have a staff member who is in danger of quitting because of frustration with her manager. What next? • You have a huge presentation for the board, two important funder meetings, and a performance evaluation. All are due tomorrow and you are not yet prepared for any. What next?	You want evidence that your candidate has the instinct and skill to pause, plan, reassess what matters, align with others, and communicate for agreement.	You do not want someone who says, "I would just stay up all night to get it all done!" Sure, getting it done is great, but this is not a sustainable solution over time.

SHOWCASE AND MODEL TOGETHERNESS AT THE ONSET

Once you've selected a candidate with average to above-average Togetherness skills, you need to acclimate him or her to your organization and team's particular culture and expectations. "Be responsive to e-mail" means different things in different places. You want to set up your new hire for success and ensure he or she models Togetherness from the start.

As a former chief talent officer for a charter school district, you can probably guess that I think a lot about hiring and preparing people for success. An Onboarding Overview is the plan to welcome and acclimate someone to your school or organization. In my experience, I've been welcomed to new jobs in a wide variety of ways, from nothing but a cubicle full of crumbs to a detailed set of meetings and expectations. You may be able to guess which option I prefer.

In the next section, you will find samples of Onboarding Overviews that spell out systems and expectations. As you think about your own time, you will want to block off *more* time to spend with your new hires at the beginning. It is far better to be clear on the front end than give a bunch of after-the-fact feedback. Trust me, it will pay you back.

Make Sure the Basics Are in Place

There's nothing quite so demoralizing as showing up to your first day of work to a messy cubicle, office, and no idea what on earth to do next. It also sends the signal that Togetherness doesn't matter in your organization. Show you care: take the time to ensure your new hire has a working phone, computer, smartphone (if you issue one), and e-mail address. Make certain that the benefits, health care, and payroll process is seamless and that he or she has a place to go with questions. Get the basic meetings calendared well ahead of time. Now, if you showed up and none of these things were in place, fine, but let's take the time to make it better for future hires. As you read the next section, you can take the point of view of a manager hiring someone new *or* facing an upcoming transition you may have yourself.

Determine Necessary Systems Up-Front

Starting a new role is almost always like drinking from a fire hose. It is almost impossible to know what to start working on first, what to pay attention to now versus later, and who is who. Genna Weinstein, a leader in an education tech start-up in Boston, described to me how she put systems in place. As told by Genna, some of the more specific issues she considered were as follows:

- Align your goals and priorities with *someone*. It may be a manager, the board, or a thought partner. Whether you have SMART goals, a scorecard, or a Priority Plan, make sure you know what you are shooting for.

- Create a way to track relationships. I'm not talking about a cold, calculating relationship tracker, but you will be meeting tons of people. It can be helpful to record items about each person, such as the things he or she is responsible for, how long he or she has been with the organization, and what motivates that person. You may be lucky enough to have a pictorial photo directory, but it can still be useful to track your own information.

- Track your observations and questions and see who can answer what, if your manager can't. As you track the questions, be sure to bucket them so you can easily say, "Hi, member of the finance team. I have five questions I've stored up that I'm hopeful you can assist me with."

And on the more technical, but still important side, don't get blindsided by the vast amount of information that can come your way. Genna explains other ways she avoided information overload.

- Set up your email inbox for the first time: What folders should I set up from the beginning so I can process my inbox as efficiently as possible?

- Create folders in your new computer. How should you think about the categorization you need now vs. later?

- Track the systems: There are directions, links, wiki pages, new tools and logins … I ended up creating a simple spreadsheet to keep track of them all. I probably won't continue to use the spreadsheet after the first couple of weeks once I internalize it all, but it was helpful to have one place to dump all of that information coming at me at once. I created about 10 new passwords that I needed to write down as well.

Calendar synching: Luckily I had moved all of my personal commitments to Google Cal knowing that this company used Google. I was able to quickly merge my personal calendar with my work calendar. That was something I did on Day 1 just realizing that invites were coming in and I couldn't see the conflicts on the personal side. I also quickly added my "recurring work time" and "recurring exercise time" to my work calendar on day 1 so that those would be preserved as my calendar filled up with new commitments!

CREATE AN ONBOARDING OVERVIEW

In most dynamic mission-driven organizations, we tend to just throw smart people in to figure it out—just like you did, huh? Whether starting a new role yourself or managing a new hire, with a little forethought and a bit of time, we can do more to prepare our people to hit the ground running. I want to introduce one more tool that could help you put everything Together when bringing someone new into your fold.

Definition

An **Onboarding Overview** is a document that shares resources to orient your new hire to the organization, provide him or her with prioritization guidance, and sets expectations for the early stages of the role.

Elements of an Onboarding Overview

- Key questions for the new hire to answer in the first few months on the job about topics such as goals, culture, and team talent
- Suggested ways to retrieve the answers
- A reading list of key organizational documents
- A detailed schedule of introductory meetings for the first two weeks on the job
- Your expectations as a manager for dress code, work hours, and communications
- Directions on how to structure the first three months and a clear deadline to discuss
- A suggested way to capture and answer questions as they arise

Clarify the First Three Months: Set Priorities and Calendar

Although there are many, many items to include in an Onboarding Overview, I'm specifically focused on how you are helping others set goals and manage time and To-Dos accordingly. Developing a clear picture of priorities and gaining calendar alignment are the two most important steps in onboarding a new employee. Your team member should have a good sense of the goals, culture, and planning cycle of your organization. I like to ask the person to create a Priority Plan (see chapter 4) to share back and align with you. Sometimes, it makes sense to give the new hire his or her top-level priorities to help with focus, but in other cases, you may want to let him or her take the first cut. If it is a very senior hire and someone with strong planning chops, let them take the lead!

This may feel like micromanagement, but most people do need guidance and direction in their first few months on the job. This is especially true in mission-driven work, where To-Dos are endless, priorities are never-ending, and pressure is high. Instead of feeling intrusive, consider this a huge investment in setting up your new team member for success! And, of course, you can and will scale back as the person succeeds in your organization.

> **Suggested Priorities**
>
> - Suggested Danielle Priorities
>   1. Understand context of Citizen Schools CA team and organization
>   2. Start the work:
>   - **Talent:** Head of External Engagement; Ops Coordinators; CCA CD
>   - **Strategy:** Strategy engagement
>   - **New site cultivation:** Focus on RWC, Alum Rock and OUSD
>   - **Reach credentialing project:** Recruiting and program strategy development
>   - **Admin assistant (Guy/Paul):** strategy/scope/role
>   3. Build your vision of excellence
>   4. Build annual goals and quarterly maps
>   5. Build state office, campus, board and HQ relationships/credibility
>   6. Invest in team management and communications systems
>   7. Establish ops team priorities
>   - **Role development / hiring:** CSC ops coordinator and EE ops coordinator
>   - **Seasonal work:** Fall semester WOW support and annual appeal

Figure 15.5   Joe's Onboarding Plan of Suggested Priorities

Let's look at a great example of how to orient someone to the planning culture of an organization. Joe Ross, executive director of Citizen Schools in California, worked on this onboarding plan for his incoming chief of staff, Danielle Sharon (see figure 15.5).

There are three things that stand out to me about Joe's thoughtful outline (for a complete view of his onboarding deck, check out my website, www.thetogethergroup.com).

- **Build Annual Goals and quarterly maps (Priority Plans).** This helps Danielle focus on what is most important in her actual job.

- **Invest in team management and communication systems.** Joe names that relationship building and communication work is important, which could have easily been overlooked in the hustle and bustle of starting a new position.

- **Establish ops team priorities.** Joe challenges Danielle to make her own observations and develop priorities accordingly.

With all that needed to get done, it would be very easy just to tell Danielle to "Get the work moving!" Instead, Joe sets clear expectations for planning, prioritizing, and investing in others. His onboarding deck then provides the resources necessary to do so.

Although it may feel intimidating to prepare something as detailed as an onboarding overview for a new hire before he or she starts work, I've continually seen people give thanks for the clarity after they got a successful start. Jon Schwartz, someone I hired as a VP of operations, had this to say: "All any new hire wants is to be fabulously successful in his new role. And, from the perspective of a new hire, nothing is more demoralizing than failing to meet expectations and organizational norms that you were not aware of. If you truly want to see your new hires succeed, a comprehensive onboarding deck is critical." You can find more examples of onboarding overviews on my website (www.thetogethergroup.com).

Reader Reflection

How is this process the same or different from your current practice? How can you strengthen your onboarding process?

UP AND RUNNING: OBSERVE AND COACH

Your new colleague has been hired and started the job. What now?

Around week four, your hire should have a clear sense of the pace, volume, and content of his or her role. Although I'm not asking you to review his or her Outlook or Google Calendar in great detail, I think it is worth having him or her reflect on the systems self-assessment in chapter 2. For example, keep an eye on these issues:

- If time is aligned to overall priorities
- Preparation and follow-up for meetings (I would even ask some colleagues.)
- Keeping up with volume of e-mail and phone calls

At this point, if you are managing a manager, I would also want to see the following:

- A Management Memo, from the "See It in Action" after chapter 13, to understand how and when he or she is spending time with the team
- Personal systems, such as how his or her time is aligned with priorities and how he or she will capture long-term thoughts and track team feedback
- Team systems such as meeting agendas and Project Plans.

Okay, I can hear you. *Really, Maia?! You want people to* prove *they are staying Together?!?* Yes, I do. And here's why: how many times have you ever had to follow up with someone on a late deadline or lack of preparation for a meeting with *your* own boss? Me, too. It's much easier to prevent as much of this as possible on the front end by setting expectations and making sure systems can hold up under the pressure of our demanding jobs. When you explain this thinking to your team member, he or she will appreciate your investment. The more you do up-front, the more you can get out of the way later. And this is a tremendous opportunity for coaching, investing in your new hire, and building a strong relationship.

Reader Reflection

How will you acclimate your new team member to your definition of Togetherness?

HOW TO OBSERVE TOGETHERNESS

Inevitably, whether you like it or not, you may find yourself in a position in which coaching, directing, or supporting Togetherness is required. One of your direct reports may be scrambling to prepare for an event and has completely ambushed an entire team with a last-minute ask. A seasoned executive may frustrate her colleagues by not preparing for meetings. No matter the reason, you'll be asked to weigh in. In this section, you will find helpful tips, mind-sets, and exercises for coaching others—even if you are not yet an expert yourself! In this section, I share some ideas for practices and activities you can use to support someone who is struggling.

Time Tracking

First, you'll need to understand where someone's time is actually going. Too often, we rely on people retelling their struggles or suffering silently. Use fancy software such as Toggl or an old-fashioned spreadsheet to look at a week's worth of data on where time is spent. Your ultimate goal is to better help your team align their time to what matters most!

Questions to Ask When Reviewing Time Data

- Let's look at your priorities. How well is your time aligned with what matters most?
- What gets in the way of spending time on your priorities?
- What took more time than you thought it would?
- What took less time than you anticipated?
- How well are you able to use small pockets of time?
- Are there opportunities to batch process?
- What percentage of your work is proactive versus reactive?

Your goal here is to get the right stuff on the calendar, minimize the wrong stuff, and help people stay true to their time allocations. Once you discuss this data, there are a few other next steps you can take, depending on the particular challenges a person is having.

Align Priorities to Calendar

Cocreate a Priority Plan to align with your direct report but take it a step further by going into his or her Comprehensive Calendar. Start scheduling Time Blocks to accomplish priorities. Work backwards from deadlines to ensure there is enough time to complete important work. And be sure there is adequate time for the Standard Stuff.

Shadow

This is an intensive option, but sometimes you really cannot tell what is happening until you see it. If you are not available to shadow the person, find a trusted other who can. And yes, I'm really talking shadow. Join that person for a full day and see what unexpected emergencies come his or her way. You are in pure observation mode here; no judgment please. Then share the data with your team member and discuss if the results are in line with priorities. Who knows? You may discover something about your organization that you didn't know.

FAQ: What if someone you manage is *really* struggling with their Togetherness?
The first questions to ask are these: What is the impact of this struggle? Are his or her team members frustrated? Are big deadlines getting missed? Are the wrong things getting done first—or worse, are the right things not done at all? Once you identify the impact, it's very important that you and your employee share the same understanding of this. Lean in, and lean in heavily, using some of the strategies mentioned previously in the chapter. The effects of unTogetherness can snowball quickly and employees can easily develop a reputation that is hard to undo.

Share Exemplars

You probably know what you are looking for in Project Plans, Priority Plans, and Meeting Agendas. Why not set people up for success by sharing exemplars? Planning can be intimidating, stressful, or a total snoozefest for most of the world. Don't make someone suffer through creating something that isn't useful to them. Help them see the purpose and functionality of the tool. The downside of showing exemplars is that people may conclude there is only one way of doing things, which is decidedly what we *don't* want. For this exact reason, I try to keep at least three to five examples of all tools on hand. I look at all of them with my team and determine which elements they find most useful in each. This enables them to ultimately build their own tools, or at the very least, adjust what they see.

FAQ: What if my manager is completely *not* Together?

Yup, unTogether managers completely exist. Who knows, maybe you have even been one of them! Past tense! But we have all had bosses who are at varying levels of Togetherness. At its worst, goals are completely nonexistent or constantly shifting. At its most annoying, it looks like lack of preparation for important stuff, last-minute delegation, or endless non-priority meetings. Whatever position you may find yourself in, I would encourage you to align, align, align using various tools from this book. In years of coaching on this topic, I've never met a manager who reacted poorly to someone sharing a Goals Overview or a Priority Plan and saying, "Here is how I best think I should spend my time to meet our goals. Where do you agree and disagree?" And if there was pushback about spontaneity and flexibility, there's a simple reply: "I can actually be *more* flexible if I have a full handle on my work." You may never be able to change your boss, but Togetherness is contagious if framed positively.

Reader Reflection

When have you successfully coached someone toward Togetherness? What do you need to add to your toolkit?

MAINTAINING TOGETHERNESS IN YOUR ORGANIZATION

Congratulations! Togetherness is now up and running! You've connected it to your hiring processes, trainings, coaching, and evaluations. In this section, I will share some other ideas to help create a culture of Togetherness, keep it alive, and restart when it goes off track.

Kick Off the Year

Whether through a Management Memo, Meeting Matrix, or just a plain old Kick-Off Meeting, it is important to align on Togetherness expectations at the beginning of the year. Your year may be fiscal, academic, or of some other definition, but an outline of what matters the most (goals), how to get there (Priority Plan), and how resources (time) align is useful. Many Together Leaders insert some aspects of Togetherness into a beginning-of-year retreat, including items such as these:

- Setting communication agreements
- Agreeing on intervals for sharing and reflection on progress toward goals
- Cowriting Priority Plans
- Reviewing the Meeting Matrix

Amy Christie, a leader of a college readiness team at Achievement First, describes how and why she sets the tone at the beginning of the year: "I required Priority Plans of my team. To do this, I gave a few examples, being very neutral on format and being clear what the essential elements were. I explained the why around how this planning can help you communicate, how it can give me a window into the ebb and flow of work, and how we can anticipate crazy periods in advance. Eventually, everyone got behind it."

Set and Honor Regular Planning and Reflection Intervals

If you use an annual or quarterly planning process, consider carving out specified times for teams to plan and reflect at existing retreats or in small groups. I even know teams who hold a weekly "power hour" to sit together in a room and get their Weekly Worksheets completed for the following week. Ron Gubitz, a principal in New Orleans, holds Tuba Time (he leads an integrated arts school), when the whole team is focused on planning for the week ahead (see figure 15.6).

FAQ: What if people leave boxes out on the floor, start replying all, or generally just go unTogether hog wild?

Being the Togetherness police is generally no fun. Let's think back to your original purpose for getting Together. My guess is that you picked up this book because you wanted a great sense of accomplishment and an even greater sense of calm. If you see your team running around all frenzied, don't be afraid to call for a pause-and-plan moment. You can reevaluate Communication Agreements, recommit to the why of having prepared meeting agendas, or even adjust expectations. Or you may actually be worried your team is checking things off lists very productively, but they may not actually be the right tasks to meet your goals. See table 15.2 for some sample steps.

Figure 15.6 Tuba Time Sign

Table 15.2 Steps to Get Your Team Back on Track

Action Step	Possible Language
Name the evidence you are seeing.	*"Hey folks, I've noticed our meetings are all running at least fifteen minutes past time. Has this happened to anyone else?"*
Note the impact the lack of Togetherness is having.	*"For those of us who work with external constituents, and even for those of us with internal meetings only, this often means we arrive late, unprepared, or lose credibility."*
Recommit to the why Togetherness is necessary.	*"I want to go back to tighter agendas with a timekeeper to alert us to trade-offs if we need to adjust."*
Commit to the agreements resurrected or created.	*"Can we commit to bringing this back for the next month and we will assess again here."*

Reader Reflection

How will you keep Togetherness alive in your organization? What is your plan if Togetherness goes off the rails?

AGREEING ON STANDARD TOGETHER TEAM TOOLS

Earlier in the chapter, I discussed ways to intervene if someone is totally floundering in their Togetherness, but what about proactively introducing the tools, routines, and mind-sets in this book to your team? I do *not* recommend micromanaging e-mail habits and suddenly mandating that everyone turn in Priority Plans and Weekly Updates. Here are a few ideas to help promote a more organic Together adoption:

Start Small. Pick a couple of talented team members, introduce tools that you think may help them, and let them become the evangelists.

Figure Out What Problem People Are Trying to Solve. Everyone's motivation on this stuff is really different. Maybe some of your team members want to work shorter hours, get others to stop making last-minute requests of them, or reclaim some focused work time. Just pause to ask, such as we did for you.

Name the Impact. If people are drowning so much that they cannot even think about the problem they are trying to solve, gently point out the impact their lack of Togetherness is having on the team and the work. For example, "When you are late with your time sheets, it throws off an entire team's payroll process."

Remain Focused on Outcomes. The minute you try to require your team to use your *perfect* MS OneNote Later List, you lose. Make sure team members have established *habits* for tracking their long-term To-Dos, but don't mandate the *tool*, because this is a surefire way to inspire rebellion. At the same time …

Normalize Certain Terminology and Tools. I have seen a lot of success when schools say "All teachers need to have Comprehensive Calendars" or "My whole staff should complete Priority Plans on a monthly basis." Some shared tools can be beneficial for efficiency and communication.

Evaluate It

Eventually, if you have a performance management cycle in place, you will want to evaluate your employees' Togetherness. It's important to keep in mind, as always, that keeping Together is a means to a greater end—living out your mission! But a deficit in Togetherness can hugely affect effectiveness, credibility, and team morale.

Reader Reflection

How will you roll out any tools or habits to your team? How will you ultimately evaluate Togetherness?

START STRONG

There are many ways, formal and informal, to bake a culture of Togetherness. As a leader, you are a model and torchbearer of this value. I want you to take full responsibility for ensuring your team is as Together as possible! The positive impacts on someone's work experience and results are worth it. Tackle Togetherness proactively—before there is a problem!

- Write an organizational or team definition of Togetherness.

- Determine how and when you will incorporate Togetherness into your interview and selection process.

- Map out a strong training plan to get your team member up to speed on how your organization functions.

- Plan how you will keep Togetherness alive—proactively and reactively.

Togetherness Talks: Stephanie Patton

Name: Stephanie Morgan Patton

Title: Head of school, Excel Academy Chelsea (MA)

Why Togetherness matters: If my time is not maximized and organized, there is no way I would be able to accomplish the goals and tasks of my work.

Tell me about the mission and scope of your work. What are you most proud of?

The mission of my work is to effectively lead a middle school that prepares students for success in college. That is done through strategic development of my leadership team and teachers so that our school has the right balance of structure, joy, and support for our students to reach our mission. I am most proud of the growth both teachers and leaders have made over the last four years and the high level of student achievement.

At 10 AM on any given workday, what might I find you doing?

I might be interviewing a candidate for a role, observing classrooms and coaching teachers, or participating in a school leader meeting with other leaders in the Excel Network.

What is your favorite Together Tool and why?

My Weekly Worksheet that I have adapted to make two weeks long. As a leader, this helps me effectively use every minute of every day. My recurring meetings are set in my worksheet and I am able to schedule observation blocks and project work-time blocks effectively each week.

Tell me how you start and end each day to remain Together.

In the morning, the first thing I do is check my schedule on my Weekly Worksheet and check all e-mail that has come in since the night before—making sure everything is set and ready to go. At the end of the day, I look back on the work from that day and make any adjustments or notes I need to for the following day/week.

What is a challenge you still face with Togetherness?

I have my Meeting with Myself set for every Friday morning, and find that 50 percent of the time it spills into the weekend. I really want to have everything set by 9 AM Friday for the following week.

How do you remain focused when the work is swirling around you?

I like the swirl and work better if there is some slight distraction. With that said, if I am struggling to focus, I move locations, or take a two- to three-minute walk before getting back to work.

What happens when you get interrupted or ambushed?

I handle the urgent matter and then adjust my schedule as needed. I block project time each week, which is usually where this comes from.

It's 10 AM on a Saturday morning! What keeps you rejuvenated and renewed?

I try not to work for twenty-four hours each weekend—which usually takes place on Saturday. At 10 AM it is usually coffee, house organization, and spending time with my husband to make a plan for the rest of the day.

What have you learned to let go?

Everything does not need to be perfect and it is important to prioritize well. There is always more work to do, and finding the best and most productive times to do that work is important so that you do not feel like you are working twenty-four hours every day.

CHAPTER 16

Conclusion
Keep It All Together

SEEN AND HEARD

"I have tried and abandoned organizational systems multiple times over the years. At the beginning of each year I do it, but it only lasts one to two weeks and then it slowly unravels."

"I believe in organizational strategies but sometimes I try too many at once and things don't stick."

"There's so much I need to fix—I don't even know where to start!"

OVERVIEW AND OBJECTIVES

Thankfully, I've come a long way from my midday car nap in Houston many summers ago. But it hasn't been easy. I've shifted jobs twice, moved five times, given birth to two children, and started my own business. And with each and every transition, I've had to examine my tools, routines, and mind-sets to make sure they still held up. More often than not, they have required revisions and adjustments along the way. Yours will, too.

However, my intentions remain the same in my pursuit for Togetherness. I want to be Together so I can make huge positive contributions to the world and be fully present with my family and friends. And to accomplish those things, I have to remain focused on priorities, be reliable and responsive—and sleep enough at night! So although not always perfect, I can now ensure I'm planned well enough in advance for a large workshop. And I can make time to have a career conversation with a friend while en route to the airport—and not lose my taxi receipts while exiting the car because I have an envelope for my small papers! After that, I can sit quietly at the airport (because I got there with time to spare) to complete two smaller tasks prior to boarding. Once I get called, I load up one of my favorite podcasts and listen to it until I can work on the plane. And on that plane ride, I can edit the conclusion of my second book (you are reading it!) while eating a squash and bean salad I packed the evening before. The presentation will run smoothly tomorrow because I delegated the logistics to my director of operations well in advance. I will be able to be fully present and engaged with my participants. And when I return home thirty-six hours later, I will be able to be present and energetic with my family because I had already prepared for the next few days on the flight home. *That* is Together. A balance of mission-driven professional work with ample attention paid to energy, sustenance, and well-being.

So, what about you? We've tackled systems for self, systems for your team, and systems for your entire organization. Along the way, we've learned about different types of technology and various routines to keep it alive, as well as ways to protect our time from others. Let's close strong by putting it all Together.

In this chapter, you will do the following:

- Identify which areas of Togetherness to tackle first and why.
- Practice explaining your new venture to your colleagues.
- Transfer some learnings to home to help establish balance.
- Establish recovery methods for when you fall off.

REMEMBER THE WHY

Wayyyyy back in chapter 2, I asked you to think about what you were shooting for. Maybe you pasted a sticky note to your computer, made yourself a sign like the ones in figure 16.1, or wrote up your vision in your Reader Reflection Guide. Whatever you did back then, resurrect it now.

My hope for you is that through careful planning, intentional use of your time, and management of others' expectations, you *can* and will achieve your desired outcomes. Remember, your ultimate goal can change over time. Asking yourself to refine or define it is worth doing a few times per year.

Reader Reflection
Describe a Together event or time in your future life. What does it look like? How far from this are you now? What will it take to get there?

Figure 16.1 Balanced! Effective!

WHAT TO TACKLE FIRST

As mentioned in chapter 2, I do *not* recommend jumping in and adopting this entire book at once. Do not binge on organization. It will simply be too much. As I keep saying, let's prioritize! Instead, build your new habits over a six- to twelve-month period. Consider which

Table 16.1 Where to Start

Your Challenge	Start Here
E-mail management	Chapter 11: Keep E-mail in Its Place
Planning for beyond a week	Chapter 4: Break Down the Goals: Create a Priority Plan Chapter 6: Get Macro: Design a Comprehensive Calendar Chapter 7: Strategic Procrastination: Design a Later List
More effective meetings	Chapter 5: Align Your Meetings: Make a Meeting Matrix
A messy office or workspace	Chapter 14: Keep Track of Stuff, Space, and Knowledge Chapter 15: Create a Culture of Togetherness
Coaching others	Chapter 10: Hold That Thought: Save It for Later! Chapter 12: Project Design, Planning, and Communications: More Than Just Spreadsheets! Chapter 15: Create a Culture of Togetherness
Working with an assistant	Chapter 13: Become a Dynamic Duo: Maximize Your Assistant
Sticking to goals and priorities	Chapter 3: Set Goals: Define the Direction Chapter 4: Break Down the Goals: Create a Priority Plan
Implementing new programs and projects	Chapter 12: Project Design, Planning, and Communications: More Than Just Spreadsheets!
Tightening up your week	Chapter 8: Reconcile Your Time and To-Dos: Create Your Weekly Plan Chapter 9: Keep It Together: Routines and Checklists

actions, tools, and habits will have the biggest impact for you and choose accordingly. You can always add in other routines later.

Table 16.1 presents common challenges to help you think about where to get started.

Reader Reflection

Moving forward, what will you tackle? In what order? Jot down your ideas in the table in your Reader Reflection Guide.

EXPLAINING YOURSELF TO OTHERS

You know how when you start to eat healthy and everyone asks you at dinner why you are not having the bread or why you are turning down that second glass of wine? Togetherness works the same way. People may look at you funny when you say that you need at least forty-eight hours to respond to an e-mail or that you don't have time to review a document on such short notice!

It's important to give your colleagues a heads-up about what you are trying to accomplish—and, most important, what you want the result of all this change to be for you and others.

You don't want to be written off as a nitpicky stickler who doesn't collaborate. That's why it's so important that, as a leader, you continually emphasize *why* Togetherness matters so much—for you, your team, your clients, and your organization.

Reader Reflection

When and how will you introduce your team to your new habits?

WHAT HAPPENS WHEN YOU FALL OFF

Get ready because it's gonna happen. There will be a week, or two, or three or even a *month* when you are just plain slammed. Everything comes crashing down at once: a media storm at work, your kid breaks her arm, four snow days, and some data come back that require extra meetings with every team member. You will skip a Meeting with Myself, forgo a Daily Closeout, and then all of a sudden, the Priority Plan is outdated by four months. Been there. It's times such as these that we need to hug our plans the closest. And believe it or not, you can often predict when they are going to happen. Let's try it.

You will get more done if you can be the person to help your team, or *yourself,* refocus. Corey Crouch, a school leader in Houston, described a "retreat with herself" that she scheduled when she felt her Togetherness falling apart: "I'm Together enough to know when I need to get it Together. I've actually planned a Corey Retreat for a refresh of systems, recommitment to Meetings with Myself and systems, and some long-term strategic planning for my leadership team and campus. I needed something to kick-start a recommitment to balance, my Priority Plan, and my sanity. When systems get unhealthy, take a day that is *not* a weekend and get it Together!"

Go into your Comprehensive Calendar (because it is now in *great* shape) and look for these Time Blocks:

- Any time you will be out of the office for more than a week

- The week before any vacation

- The week before any conference, board meeting, or other major event

- Performance evaluation time

- Goal-setting time

Now, block a little extra Meeting with Myself or Opening and Closing times in those weeks. And block some buffer time to clean up on the back end similar to what Max did in the "Common Challenge" after chapter 8. Consider shortening or canceling meetings. Or plan a massage for when the event is over! The key is to hold tight to your tools and routines because they are what will get you through the storm.

Reader Reflection

When do you anticipate needing to get back Together? What will you do when this happens?

TRANSFERRING TOGETHERNESS TO THE HOME FRONT

This is not a work-life balance book. This book is explicitly about how to align your time to what matters most in mission-driven work. That said, many mission-driven leaders I've met are in danger of burnout, not getting enough sleep, not delegating well, and hopping from crisis to crisis. I've peppered the book with many tools that combine the personal and professional. Without getting too much in your business, I do want to make sure that some of your systems for home, if you choose to have them, are in line. This way, the home stuff doesn't become another crisis you have to manage.

- **A Comprehensive Calendar.** Or at least have a place where you can see work and home events overlapping.

- **A Later List.** Many household items, such as creating holiday cards, making annual pediatrician appointments, or preparing for an important anniversary, can sneak up on us.

- **Hold a great weekly family meeting.** You can find a sample agenda on my website (www.thetogethergroup.com).

- **A clear entryway.** I don't dabble much in stuff management, but some place to put mail, keys, wallets, and phones can save you a lot of time on the back end.

- **A safe spot for important documents.** Whether it's a fire safe or safe deposit box, get those passports, car titles, and house deeds in one singular, safe location.

- **A safe spot for important information.** I don't care where you keep it, but create one single document with Social Security numbers, blood types, credit card passwords, and more.

- **A method to deal with food procurement, planning, and preparation.** We all need to fuel ourselves to do good work.

- **A screen-free sleep sanctuary.** Sleep matters. Get lots.

I promise I'm not asking you to forgo all spontaneity. I just know that stressed-out leaders on the home front (who have to run out to cash machines late at night to pay the babysitter) won't help further anyone's mission. So, let's plan ahead for what we can at home.

WHY THE WORLD NEEDS TOGETHER LEADERS

As discussed throughout this book, mission-driven work is unique because goals are ambitious and urgent, we are managers and makers, resources are constrained, and stakes are high. This doesn't give us an excuse to toss our hands in the air and just react to whatever crosses our desks or in-boxes that particular day. Great organizations needed disciplined leaders who make strategic decisions, plan carefully, and execute smoothly. If we allow ourselves to be scattershot or unprepared, there is no way we can meet our goals. And if we allow ourselves to work around the clock on little sleep, eat nothing but donuts all day, and never get physical exercise, we will lose motivation and eventually burn out.

Mission-driven work is so challenging. Our job is never done, and our bottom line is often made up of the very real people we meet with every single day. It can feel painful to prioritize. Because it *is* all critically important. Whether you manage professional development for a school district, fund-raise for a food bank, or oversee outreach for your church, you owe it to the people you serve—and yourself—to have a rigorous and systematic approach to *how* you get your work done. With Together habits, mind-sets, and tools in hand, your outcomes can have an even greater impact.

Feel free to contact me through my website (www.thetogethergroup.com) or come cyberloaf with me on various forms of social media. I love seeing pictures, hearing stories, and celebrating your success!

I hope that being Together supports you in doing great things for the world. Mission-driven work is some of the most challenging—and most important—work out there. Good luck!

Bibliography

Allen, David. *Getting Things Done*. New York: Penguin Books, 2015.

Bilton, Nick. "Disruptions: For a Restful Night, Make Your Smartphone Sleep on the Couch." Web blog post. *Bits*. The New York Times Company, February 9, 2014.

Covey, Steven. *First Things First*. New York: Fireside, 1994.

Covey, Steven. *The 7 Habits of Highly Effective People: Powerful Lessons in Personal Change*. New York: Simon & Schuster, 2004.

Coyle, Daniel. *The Talent Code: Greatness Isn't Born. It's Grown. Here's How*. New York: Bantam Books, 2009.

Duhigg, Charles. *The Power of Habit: Why We Do What We Do in Life and Business*. New York: Random House Trade, 2012.

Gawande, Atul. *The Checklist Manifesto: How to Get Things Right*. New York: Metropolitan Books, 2009.

Green, Allison, and Hauser, Jerry. *Managing to Change the World: The Nonprofit Manager's Guide to Getting Results*. San Francisco: Jossey-Bass, 2012.

Henry, Alan. "The Weekly Review: How One Hour Can Save You a Week's Worth of Hassle and Headache." Web blog post. *Lifehacker*. Gawker Media, May 9, 2012.

Hseih, Tony. "Yesterbox." http://www.yesterbox.com/, 2013

Leistner, Frank. *Mastering Organizational Knowledge Flow: How to Make Knowledge Sharing Work*. San Francisco: Wiley, 2010.

Lencioni, Patrick. *Death by Meeting: A Leadership Fable … about Solving the Most Painful Problem in Business*. San Francisco: Jossey-Bass, 2004.

Levitin, Daniel J. *The Organized Mind: Thinking Straight in the Age of Information Overload*. New York: Plume Books, 2014.

Linenberger, Michael. *Total Workday Control Using Microsoft Outlook*. San Ramon, CA: New Academy Publishers, 2013.

Mullainathan, Sendhil, and Shafir, Eldar. *Scarcity: The New Science of Having Less and How It Defines Our Lives*. New York: Times Books, 2013.

O'Dell, Carla, and Hubert, Cindy. *The New Edge in Knowledge: How Knowledge Management Is Changing the Way We Do Business*. Hoboken, NJ: Wiley, 2011.

Rath, Tom. *Eat Move Sleep: How Small Choices Lead to Big Changes*. Arlington, VA: Missionday, 2013.

Rath, Tom. *Are You Fully Charged? The Three Keys to Energizing Your Work and Life*. Arlington, VA: Missionday, 2015.

Rhodes, Justin. "Why Do I Think Better after I Exercise?" *Scientific American*, http://www.scientificamerican.com/, June 6, 2013.

Rubin, Gretchen. *Better Than Before: Mastering the Habits of Our Everyday Lives*. New York: Crown Publishers, 2015.

Smart, Geoff, and Street, Randy. *Who: The A Method for Hiring*. New York: Ballantine Books, 2008.

Vanderkam, Laura. *168 Hours: You Have More Time Than You Think*. New York: Portfolio, 2010.

Womack, Jason W. *Your Best Just Got Better: Work Smarter, Think Bigger, Make More*. Hoboken, NJ: Wiley, 2012.

INDEX

Page references followed by *fig* indicate an illustrated figure; followed by *t* indicate a table.

Hsieh, Tony, 276
Hubert, Cindy, 384

I

Ideal Week: completed, 137*fig*; impose onto your digital calendar, 138–141; macro time blocks, 135*fig*–136*t*; scheduled meetings, 136*fig*; on weekly priorities, 133, 134*fig*. *See also* Comprehensive Calendar
"Inbox Zero" movement, 278
Internal time crushers: common types of, 200*t*; description of, 199; solutions for, 202; tracking your, 203*t*–204
Inventory tracking, 383

J

Job candidates: hiring the right assistant, 326–331*fig*; hiring those that will support Togetherness, 397–406; interview process to assess Togetherness, 398, 399*t*–400*t*; observable Togetherness behavior, 398
Job description: Residential Ops, 300*fig*; to secure Project Plan resources, 299–301, 302*t*
Johnson, Sharon: stationary space examples from, 368, 369*fig*; weekly team meeting and agenda examples from, 110–112
Junk E-mail folders, 263, 264

K

Kanth, Indrina: on the Calendar and To-Do list colliding challenges, 172–175; her E-mail Audit, 259–260; meeting preparation checklists by, 221–223*fig*
Kennedy, Riley, daily closing routine of, 211*fig*
Key actions: spell out the one required to archive priorities, 67, 70–71, 75–76*t*; spread out across three-month period to achieve priorities, 67, 71–73, 77*t*–79. *See also* Annual activities
Kick-Off Meetings: maintaining organizational Togetherness through, 408–409; Project Plan, 292*fig*, 305–307
KIPP Austin Public Schools, 56
KIPP Foundation, 376
Klos, Maggie, 133, 136*fig*–137, 138
Knowledge management: examining the multiple approaches to, 383–384; Reader Reflection on, 387; TNTP's wiki as example of, 384–389*fig*. *See also* Office space organization
Koltuv, Max, 206–207

L

Later List benefits: avoid ambushing others, 157, 158; be a thoughtful human, 157–158; be flexible, 157, 158; delegate, 156, 158; manage expectations (proactively and reactively), 156–157, 158; plan for input from others, 157, 158; stay focused, 157, 158; track the teeny-tiny things, 158
Later List process: Ashley's combo Priority Plan and, 168*fig*; complete the content, 167; connect it to your Priority Plan, 167, 168*fig*; overview of the, 169*fig*; select a tool, 166–167; select your categorization method, 165
Later List routines: determine how you will keep your List accessible, 170; make sure the To-Dos don't get stuck, 170; systematic weekly review of your Later List, 169
Later Lists: Assistant Alert on maintenance of your, 168; benefits of a, 156–158; building your own, 165–170; definition of, 152; description of tool, 17*fig*, 18, 153*fig*; differentiating between Thought Catchers and Priority Plan and, 242, 244*t*; differentiating between To-Do lists and, 154; entering tasks directly on Calendar versus your, 161–162; Johanna's Later Lists, 152*fig*, 163–164*fig*; as one of your most valuable tools, 20; overview and objectives for using, 151–152; Reader Reflections on, 166, 167, 169; Ron's, 251*fig*; routines to use with your, 169–170; Steve's, 154–156; template for, 154*fig*; time commitment for, 171; used for your home life, 418. *See also* To-Do Lists
Lateral colleague meetings, 103
Leader-assistant communication structures: Daily Update, 345–346*fig*, 347*fig*; Meeting Scope and Sequences used as, 355; Monthly Step Back, 351–353; Our Communication Plan for, 353*t*; special project meetings, 353; Weekly Check-in, 346, 348*fig*–351*fig*
Leader-assistant tools: batch process, 356; daily or weekly Briefings Folder, 354*fig*–355*fig*; receipt and expense tracking, 356; stock e-mail responses, 355–356
Leadership: mission-driven context of, 3–4; Togetherness as just one asepct of effective, 5–6. *See also* Together leaders
Leadership meetings: description of, 103; YES Prep meeting agenda for, 112, 113*fig*–114*fig*
Leistner, Frank, 384
Levitin, Daniel, 156, 257–258
LIFT, 192

How to Access the Website Resources

- If you purchased a new paperback copy of this book, you will find a unique single-use access code for the video clips and downloadable tools inside the back cover.

- Go to **my.thetogethergroup.com** and click "**Activate Pin**."

- If you don't have a pin, simply answer our verification question to then create an account.

- Follow the instructions on the website for registration.

About the Author

Maia Heyck-Merlin is the founder and CEO of The Together Group, a business focused on training educators on topics such as time management, prioritization, organization, and efficiency. Her clients include many leading charter operators, large traditional school districts, and innovative education nonprofits. Before becoming a full-time entrepreneur in 2013, she served as chief talent and operating officer for Achievement First for five years, where she oversaw human capital, operations, recruitment, leadership development, and evaluation of school leaders and teachers.

Prior to joining Achievement First, she worked at Teach For America in a variety of capacities. Maia began as a 1999 corps member in South Louisiana, where she taught fourth grade for two years and was named Teacher of the Year at her placement site. Following her TFA commitment, she went on to teach fifth grade at Children's Charter School and direct Teach Baton Rouge's first summer training institute for TNTP. In 2002, Maia returned to Teach For America as the executive director in South Louisiana, overseeing programmatic efforts for a corps that had doubled in size. She then served for three years as the Houston institute director, leading training and development for the incoming corps. In her last role at Teach For America, Maia founded and led the national institute operations team, which managed national operations for all five summer training institutes.

Maia has also authored *The Together Teacher: Plan Ahead, Get Organized, and Save Time*. She grew up in rural Maine and holds a BA in child development from Tufts University. She lives in the Washington, DC, area, with her husband Jack, their two young children, and two unruly cats. In her free time, she trains for (short) triathlons and tries to figure out how to make green smoothies that actually taste delicious. You can reach out to Maia directly via The Together Group's website, www.thetogethergroup.com.